Canada's Party of Socialism
History of the Communist Party of Canada
1921-1976

Best wishes to a dear friend

Evan Hunter

Canada's Party of Socialism

History of the Communist Party of Canada 1921-1976

Progress Books Toronto 1982

Paperback ISBN 0-919396-46-1
Clothbound ISBN 0-919396-45-3

Printing: Eveready Printers, Toronto

Published by Progress Books
71 Bathurst Street
Toronto, Canada M5V 2P6

Canadian Cataloguing in Publication Data

Main entry under title:
Canada's party of socialism

Includes index.
ISBN 0-919396-45-3 (bound). — ISBN 0-919396-46-1 (pbk.)

1. Communist Party of Canada — History.

JL197.C5C36   324.271'0975   C82-094153-0

Contents

Foreword

This is not a history of just another party. It is the history of a party dedicated to fundamental social change, a party which gives expression to the fundamental interests of the working class and to the fulfillment of the historic mission of that class.

This history has been written, first to register the impact of the Communist Party of Canada on political events in Canada and internationally. This history will also acquaint new members with the party's rich history.

Secondly, more and more Canadians are interested in a working class interpretation of Canada's history. Those who dig into the history of the working class find that the Communist Party of Canada played an important role, indeed a significant role, on a whole number of fronts: the fight-back against the great economic crisis of the 1930s when capitalism attempted to place the entire burden of that crisis on the working people; the leadership given by the party to the organization of the unemployed, as well as the unorganized in the mass production industries; the formation of the Mackenzie-Papineau Battalion as democratic Canada's contribution to the struggle against fascism in Spain and, indirectly, in Europe; the establishment of Dr. Norman Bethune's blood transfusion unit in Spain; the struggle against fascism and imperialist war, and for democracy and peace.

Indeed, wherever diligent students of working class history probe, they cannot but note the initiatives and important organizing role of the Communist Party and of Communists in the struggles of the working people against capitalist exploitation and imperialist oppression, and for improved living standards and social advance, in defense of peace, democracy and Canadian independence.

There are others though, apologists for the exploitive capitalist system who, like their masters, fear fundamental social change, strive to blacken the party's name and its record. It is therefore necessary to set the record straight.

This is particularly important because books have appeared in the post-war period that twist and distort the history of the Communist Party of Canada and deny its Canadian birthright. The aim of such deception is to create an image of the party as a foreign importation, alien to the working class and democratic movement in Canada, a sinister conspiracy against democracy.

This history unmasks those falsifiers of working class history. It shows indisputably that the Communist Party of Canada was born on Canadian soil, arising out of the struggles of the Canadian working class for trade union organization, class solidarity regardless of national origin, and, above all, the acquisition of socialist consciousness by the broad labor movement.

The history pays tribute to the immigrant workers who played a significant role in the building of the Communist Party. They played an equally significant role in building the trade union movement, the unemployed movements and the militant farm movements in the prairies, and in the building of Canada.

In addition to those who try to rewrite or falsify history, there are those who, while compelled to recognize the role the Communist Party played in the past, deny the party's validity today. They argue that the party has outlived its usefulness by suggesting that capitalism has fundamentally changed, that imperialism has all but disappeared, that the evils of capitalism such as crises, poverty, inequality and the worst features of exploitation have been eliminated.

True enough, the world has changed and the relationship of forces between imperialism and socialism has changed. But imperialism remains an aggressive predatory force in the world, and modern capitalism — monopoly merged with the state, state-monopoly capitalism — has become a highly sophisticated system for the exploitation of the working people. The chief purpose of this merger is the preservation and stabilization of the capitalist system. However state-monopoly capitalism is unable to accomplish this. Rather than bring an end to crises, monopoly intensifies all the contradictions of the system of capitalism.

Keynesianism, which was to have replaced Marxism and given us a crisis-free capitalist world, has proven unable to cope with the problems of modern-day capitalism. Rather than being crisis-free, capitalism staggers from crisis to crisis. The replacement of capitalism by socialism has become a historic necessity.

State-monopoly capitalism created and spread the illusion of the affluent society in which classes are disappearing, in which the working class has become bourgeoisified and therefore unable to fulfil its historic mission as the grave-digger of capitalism. But monopoly capitalism intensifies exploitation of man by man. Inequality and insecurity are becoming more acute. The process of the relative deterioration of the conditions of the working class has accelerated. Far from becoming bourgeoisified, the working class is asserting itself more and more as a class for itself.

Thus, all the myths about the transformation of capitalism into an egalitarian society, spread by monopoly, liberal reformists and social reformists alike, are coming apart at the seams. So is the idea that class peace and collaboration have replaced the class struggle. Instead, the contradictions between labor and capital are growing.

Indeed, history denies not the validity of the Communist Party, but of capitalism itself. History shows that capitalism is not immune from its own laws of development, including the laws of its decay and replacement by a higher, more advanced form of society, socialism.

The working class and all working people are learning through their own bitter experience that no gains are permanent under capitalism, that what is needed is to end capitalism through a fundamental reorganization of society.

Lenin pointed out that owing to the unevenness of capitalism's economic and political development in the epoch of imperialism, the conditions for social revolutions ripen at different times in different countries, and that the social liberation struggle in the capitalist world develops unevenly. But in no way does this unevenness exclude any country from the forces of revolutionary change. Unevenness of development is reflected most clearly in the different strategic stages of the struggle in different countries.

The two world wars and their respective post-war periods made it possible for Canadian imperialism to benefit materially at the expense of other countries and peoples. This in turn enabled monopoly to make concessions to the Canadian people, concessions wrested from monopoly as a result of the economic and political struggles of the working class and working people for economic gains and democratic advance. This widened the base of reformism, both bourgeois and social, and dampened the class struggle which, of course, slowed down the development of class consciousness among working people. Such conditions could not help but serve the interests of the ruling bourgeoisie. These problems were added to by imperialism's cold war against socialism and the national liberation movement, which monopoly and the state used in attempts to isolate the party from the working people, the trade unions and people's movements. Despite temporary successes, the forces of the state, right-wing social democracy and the cold warriors of capitalism failed in isolating the party because the laws of social development are much stronger than they.

During the course of its history the Communist Party has had to contend with a variety of opportunist and revisionist schools of thought. All reflect the pressures of bourgeois and petty-bourgeois ideology on the working class and on the Communist Party.

There was the "new left" which set out to replace the "old" Communist Party on the assumption that the working class had become bourgeoisified, that other social strata such as the students and intellectuals were going to bring about social change. There was the "Waffle" and their narrowly conceived nationalism divorced from the working class and from international solidarity based on consistent class struggle. Both of these "replacements" for the Communist Party have passed away as organized political movements.

There were the revisionists within the Communist Party who wanted socialism without working-class power, without the sure guidelines of Marxism-Leninism, creatively developed and applied to the specific conditions in Canada and, last but not least, without internationalism and with an anti-Soviet bias. Somewhat akin to the foregoing are the Maoists who, in their betrayal of the international working class, have swung from extreme leftism to right opportunism of the worst kind — and have landed in the lap of U.S. imperialism, the cold war, opposition to the national liberation movement and real socialism, and above all the Soviet Union.

A relatively new phenomenon is eurocommunism, which under the guise of a "creative" development of Marxism-Leninism advances pluralism as the path to socialism, and rejects as a whole the laws of historical development and revolutionary struggle discovered by Marx, Engels and Lenin — laws which are indispensable in the creative quest for specific roads to socialism. These laws include the political power of the working class and its allies, the elimination of the private ownership of the means of production, the democratic participation of the people in planned socialist construction with the working class and the Communist Party playing the leading role, and the ability to defend the revolution. All of these are universal truths. Without them revolution and the building of socialism are not possible.

It should be noted that in all these various revisionist and opportunist manifestations there is one constant, namely, a negation of the historic mission of the working class in achieving fundamental social change, and with it a denial of the leading role of the Communist Party and of Marxism-Leninism in this revolutionary process. Further, all of them are steeped, in one form or another, in anti-Sovietism. It is therefore not surprising that nationalism, not internationalism, permeates the activities of revisionists and opportunists.

As the history of the Communist Party shows, our party has never shied away from the historical significance of existing socialism in the Soviet Union and what that means for social progress the world over. The existence of the Soviet Union strengthens the communist movement, serves as the main guarantee of universal peace, and creates the necessary conditions for developing peaceful, democratic forms of struggle in the interests of the working people and the cause of socialism in the capitalist world.

This does not mean that the Soviet Union is a universal model. Each country develops its own specific forms of social advance within the framework of the universal laws of social development and revolutionary change which are applicable to all countries. The Communist Party's program, *The Road to Socialism in Canada,* spells out the stages of struggle for realizing revolutionary change and the specific conditions in which it will be achieved.

As this history amply proves, the Communist Party has no interests separate and apart from those of the working class. In the struggles of the workers today, Communists see the socialist future. The 55 years of class and democratic struggles recorded in this book, show that the party and the class-conscious section of the working class attain theoretical clarity and political maturity in unremitting struggle against capitalist ideology and its social reformist apologists. The party's experience shows that such struggle demands the exposure and defeat of right and left opportunism, dogmatism, sectarianism, bourgeois nationalism, anarchism and ultra-left adventurism.

This history shows also that the party works incessantly for the political advancement of the workers, farmers and the middle sections of the population, so that in the course of a consistent struggle for democracy, the majority of the Canadian people by their own united action and decisions, and under the leadership of the working class will achieve socialist democracy. The party's history is also one of untiring work for cooperation with all democratic forces to bring about a new people's majority, to bring into being an anti-monopoly people's government as a transitional stage to a socialist government.

Communists have every reason to take pride in the fact that throughout its history, the Communist Party has staunchly upheld the banner of scientific socialism and unceasingly sought to integrate Marxism-Leninism with the broad labor movement. The party has upheld the interests of the working class and all working people. Despite errors made in the course of its varied activities, the Communist Party has always remained true to itself, to its class, to the national interests of our country and to internationalism. It has always striven to correctly combine patriotism with working class internationalism.

The task set by the founders of the party to bring scientific socialism, that is Marxism-Leninism, to the broad labor movement has still to be completed. It is the permanent long-term task of the Communist Party around which the working class will fulfil its historic mission. That mission will be achieved.

William Kashtan
General Secretary
Communist Party of Canada

Preface

This history covers a period of 55 years, 1921-1976, and is documented from the Communist Party of Canada's extensive archives.

The history of any Communist Party is very complex, specifically with regard to the relationship between theme and chronology. There are many themes, the development of which is closely connected to the development of other aspects of the party's life and policies. In general, the party's history lends itself to division into periods of five to six years. Each period became a chapter, within which certain themes assumed particular importance. Hence each section within a chapter explores a particular theme and related subjects.

Not every chapter follows this general rule however. The introductory chapter necessarily outlines the historical conditions which gave rise to the revolutionary working class movement in Canada and the foundation of the Communist Party of Canada. This process naturally took a number of decades. Chapters 3 and 10, which deal with the two major ideological crises in the party's history, cover a much shorter period of time. These two periods were watersheds in the history of the party. The well-known upheavals which shook Canada during the 1930s demanded extensive coverage, and hence three chapters are devoted to that decade. Chapter 13 is devoted entirely to the singular contribution of Canadian Communists to the national question, a central feature of Canadian life. Each section represents a stage in the development of the party's policy on this question.

Gerry van Houten was given the task of research and writing the manuscript under the supervision of a History Commission which included William Kashtan, Alfred Dewhurst, Bruce Magnuson, Mel Doig, William Sydney and Robert S. Kenny. The writing of the history was a collective effort, which greatly benefited from the work first started in 1965. Tim Buck, then John Weir and later Norman Freed accepted the assignment, but unfortunately ill health prevented them from continuing this work. Intensive discussion in the Central Executive Committee on important questions in the party's history and the valuable contributions of many other members of the Communist Party of Canada enriched the analysis of the development of the party. Although not members of the History Commission, John Weir and Sam Walsh made important contributions to the manuscript.

Appreciation must be recorded for the work of the late Eva Kulha, the party's office secretary for 17 years. Eva Kulha meticulously collected and stored materials and photographs related to the history and activities of the party. While the Communist Party was making history, Eva Kulha made sure that it was also preserved.

Valuable photos were contributed to the party archives and this book by the *Canadian Tribune, Combat,* and the *Pacific Tribune.* We would like to give special thanks to the many members of the Communist Party who contributed photos and other materials.

A number of institutions kindly gave permission for the use of photos from their collections: the Saskatchewan Archives Board, the York University Archives, the Toronto Star, the Glenbow

Archives in Calgary, Alberta, the Thomas Fisher Rare Book Library (particularly Marjorie Pearson) of the University of Toronto, the United Electrical, Radio and Machine Workers Union, and the Public Archives of Canada.

We would like to extend our appreciation to the Public Archives of Canada, especially Photo Archivist Andrew Rodger and Labor Archives Coordinator Danny Moore for their assistance.

Finally, but certainly not least, we would like to thank Progress Books and the workers of Eveready Printers for their particularly important contribution.

1. The Roots of the Communist Party of Canada

May 28, 1921 will go down in the history of Canada as marking the dawn of a new stage in the struggle of the working people of our land for economic, social and political emancipation. On that day in Guelph, Ontario, a party of a new type — based on the world outlook of Marxism-Leninism, revolutionary in thought and deed — came into being. From its very first days, the Communist Party of Canada has been inseparably linked with the growth and political development of the working class movement. The history of the party is one of selfless struggle for the vital needs of the working people, of Canada and her two nations. In that struggle, Communists faced blacklisting, prison, physical abuse, in some cases death. The long and difficult road of these 55 years of Communist Party history is rich in lessons which will prove invaluable for the working class and all who strive for a socialist Canada and a world of peace.

1. Beginnings of the Working Class Movement

Long before the formation of the first union, in fact as early as 1794, Canadian workers conducted unorganized and usually unsuccessful struggles for better working conditions and decent pay.[1] In spite of these early efforts, the labor movement of the 19th century was generally too weak to obtain anything more than very limited and isolated successes. Virtually no laws favorable to the workers existed; employers enjoyed a heyday.[2] In those days, the balance of class forces overwhelmingly favored the capitalist class. It was a period which gave Canada's capitalist class the opportunity to consolidate itself, to find the ways and means of overcoming obstacles to its unfettered development. It was a period which saw a massive influx of immigrant workers and farmers, a specific feature of North America which was a boon to capitalist development and left an imprint on Canadian politics, and particularly on the Canadian working class.

British North America's fragmentation into a number of small colonial provinces restricted the development of the economy. Confederation was the Canadian bourgeoisie's answer to overcoming these political and economic barriers to capitalist development. It also served British interests which feared U.S. annexation of Canada.

While striving for at least a certain degree of independence, the Canadian capitalist class remained heavily dependent on British loan capital, most especially for the construction of a Canada-wide railway system.

At Confederation the British government confirmed the claim of the Canadian capitalists to legislative sovereignty within Canada, while they in return undertook to keep the Dominion within the Empire.[3]

Confederation enshrined political, economic and social inequalities between Canada's two nations — English-speaking and French Canadian — which originated with the British conquest of New France in 1759-60.

In other respects, Confederation was a boon to the Canadian bourgeoisie as it not only struck down provincial economic and political barriers but also led to the formation of a single internal market as the basis of Canada's economic unity and the centralization of the financial resources of the former British North American colonies into a single Canadian state. The new federal government was then able to direct these financial resources toward building the necessary economic infrastructure for further Canadian capitalist development. The government's economic policies stimulated the growth of Canada's privately-owned railway systems and gave impetus to the growth of Canada's private banking system. Although the federal, provincial and municipal governments provided the largest share of the capital for Canada's economic development, they never departed from the principle that ownership should remain in the hands of private entrepreneurs.

The birth of Canada as a sovereign country promised a new era of growth and expansion. Workers too wanted to improve their position. The class struggle intensified during the 1870s forcing the working class to think in terms of direct labor political action. Soon after the foundation of Canada's first trade union center in 1873 (the Canadian Labor Union which lasted only until 1877), the labor movement took on the task of fighting for its rights in the political field. At that time, most unionists advocated reforms within the capitalist system, but as early as 1874, voices could be heard promoting the supersession "of the present system, as the present system superseded the serf system of the past."[4] The wording was vague, but the sentiment was clear.

The 1880s saw the eight-hour day movement sweep across both the United States, where it originated, and Canada. In Chicago, the Knights of Labor led a mass strike, beginning on May 1, 1886, in support of the demand for the eight-hour day. The employers, backed by company goons, the police and anti-labor laws, bloodily smashed the strike. This strike expressed the hopes and aspirations of workers around the world and was supported by the international working class movement. In 1866, the Geneva Conference of the International Workingmen's Association (the First International), had adopted the demand for the eight-hour day. The Second International, in honor of the Chicago strike, declared May 1 a day of international working class struggle and solidarity.

Two characteristics distinguished the Knights of Labor from previous labor organizations. Firstly, it opened its membership to all workers, including the unskilled.[5] This earned it the enmity of the craft unions which, in view of the rapid growth of the Knights of Labor in Canada, felt compelled to unite, forming the Trades and Labor Congress (TLC). Secondly, the Knights of Labor advocated the replacement of capitalist society with a cooperative society.[6] Although wishing to go beyond the confines of the capitalist system, the Knights of Labor had only the vaguest notions of what should replace capitalism. Nevertheless, the Knights of Labor's relatively radical views led to persecution by the employers, the government and the craft unions; this in turn contributed to its demise by the end of the century.

The period of the 1890s to the end of the First World War constituted a watershed in the development of capitalism in Canada. It was a period characterized by the country's rapid industrialization and the strengthening of the positions of Canadian capitalism in relation to British imperialism. From 1890 to 1920, numerous corporate mergers took place as industry became more and more concentrated and centralized. The years between 1896 and 1912 in particular witnessed the rise of monopolies and near-monopolies in many branches of the economy. Canada was well on the way to becoming an imperialist power.

The prospect of full control over the Canadian state whetted the appetite of Canada's ruling classes for more political independence from Great Britain. Control over its own state would help the young Canadian monopoly bourgeoisie find a place of its own in the imperialist world. World War I accelerated this process as it enabled Canadian capitalists to take advantage of British dependence on Canadian war materials to take British investments in Canada into their own hands. The Imperial Conferences of 1917 and 1921 saw Canada demand control over its international affairs commensurate with its growing control over the economy.

The decades between 1890 and 1920 also saw the penetration of U.S. capital into Canada, particularly in the manufacturing and natural resources industries. This process began after the federal government's implementation of the so-called National Policy in 1879 when a high tariff was placed on goods manufactured in the USA. U.S. companies circumvented these tariffs by using their capital to invest in and take over manufacturing and other concerns in Canada.

These developments occurred on a background of growing labor unrest.

Stimulated by the growing militancy of the labor movement, workers began to create their own political organizations. The economic depression of the 1890s convinced many workers of the need for social change. Marxist, social-reformist and anarchist ideas spread into Canada from the United States and Europe. The working class and socialist movements in Canada were as yet politically immature and inexperienced. The concepts of scientific socialism were at best only imperfectly understood by Canadian workers. Although a few works of Marx and Engels had made their way to Canada, they were not yet sufficient to overcome the lack of theoretical clarity that prevailed in the working class and socialist movements.

Nevertheless, workers' parties mushroomed across the country. One of the first was the Socialist Labor Party which was founded in the USA by Daniel De-Leon. Although this party spread the works of Marx and Engels in North America, it gave Marxism a very sectarian interpretation.[7]

After a few years of especially acute class struggle in British Columbia, a militant Socialist Party was founded in 1901 through the merger of five smaller socialist parties. It achieved the election of the first Socialist to a provincial legislature.[8] Shortly afterward, the newly formed Socialist Parties of Manitoba, Ontario and New Brunswick joined their senior fraternal party in British Columbia to establish the Socialist Party of Canada.[9]

The new united Socialist Party declared its allegiance to "the principles and programs of the revolutionary working class."[10] It advanced an economic

In August 1913, the striking miners of Ladysmith, British Columbia, are marched to prison under the guard of the armed militia for demanding an improvement in their living and working conditions.

program for radical change in the social system.[11] This party received its main support from among the industrial unions which had come into existence in the 1890s because of the persistent refusal of the craft unions of the American Federation of Labor (AFL) to organize unorganized workers along industrial lines. It was no coincidence that the party was strongest and most influential in British Columbia, precisely because it was here that the militant industrial unions were the most powerful.

The growing influence of these unions as a result of their leadership in some important strike struggles and the rapid spread of revolutionary ideas among Canadian workers compelled the leaders of the TLC to seriously consider direct involvement in working class politics. The TLC had maintained close ties with the Liberal Party, but these relations were beginning to sour. To avoid further isolation from an increasingly militant working class, the TLC decided to throw its resources behind the creation of a reformist labor party. The first such attempt had been made in Winnipeg in 1895 with the formation of the Independent Labor Party. It was so conservative that it was even afraid to call itself socialist. In 1902, its left-wing members had broken away to form the Socialist Party of Manitoba.[12] Subsequently, other parties of the reformist type were set up throughout the country as a counterweight to the growing influence of the Socialist Party.[13] An attempt to consolidate these labor parties into a single party collapsed "mainly because it satisfied no real need, but had been imposed on the groups from above."[14]

It was nevertheless clear that the working class movement was dividing into two trends in both union organization and political orientation. On the one side, there were the industrial unions which tended to support a radical, even revolutionary socialism. On the other side, there were the craft unions of the TLC which supported labor politics aimed at immediate trade union and reformist demands. Historically speaking, the emergence of these two political trends in the working class crystallized the division of the working class movement into its reformist and revolutionary wings, although the latter still had a long road to travel before it would mature into a party of the new type, a party based on the principles of Marxism-Leninism.

In spite of their revolutionary programs, the Socialist Party and the Socialist Labor Party were heavily influenced by economic determinism. Tim Buck, an active participant in these debates, observed that these two parties were actually adhering to certain opportunist misconceptions promoted by Karl Kautsky in Europe.[15] Economic determinism caused these parties to adopt positions of a left-sectarian nature.

Anti-parliamentarism seriously afflicted the Socialist Party and gave rise to contradictions within its ranks. While Socialist members of the British Columbia legislature fought effectively for reforms and trade union rights, their fellow party members accused them of betraying the revolutionary cause.[16] Many party activists regarded political action around immediate demands as reformist and diversionary because it allegedly deflected the attention of the working class from the imminent collapse of the capitalist system. The Socialist Party's attitude became a barrier to working class unity especially when cooperation was offered by reformists. As a consequence, by the time of the First World War, the Socialist Party had degenerated into a small educational sect with little real influence.

The controversy within the Socialist Party concerning the role of reforms in the revolutionary process and the party's extreme sectarianism provoked a number of organizational splits.[17] Some of these breakaway groups merged to form the Social Democratic Party of Canada.[18] By 1914, it was the largest socialist party in Canada. The majority of its membership consisted of European immigrants, largely Finns, Ukrainians and Jews, who arrived in Canada in the 1890s and 1900s. Most had fled the scourges of war and national oppression which often marked life in their homelands. Affected by the political and economic struggles occurring in the countries they had left, many were supporters of socialism before they came to Canada. When they arrived in Canada, they set up their own organizations (for example, the Ukrainian Labor-Farmer Temple Association) and their own political parties (such as the Ukrainian and Finnish Social Democratic Parties).

In the winter of 1910-11, still another split occurred in the Socialist Party, this time in Toronto.[19] The newly-formed Socialist Party of North America accused the Socialist Party of being reformist and opportunist despite its rev-

Delegates to the Ukrainian Social Democratic Party of Canada convention in 1917. Its left wing became a part of the Communist Party four years later. Matthew Popovich and William N. Kolisnyk (middle row, fourth and sixth from the right respectively) were to play prominent roles in the Communist Party and the Ukrainian-Canadian working class movement.

UKRAINIAN LABOR TEMPLE, WINNIPEG/PAC C-54117

olutionary program. The members of the new party were obliged to know the three fundamental tenets of Marxism — historical materialism, the theory of surplus value and class struggle. The party obliged its members to join trade unions whenever possible. The emergence of this party reflected the fact that the scientific ideas of Marx and Engels were now more widely known and seriously studied.

The militancy of the class battles preceding the outbreak of the world war and the spread of revolutionary ideas in the working class movement stimulated the further dissemination of Marxism, but it also kept alive the spirit of anarcho-syndicalism. In 1905, the ideas of a continental industrial union and the replacement of capitalist society by a cooperative one which had emerged

with the formation of the Knights of Labor, were revived in a different form in the establishment of the Industrial Workers of the World (IWW). Although the IWW fought heroic battles, it suffered from serious ideological weakness stemming from the contradictory nature of its program. The union put itself forward as a revolutionary organization aimed at the overthrow of capitalism, a political objective, while simultaneously serving as an ordinary union fighting for the immediate demands of the workers for better wages and working conditions.[20] This contradiction prevented the IWW from becoming more than a passing phenomenon.

In spite of the continued fragmentation of the working class movement in Canada and the ups and downs of the revolutionary struggle, the ideology of

Members of Local 145 of the Western Federation of Miners, a militant industrial union, celebrate the construction of their new hall in South Porcupine, 1912.

the revolutionary working class made headway among the most advanced workers. Although strongly influenced by the socialist movements of Europe and the USA and the 1905 revolution in Russia, the main reason for the growth of the young revolutionary movement in Canada lay in the very nature, the objective laws, of Canada's capitalist development. Canada was a class society where the few, the capitalist class, exploited the workers. Long before Marx and Engels and later Lenin made an appreciable impact on the ideological and political development of the Canadian working class, the need for collective working class action against capitalist exploitation had spontaneously brought about the formation of the trade union movement, and later, of working class parties.[21] The experience of class struggle against the negative effects of capitalist society in Canada impelled many advanced workers to come to the conclusion that the status quo had to be changed in favor of the workers. When the revolutionary ideas of Marx and Engels reached these workers, the impact was immediate. Not only did this theory embody and elaborate the conclusions the workers had reached by themselves, but it also showed that they shared experiences and interests with workers of other countries. The essential unity of the international working class was expressed in the concept of proletarian internationalism.

The growing militancy and internationalism of Canadian workers was put to the test with the outbreak of World War I. From the beginning of the war, the monopolies proceeded to foist the cost of Canada's participation on the workers and other sections of the Canadian people. Inflation fell with full force on the working class "which at the time saw others growing wealthy on war profits."[22] In 1917, social antagonisms were further aggravated by the introduction of conscription, which compelled the sons of the working class to serve as cannon fodder in a war which so obviously enriched the owners of the war industries.

The working class was not alone in its opposition to monopoly exploitation and imperialist war. Years of exploitation by land speculators and by the financial and railway monopolies who acted as middlemen between agricultural producers and consumers brought about a desire for social change among Canada's farmers. As inflation and war profiteering made their impact, the farm-ers' opposition to Canada's participation in the imperialist war grew.[23]

The people of French Canada were vociferous opponents of the war as well. Having experienced decades of national oppression themselves, French Canadians did not care to be embroiled in a war between oppressor nations, including Great Britain. The introduction of conscription heightened anti-war sentiments in French Canada to fever pitch and acted as a catalyst to the growth of the national consciousness of the French Canadian nation. Along with the advanced farmers, French Canada became an objective ally of the working class in the struggle against Canada's participation in the imperialist war.

Prime Minister R.L. Borden's Tory government, conscious of the profound unpopularity of the war and of conscription among many Canadians, decided to invite the Liberal Party to join in a coalition government, an invitation which was accepted by that party's English-speaking majority but rejected by its French Canadian members, including its French Canadian leader and former Prime Minister, Wilfred Laurier. In October 1917, three months after the imposition of conscription on an unwilling population, Borden formed his so-called Union Government. Federal elections were held in December. Given the lack of organization and unity of the anti-war forces and the intense pro-war propaganda campaign which sucked in many English-speaking Canadians under the banner of chauvinism disguised as patriotism, the Union Government won handily.

This anti-conscription march in Montreal in May 1917 was one of many actions throughout Canada protesting the policies of the Borden government.

The main factor aiding the plans of Canada's capitalist ruling circles was the fact that the working class itself was not united on the question of Canada's participation in the war. As in the case of the Second International, there were elements which tended to support the Canadian imperialist bourgeoisie. The TLC reacted to the war by attempting to reconcile views which were in fact irreconcilable. At the 31st TLC convention in 1915, the right-wing reformist leadership put forward a resolution recognizing labor's opposition to the war but calling for support as the only way "to secure early and final victory for the cause of peace and freedom."[24] Although the TLC leadership dared not withdraw its official opposition to conscription, it also declared that it would take no action to prevent the government from enforcing compulsory military service.

A substantial section of the TLC opposed these policies. As the war progressed, the anti-war and left-wing forces grew stronger and compelled the TLC to make concessions. For some of the radicals, this was too little, too late. At the 34th TLC convention in 1918, the split between the reformist leadership and the left-leaning syndicalists reached the breaking point. Shortly afterward, the One Big Union (OBU) was formed. Based mainly in western Canada, the OBU became a militant organizing center. It was in this period that the working class movement received news of an event which had a profound impact on Canada as a whole and which inspired class conscious workers to step up their activities.

2. The Impact of the Russian Revolution

Against the background of extensive opposition to the war, the Bolsheviks led a successful revolution in Russia. News of the 1917 revolution sent shock waves throughout the world. The immediate reaction of the ruling classes of the imperialist countries was an almost hysterical fear and rage — somewhere the working class had actually dared to seize power. From imperialism's standpoint, an extremely dangerous precedent was set. Lenin and the Bolsheviks had proven that it was possible to turn the imperialist war into a revolutionary war of workers and peasants against the ruling classes of capitalists and landowners. Equally distressing for the imperialists was the fact that the successful socialist revolution in Russia acted as a catalyst for the revolutionary activity of the working class in other capitalist countries and for the anti-colonialist movements in Asia and Africa. In fact, after the war ended, the working class in several European countries attempted to seize power. In Germany, Hungary, Finland, Estonia, Latvia and Lithuania, the workers achieved temporary successes, but these revolutions were drowned in blood.

World imperialism sought to strangle the socialist revolution in Russia and isolate it from the international working class movement. A vicious campaign of lies and slanders was accompanied by material and military support for the counter-revolutionaries in Russia. Fourteen capitalist countries including Canada intervened militarily to tip the balance of forces in the Russian civil war in favor of the deposed ruling classes. But the struggle of the workers and peasants of Russia led by the Bolsheviks, and the unprecedented solidarity of the international working class assured the triumph of the world's first socialist state.

News of the successful socialist revolution caused near panic in Canada's capitalist class. An anti-Soviet smear campaign was inaugurated to distort the true character of the revolution taking place in Russia. In addition to dispatching troops to Siberia, the Borden government took measures against what it perceived as the revolutionary threat inside Canada. In September 1918, it issued an Order-in-Council banning a number of working class political organizations such as the Socialist Labor Party, the Social Democratic Party, the IWW and 11 other political groups. In November, the Union Government passed another Order-in-Council banning several other organizations, among them the Socialist Party of North America.[25] The War Measures Act, under whose provisions the bans were made, also outlawed all organizations of workers who came from central and eastern Europe. In fact, many immigrant workers had been interned during the war as "enemy aliens." Left-wing literature was prohibited and vigilante groups were organized to forcibly suppress dissent. These anti-working class and anti-democratic measures revealed the tenuous nature of democracy in a capitalist country.

The hostile propaganda of the bourgeois press, the government's denial of basic human rights to workers and the misleadership of the reformist

Canada was one of fourteen imperialist countries to participate in the Russian civil war on the side of the deposed capitalist and landlord classes. Above, troops of the Canadian Expeditionary Force boarding a train near Vladivostok (January 1919). Below, Canadian officers near Vladivostok (April-May 1919).

RAYMOND GIBSON PAC/ABOVE: C-91761/BELOW: C-91743

elements in the labor movement could not stop the working class from becoming more militant and class-conscious or from lending its support to the working people of Soviet Russia. From the time news of the revolution arrived in Canada, there was a massive and spontaneous outpouring of support for the workers and peasants of Russia. Demonstrations and mass public meetings in solidarity with the first socialist state took place throughout the country. Money was collected to aid the victims of the 1922-24 famine which had been caused by the devastation of the civil war, foreign intervention and blockade. These expressions of solidarity reflected the depth of the proletarian internationalism of the Canadian working class.

At the ninth annual convention of the British Columbia Federation of Labor held in March 1919, Jack Kavanagh, the president, moved a resolution protesting foreign intervention in Soviet Russia and recommending that the Federation "refuse to assist in the forwarding of men, money and materials intended for use against the workers of Russia and that the executive committee carry on a system of propaganda with this in view."[26] Many spoke in favor of the resolution which was then adopted.

A few days later, most of the delegates to this convention attended the Western Labor Conference which resolved to found the OBU. The conference sent messages of solidarity to the Bolsheviks, the Soviet government and the Spartacists in Germany. Delegate Joseph R. Knight of Edmonton, Alberta, summed up why Canadian workers had to and did support the workers of Soviet Russia:

> I don't think that we should fail to understand that when the working class over in Russia is being oppressed by the capitalist class of the world, that is our oppression and whatever we can do to assist our fellow workers in those countries it is up to us to do it and to put our ideas into operation, which are identical to those of the workers there and not in our own capitalist class.[27]

J.R. Knight's speech was received with loud approval. The delegates understood that solidarity with the working class of Russia served their own class interests. Canadian workers knew that those who were trying to subvert Soviet power were the same as those who were denying them their basic rights and decent living and working conditions.

On May Day 1919, Canadian workers from Vancouver to Montreal, English and French-speaking, celebrated the holiday of the international working class by demonstrating their support for Lenin and Russia.[28] These demonstrations symbolized their recognition of the new socialist country as the bastion of the international working class against imperialist war and capitalist oppression.

The movements of solidarity with the Russian workers merged with the upsurge in the class struggle which followed World War I. Workers in their thousands were organizing, striking for higher pay; returning war veterans were demanding jobs; farmers too were actively involved in the struggle for social change.

The struggle of the Canadian working class reached a peak during the Winnipeg General Strike in the spring of

1919. The workers had already gone through several tough struggles against their recalcitrant bosses. Through these experiences they became more conscious of the need for mass workers' unity and independent labor political action. In December 1918, the growing political awareness of the city's workers was expressed during a mass meeting sponsored by the Socialist Party and the Winnipeg TLC. The meeting demanded the repeal of the Orders-in-Council passed under the provisions of the War Measures Act because they were a "distinct violation of the principles of democracy."[29] It urged the federal government to release all political prisoners and expressed the solidarity of Winnipeg workers with their class brothers and sisters in Soviet Russia. Local reactionaries interpreted these resolutions as proof that the workers were falling under Bolshevik influence.

In May 1919, solidarity with striking metal workers prompted the general strike. Approximately 30,000 workers, including the city police, went on strike, thus paralyzing the city except for essential services which were run by the workers themselves under the aegis of the Strike Committee.[30] Winnipeg authorities were convinced that what they were witnessing was an attempt to seize power. In actual fact, the strike's aims were far more limited: its two main demands were the right to collective bargaining and the right to a living wage.[31] To the reactionaries these were revolutionary demands because the workers dared to challenge the status quo. What particularly frightened the capitalists was the fact that the workers ran essential services *without the direction of the capitalist class,* a characteristic of the strike which implied that capitalists were unnecessary for the functioning of society. As far as the bourgeoisie was concerned, the general strike had to be crushed at all costs.

Soon after the general strike began, the city's business community organized the Citizens' Committee of 1,000 whose principal aim was to break the strike. Alarmist reports that riots and revolution were impending were deliberately spread by the bourgeois press, despite the explicit denials of the Strike Committee.[32] The reactionary Committee openly plotted the violent suppression of the strike.[33] The armed forces provoked the riot they needed by smashing a peaceful demonstration. Two workers were shot dead and 30 others seriously injured.[34] With the strike broken, a campaign of intimidation, arrests, trials and deportations was begun to suppress the growing militancy of the working class movement not only in Winnipeg but throughout Canada as well.

Thousands of workers across the country had demonstrated their solidarity with the Winnipeg workers in sympathy strikes, meetings and rallies. Although victory was denied them, the Winnipeg General Strike heightened the class consciousness of Canadian workers.

3. The Foundation of the Communist Party of Canada

The conjuncture of the Russian Revolution, the negative aftermath of the imperialist war and the fight to improve

Top left, in the Winnipeg General Strike of 1919, World War I veterans demonstrate their militant solidarity with the striking workers on Broadway Avenue. Top right, the first charge by the RCMP on the demonstrating workers. Bottom, mounted and special police attack the striking workers at the corner of Portage and Main.

PAC C-34025

W. GOODALL PAC C-3339

FOOTE PAC C-3402

living standards and extend labor's rights stimulated the development of the revolutionary movement toward the foundation of a scientifically-based revolutionary working class party of a new type.

Among the socialist parties, sympathy and support for the socialist revolution in Russia was extensive. The Socialist Party of North America and the left wing of the Socialist Party and the Social Democratic Party threw their support behind the efforts of the Bolsheviks to establish a socialist system of society.

The building of a united revolutionary party of the Canadian working class was clearly on the agenda. Attempts were made to call a unifying convention of all the existing socialist parties in the country. Local branches of the Social Democratic Party and the Socialist Party adopted resolutions to this effect.[35] However, the movement toward socialist unity was hampered by the existence of substantial ideological differences not only between parties but also within the parties. Furthermore, the lack of access to the illuminating classics of Marx and Engels and the virtual absence of the works of V.I. Lenin made the struggle for ideological clarity much more difficult. News items in the capitalist press reporting on what Lenin had to say on various issues were often the only source of information on what the Bolsheviks thought and did.

A number of the smaller classics of Marx and Engels such as the *Manifesto of the Communist Party; Socialism, Utopian and Scientific; Value, Price and Profit; Wage-Labor and Capital* and the famous *Preface to A Contribution to a Critique of Political Economy* were available but not well known.[36] In the year following the Bolshevik Revolution, some of Lenin's writings in English began to find their way to Canada. Among them were his *Letter to American Workers* and limited copies of *The State and Revolution.*[37] By 1920, a few more of Lenin's works such as *The Tasks of the Third International* and parts of *What Is to Be Done?* had arrived in Canada in spite of the fact that all Marxist literature had been banned under the War Measures Act. These works influenced many members of the various socialist parties to favor the creation of a single, unified revolutionary party based on the principles of scientific socialism.

Lenin's ideas played a particularly significant role in clarifying the ideological positions of Canada's revolutionary socialists and thereby helped to create the necessary ideological conditions for the formation of a revolutionary working class party. His pamphlet on *The Vote in the Elections to the Constituent Assembly,* for example, impressed upon Canadian socialists the need to take into account the relationship of class forces in the struggle to achieve and retain state power. Much depended on the ability of the working class to win over the non-proletarian masses. Working class political power functions not only to suppress the resistance of the capitalist class but also to build socialism and establish socialist democracy. Studying this pamphlet, the most advanced and class-conscious workers "began to sense how profound was the reality of the genius of Lenin."[38]

Despite continuous government re-

John Boychuk (1891-1976)

pression under the War Measures Act even after the end of the world war, revolutionary-minded workers were intent on setting up a Communist Party.

An attempt was made in the spring of 1919, but police raids prevented the party from establishing itself. A number of people were arrested in these raids, among them Arthur Ewert, John Boychuk and Tom J. Bell. Arthur Ewert was deported. In the 1920s, he became a member of the Central Committee of the Communist Party of Germany and was elected to the German Reichstag.[39]

CANADIAN TRIBUNE

Despite unabated repression, agitation for the foundation of a Communist Party continued. Revolutionary workers did not want to return to the dogmatic and passive Socialist and Socialist Labor Parties, nor did they care for the opportunistic mistakes of the Social Democratic leadership, some of whom were gravitating toward right-wing European social democracy. Revolutionary Canadians joined either one or the other of the two Communist Parties formed in the United States in September 1919.[40] Their separate formation arose out of organizational and tactical differences, but due to the offices of the Third International (Comintern) and the influence of Lenin's theoretical works, the schism between the two parties was soon healed. *"Left-Wing" Communism — an Infantile Disorder* in particular helped to clear up controversies over such questions as the role of Communists in parliament and in mass organizations. In May 1921, the two parties merged to form a united Communist Party of America.[41]

A similar merger took place between the Canadian membership of the two parties. On May 28 and 29, 1921, the famous clandestine meeting in the Guelph barn was held.[42] This was the meeting which officially marked the foundation of the Communist Party of Canada. Twenty-two delegates representing a total membership of 650 were in attendance.[43] They met in "accordance with the mandate of the Pan-American Council of the Third International to bring about the formation of a Communist Party of Canada. . . ."[44] Tom Burpee was elected secretary of the new party.

The program of the new party outlined the objective laws of capitalist development which bring about the class struggle between the proletariat and the bourgeoisie. It pointed out that Canada was developing in a period dominated by world imperialism and that imperialist competition was responsible for the bloody world war. It agreed with Lenin's thesis that the general crisis of capitalism had begun and that its main content was the world's transition from imperialism to socialism. In this context, Canada was schematically characterized as a self-governing colony with a "privileged status which made Canada an auxiliary

Tom Burpee (1885-1972)

of British imperialism."[45] The program made no mention of the striving of the bourgeoisie for political independence from Great Britain nor did it take into account the growing penetration of U.S. capital into key sectors of the Canadian economy.

Noting that bourgeois democracy "is nothing but the concealed dictatorship of the bourgeoisie," the convention called for the establishment of the dictatorship of the proletariat which "realizes true proletarian democracy, the democracy for and of the working class and against the bourgeoisie."[46] This would make possible the transformation of capitalist society into a communist society. Mass political action on the part of the working class and its allies had a vital role to play in the achievement of this goal. Special attention was therefore paid to the poor farmers as allies of the working class in their common struggle against capitalist exploitation. Great significance was placed on the farmers' militant struggle against conscription and exploitation by the banks, transportation companies, farm machinery trusts and so on.

On the trade union question, the program of the newly-formed Communist Party declared the party's support for industrial unionism as the superior form of labor organization. While emphatically opposing the splitting of labor's ranks, the party reserved the right to criticize the policies of the

(ARCHIVES CPC) PAC PA-124395

social-reformists. The program also criticized the anarcho-syndicalist leaders of the OBU and the socialist parties for failing to understand the separate roles played by labor unions and the revolutionary party of the working class in the fight for socialism. The socialists tended to ignore the role of the trade unions in the revolutionary struggle while the anarcho-syndicalists refused to acknowledge the political necessity of having a Communist Party.

The convention recognized the contribution of the Comintern in reorganizing the world revolutionary movement. During the war, the right-wing leaders of the Second International had supported the bourgeoisie of their own countries, leaving the revolutionary working class movement in disarray. On Lenin's instigation, the Third or Communist International was formed in March 1919, and the Red International of Labor Unions (RILU) in July 1921. By unanimously adopting the 21 conditions of admission into the Comintern, the delegates demonstrated their determination to become a part of the world communist movement and in this way to advance the long-term interests of the Canadian working class. As history was to show, the Communist Party of Canada's affiliation to the Comintern greatly enriched the party's experience and deepened its theoretical basis.

The unity convention adopted a constitution outlining the organizational principles of the new party. The basic unit was to be the nucleus (or the club in present-day terminology) which would consist of not less than five members and not more than ten, grouped according to language and territory. Ten language clubs in a given territory would constitute a branch and every branch would be part of a subdistrict. The convention, to be called at least once a year, was the party's supreme body. It decided the program, constitution and policies of the party and elected the members of the Central Committee (CC) and the Central Executive Committee (CEC) which directed the party's day-to-day work.

The major foreign language groups, called sections, were given a certain measure of autonomy because they had joined the Communist Party from the Social Democratic Party en bloc. A language group could not form a section unless it had a minimum of 200 members. It elected a bureau of three members and was responsible for the publication of a party organ in the language concerned. Language sections were obliged to report regularly to the CEC. Organized on a language and geographical basis, it was not until 1924 that the party began its reorganization on the basis of factory clubs.

One of the first tasks of the Communist Party of Canada was the consolidation of its organizational unity. In a report accompanying the party's application to join the Comintern, the CEC noted that the party was in the process of perfecting "the technique of the illegal organization," as the War Measures Act was still in effect.[47] The party's application, made in the summer of 1921, out-lined the principal points of the party's program and constitution to show that they corresponded with the Comintern's 21 conditions of admission. In December 1921, Otto W. Kuusinen, a member of the Secretariat of the Executive Committee of the Communist International (ECCI) informed the Communist Party of Canada that its application for affiliation had been unanimously accepted. Under the slogan "Into the Masses!" he emphasized the party's responsibility to work and agitate in the labor movement, advising that communist work must be both theoretical and practical.[48]

While continuing to consolidate its clandestine organization, the party participated in the public political life of the country to draw wider sections of revolutionary-minded workers into organized revolutionary activity. Communists participated in a wide range of legal organizations. In the spring of 1920, a group of young Canadian Marxists, among them Annie S. Buller, Bella Hall Gauld, Beckie Buhay and her brother Mike, set up the Montreal Labor College as a center for progressive education. The Labor College quickly became a very influential force in the city's progressive community and was instrumental in the establishment of the Communist Party and the Young Communist League (YCL) there.[49] In Toronto, the Plebs League and the Ontario Labor College, both led by Florence Custance, played a similar role.

Like the labor organizations, these bodies were limited in what they could do. The party therefore decided to call a special conference for December 11, 1921 to establish a legal and open rev-

Many of the people at this picnic on Toronto Island were leaders and activists in the Plebs League, the Ontario Labor College and the Socialist Party of North America, organizations which provided much of the initial membership and leadership of the Communist Party in Toronto.

1. Ted Buck; 2. Tim Buck; 3. Carol Kahn; 4. Mina Kahn; 5. Mildred Uspich; 6. Ron Buck; 7. Rae Uspich; 8. Mrs. Shapiro; 9. Alice Buck; 10. Florence Custance; 11. Rose Davidson; 12. Rose Kogan; 13. Dinah Kahn; 14. Marie Tiboldo; 15. Helen Burpee; 16. Walter Swift; 17. Shapiro; 18. John Ingham Sutcliffe; 19. Jack Held; 20. Max Armstrong.

olutionary working class party. Fifty-one delegates from as far away as Timmins, Winnipeg and Montreal arrived in Toronto to participate. The conference decided to found the Workers' Party of Canada. As the basis for the new party, the delegates adopted a five-point program around which the party would be organized: (1) the establishment of a workers' republic; (2) participation in electoral campaigns as a means of exposing the capitalist system; (3) the education of the workers on the potential of their organizations as genuine fighting units while opposing the "tyranny and treachery of the reactionary labor bureaucrats;" (4) democratic centralism; and (5) the eventual establishment of a party press under the control and direction of the party leadership.[50] William Moriarty was elected secretary of the provisional committee; he also replaced Tom Burpee as secretary of the Communist Party because the latter preferred less public and more administrative types of work.

Firm links were maintained between the Communist Party and its open, legal arm, the Workers' Party. The latter worked under the strict control and direction of the underground organization.[51] The Communist Party went under the code name "Z" while its legal counterpart was known as "A". "Z" was smaller, 650 members in the summer of 1921. In 1922, to ensure the safety of the underground organization, its membership was reduced. The Workers' Party, on the other hand, had 3,000 members by the time of its constituent convention in February 1922.

Attending this convention were 42 delegates from Ontario, 5 from Quebec and 16 from western Canada. The latter were given weighted votes of two each because the time and expense of travelling across Canada's vast distances in those days did not make it practical for Communists in western Canada to send all the delegates to which they were entitled.[52]

The first convention of the Workers' Party was characterized by its determination to advance the revolutionary struggle and by its proletarian internationalism. The delegates expressed their solidarity and admiration for the Russian Revolution and the world's first socialist state. They passed a resolution calling for the creation of a Canadian Famine Relief Committee to aid the young Soviet Republic. The resolution drew attention to the fact that most of the Soviet Republic's difficulties stemmed from the sabotage of production on the part of the old regime's sympathizers. The motion emphasized that the success of the Russian Revolution would hasten the day of the emancipation of the workers of the world. The delegates, most of whom were workers and trade unionists, thus showed remarkable perception with regard to the historical significance of the events which had taken place in Russia. They very well understood the connection between the struggles of Canadian workers against capitalist exploitation at home and the need to weaken world imperialism through support for the first workers' state so that the balance of world forces would tip in favor of the world revolutionary movement.

The convention occupied itself with the immediate demands of the Canadian working class as well. Unemployment,

Killed by police for his anti-conscription and labor activities, Ginger Goodwin had been a past president of the British Columbia Federation of Labor and an organizer for the Mine, Mill and Smelter Workers. His murder provoked a one-day general strike throughout much of British Columbia, the first general strike in Canadian history.

for example, was characterized as a permanent feature of the capitalist system. The Workers' Party identified itself with the plight of the unemployed and put forward a program of immediate demands on their behalf: (1) public works providing jobs at union rates; (2) unemployment insurance at not less than the average wage and supplemental grants for part-time workers; (3) cessation of all interest payments on war bonds until unemployment payments were made; and (4) trade with and the extension of credits to Soviet Russia.[53]

The convention adopted a constitution which differed little in its essentials from that of the Communist Party.[54]

To spread the new party's message among the workers, the delegates agreed on the necessity of beginning publication of a legal communist newspaper to be called *The Worker*. The newspapers of the Communist Party had had to face great difficulties. *The Communist*, the *Workers' World* and the *Workers' Guard* had been victims of police raids and the difficulties of circulating an illegal newspaper.[55]

The first issue of *The Worker*, dated March 15, 1922, explained succinctly the reasons why a communist press was a necessary part of the revolutionary working class movement in Canada. To realize its aims, the working class needed its own militant organ expressing its class demands and reporting on its everyday experiences. The function of the communist press was to act as a collective organizer and agitator of the working class. It had to educate the workers on the need to achieve socialism and was an ideological and political weapon of the working class in its struggle against the bourgeoisie.

The Communist and Workers' Parties existed side by side for three years. The Orders-in-Council passed under the authority of the War Measures Act were finally allowed to lapse in 1923. At the third convention of the Workers' Party in April 1924, the party's name was changed to the Communist Party of Canada and the underground organization was dissolved.[56]

1. H.A. Innis, *The Fur Trade* (Toronto, 1970), p. 242.
2. M.Q. Innis, *An Economic History of Canada* (Toronto, 1935), p. 212.
3. *The Road to Socialism in Canada* (Toronto, 1971), p. 18.
4. M. Robin, *Radical Politics and Canadian Labour* (Kingston, 1971), p. 20.
5. M. Mackintosh, *An Outline of Trade Union History in Great Britain, the United States and Canada* (1946), p. 11; also reprinted by the Mine, Mill and Smelter Workers (Canada) in 1966.
6. Robin, p. 20.
7. J.F. Cahan, "A Survey of the Political Activities of the Ontario Labor Movement, 1850-1935" (Toronto, 1945), Master's thesis, p. 9.
8. Robin, p. 40.
9. H. Griffin, *British Columbia: the People's Early History* (Vancouver, 1958), pp. 79 and 84.
10. Quoted in Cahan, p. 23.
11. Ibid., p. 24.
12. Robin, pp. 38-39 and 62.
13. Griffin, p. 74.
14. Cahan, p. 16.
15. T. Buck, *Lenin and Canada* (Toronto, 1970), p. 10.
16. Robin, p. 99.
17. Ibid., p. 110.
18. Cahan, p. 30.
19. Ibid., pp. 30-31.
20. W. Bennett, *Builders of British Columbia* (1937), p. 42.
21. Buck, p. 19.
22. Cahan, p. 39.
23. P.F. Sharp, *The Agrarian Revolt in Western Canada* (St. Paul, 1948), passim, pp. 105-127.
24. *Report of the Proceedings of the Thirty-First Convention of the Trades and Labor Congress of Canada*, September 20-25, 1915, p. 14.
25. Cahan, p. 41.
26. *Report of the Proceedings of the Ninth Annual Convention of British Columbia Federation of Labor*, March 10-13, 1919, p. 24.
27. *One Big Union Bulletin*, March 10, 1927.
28. Buck, p. 22.
29. Defense Committee composed of the various labor organizations in Winnipeg, *The Winnipeg General Sympathetic Strike* (no date), p. 11.
30. *Western Labor News*, May 19 and 22, 1919.
31. Ibid., May 21, 1919.
32. *The Winnipeg General Sympathetic Strike*, pp. 47 and 55.
33. A.E. Smith, *All My Life* (Toronto, 1977), p. 58.
34. *Western Labor News*, June 23, 1919.
35. Robin, p. 146.
36. Buck, p. 12.
37. Ibid., p. 19.
38. Ibid., p. 24.
39. T. Buck, *1917-1957: Forty Years of Great Change* (Toronto, 1957), p. 27; and *Canadian Tribune*, July 20, 1959.
40. W.Z. Foster, *History of the Communist Party of the United States* (New York, 1970), p. 171.

41. Ibid., pp. 180-181.

42. The barn was owned by A. Fred Farley, a member of the United Communist Party of America.

43. *The Application of the Communist Party of Canada for Affiliation with the Communist International* (no date but sometime in 1921), Archives of the Communist Party of Canada (Archives CPC).

Those who are known to have attended the Guelph unity convention are Tim Buck, John Boychuk, Tom Burpee, Max Dolgoy, Jack MacDonald, Tom Bell, William Moriarty, John Latva, John Ahlqvist, Mike Buhay, Alex Gauld, Matthew Popovich, John Navis, Trevor Maguire, Jack Margolese, Maurice Spector, Florence Custance and Comintern representative Caleb Harrison — 18 of the 22 who attended.

Tim Buck's list of the 22 delegates who attended the Guelph convention given in his 1965 interview with the Canadian Broadcasting Corporation is inaccurate. It excludes Tom Burpee and Max Dolgoy who were definitely present (see B.C. Hughes, "Arise Ye Prisoners of Starvation..." in *The Canadian Magazine*, January 22, 1972, p. 24). On the other hand, it includes J.R. Knight and his wife, but as Tim Buck states elsewhere, J.R. Knight did not join the Communist Party until *after* his return from Moscow in July 1921 (see T. Buck, *Canada and the Russian Revolution*, p. 88 and the Department of Labour, *Labour Organization in Canada* for the calendar year 1922, p.

173). According to John Boychuk, only one woman, Florence Custance, attended the convention and therefore J.R. Knight's wife was not present. Tim Buck's list also includes Malcolm Bruce and Jacob Penner (among others) who did not join the Communist Party until after its foundation. It seems probable that Tim Buck confused the Guelph convention with the preliminary conference of December 1921 and the first convention of the Workers' Party in February 1922.

44. *The Communist*, June 1921.

45. Ibid.

46. Ibid.

47. *Decisions and Activities of the Central Executive Committee* (June or July 1921), Archives CPC.

48. O.W. Kuusinen, letter to the Communist Party of Canada, December 28, 1921, Archives CPC.

49. L. Watson, *She Never Was Afraid* (Toronto, 1976), p. 11.

50. *To the Workers of Canada* (December 1921); reprinted in *Labour Organization in Canada*, pp. 174-177.

51. W. Moriarty, letter to the ECCI, August 1922, Archives CPC.

52. *The Worker*, March 15, 1922.

53. Ibid.

54. See *Labour Organization in Canada*, pp. 180-183.

55. L.T. Morris, *The Story of Tim Buck's Party* (Toronto, 1939), p. 12.

56. *To the Third Convention of the Workers' Party of Canada*, April 18-20, 1924.

adopted policies. Worse, the ACCL, whose president was the reformist A.R. Mosher, was very much inclined to pursue class-collaborationist policies. In this fundamental sense, Mosher and his cohorts were little different from the right-wing leadership of the TLC.[63] The main difference between the two union centers lay in the ACCL's opposition to the AFL, solely on the basis that it was American. Otherwise, there was no real difference between them in either ideology or practice.

In the context of their fierce anti-communism, their refusal to take up the issues of the day and their gross violations of union democracy in the name of democracy, the class-collaborationism of the TLC and the ACCL led only to greater frustration on the part of many Canadian workers. The workers were becoming more militant. They wanted organization and leadership. They wanted militant unionism which would put an end to sell-outs and defeats and bring about authentic unity and victories.

As in the case of the workers, conditions impelled Canadian farmers to act, to join the political struggle. The Communist Party paid much attention to the struggles of Canada's small farmers and agricultural workers who by and large were extremely poor and at the mercy of the railway companies and the banks. In the early 1920s, the United Farmers of Manitoba, Alberta and Ontario were elected to their respective provincial governments with the substantial support of the poor farmers and in alliance with the provincial labor parties. However, the reformist leadership of the United Farmers failed to carry out their

policies and consequently lost popular support. In Ontario and Manitoba, the United Farmers were defeated in the following provincial elections while in Alberta they managed to hang on until 1935. A similar fate befell the Progressive Party which in 1921 had elected 63 representatives to the House of Commons. Its support also came from the farmers but its leadership and most of its Members of Parliament soon defected to either the Liberal Party or the Conservative Party.

Nevertheless, progressive ideas were still strong among the farmers. With the decline of the United Farmers, a new militant Farmers' Union of Canada was founded in the spring of 1923.[64] After two years of rapid growth, it too fell under the influence of more conservative elements. Given these circumstances and the achievements of the TUEL, the Communist Party, which had considerable support among poor, particularly Ukrainian farmers, considered it appropriate to set up the Progressive Farmers' Educational League (PFEL) in early 1925. Serving much the same function in relation to farmers' organizations as the TUEL did to the trade unions, its purpose was to educate farmers on the need for progressive policies.[65] In practice, the work of the PFEL was more difficult than that of the TUEL because of the class character of the movement it was trying to influence. Speaking to the Communist Party's fifth convention, Walter E. Wiggins pointed out that the worker could see his enemy in the boss "but the farmer was under the illusion that he was a property-owner and could not see how he was being exploited."[66] The farmers' owner-

2. A Party of the New Type

Throughout the twenties, the Communist Party worked to consolidate itself on a basis of consistent democratic centralism, a process in which both inexperience and ideological deviations were factors. Neither, however, prevented the party from being actively involved in the workers' and farmers' movements across the country and at the international level. This was a period in which the party's policy of unity in the working class movement had a clear impact; the Trade Union Educational League (TUEL), the Progressive Farmers' Educational League (PFEL) and the Canadian Labor Party (CLP) entered the political arena.

1. The Communist Party in Action

After the acute economic and political crisis of 1920-1923, imperialism embarked on a period of temporary stabilization of capitalism. It was a time when the revolutionary upsurge of the early 1920s receded. Until the market crash of 1929, there was a relatively high degree of economic prosperity. World capitalism managed to reduce unemployment and raise the living standards of certain sections of the working class. Other sections, however, became the victims of an effective capitalist economic and political offensive. In the ideological sphere, imperialism gained ground in strengthening bourgeois and reformist illusions among working people. In most imperialist countries, the left suffered some decline.

Similar processes were at work in Canada. The fourth convention of the Communist Party of Canada in 1925 observed that the "acute industrial and agrarian crisis of 1920-23 has been partially liquidated."[1] Reflecting the objective process of capitalism's development, Canada's industries were increasingly concentrated and centralized in the hands of finance capital. The party's fifth convention in 1927 took note of the continuing prosperity of capitalism in Canada. Although pointing to "the very unstable equilibrium of world capitalism as a whole," the convention report did not foresee any immediate alteration of the prevailing economic situation.[2]

Economic circumstances affected the political work of the party. One of the first tasks of the Workers' Party was to organize the unemployed around a program of immediate demands. The party helped to organize a demonstration of the unemployed as early as March 1922 when 5,000 jobless workers marched in Vancouver, demanding jobs or unemployment insurance. Similar demonstrations were held in other Canadian industrial centers as well. As a year of economic crisis and high unemployment, such actions were frequent during 1922, but in the later 1920s, the organizations of the unemployed found themselves struggling to survive.

The effectiveness of the capitalist offensive against the working class was reflected in the fortunes of the labor movement. In 1919, the year of the Winnipeg General Strike, union membership reached an all-time high of 378,000. In the course of the next few years, total union membership suffered a drastic decline, falling to a low of 271,000 by 1925.[3] Wage rates declined very sharply as well. In terms of 1939

wages equalling 100, the general average wage rate in 1920 was 107.0, but two years later, it tumbled to 91.1. The economic boom of the later 1920s gave the working class a chance to regain some of its losses, and by 1930, the general wage rate had reached 99.9. (The working class did not regain its 1920 position until 1940.)[4] As the working class recouped some of its losses, so too did the trade unions which made a limited comeback in terms of membership.

The level of the class struggle, which is largely determined by the prevailing economic and political conditions and the balance of class forces, affected the communist movement too. As the class struggle ebbed in the mid-1920s, the party experienced a sharp falling off in the number of its members.[5] In 1929, it was reported that the party was still suffering what was called a "general loss of membership."[6]

The Worker's fortunes at first reflected the problems of the party. Initial growth in the newspaper's first two years of operation was succeeded by growing financial difficulties and a decline in circulation.[7] But hard systematic work by Annie Buller, Beckie Buhay and others brought about a reversal by late 1925. A significant gap began to develop between the falling membership of the party and the rising readership of the newspaper.

Despite changing economic and political conditions, the Communist Party paid especially close attention to solidarity work and to the promotion of proletarian internationalism. In this, it remained true to the traditions established by the Canadian working class movement. The very first organization initiated by the newly-formed Communist Party was in fact the Canadian Friends of Soviet Russia in August 1921, an organization of solidarity with the struggles of the revolutionary workers and peasants of Russia. The fact that it was established even before the preliminary conference of the Workers'

From left to right: Florence Custance (1881-1929), Bea Colle who became a secretary of the Friends of the Mackenzie-Papineau Battalion in the late 1930s, Beckie Buhay (1896-1953) and Annie Buller (1895-1973).

Party and that Florence Custance, a prominent party leader, was made its first secretary, symbolized and testified to the Communist Party's determination to make proletarian internationalism a cornerstone of its ideology and its practice. The Canadian Friends of Soviet Russia soon joined the Workers' International Famine Relief Committee.[8] At the Workers' Party's constituent convention, a Canadian Famine Relief Committee was formed to collect financial and material aid for the young struggling Soviet Republic.

Working under the slogans "Hands off Russia" and "Trade with Russia," the Canadian Friends of Soviet Russia developed a widespread movement to compel the imperialist states, including Canada, to end their military intervention in Russia. This movement merged with the efforts of the international working class and communist movements.[9] Once this aim was achieved, the next thrust of the activities of this solidarity organization was directed toward agitating for the Canadian government's recognition of the Soviet government. In less than a year, its efforts were crowned by partial success when, in 1924, trade relations were agreed upon by the two countries.[10] Three years later, however, trade relations were unilaterally broken by Canada under pressure from British and U.S. imperialism.

From the very beginning, the Canadian Friends of Soviet Russia and the Canadian Famine Relief Committee successfully mobilized broad public sympathy in support of the young Soviet state. From August 17, 1921, to February 28, 1923, over 64,940 dollars was sent to the Russian Red Cross, in those days a phenomenal sum of money.[11]

Canadian Communists expressed their solidarity with the workers and the Communists of other countries throughout the 1920s. In 1922, solidarity work was carried out in support of the German working class movement which, after its unsuccessful revolution, suffered bloody repression from both the German bourgeoisie and foreign imperialist powers.

France seized Germany's rich coal fields in the Ruhr region in January 1923 on the pretext of making Germany pay war reparations. The CEC issued a statement roundly condemning the French military action, charging that France was selfishly motivated to develop these coal fields in its own interests. It warned that the invasion "promises to revive the ghosts of 1914-18."[12] It called for the abolition of the iniquitous Versailles Treaty because in practice the treaty made the German workers rather than the German imperialists pay for war reparations.

The party took a great deal of interest in and supported the British General Strike of 1926 and issued a special statement analyzing its lessons. The reformist leaders of the British Labour Party had abruptly called off the strike on the grounds that it was "unconstitutional." What failed, declared the Communist Party of Canada, was not the strike, but the reformist leadership of that strike.[13]

Communists, along with the trade union movement and other democratically-minded Canadians, were extremely active in the movement for the defense of the democratic rights of two Italian-born Americans, Nicola Sacco and Bartolomeo Vanzetti, who had been falsely accused of murder. The party's fifth convention in June 1927 adopted a resolution demanding the unconditional release of the two union organizers and characterizing their impending execution as a "judicial murder" and the "latest exhibition of capitalist class justice."[14] Mass meetings and demonstrations in their defense were held throughout Canada up to the night of the scheduled execution. Despite extensive international protest, the judicial murder of Sacco and Vanzetti was carried out on August 23, 1927.

The Communist Party played an active role in the congresses and plenums (ECCI meetings) of the Comintern and the RILU during the 1920s, but attendance was rather sporadic because of financial limitations. J.R. Knight attended the congresses of the Comintern and the RILU in the summer of 1921 but not as a party representative. Influenced by his experiences, he joined the party on his return to Canada.

Florence Custance, Jack MacDonald and Maurice Spector attended the fourth Comintern congress in November and early December 1922. The latter two also represented the party at the second congress of the RILU which took place at the same time. The main topics for discussion at the Comintern congress were the tactics of the united front, Lenin's report on the first five years of socialism in Soviet Russia and the prospects of the world revolutionary movement, the slogan of the workers' government and the draft program of the Comintern.

Unable to attend the ECCI meetings of 1923 and 1924, the party sent delegates

The fifth congress of the Comintern took place in 1924, when Soviet Russia was still recovering from the devastating effects of the civil war. Tim Buck (1891-1973) attended the congress, during which he met these two children orphaned by the war.

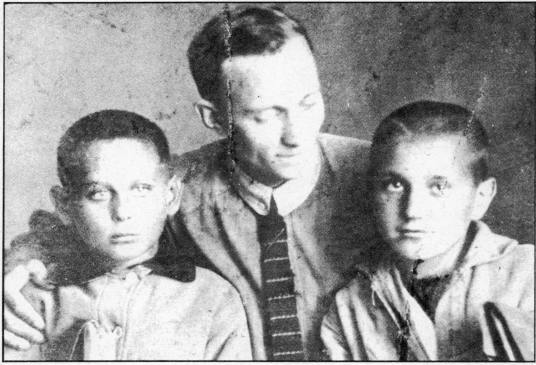

ARCHIVES CPC/PAC/PA-124380

to the Comintern's fifth congress held in June and July of 1924. Tim Buck, A.T. Hill and Malcolm L. Bruce represented the party. Tim Buck also attended the third congress of the RILU which was held immediately after the end of the Comintern congress. The fifth Comintern congress observed that the capitalist offensive against the working class movement had receded and that it was now necessary to strengthen the world communist movement ideologically and organizationally under the slogan of bolshevization.

After he came back from the fifth Comintern congress, Tim Buck raised the question of the reorganization of the party in an article in *The Worker*. Ex-

plaining why it was necessary and the difficulties involved, he stated that the Comintern's call for bolshevization meant the restructuring of the Communist Party on the basis of factory and street clubs, that is, in a way consistent with the principles of democratic centralism and with the party's political aims and character. Reorganization had to be made party policy.

The Communist Party of Canada, although an overwhelmingly working class party, initially included affiliated immigrant associations. There were a number of reasons for this: the party's inexperience in the application of the principles of democratic centralism, the need to consolidate the party in conditions of illegality which tended to divert attention from organizational matters to the problem of how to obtain legality and, above all, the fact that the federative structure was inherited from the Social Democratic Party when its Ukrainian and Finnish sections joined the party *en masse*. In fact, Finns and Ukrainians constituted a large section of the party membership at that time. As workers, they were actively involved in organizing trade unions and leading strikes. Much cultural and political work was done by Communists of Finnish and Ukrainian origin in their respective communities. They worked to involve workers and farmers in their communities in Canadian labor and farm struggles and progressive political action.

The scattered nature of the party membership, the tendency to work on a territorial basis and the resistance to party reorganization which could be expected from the language group sections because they feared the removal of "the bond which their present language branch supplies" were, in Tim Buck's opinion, the three main obstacles to reorganization.[15] On the other hand, what favored party reorganization on the basis of industrial clubs was the fact that the majority of party members were industrial workers. Of the party's 4,500 members in 1925, 800 were miners, 800 lumber workers, 400 railroad workers, 800 to 1,000 farmers, most of whom also worked in the mines or the lumber camps, and most of the remainder were city workers employed in the needle, leather and metal trades.[16]

Party reorganization proved to be a slow and difficult process. In fact, Tim Buck foresaw that the party's organiza-

tional transformation would take considerable time.

Transformation of the party from what it is, to a party rooted in the factories, mines and shops, means much more than the mere physical reorganization. It presupposes a complete change in the whole basis of its work. It means transferring the principal sphere of party activity 'and influence' from the branch meetings in the party hall — to the shops.

It means the establishment of close and unbreakable contact between the party and the masses, the organization and leading of the revolutionary struggle against the employers, for shop committees and workers' control. It provides, in fact, the Communist base in the struggle for power.[17]

The object of the reorganization was to increase the proportion of industrial workers in the party, thereby changing its social composition even more in favor of the industrial proletariat and bringing the party still closer to the workers.[18] It was, in short, a form of what the Communist Party now calls industrial concentration.

Three years later, little progress had been made in restructuring the party. At the fifth convention, Jack MacDonald, the party leader, reduced the difficulties to the fact that many party members who could not speak English were experiencing problems in conducting group discussions in the English language.[19] These problems were still being encountered at the sixth convention in 1929. Mike Buhay reported on behalf of the organization department that "in the organizational sphere the Communist Party of Canada has not yet fulfilled the tasks raised before it. ..."[20] The party had failed to achieve its organizational aims as embodied in its 1925 constitution.[21] The solution, according to Mike

Buhay, lay in strengthening the party's organizational apparatus and in raising the ideological level of the party membership.

The real cause of the party's problems was to be found in the unwillingness of some party leaders to carry through the decisions of the fifth convention. As the Comintern had pointed out, a temporary objective basis existed for the growth of opportunism in both the working class and communist movements due to the partial and temporary stabilization of capitalism.

Jack MacDonald, who had succeeded William Moriarty as party leader in 1923, was becoming the ideological leader of a political current within the party which later became known as North American exceptionalism. His opportunism led him away from the organizational principles of the Leninist party. The report of the 1929 convention on the organizational and inner problems of the party placed the blame on the persistence of federalist and social-democratic remnants in the party's leadership.[22] The leadership, in fact, wanted to maintain the federative structure which had given the language sections a certain degree of autonomy, a form of organization which contradicted the working class orientation of the party and prevented it from establishing itself on a consistent basis of democratic centralism.

Another weakness in the party's work was the difficulty it had in establishing itself in French Canada. In Quebec, industrialization on a massive scale had occurred relatively recently, bringing with it the rapid growth of the French Canadian working class. William Kashtan (who became General Secretary of the YCL in 1929) explained that this growth was interlocked with the social and ideological hangovers of the past. The historical ideological domination of the Catholic Church over French Canadian society acted as a serious obstacle to the organization of French Canadian workers on a class basis and thus reinforced a situation in which French Canadian workers were the lowest paid and the least organized.[23]

Beckie Buhay noted in *The Worker* that the ideological domination of the Church was further strengthened by the history of national strife in Canada which made it possible for the Church to pose as the defender and bearer of French Canada's national consciousness.[24] English Canadian chauvinism and French Canadian nationalism inhibited the achievement of unity between the two national sections of the Canadian working class.

The national question in Canada was much deeper and more complicated than the Communist Party realized at that time and the party tended to underestimate its importance. As Tim Buck summarized years later, the basic weakness of the party's approach was the fact that "the party did not grasp the full historical significance of the national status of the people of French Canada and therefore failed to put forward the necessary demand for the right of French Canada to national self-determination up to the right of secession."[25]

There was certainly no lack of attempts to establish Communist groups among French Canadians. In 1923, Albert St. Martin tried to set up a French

In addition to taking up issues concerning women and international solidarity, the Women's Labor League was involved in other activities including the maintenance of children's homes, such as this one in Drumheller, Alberta.

Canadian section of the Comintern but was refused affiliation because a Communist Party already existed in Canada.[26] In addition, St. Martin was heavily influenced by nationalism. He strongly opposed the international craft unions and preferred the Church-dominated Catholic unions, in spite of his avowed anti-clericalism, because the latter were at least "Québécois." He founded the Université Ouvrière but as the process of differentiation among French Canadians developed, a section of St. Martin's group decided to break away and join the Communist Party of Canada.[27]

The Communist Party made its own attempts as well. In the mid-1920s, a left-wing newspaper in the French language was founded but the lack of both funds and experienced cadre ended its existence after only a few issues. Work among French Canadians was further hampered by the fact that the basic works of Marx, Engels and Lenin were practically unavailable in French. Capable organizers were extremely scarce.[28] Similar problems plagued the YCL. In May 1930, the party once again set up a French language newspaper, *l'Ouvrier Canadien*, but it was suppressed by the provincial government a month later.[29]

At this early stage, the party recog-

31

nized the urgent task of drawing women into active participation in the fight for better wages and working conditions. At the same time, the party fought reactionary ideas which tended to separate women from the organizations of the working class. As early as 1922, Florence Custance, who was in charge of work in this sphere, noted that women were a source of cheap labor for capitalist employers.[30] At the party's third convention, she pointed out that from a political standpoint women enjoyed nominal equality with men, but from the economic standpoint the opposite was the case.

Communists participated in the Women's Labor Leagues which had been founded prior to World War I. This organization campaigned actively to collect funds for the women and children of the striking steelworkers of Nova Scotia; it sponsored a "No More War" demonstration; those of its members who also belonged to the TLC participated in the unemployed movement in Toronto. In 1924, the Women's Labor Leagues became the first Canadian women's organization to celebrate International Women's Day on March 8. This celebration highlighted the internationalist theme of solidarity with German working class women suffering under bloody reaction and bourgeois terrorism which had followed in the wake of the unsuccessful post-war revolutionary insurrection. The Women's Labor Leagues were also deeply involved in issues of immediate interest to women such as the raising of the minimum wage and the organization of the unorganized women into trade unions.[31]

2. The Trade Union Educational League

From its inception, the Communist Party supported and promoted trade union unity. In this, it followed the finest traditions of the Canadian working class movement. The founding convention adopted a program which opposed splitting the ranks of labor but which also supported the fight for industrial unionism as a form of labor organization superior to craft unionism. At the same time, the delegates expressed their opposition to any policy which hindered trade union unity on a class struggle basis and thereby served notice to the social-reformists of the labor movement that their class-collaborationist policies would not be allowed to go unchallenged. The "Resolution of Policy on Trade Unions," adopted by the 1922 convention of the Workers' Party, expanded on this theme to include the unity of the working class as a whole in a united front. In the Communist Party's view, there was no other alternative for combating the capitalist offensive against living standards and the trade union movement, and for overcoming the "disorderly retreat" experienced by the labor movement in the early 1920s.[32]

Opposition to the party's policy of working class unity came almost immediately from the opportunists within the labor movement. The OBU became one of the centers of this opposition even as many of its most prominent leaders joined the Workers' Party. That differences existed within the OBU became fully apparent during the course of the 1922 Workers' Party convention where R.B. Russell, who had been invited to attend as a fraternal delegate from the OBU, hoped to persuade the party to turn itself into the political arm of the OBU. Russell opposed the party's resolution on trade union unity, demanding that the delegates choose either the OBU or the reformist TLC. He claimed that his union was the ideal form of union organization. As his views held wide currency among large sections of militant workers in western Canada, the convention had to come to grips with his divisive position. Following a heated debate, most of the delegates (among them J.R. Knight and Jack Kavanagh, two former leaders of the OBU) emphatically rejected Russell's anarcho-syndicalist ideas and overwhelmingly endorsed the party resolution.[33] From then on and throughout the twenties, the Communists and anarcho-syndicalists were irreconcilable antagonists. The Communist position in favor of trade union unity prevailed among militant workers while the OBU became weaker and weaker. By the end of the decade, the influence of anarcho-syndicalism was substantially reduced.

The main organizational form for communist work in the trade unions was the TUEL. Founded by U.S. Communists in November 1920, the TUEL did not become fully active until it launched the *Labor Herald* in March 1922.[34] The Canadian TUEL was established in Toronto in April 1922.[35] It was to carry out agitational and educational work in favor of amalgamation.[36] The amalgamation movement, led by Communists and the TUEL, became a new form of the continuing struggle by militant and left-wing workers to achieve trade union unity on a class struggle basis.

The Canadian section of the TUEL was an organic part of the American TUEL. They had common aims and principles which originated out of their history of common struggles. Unlike the Canadian sections of the AFL, the Canadian TUEL enjoyed genuine autonomy and effective control over its own affairs. The Canadian TUEL derived benefits from its ties with the RILU as well, because the latter transmitted the experiences of the international working class movement to its affiliates. As the basic interests of the working class of all countries coincide despite national variations, the TUEL's affiliation to the RILU was quite consistent with its struggle for the rights and interests of the Canadian working class.

The TUEL held its first conference on August 26-27, 1922, in Chicago. Although interrupted by a police raid toward the end of the first day's session, the conference formally adopted basic principles and program.[37] The TUEL declared itself to be a purely educational body and not a trade union. To emphasize this point, it was "strictly prohibited for any of its national or local branches to affiliate or to accept the affiliation of trade unions."[38] In order to ensure no misinterpretation of the TUEL's intentions, its principles specifically prohibited the collection of dues and specified that funds would have to be raised in some other manner such as through donations, sales of literature and so on.

The TUEL's program called for the amalgamation of the craft unions into industrial unions, the organization of the unorganized, independent labor political action, fighting against class-collaborationism, the abolition of capitalism and the establishment of a workers' republic.[39]

Tim Buck, who represented the Canadian section, reported to the conference that after some initial difficulties the TUEL had already become a force among militant trade unionists. In his opinion, the conference was useful because it would help facilitate the work of the TUEL in Canada.[40] On his return to Toronto, he immediately set out on an organizational tour of western Canada in the name of the TUEL. By the time of the 1923 convention of the Workers' Party, Tim Buck was in a position to inform the convention delegates that although work was still in its initial stage, the party and the TUEL had active groups in 16 of 60 Trades and Labor Councils including all the important centers. They also succeeded in establishing their presence in the logging camps, the coal mines of Nova Scotia and western Canada and the metal mines of northern Ontario. Directly and through the TUEL, Communists were already exerting considerable influence in the labor movement and had become a major factor in its development. In order to make the TUEL still more effective, the February 1923 convention of the Workers' Party adopted a resolution urging the party membership to participate in the TUEL's activities and wholeheartedly supported its work.[41]

The resolution supported the formation of industrial unions, particularly in the railway industry, through amalgamation, that is, through the unification of existing craft unions on the basis of one union in each industry. According to the "Resolution on the United Front," amalgamation was necessary in order to overcome the disorganized and demoralized state of the labor movement in the face of the capitalist offensive.

Although the leadership of the craft unions opposed industrial unions, the sentiment of the rank and file was strongly in favor of amalgamation.[42] In time, it became apparent that quite wide sections of the craft unions wanted to strengthen the union movement through unification. The conditions of the class struggle, in fact, spontaneously gave rise to a desire to overcome inter-union bickering. Industrial unionism seemed to be the appropriate answer.

Nevertheless, the right-wing leaders of the craft unions did everything possible to discourage and obstruct the amalgamation movement and blamed Communists for the problems besetting them. At the 38th TLC convention in 1922, Tom Moore, president, went out of his way to attack the Workers' Party. He accused it of employing splitting tactics in its promotion of amalgamation and industrial unions and deliberately ignored the fact that the party actively campaigned against secession. The TLC leadership further accused the Workers' Party and the TUEL of aiming "to poison the minds of the workers against the present trade union and labor organizations and ultimately make them instruments for the establishment of Communism."[43] The 39th and 40th TLC conventions also went on record in opposition to amalgamation, but a great deal of pressure had to be exerted on the delegates to follow the leadership's lead on the question.[44]

The resistance of the TLC leadership to industrial unionism was buttressed by their financial and organizational dependence on the U.S. parent unions. Most craft unions in Canada were extensions of the so-called Internationals which were U.S.-based and dominated unions. In most cases, the Canadian membership had little say in the conduct of the union's affairs in Canada. This became more than obvious when John L. Lewis, president of the United Mine Workers of America, broke the coal miners' strikes of District 18 (Alberta and eastern British Columbia) and District 26 (Nova Scotia) through administrative fiat and open collaboration with the coal companies and the government.[45] Meanwhile, the attempted amalgamation of the railroad shop crafts was frustrated by the AFL unions despite the demonstrated need and desire for such a merger.

As the activities of the TUEL expanded, it became subject to the hate of the AFL bureaucrats. While the RILU welcomed the TUEL's foundation, at its 1922 convention the AFL, led by the notorious "business unionist" Samuel Gompers, condemned the TUEL as an organization of disrupters bent on "a gigantic campaign of deception, plunder and greed."[46]

At the 1923 U.S. convention of the

UTL. TF/MS. COLL. 179/KENNY COLLECTION

AFL, the leadership attacked proposals for amalgamation as Communist-inspired.

This propaganda to which we refer is frankly revolutionary, and has for its ultimate purpose not only the destruction of the trade union movement but the eventual overthrow of the government of the United States.

Propaganda in the United States is carried on in accord with the tenets of the Red International, an organization which is completely under the domination and dictation of the Russian Communist oligarchy.

The catchword of the campaign in the United States has been 'amalgamation.'[47]

These words were echoed by the leaders of the TLC. Under the guise of defending democracy and the integrity of the labor movement, they used anti-communist lies and distortions to smear the real aims of the Workers' Party and evade the pressing issues facing the labor movement. Yet despite these unjust attacks on their motives, Communists still pursued the fight for working class unity and the advancement of its class interests.

In August and September of 1923, the Canadian section of the TUEL organized eastern and western Canadian conferences. At both conferences, the main report was delivered by Tim Buck who at the time was both leader of the Canadian TUEL and the industrial organizer of the Workers' Party. Both reports dwelt on the progress and tasks of the TUEL and the conferences helped to consolidate the organization in Canada. Resolutions were adopted relating to amalgamation, industrial unionism and the organization of the unorganized.[48]

The persistent refusal of the right-wing social-reformist leaders of the AFL and the TLC to adopt progressive policies and in fact their betrayal of the class interests of the workers even to the point of aiding strikebreaking, compelled the TUEL to take a more active role, that is, to become more than just an educational body. The 1924 TUEL conference drew attention to the growing contradiction between the workers' desire for industrial unionism and the obstacles raised to its realization by the TLC leadership. Concluding that failure to extend the TUEL's activities would have dire consequences for the working class, the conference formally incorporated the demand for Canadian autonomy into its program.[49] To be more effective in propagating its views, the TUEL began publication of its own newspaper, *The Left Wing*, in 1925.

Industrial unionism retained its appeal among many workers. When confronted with the divisive activities of the AFL and TLC leadership, many workers began to take up the demand for Canadian autonomy, a demand which spread rapidly in the Canadian sections of the AFL unions due to the refusal of the Internationals to allow Canadian workers to run their own affairs. The leadership of the AFL and the TLC regarded Canadian autonomy as dangerous because they feared it would open the door to militant industrial unionism. In their view, autonomy would run counter to their pursuit of class-collaborationist policies. In the Communists' view, however, autonomy would facilitate working class unity on a class struggle basis. For this reason, the third convention of the Workers' Party decided to incorporate the demand for Canadian autonomy in its program.[50]

The Communist Party took pains to explain that the demand for autonomy was not to be confused with secession nor was it inspired by Canadian chauvinism. The party wanted Canadian locals to remain members of their respective International unions. Canadian autonomy was meant to ensure that Canadian workers would be able to pursue their special interests and function as a unit in the struggle against employers in Canada.[51]

For the party, the demand for an all-inclusive Canadian trade union center was as necessary as Canadian autonomy to facilitate the unity of the Canadian working class. Tim Buck wrote in 1925:

Our puny organizations, demoralized by sectionalism, weakened by isolation and the conflicting ideologies inevitable under present conditions, are split and smashed with a regularity that is appalling.

There is only one way at the present time, but that way is simple. Freedom of action for Canadian workers; every union in the country affiliated to one central body.[52]

Thus freedom of action from the AFL's class-collaborationist leadership had to be accompanied by the formation of a union center capable of overcoming the isolation of the individual unions and of strengthening the union movement as a whole. This principle was officially adopted by the fourth convention of the Communist Party in September 1925.[53]

The 1925 convention also took up the question of organizing the unorganized which was regarded by the party as one of the most urgent tasks of the Canadian labor movement as early as August 1924.[54]

The AFL and TLC leadership chose to ignore the growing demands for amalgamation, autonomy, an all-inclusive trade union center and the organization of the unorganized. As a result, a divided labor movement became even more divided. Rejected by the TLC, the independent Canadian unions decided to form their own central body, the All-Canadian Congress of Labor (ACCL), in 1927. Most of its member unions were industrial unions who initially proclaimed their intention of organizing the unorganized on the basis of militant industrial unionism. Meanwhile, secessionist tendencies grew in the Canadian sections of the AFL unions and in several cases actually led to splits. The Communist Party combatted these tendencies. In the case of District 26, Communists successfully persuaded the coal miners not to pull out of the United Mine Workers of America (UMWA).

In District 18 events took a different turn. There, the Communist Party's campaign against the District's secession from the U.S.-based UMWA was unsuccessful. The situation in the union had deteriorated so badly because of Lewis' abject surrender to the coal companies that the miners were absolutely determined to secede. Faced with no alternative but the total disintegration of union organization among these workers, the party decided to work toward the formation of an independent, Canadian miners' union to replace the former District 18 of the UMWA. Given the state of affairs in the UMWA, the party did not adopt an "AFL or nothing" attitude.[55] Instead, the party decided to use its considerable influence among the miners "to prevent the district splitting into a dozen different sections."[56] The party's role in the creation of the Mine Workers' Union of Canada (MWUC), given the special circumstances, in no way compromised its general principle of opposing secessionism.

The TUEL and the Communist Party were deeply involved in most of the important struggles of the period. The TUEL helped the Lumber Workers Industrial Union of Canada (LWIUC) reorganize when its demise appeared imminent. This union, originally founded by the IWW in 1917, joined the OBU in 1919 but withdrew in 1920. In 1922, the union's convention decided to apply for affiliation to the RILU and was accepted, so becoming the only Canadian union ever to formally join the RILU.[57] As a militant industrial union, it was hated by the bosses and the TLC bureaucrats alike. A campaign to smash the union was launched and by 1925 had almost succeeded. It was at this point that the TUEL became involved.[58] With the re-emergence of the union in the logging camps, company resistance stiffened even more. In an effort to frustrate the union's organizational drive, company goons brutally murdered two Finnish-Canadian Communist union organizers, Viljo Rosval and John Voutilainen, in the fall of 1929. Nevertheless, the union achieved major successes and later, as a member of the Workers' Unity League (WUL), played an important role in the organizing drives of the 1930s.

Finnish-Canadian Communists played a particularly prominent role in the Lumber Workers' Industrial Union of Canada. Among the participants at the union's 1928 convention were union organizers Viljo Rosval (second from the left) and John Voutilainen (seated on the left of the middle table) who were later murdered by company goons for their organizing activities. Karl Salo (1900-1962) (seated on the right of the middle table) was the union's secretary, and editor of the Finnish-language newspaper Vapaus, for a number of years. (Bottom photo) The body of Viljo Rosval. Murdered in the winter of 1929, Rosval and Voutilainen were hidden under snow and ice and found the following spring.

Communists and the TUEL played a key role in the heroic struggles of the coal miners and steelworkers of Nova Scotia. From 1923 to 1925, several long and bitter strikes took place during which the workers were faced with the combined opposition of the companies, the federal and provincial governments and the treachery of the Lewis leadership of the UMWA. The coal miners were ably led by the colorful J.B. McLachlan and Dan Livingstone, secretary and president of District 26 respectively. At the height of the miners' struggle, when it seemed that they stood virtually alone against the attacks of the courts, the police and even troops, the TUEL and the Communist Party came through with substantial aid in the form of money and personnel.[59] Tom Bell, for instance, took over the editorship of the *Maritime Labor Herald* during the most difficult phase of the strike. Tim Buck, Jack MacDonald, Malcolm Bruce, Beckie Buhay, Annie Buller and others made organizational tours to Nova Scotia and then followed up with tours to other parts of the country in order to popularize the plight of the miners and organize solidarity work.

In Alberta and eastern British Columbia, Communists such as Roy Reid, Jan Lakeman, James Sloan and John Stokaluk, to name only four of the most outstanding, actively assisted in the organizing of the MWUC.

The TUEL, which called itself the representative of the Canadian trade union minority, gained wide popularity as the years went by. The circulation of *The Left Wing*, a monthly, stood at 6,000 after just three years. A more significant indicator of its influence was the fact that by 1925 about 50 per cent of Canadian union locals had declared themselves in favor of amalgamation and Canadian autonomy. In 1925, Communists were elected to the Montreal executive of the Amalgamated Clothing Workers Union, Canada's largest needle trades union at that time. This victory was achieved after a long struggle against the old administration. Substantial inroads were also made in other needle trades unions such as the Furriers and the International Ladies' Garment Workers' Union. The TUEL in the United States, meanwhile, had achieved even greater successes.[60]

From the foundation of the TUEL, the union establishment had been per-turbed by the TUEL's activities and successes. What had begun as verbal condemnation and relatively isolated anti-communist acts in the 1923-25 period became a systematic campaign of persecution in 1926. The signal for carrying out this campaign came from the new AFL president, William Green, who wrote an editorial in the December issue of the *American Federationist* urging AFL affiliates to expel supporters of the Communist Party.[61]

This anti-communist war cry was taken up in Canada as well. The general office of the Amalgamated Clothing Workers Union rejected the candidacy of Local 209's left-led executive on the day of the election so that its own slate could be elected. Shortly afterward, Sidney Hillman, the union's U.S. president, made a special appearance at a meeting of the local where he manipulated the expulsion of nine left-wingers for having distributed a TUEL leaflet. In March 1928, a strike by union members was broken when the union leadership expelled the strike committee.[62] By late 1928, expulsions were a feature in other needle trades unions as well. They assumed such a massive scale that the TUEL had no choice but to help in the organization of the Industrial Union of Needle Trades Workers (IUNTW) in December 1928.

Antagonisms also developed between the TUEL and the leadership of the ACCL. Although the TUEL initially welcomed the ACCL's formation and in fact encouraged the MWUC and the LWIUC to join, the ACCL leadership soon began to move away from militant unionism. It did very little to organize the unorganized, one of its officially

Delegates to the convention of the Canadian Labor Party (Ontario Section) in London, Ontario, 1926. Counting from left to right: sitting on curb, (4) Tim Buck; first row seated, (5) Florence Custance; (18) A.E. Smith; (19) J.S. Woodsworth; (22) A.T. Hill; second row, (4) David Goldstick; (8) Maurice Spector; (10) Jack MacDonald; (11) Mike Buhay; (22) Oscar Ryan; (28) Arthur Mould; last row, (4) Phillip Halperin.

ARCHIVES CPC/PAC/PA-125186

ship of land gave rise to petty-bourgeois illusions of economic independence, an illusion which was reinforced by the economic prosperity of the mid and late twenties. Despite these obstacles, the PFEL kept alive the progressive and militant traditions of the Canadian farmers' movement and laid the basis for the work of the Farmers' Unity League (FUL) in the 1930s.

3. The Canadian Labor Party

In the estimation of the Workers' Party, the conditions of the twenties demanded militant, united class struggle. The first convention of the Workers' Party had adopted a resolution which urged "the establishment of a united front to resist the aggressions of the capitalist class."[67] The TUEL and the PFEL were two forms of this policy, organized to defend the interests of the workers and farmers. The Workers'

Party also supported the Canadian Labor Party (CLP) as a form of organization which could unite all those who believed in independent labor political action.

The essence of the united front had been first enunciated at the third Comintern congress in 1921. It combined two essential factors — unity of the working class, and class struggle against exploitation and oppression by the capitalist class. Unity between revolutionaries and reformists based on militant policies advancing the class struggle was the way forward. Unity on the basis of class-collaboration was a dead-end.

The CLP had been founded in 1917 on the TLC's initiative, at a time when it was under heavy pressure from the union membership to organize a political party which would unite all those who believed in independent labor political action and who opposed the imperialist war and conscription. Its declared intention was "to solidify the different groups of the working class political movement . . ."[68]

The August 1921 CLP conference declared that its aim was "a complete change in our present economic and social system."[69] In contrast to the vagueness of its general long-term aim, the CLP's immediate program was quite concrete. It contained a number of demands (unemployment insurance, nationalization of the banks, etc.) which were consistent with the demands of the Workers' Party.[70] In the opinion of the Workers' Party, the struggle for the realization of these demands would further the class interests of the workers. The Workers' Party applied to the CLP through its provincial organizations for affiliation, applications which were accepted by the provincial sections of the CLP during 1922-24.

The two parties differed in their organizational structures. Whereas the Workers' Party (renamed the Communist Party in 1924) was a revolutionary party generally based on democratic centralism, the CLP was a federated labor party whose membership was open to both individuals and working class organizations such as the unions and political parties. While the Communist Party also had elements of a federated structure, this was due to its ethnic composition and was not supposed to conflict with its Marxist-Leninist ideology. The CLP incorporated not only different groups but also their various ideological tendencies ranging from the revolutionary ideology of the Communists to the social-reformism of the TLC and the Independent Labor Party.[71]

Nevertheless, all these divergent groups officially adhered to the immediate program of the CLP, a program of struggle for the short-term interests of the working class. But within the CLP there lay a contradiction between the left and the right which broke into the open in the mid-1920s.

The policies of the Communist Party enjoyed wide support in the CLP. At the September 1922 convention of the CLP's Quebec section, Jack MacDonald in his capacity as a trade unionist "captured the hearts and minds of 90 per cent of those present with a splendid exposition of our party's [the Communists'] program and policies."[72] However, Jimmy Simpson, secretary-treasurer of the CLP, future mayor of Toronto and erstwhile TLC radical who had opposed conscription and who had even called for the formation of a united front to include Communists, revealed his true political colors by attempting to exclude three representatives of the Workers' Party from participating in the convention. Nonetheless, the Quebec section of the CLP accepted the affiliation of the provincial organization of the Workers' Party over his objections.[73] Other provincial sections of the CLP followed suit, although not without strong resistance from the right wing.

While affiliated with the CLP, the Communist Party did not run candidates for electoral office under its own banner. In strict observance of the CLP's rules, Communists ran only as CLP candidates and supported the CLP's non-communist candidates even though the party had little confidence in some of them. Communists never knowingly split the united front; when splits did occur, they could usually be traced to the activities of right-wing social-reformists.[74]

As the class struggle ebbed in the 1920s, the right wing stepped up its anti-communist activities. In the winter of 1925, the right wing in the CLP's Quebec section successfully manoeuvred to have the Communist Party expelled, by a narrow margin, on the specious grounds that it was trying to direct the CLP into the Comintern. Rejecting the charge, the Communist Party pointed out that the CLP's federated structure was sufficient in itself to make it ineligible for membership in the Comintern. A similar attempt to have the Communist Party expelled was made at the April 1926 Ontario CLP convention but was overwhelmingly defeated.

A few months later, the reformist Manitoba Independent Labor Party, which stood outside the CLP, suffered a humiliating defeat in the Winnipeg municipal elections at the hands of the CLP and the Communist Party. William N. Kolisnyk defeated a candidate of the Independent Labor Party for a seat on city council, thus becoming the first Communist ever elected to public office in North America.[75]

The right-wing social-reformists were not about to give up, however. At the April 1927 convention of the Ontario CLP, they caucused openly for the formation of an Ontario Independent Labor Party which they would dominate. It was an action which coincided with a vociferous anti-communist campaign within the TLC. The CLP in its majority was consequently obliged to remove Simpson from its slate of electoral candidates because of his participation in the right-wing's divisive manoeuvres. The TLC retaliated by quitting the CLP and joining the newly established Independent Labor Party.[76]

By splitting the CLP, the right wing achieved its aim. An atmosphere of pessimism and defeatism began to permeate the CLP.[77] Sabotaged by the reactionary and divisive policies and activities of the right-wing social-reformists, deprived of a major base of support, the provincial sections of the CLP folded one by one during 1928-29.

Despite the ultimate demise of the CLP, the Communist Party's experiences in working with it were on the whole positive. As long as the CLP's political and organizational unity was maintained (and Communists played a very constructive role in this respect), its influence and prestige grew. The experience of the CLP clearly demonstrated the need for and potential of the united front of the working class based on a program fighting for the real interests of the workers. What prevented the CLP from becoming a success was the divisive role played by the class-collaborationists. By means of anti-communism, they blatantly undermined working class unity and thereby objectively upheld the class interests of the bourgeoisie inside the working class movement.

1. *Proceedings of the Fourth National Convention, Communist Party of Canada,* September 11-13, 1925, sheet one of the "Political Resolution."
2. *Report of the Proceedings of the Fifth Convention of the Communist Party of Canada,* June 17-20, 1927, p. 50.
3. Department of Labour, *Labour Organization in Canada, 1970* (Ottawa, 1971), p. xiii.
4. Department of Labour, *Wage Rates and Hours of Labour in Canada, 1943* (Ottawa, 1945), p. 9.
5. *Organizational Report — Communist Party of Canada,* January 1927, Archives CPC, p. 5.
6. Letter of the Politsecretariat of the ECCI to the Central Committee of the CPC, no date, Archives CPC.
7. W. Moriarty, *The Worker Business Manager's Report,* 4th convention of the CPC, September 11-13, 1925, sheets 2-3; and *Fourth Convention,* sheet 1.
8. *The Worker,* April 1, 1922.
9. Ibid., May 30, 1923.
10. Ibid., April 5, 1924.
11. Ibid., May 16, 1923.
12. Ibid., February 15, 1923.
13. CEC of the CPC, *Lessons of British General Strike,* 1926, Archives CPC.
14. *Fifth Convention,* p. 105.
15. *The Worker,* September 20, 1924.
16. *Organizational Report — CPC,* p. 5.
17. *The Worker,* October 25, 1924.
18. Ibid.
19. *Fifth Convention,* p. 10.
20. *Report of the Sixth Convention of the Communist Party of Canada,* May 31 — June 7, 1929, p. 3.
21. Constitution (1925), pp. 6-8.
22. *Sixth Convention,* p. 91.
23. *The Young Worker,* February 1929.
24. *The Worker,* November 22, 1924.
25. T. Buck, *Thirty Years* (Toronto, 1952), p. 29.
26. In principle, the Comintern accepted the membership of only one Communist Party in each country.
27. M. Fournier, *Communisme et anticommunisme au Québec (1920-1950)* (Montreal, 1979), p. 21.
28. *Organizational Report — CPC,* p. 10.
29. *The Worker,* May 24 and June 28, 1930.
30. Ibid., May 1, 1922.
31. *To the Third Convention of the Workers' Party of Canada,* sheet 1 of "Progress of the Toronto Women's League and the Results of its Activity of the Year."
32. *The Worker,* March 15, 1922.
33. Department of Labour, *Labour Organization in Canada (For the Calendar Year 1922)* (Ottawa, 1923), p. 180; and *The Worker,* March 15, 1922.
34. C. Krumbein, "A Year of the League" in *Labor Herald,* February 1923, p. 3.
35. *The Worker,* August 22, 1923.
36. Department of Labour, *Labour Organization in Canada (For the Calendar Year 1923)* (Ottawa, 1924), p. 160.
37. *Labour Organization in Canada 1922,* pp. 189-190.
38. *Labour Organization in Canada 1923,* p. 186.
39. W.Z. Foster, *History of the Communist Party of the United States* (New York, 1952), p. 203.
40. *Labour Organization in Canada 1922,* pp. 189-190.
41. T. Buck, *Report of Industrial Organizer* to the second convention of the Workers' Party, February 22-24, 1923, sheets 1-2; *Resolution on Trade Unions* of the second convention of the Workers' Party, February 22-24, 1923, Archives CPC.
42. *Labour Organization in Canada 1923,* pp. 196-198.
43. *Labour Organization in Canada 1922,* p. 192.
44. *The Worker,* September 15, 1922; *Labour*

Organization in Canada 1923, p. 198; and TLC, *Report of the Proceedings of the Fortieth Convention*, September 15-19, 1924, pp. 101-105.

45. *Labour Organization in Canada 1923*, pp. 187-188.

46. *Labour Organization in Canada 1922*, pp. 188-189.

47. *Labour Organization in Canada 1923*, p. 199.

48. *Report of Conference of Eastern Sub-division of Canadian Section of Trade Union Educational League*, August 4-5, 1923, Archives CPC; *Report of Conference of Western Sub-division of Canadian Section of the Trade Union Educational League*, September 22-23, 1923, Archives CPC.

49. Buck, *Thirty Years*, p. 46.

50. *Resolution on Industrial Policy* of the third convention of the Workers' Party, April 18-20, 1924, Archives CPC.

51. *The Worker*, August 30, 1924.

52. T. Buck, *Steps to Power* (Toronto, no date), pp. 43-44.

53. *Resolution on Industrial Policy*.

54. *The Worker*, August 30, 1924.

55. *Report on the Canadian Situation* (1926), Archives CPC, p. 2.

56. *Fourth Convention*, sheet 8.

57. *Labour Organization in Canada 1922*, p.173.

58. *Report of the Canadian Section of the RILU for July, August and September 1925*, October 17, 1925, Archives CPC, sheet 2.

59. *The Worker*, May 23, 1923.

60. *Report to RILU for July-September 1925*, sheet 8; *Fourth Convention*, sheet one of the "Resolution on Industrial Policy;" and Foster, p. 253.

61. Department of Labour, *Labour Organization in Canada (For the Calendar Year 1926)* (Ottawa, 1927), p. 163.

62. *The Worker*, November 27, 1927, and March 24, 1928.

63. *Sixth Convention*, p. 34.

64. *The Worker*, January 5, 1924.

65. Ibid., February 13, 1926.

66. *Fifth Convention*, p. 94.

67. *The Worker*, March 15, 1922; and also *Labour Organization in Canada 1922*, p. 179.

68. CLP circular to trade unions, Trades and Labor Councils, local Labor Parties, Socialist Societies, farmers' organizations and cooperators, p. 1.

69. A.E. Smith, *All My Life* (Toronto, 1977), p. 69.

70. Ibid., p. 69; also the *Manifesto* of the CLP for the general election of September 14, 1926, Archives CPC; and *Labour Organization in Canada 1923*, p. 202.

71. Minutes: *Emergency Convention, Ontario Section, Canadian Labor Party*, August 7, 1926, Archives CPC; reprinted in the appendix of the second (1977) edition of A.E. Smith's *All My Life*, pp. 225-227.

72. *The Worker*, September 15, 1922.

73. Smith, p. 73; and *The Worker*, September 15 and December 1, 1922.

74. *The Worker*, December 5, 1925.

75. Ibid., December 11, 1926.

76. Ibid., April 30, November 26 and December 3, 1927.

77. *Fifth Convention*, p. 101.

3. The Struggle
for Theoretical Clarity

The struggle for theoretical clarity is a continuous process in the Communist Party. Toward the end of the twenties, however, it assumed large proportions, partly because the party was still in its infancy, but mainly because capitalist prosperity gave rise to reformist illusions.

At first, the opportunist trends within the party manifested themselves as seemingly isolated cases. Departures from Leninism were concealed in tactics which appeared to give the party some immediate advantage. Some party members, for example, began to submerge the party's independent identity in the mass organizations in which they worked, to confuse the role of the party with the function of the mass organizations. The aim of mass organizations is to struggle for the immediate interests of their members while the party's aim is to unite the different strands of the anti-monopoly and anti-capitalist struggle into one powerful force to bring about the replacement of capitalism with socialism. The united front was interpreted not as the unity of the working class despite differing outlooks among its component forces, but as a substitute for the independent political action of the Communist Party. There was also resistance to the idea of having Communists run in elections for fear that it would damage cooperation between Communists and social-reformists.

From these isolated instances of opportunism, two definite ideological trends of left and right-opportunism surfaced in the twenties — Trotskyism and North American exceptionalism. These trends caused much difficulty in the party's struggle to organize on a Leninist basis, to reorient its trade union work and to determine the nature of Canada's status in the imperialist world. The first challenge came from Trotskyism, as Maurice Spector, the party's chairman and editor of both *The Worker* and the *Canadian Labor Monthly,* revealed his true political colors.

1. Against Trotskyism

Spector had become infatuated with the theories of Leon Trotsky, a Russian petty-bourgeois revolutionist. As early as 1906, Trotsky advanced a series of anti-Leninist theoretical propositions which later became known as the theory of permanent revolution.*

After the bourgeois-democratic revolution in Russia in February 1917, Trotsky and his sympathizers publicly renounced their views and declared that the political and theoretical line of the Bolsheviks led by Lenin had been correct all along. Trotsky and his followers were then allowed to join the Bolshevik Party.

In actual fact, Trotsky had not changed his views as expressed in his concept of the permanent revolution, but instead, chose to conceal them. Nevertheless, his differences with the Bolsheviks surfaced on several occasions and compelled Lenin to refute Trotsky's positions in several lengthy articles. Trotsky in 1918 even went so far as to stall on the signing of the Brest-Litovsk treaty with imperialist Germany despite specific instructions from the Soviet government and the Bolshevik Party to do so immediately. As a result of Trotsky's treacherous policy, Germany,

ARCHIVES CPC PAC

which would otherwise have concluded an armistice with Russia, occupied even larger tracts of Russian territory.

After Lenin died in January 1924, Trotsky renewed his advocacy of the theory of permanent revolution and organized an opposition faction in both the Comintern and the Communist Party of the Soviet Union (CPSU). As Trotsky came to hold high positions in both the Comintern and the CPSU, his ideological deviation became a major concern of the world communist movement. In the winter of 1926, the seventh enlarged plenum of the ECCI, which Tim Buck and Matthew Popovich attended on behalf of the Communist Party of Canada, discussed the question of Trotskyism as well as events in China and questions of socialist construction. In late 1927, Trotsky was expelled from both the Comintern and the CPSU. He then went into exile where he continued his anti-Soviet and anti-communist agitation.

Leading members of other Communist Parties such as Spector in Canada and Max Schachtman and J.P. Cannon in the United States, fell under Trotsky's influence. Although Trotskyists usually constituted only a small sect in most Communist Parties, they were able to inflict various degrees of damage and harm depending on the circumstances prevailing in the individual parties.

Spector, like his mentor Trotsky, deceitfully concealed his sympathies for Trotskyism. No one was aware of the fact that he was in Trotsky's ideological camp until after he returned from the sixth congress of the Comintern in the fall of 1928. For a long time, Spector kept silent about the struggle against Trotskyism that was taking place in the Comintern and the CPSU. Yet indications of his true sympathies existed even if they were not immediately perceived. While he was editor of *The Worker* (from May 1924 to November 1928), Trotsky's factionalism inside the world communist movement was almost never mentioned until the newspaper printed the announcement that Trotsky had been expelled from the Comintern and later the CPSU.[1] During Spector's editorship of the newspaper, only one article, authored by Tim Buck, ever discussed Trotskyism as a definite ideological trend. Clearly Spector was utilizing his position as editor of *The Worker* to prevent the party membership from becoming cognizant of the vital ideological issues being debated by the world communist movement.

Further indications of Spector's actual sympathies were manifested in his refusal to discuss Trotskyism at CEC meetings. In fact, he avoided all situations where this topic came up for discussion.

From 1923 until today, the years when this questioning [of Trotskyism] was under discussion in the Communist International, Maurice Spector at no time raised his voice to explain his viewpoint to the Canadian Party. At the enlarged executive sessions in December 1927, he absented himself on the grounds of illness during the discussion and voting on this question. At the sixth congress of the Communist International, he absented himself during the consideration and voting on the question of Trotskyism.[2]

Two other incidents, however, finally exposed Spector's deceit and led to his expulsion from the party. On October 26, 1928, he made a speech at the Alhambra Hall in Toronto which was supposed to inform the Toronto party membership of the results of the sixth congress of the Comintern. As Spector himself wrote in a letter to the U.S. Trotskyist, J.P. Cannon, the audience had expected good news, but what he gave them was, to use Spector's own words, "a sober analysis of what led up to the grain crisis, stressing the role of class differentiation in the village and the menace of the Kulak."[3] Other party members were not so glib about the speech. A.E. Smith, who was in attendance, recalled that the address "consisted of a calculated array of slanders against the Soviet Union and its leaders. The speech left everybody cold with astonishment."[4] Spector was then called before the party secretariat to explain "the pessimistic and hidden Trotskyist character of his speech, but he denied his Trotskyist leanings."[5]

News of the expulsions of Cannon and Schachtman from the U.S. party and the discovery of correspondence between Cannon and Spector brought the controversy to a head. The correspondence revealed the true extent of the duplicity and anti-party machinations practised by Spector. On October 9, the day after his return from the sixth congress of the Comintern, Spector had written to Cannon congratulating him on winning over four members of the U.S. party to

By the mid-1920s, the Young Communist League was firmly established all across Canada. This photo taken about 1926 shows some Winnipeg members of the YCL. From left to right: unidentified, Alice Saliga, Saul Simkin, Bertha Guberman (née Dolgoy), Freda Coodin and unidentified.

his faction. Later, he wired the U.S. Trotskyist leader that he had been successfully evading the Trotskyism issue at CEC meetings. Cannon replied by advising him to continue his tactics of evasion and abstention. His aim was to gather his forces together as much as possible so that when the time was ripe, the Trotskyist faction would be able to exert maximum disruption of the Comintern and the Canadian and U.S. parties. Spector was assigned a key role in the conspiracy against the world communist movement in his capacity as a member of the ECCI, a post to which he was elected at the sixth congress while concealing his Trotskyist beliefs. On

November 5, Cannon informed Spector:

We thought in view of *your position on the ECCI* your most effective entry into the situation would be in the form of a letter of protest to the ECCI against our expulsion which we would publish and which would be the signal for your openly joining forces with us in the publication of the paper. *This would give the appearance of the fight spreading on a wider front* and should have a valuable moral effect.[6]

Cannon also asked Spector to obtain *The Worker*'s subscription list but Spector was suspended by the CEC before he had the chance to do so. In anticipation of further actions against him, Spector suggested to Cannon that "we must put ourselves in immediate communications with the Oppositional elements (who stand on the legitimacy of the Trotsky program) in order to give our expulsions the widest possible Comintern publicity."[7] Clearly this exchange of correspondence between Spector and Cannon left no room for doubt that Spector had been deceiving and lying to the party for years. (As it turned out, Spector confessed that he had had doubts about the Comintern's line as early as 1923.)[8]

Once again the party confronted Spector with his political beliefs, this time at a meeting of the Central Committee (CC) on November 11. Faced with the incontrovertible facts, Spector openly declared his support for Trotskyism.[9] The CC expelled him "on the grounds of his open alliance with Trotskyism against the Leninist policy of the Communist International."[10]

The Communist Party made a thorough examination of its experience with Trotskyism. A joint statement issued by the party and the YCL analyzed the origins and nature of this petty-bourgeois trend.

Bourgeois ideology, with the tremendous powers at its disposal, constantly forces itself upon the working class, and finds its representatives among the upper strata of the workers, and petty-bourgeois intellectuals on the fringe of the working class.[11]

Maurice Spector, a son of a small shopkeeper and a student at the University of Toronto, was one of the latter. He

twice abandoned his studies in order to be a full-time party functionary.[12] Lacking experience in and concrete ties with the working class movement, he was mainly interested in the more abstract fields of theory and international affairs. Despite pretensions that he was a brilliant theoretician, Spector's view of the world was not tempered by the sobering realities of the class struggle. Spector, in fact became the archetype of a Trotskyist. Even his factionalism, deceitfulness and underhanded machinations became typical methods of his followers, now as then.

The Communist Party drew the important conclusion that Trotskyism was an objective ally of social-reformism and right-opportunism. In common with the anti-Soviet opportunism of the Russian Mensheviks and European social democracy, Trotskyists such as Spector refused to believe in the possibility of building socialism in the Soviet Union. This led him to oppose the Soviet Union and objectively join hands with openly counter-revolutionary forces. Even in the specifics of the Canadian party's policies, Spector made essentially the same errors as the right-opportunists. For example, he opposed the party's reorganization on a more consistent basis of democratic centralism and accepted the slogan "Canadian Independence under a Workers' and Farmers' Government," a demand for Canada's constitutional independence from Britain.[13] These mistakes, and others, if they had been implemented as party policy, would have effectively subordinated the revolutionary struggle to spontaneity in the former case and the policies of the national bourgeoisie in the latter case. Organizationally, ideologically and politically, Trotskyism has nothing in common with Marxism-Leninism and thus the Communist Party; it is an expression of right-opportunism and counter-revolution. Revolutionary and left-wing in words, Trotskyism is counter-revolutionary and reactionary in practice. Although a threat to the world communist movement at one point, Trotskyism was decisively defeated as a trend in the working class movement.

2. Against North American Exceptionalism

The CEC statement on Spector's expulsion, while noting the need to continue the fight against Trotskyism, nevertheless drew attention to the fact that the main danger to the party and the world communist movement came from the right.[14]

The struggle of the Comintern against the right danger within its own ranks facilitated the realization in the Communist Party of Canada that an opportunist ideological trend was developing. Although the struggle against Trotskyism had temporarily suspended the growing conflict between the two op-

ARCHIVES CPC/PAC

posing forces, it was resumed with full vigor almost immediately after Spector's expulsion.

While bourgeois ideology had influenced some Communists to adopt Trotskyist positions, a still larger number moved in a right-opportunist direction. Like bourgeois ideology and social-reformism, right-wing opportunism was an international phenomenon. Its specific features in the context of the 1920s were the overestimation of capitalist stabilization, the underestimation of the threat of war and repudiation of the principles of democratic centralism.[15]

In the USA, the right deviation led by Jay Lovestone advocated a theory which later became known as American exceptionalism, a theory which claimed that "in its essence capitalism in the United States is different from and superior to capitalism in other countries and is, therefore, exempt from that system's laws of growth and decay."[16] In 1929, Lovestone and his followers were expelled from the U.S. party after a protracted ideological struggle lasting several years. Lovestone eventually became George Meany's right-hand man in the reactionary leadership of the AFL-CIO.

As the Canadian economy was experiencing a similar, relatively long period of growth, and as the Canadian and U.S. Communist Parties maintained very close fraternal ties, it was not surprising that the theory of American exceptionalism should find sympathizers in Canada. Here the theory became known as North American exceptionalism since it was amended to include Canada. Like its U.S. counterpart, the Communist Party of Canada had to wage a long and difficult struggle against this theory and its proponents.

Jack MacDonald, the party's General Secretary, became the leading Canadian exponent of North American exceptionalism. Hints of his shift away from consistent Marxist-Leninist positions were in evidence as early as the party's 1927 convention. His report focused on Canada's industrial expansion but avoided any mention of tendencies in the Canadian economy which indicated a possible economic crisis. MacDonald concluded that the strategy of the working class ought to be based on the fact of industrial expansion, "a fact which opens up the possibility for a renewed offensive in the direction of an even greater share of the national income, higher wage standards, improved working conditions, shorter working hours, more adequate social legislation."[17] Although the Communist Party actively supported the struggle for the achievement of these just demands, MacDonald failed to connect them to the wider perspective of the struggle for socialism. When Tim Buck criticized the report on the grounds that it was difficult to say whether prosperity would continue or turn into something else, MacDonald retorted that "the statement on the increase in the productive forces may not sound nice, but the facts substantiate."[18] The battle line between Leninists and North American exceptionalists was thus already drawn.

Following Spector's expulsion in November 1928, MacDonald went on a Canada-wide tour on behalf of the party leadership, but news filtered back to party headquarters in Toronto that the political line enunciated by MacDonald in his criticism of Spector was actually inconsistent with the line of the party and the world communist movement.

The depth of the division in the party was more clearly revealed in the period prior to the sixth convention. In the spring of 1929, The Worker carried preconvention discussion of MacDonald's draft thesis for the convention. This thesis devoted a great deal of attention to Canada's economic and industrial growth but made only the most general of statements about the possibility of a future capitalist crisis. It was in fact a more elaborate repetition of statements he had made at the fifth convention in 1927.

MacDonald then expounded the thesis that the Communist Party was faced with a danger from the left which expressed itself in "the danger of degeneration into a propaganda sect substituting the revolutionary phrase for everyday work among the workers."[19] Stewart Smith immediately accused MacDonald of taking a line contrary to the party and the world communist movement. The accepted position was that there were only two immediate dangers in the world communist movement — one from the right and the other from Trotskyism. The former was considered to be the main danger whereas the latter was regarded as a

During the 1920s and 1930s, the YCL was responsible for organizing the Young Pioneers and for publishing a children's newspaper, Young Comrade. YCL members Jennie Freed (rear left) and her sister, Julia Carr (rear right) posing with a group of Young Pioneers, Toronto, 1928.

"right danger in Marxist disguise."[20] By focusing attention on the so-called left danger, MacDonald's aim was to attack his opponents' Leninist positions as leftist while simultaneously justifying and cloaking his own right-opportunist inclination.

Other aspects of the draft thesis also drew severe criticism. So glaring were the weaknesses of the draft, that the decision was made to postpone the convention from the end of March to the end of May.[21] Postponement gave the party more time to thoroughly debate the main issues. Fred Rose, who was briefly General Secretary of the YCL, pointed out that the document completely ignored the French Canadian question.[22] The leadership's failure to carry through the party's reorganization on a con-

sistent basis of democratic centralism was another target of criticism. The party still retained strong elements of a federative structure.

MacDonald's draft thesis had pointed to the inactivity of party units, the marked looseness in organization as examples of the party's work and charged that their source was to be found in leftism. But in Beckie Buhay's opinion, these problems stemmed from the weakness of the party leadership, an incorrect organizational structure and serious right-wing deviations. She argued that most of the party's mistakes could be traced to the leadership's right-opportunist positions.[23] John Weir supported her contention in an article published in *The Worker*. He argued that party activity tended to be concentrated in the language field and not in the factories where the mass of the Canadian workers was to be found. The problem was that the party leadership had failed to consistently apply the policy of reorganizing the party and this was reflected in the retention of a basically social-democratic structure of organization.[24] He thus agreed with Beckie Buhay's earlier observation that party leaders were not properly leading the party with the result that party clubs were unsure how to act. This situation caused party clubs to tail behind events rather than lead or guide them. The strikes at General Motors in Oshawa and at National Steel Car in Hamilton were cases in point. Local party clubs had not played an adequately active role in either struggle.

The Communist Party also had the benefit of a contribution from the Comintern. Well experienced in the ways of opportunism, the Comintern grasped the implications of Mac-Donald's draft. In a closed letter to the CC dated April 8, 1929, the ECCI expressed the belief that it "contains needless repetition of the resolutions of the sixth congress and is overloaded with statistics to the exclusion of an adequate treatment of the actual problems facing the Communist Party of Canada."[25] The ECCI letter criticized the thesis for overemphasizing Canada's economic prosperity and for not indicating the contradictions which could lead to a crisis. The majority of the CEC subsequently adopted a resolution accepting the ECCI's criticism.[26]

Accepting the ECCI's criticism proved to be a tactic aimed at putting off further criticism and concealing continued adherence to opportunist concepts. Mac-Donald's report to the 1929 convention admitted to past errors but then proceeded to repeat them.[27] In a joint statement, Tim Buck and Stewart Smith charged that the report contained elements of right-opportunism despite the efforts of the Comintern, the Communist Youth International and the U.S. fraternal delegate, C.A. Hathaway, "to convince him of the correct line."[28]

The struggle against North American exceptionalism also entailed a struggle against opportunist interpretations of the party's trade union policy. Mac-Donald, J.B. Salsberg and Mike Buhay, among others, persisted in underestimating the radicalization of the working class. They could not, or would not, understand that its class consciousness had risen considerably as a consequence of the development of mass production industries in the two decades preceding the onset of the Great Depression. These industries, such as steel and auto, incorporated many new technological innovations which reduced or even rendered obsolete the privileged craftsman. Large numbers of unskilled or semi-skilled workers which were concentrated in one workplace could quickly learn to operate modern machines or work on the assembly line. This relatively new form of capitalist industrial organization required a new form of trade union organization. As the craft unions were not able to protect or promote the interests of the workers in the mass production industries, these workers, stimulated as they were by the ideas of the TUEL, looked toward industrial unionism.

The right-opportunists at the sixth

C.A. Hathaway (1894-1963) the fraternal delegate of the Communist Party of America to the 1929 convention of the Communist Party of Canada, and Tom Bell (right), party organizer in Manitoba in the early 1920s.

ARCHIVES CPC/PAC/PA-124372

party convention understood capitalist development in Canada in a one-sided way. By emphasizing capitalism's industrial expansion without also examining the internal contradictions of capitalist development, the North American exceptionalists implied that Canadian workers were becoming more prosperous and contented with their lot and would therefore not pursue the class struggle so intensely. Furthermore, the belief that British imperialism was the main enemy tended to divert attention from the internal source of class struggle in Canada, namely the ongoing contradiction between the working class and the bourgeoisie. In practice, the convention noted, such views would mean that "we will find ourselves at the tail end of the growing radicalization of the work-

ers, the workers will be in advance of us."[29]

The tendency to underestimate the level of class consciousness expressed itself in a number of weaknesses in the Communist Party's trade union work such as the inadequate elaboration of a clear-cut program of action, inconsistency of fraction work, insufficient training and development of cadre for trade union work, failure to organize campaigns and conferences, the lack of direction from the party's industrial department and a tendency to confuse the TUEL with the party. Although constructive work had been done since the fifth convention, shortcomings in the party's trade union work tended to overshadow achievements.[30]

Resistance to the right-opportunist

Delegates to the 1929 YCL convention: 1. Fred Rose; 2. Jennie Freed; 3. Dora Leibovitch; 4. Bertha Guberman; 5. Emil Miller; 6. William Kashtan; 7. Max Kelly; 8. George Cotter; 9. Carl Steinberg; 10. Paul Phillips; 11. John Williamson; 12. Martin Parker; 13. Joe L. Farby; 14. Oscar Ryan; 15. Misha Korol; 16. Norman Freed; 17. Minnie Blackburn; 18. Charles A. Marriot; 19. Tom Chopowick; 20. Frank (Whitey) Breslov; 21. Jack Eisen; 22. Mike Golinsky.

line came from Tim Buck, Stewart Smith, Fred Rose, Beckie Buhay, Harvey Murphy and others. They supported the proposals contained in the trade union thesis of the sixth convention which called for a definite reorientation in the party's trade union work and for its more planned and systematic implementation. Previously, the main orientation of the TUEL had been to agitate and educate the workers in favor of industrial unionism; now it was to become the organizer of the great body of unorganized workers in the mass production industries, workers who were ignored by the TLC craft unions. Nevertheless, the new tactical orientation did not suggest any relaxation of effort or diminution of activity in other unions. On the contrary, work in these unions had to be stepped up so that they could be drawn into the general struggle of the workers.[31]

There was yet another aspect of the fight against MacDonald's opportunist line. A bitter debate raged around the question of the role of the language sections. Within the Communist Party's structure at this time, each language section enjoyed a certain degree of autonomy. In addition, each language section had the right to appoint a member of its section to the CEC, thus making several CEC members answerable to the language section rather than to the party as a whole. Beckie Buhay noted that as long as some CEC members were not elected by the party convention, a centralized party leadership was impossible.[32]

Neither MacDonald nor some key leaders of the Ukrainian and Finnish sections wanted to change this arrangement. Quite to the contrary, Mac-Donald sought to divert attention from the problem of the effective implementation of the party's organization policy, to charges of the alleged anti-Ukrainian prejudices of certain unnamed Anglo-Saxon party members. Although he admitted that some leading Ukrainian comrades were suffering from "conservatism," he completely avoided the question of how this conservatism was to be overcome and whether or not he would support the reorganization of the party along territorial and industrial lines to include the elimination of autonomous language sections.[33]

MacDonald avoided discussion of the Constitutional Commission's report on the organizational and inner problems of the party except to state his agreement that social-democratic remnants still existed in the party's structure. The Commission was quite emphatic about where the blame lay. The CEC, it declared, had failed to pursue a consistent organizational policy which would orient the party toward industrial workplaces. Consequently, it was necessary to liquidate all social-democratic and federative elements and thoroughly apply the principles of democratic centralism. It also recommended the election of the CEC from the convention floor.[34]

MacDonald, who admitted the leadership's weaknesses and the inadequacies of the party's organizational structure, could not openly oppose the Commission's report. He was fully cognizant of the fact that open opposition to the party line would have exposed him in the eyes of the party membership. He therefore decided to support the report although his misgivings and actual sympathies were clear at least to the more politically astute party members. Indeed, the convention adopted a whole series of policies which reflected the desire of the party membership to make the party conform more closely to its declared ideological and organizational role as Canada's revolutionary working class party. MacDonald remained silent on many of these policies rather than risk the wrath of the delegates.

Ideological deviations from the principles of Marxism-Leninism often express themselves in deviations from the principles of democratic centralism. The right-opportunists of the sixth convention were no exception. About 14 to 16 party members, among them Mac-Donald and Salsberg, attended a secret meeting prior to the June 5 session of the convention. Their aim was to consolidate the various right-opportunist elements in the party.[35] When Tim Buck and Stewart Smith accused them of holding a factional meeting, i.e., an unauthorized meeting of party members outside the framework of the party's constitution with the object of predetermining the course of the convention, Salsberg deceitfully denied that any such meeting had taken place. Instead, he accused Tim Buck and others of being "most factional in their almost every utterance and stand at this convention."[36] He waxed eloquent against Beckie Buhay and C.A. Marriot on their alleged provocative and intolerable behavior. In Salsberg's opinion, factionalism was defined as opposition to the opportunist views held by himself and MacDonald.

The Leninist section of the party received substantial support from the YCL during the struggle against North American exceptionalism. Representing the YCL at the convention and basing themselves on a resolution adopted by the YCL's National Executive Committee, Oscar Ryan and J.L. Farby declared their agreement with the criticism made by the Comintern and that section of the party opposed to MacDonald's theory. They questioned MacDonald's failure to explain the basis of the right danger and, most tellingly, drew attention to the fact that he refused to dissociate himself from open right-opportunists such as Mike Buhay and William Moriarty. MacDonald himself agreed that these two had committed serious opportunist errors.[37] He declared, however, that he would not throw Mike Buhay overboard, "but would rather throw overboard some of the champions of the new line."[38] It was a provocative and unintentionally prophetic statement.

MacDonald's tactic of appearing to reject his opportunist views while actually retaining them was characteristic of his approach to other key questions as well. He readily conceded that he was too conciliatory toward the right danger and Trotskyism, and that the party had not been properly reorganized.[39] Yet these and other admissions, draped as they were in fine-sounding generalities, could not hide the fact that he and his sympathizers lacked concrete solutions to the party's very real problems. MacDonald's only resort was double talk. In his closing remarks, he declared once again that he had made opportunist mistakes in underestimating the radicalization of the workers and in not giving a perspective to a developing crisis.[40] Al-

A.T. (Tom) Hill (1897-1978), a prominent leader of both the YCL and the Finnish Organization of Canada throughout the 1920s.

ARCHIVES CPC/PAC

though he had made this admission before, it did not result in any correction of these mistakes but merely in their repetition.

Through duplicity, demagogy and unconstitutional organized caucusing, MacDonald and his allies succeeded in electing a majority to the CC.[41] The predominance of the proponents of North American exceptionalism thus seemed assured except for the fact that the delegates had also adopted positions which were at variance with those of the leadership. MacDonald and his supporters found themselves in an extremely contradictory position. Despite having carried the day in the convention elections, they had clearly lost the ideological struggle, the struggle for the political line of the party. MacDonald realized that it would be impossible for him to maintain the appearance of having renounced ideas he in fact still held. He therefore decided to follow Mike Buhay's example, who after being severely criticized at the convention as an open right-opportunist, resigned as editor of *The Worker,* a post he had assumed after Spector's expulsion. MacDonald called a CC meeting for July. In a political manoeuvre and much to the party's surprise, his first act was to announce his resignation as General Secretary and his second act was to nominate Tim Buck to take his place. At his request, MacDonald was released from duty as a party functionary and was granted a year's leave of absence. A new eight-person CEC was elected.[42] Tim Buck was elected as General Secretary.

The struggle against North American exceptionalism did not end with MacDonald's resignation. Very strong resistance to the new party leadership, for example, came from some leaders of the Finnish language section. In November 1929, John Wirta, John Ahlqvist and Arvo Vaara, who had all participated in MacDonald's secret caucus at the convention, were suspended from party membership for refusing to carry out the party's decisions. They were quickly isolated as all the branches of the Finnish Organization of Canada except the Sudbury branch where these three people were based, came out in support of the new party leadership.[43] The Finnish Organization then transformed itself from an autonomous language section of the Communist Party into an independent progressive organization. The Communist Party was now based solely on individual membership.

Meanwhile, MacDonald and other right-opportunists continued their anti-party agitation. For a year, attempts were made to persuade them to repudiate their erroneous views, but they remained adamant. Salsberg, for example, refused to adhere to party decisions, denied the party's role in the working class movement and repudiated its leadership. He pursued his activities in the Left Poele Zion, a Zionist organization, even though its political orientation was inconsistent and incompatible with the policies and principles of the Communist Party.[44] In 1930, he was expelled but later readmitted; he then remained silent about his continuing Zionist sympathies and disagreements with the party.

In November 1930, in a decision later endorsed by the February 1931 CC plenum, Jack MacDonald, Mike Buhay and Jack Margolese, a leader of the party in Montreal, were expelled.[45] Some party members followed them out, but others overcame their differences with the party and once more became staunch party members. Mike Buhay, for example, rejoined a few months later and was to play an important role as a distinguished Montreal city councillor in the 1940s. As for MacDonald, he travelled Spector's road to political oblivion.

3. Defining Canada's Status

The struggle for theoretical clarity included the question of Canada's status in the imperialist world. Was Canada a British or a U.S. dependency? Was the main enemy, as a consequence, British or U.S. imperialism? Or should the main thrust of the class struggle be directed against the domestic Canadian bourgeoisie? On this question too, North American exceptionalism tried to divert the party from its Marxist-Leninist approach.

Communists had paid little attention to the question of Canada's status until the late twenties. Although the growing importance of U.S. investment in Canada was noted as early as 1923, and although the Canadian bourgeoisie was becoming more assertive in its demands for control over all affairs affecting Canada, the party adhered to the illusion that Canada was a British dependency.[46] The 1925 convention continued this line, focusing on British imperialism as Canada's main enemy. It declared that the revolutionary forces had to seek the abolition of the BNA Act in order to achieve Canadian independence.[47]

The party's belief that the Canadian bourgeoisie was incapable of acting on behalf of its own independent class interests persisted through the 1926 constitutional crisis and the subsequent Imperial Conference. This crisis had been provoked by the Governor-General's refusal to dissolve Parliament on the request of the then Prime Minister W.L.M. King. At the Imperial Conference later that year, Canada was one of the advanced capitalist countries in the British Empire that demanded and obtained almost complete political independence from Britain, an achievement which was formalized by the Statute of Westminister in 1931. On the other hand, Canada retained the institution of the British monarchy because the preservation of close ties with Britain provided the Canadian bourgeoisie with special opportunities to pursue its particular ambitions under the cover of British imperialism. The Communist Party, however, concluded from these events that no change had occurred in Canada's status because the Imperial Conference was followed by a shift to the right in King's foreign policy, a shift which reinforced the impression that Canada was still a British dependency.

Canada in fact followed Britain's lead in cutting off trade and diplomatic relations with the Soviet Union in 1927.[48] Misunderstanding King's motive, the party's fifth convention condemned the rupture with the USSR, declaring that it "demonstrated the colonial status of the Dominion and his [the Prime Minister's] own lack of sincerity as a champion of 'National Status' against the British Foreign Office."[49] What the party failed to understand at that time was that King's anti-Soviet turn was not an act of subservience to British imperialism but an act of imperialist class solidarity against the world's first and only workers' and peasants' state.

The theory that Canada's capitalist class was colonial and dependent did not take into account that 55 to 65 per cent of capital in Canada was Canadian-owned. In accordance with the Leninist definition of imperialism (i.e., the concentration of production and capital leading to the formation of monopolies, the merging of bank and industrial capital to form finance capital, the export of capital, the creation of international capitalist monopolies), Canada qualified as an imperialist country. Canada shared in the plunder of colonies and exported capital to colonies (mostly British) and dependent countries. Furthermore, this theory ignored the fact that U.S. capital in Canada outweighed British capital by a ratio of two to one and that the Canadian bourgeoisie had taken measures to strengthen its own independence. Lastly, it did not at all explain the existence of contradictions within the Canadian bourgeoisie itself.[50]

In November 1928, MacDonald presented his draft thesis on Canada's prospects to a meeting of the enlarged executive committee in which he attempted to reconcile economic realities with the party's mistaken beliefs and his own North American exceptionalist ideas. The draft thesis noted that the Canadian bourgeoisie was "an independent factor and with independent interests," yet it excluded the possibility of the Canadian ruling class acting in its own selfish interests in its relations with both U.S. and British imperialism.[51] In MacDonald's opinion, the Canadian bourgeoisie was divided between pro-British and pro-U.S. factions and it was therefore subject to the contradictions arising between these two imperialist powers. As rivalries between the two intensified, so the antagonisms between the two Canadian factions were supposed to intensify as well. Indeed, the party was greatly influenced by current popular prejudice that an Anglo-U.S. war was in the making. If and when that war broke out, the Canadian capitalist class was expected to split, "creating a revolutionary situation, and probably civil war."[52]

Canadian independence was thus directly tied to the threat of an Anglo-U.S. war (although this was regarded as secondary to the much more realistic danger of an imperialist war against the USSR). The enlarged executive committee accepted this right-opportunist thesis and adopted the slogan "Canadian Independence under a Workers' and Farmers' Government."[53] It was a slogan which tended to disarm the working class in its struggle against its own capitalist class.

The Comintern was unhappy with the slogan's implications because it would "lead the working masses to believe that they are oppressed more by British imperialists than the Canadian bourgeoisie."[54] MacDonald then withdrew the slogan but without giving reasons why it was formulated in the first place. Even when he had a chance to address this question in his closing remarks to the 1929 convention, he declined to commit himself on who he considered to be the main enemy of the Canadian working class.[55] His evasiveness was grounded in the fact that the slogan actually coincided with the North American exceptionalist theory that Canada, like the USA, was exempt from the laws of capitalist development. The main enemy could not be the Canadian bourgeoisie because it was not like the bourgeoisie of other countries. The same reasoning precluded U.S. imperialism from being considered the main enemy.

ARCHIVES CPC/PAC/PA-124389

In late 1929, the new party leadership shifted the focus of the class struggle from British imperialism to the Canadian bourgeoisie. Yet in every other respect, the revised theory retained the essential elements of the theory advanced by MacDonald. While the existence of a Canadian ruling class was now recognized, the party continued to hold to the belief that it was divided into pro-British and pro-U.S. factions which, if an Anglo-U.S. war broke out, would bring civil war to Canada.

Opposition to the revised theory came from three young Communists, Leslie Morris, John Weir and Sam Carr, who at that time were studying at the Lenin School in Moscow. They rejected the thesis that the Canadian bourgeoisie was divided between pro-British and pro-U.S. factions whose relations were determined by the state of relations between the United States and Great Britain. They argued that this was objectively a right-opportunist position which placed the main contradiction affecting the Canadian revolution *outside* Canada. Consequently, the internal contradiction inherent in Canadian capitalism itself was grossly underestimated. Social revolution, according to the party's then current theory, depended on external wars rather than, as the three students argued, on the internal development of the class struggle. They pointed out that Canada was an imperialist country with its own capitalist ruling class.[56] As such, the Canadian government sought to exploit Anglo-U.S. contradictions with the view of advancing its own independent selfish interests. War between the United States and Great Britain would not necessarily entail civil war in Canada.

The criticism of the three students was not initially well received. In their youthful zeal, their criticism was coupled with unjust and somewhat excessive charges that the new party leadership, like the MacDonald leadership before it, denied the radicalization of the workers and struggled against the right danger in words only. They expressed doubt that the new leadership would carry through the full reorganization of the party. In short, Leslie Morris, John Weir and Sam Carr were accusing the new party leadership of repeating the same mistakes that had been committed by MacDonald and his cohorts. Tim Buck and Stewart Smith were singled out as the chief proponents of this "false, opportunist theory."[57] They thought the party was indulging in "schematic and scholastic speculation."[58]

Being in the midst of an intense struggle against right-opportunism, the new party leadership did not take very kindly to being categorized with their irreconcilable ideological opponents. Consequently, the leadership reacted with a lengthy, strongly worded statement refuting the criticism and charges of the students and accusing them of being dishonest and of strengthening the right wing. The statement drew attention to the fact that the party leadership was not conciliatory toward the right danger, nor did it underestimate the radicalization of the workers.[59] While rejecting the accusation that its positions were similar to those taken by the right-wing opportunists, the statement nevertheless repeated the mistaken theory which put Anglo-U.S. contradictions at the center of Canadian economic and political life.[60]

The three students actually made very valid points about the definition of Canada's status in the imperialist world, but their subjective presentation led to mutual accusations of opportunism. Both sides became bogged down in misunderstandings of each other's positions. The main obstacle to the adoption of a correct decision was, however, the CEC's refusal to acknowledge its political and theoretical mistakes.

The Comintern intervened just as the debate seemed resolved in favor of the CEC. The ECCI, after studying the question, sent a letter to the CC of the Communist Party of Canada pointing out that the Canadian bourgeoisie was playing an increasingly obvious imperialist role and that the party was wrong to overemphasize external contradictions.[61] The party then re-examined its position. With the heat of the earlier debate and the bitter personal recriminations behind them, the two sides addressed themselves to the question in a much more sober manner. The mistaken theory of the new party leadership on Canada's status was separated from the correct positions it had taken in opposition to the right-opportunists on other issues. The two opposing sides became reconciled. At the enlarged plenum held in February 1931, the party agreed that the leadership had indeed been mistaken and that this error consisted "in the failure to see the imperialist interests of the Canadian bourgeoisie. ...."[62] Many years later, Tim Buck was to write in a self-critical vein that the paper of the three students "forced us, indeed it impelled the party as a whole, to study Lenin's classic, *Imperialism, the Highest Stage of Capitalism* and to re-assess our estimation of the character of the Canadian state."[63] The ongoing process of criticism and self-criticism assures a consistent and correct line on vital questions affecting Canadian working people.

The theory of North American exceptionalism and its consequent effect on specific areas of work was defeated within the Communist Party by the end of the twenties. The analysis of the Leninists was fully corroborated by the market crash of late 1929 — North America proved to be no exception to the fundamental laws of capitalist development.

---

1. *The Worker,* October 15 and November 26, 1927.
2. *Statement of the Central Executive Committee of the Communist Party of Canada on Trotskyism and the Expulsion of Maurice Spector from Party,* November 1928, Archives CPC; reprinted in *The Worker,* December 1, 1928.
3. *The Worker,* January 19, 1929.
4. A.E. Smith, *All My Life* (Toronto, 1977), p. 94.
5. *The Worker,* December 1, 1928.
6. Ibid., January 19, 1929.
7. Ibid.
8. Ibid., December 1, 1928.
9. Ibid.
10. Ibid., November 24, 1928.
11. Ibid.
12. T. Buck, *Lenin and Canada* (Toronto, 1970), p. 47.
13. *The Worker,* December 1, 1928.
14. Ibid., December 1, 1929.
15. Institute of Marxism-Leninism, *Outline History of the Communist International* (Moscow, 1971), p. 290.
16. W.Z. Foster, *History of the Communist Party of the United States* (New York, 1952), p. 271.
17. *Report of the Proceedings of the Fifth Convention of the Communist Party of Canada,* June 17-20, 1927, p. 50.
18. Ibid., p. 61.
19. *The Worker,* February 23, 1929.
20. Ibid., December 1, 1928, and March 9, 1929.
21. Ibid., March 23, 1929.
22. Ibid., March 9, 1929.
23. Ibid., March 30, 1929.
24. Ibid., May 18, 1929.
25. *Report of the Sixth National Convention of the Communist Party of Canada,* May 31-June 7, 1929, p. 6.
26. Ibid., pp. 15-18 and p. 119.
27. Ibid., pp. 108-109 and p. 119.
28. Ibid., p. 81.
29. Ibid., p. 122.
30. Ibid., pp. 39-40.
31. Ibid., p. 41.
32. *The Worker,* March 30, 1929.
33. *Sixth Convention,* p. 133.
34. Ibid., p. 91 and p. 93.
35. Ibid., p. 75.
36. Ibid., p. 79.
37. Ibid., p. 80 and p. 131.
38. Ibid., p. 80.
39. Ibid., pp. 114-116.
40. Ibid., p. 128.
41. T. Buck, *Thirty Years* (Toronto, 1952), p. 66.
42. *The Worker,* July 27, 1929.
43. Ibid., November 16, 1929.
44. T. Buck, *Statement of the Political Committee of the Communist Party of Canada on the Expulsion of Salsberg,* reel one, Communist Party Archives, Ontario Public Archives, Toronto.
45. *Resolution of Enlarged Plenum of Communist Party of Canada,* February 1931, pp. 60-61.
46. *The Worker,* July 4, 1923.
47. *Proceedings of the Fourth National Convention, Communist Party of Canada,* September 11-13, 1925, sheet 5.
48. *The Worker,* September 17, 1927.
49. *Fifth Convention,* pp. 105-106.
50. *Draft Thesis on the Canadian Perspectives Adopted by the Enlarged Executive of the CPC,* November 1928, p. 2; and reprinted in

The Worker, December 22 and 29, 1928.

51. Ibid., p. 3.
52. Ibid., p. 5.
53. Ibid., p. 6.
54. *Sixth Convention*, p. 9.
55. Ibid., p. 120 and p. 127.
56. L. Morris, J. Weir and S. Carr, *The Present Situation in the Canadian Party and Its Policies*, September 1929, Archives CPC, pp. 4-6 and 8.
57. Ibid., p. 5.
58. Ibid., p. 8.
59. *Strengthen the Struggle against the Right Danger!* (1929), pp. 1-2 and pp. 4-5.
60. Ibid., p. 20 and pp. 22-24.
61. Political Secretariat of the ECCI, letter to the CC of the CPC, October 1929, Archives CPC, p. 1.
62. *Resolutions of Enlarged Plenum*, p. 21.
63. Buck, *Lenin and Canada*, p. 74.

* In exile, Trotsky published a book, *The Permanent Revolution*, in which he reiterated and elaborated on his pre-1917 views. His main ideas were as follows: (1) denial of Lenin's theory of the two-stage revolution in Russia (the bourgeois-democratic revolution in February and the socialist revolution in October), believing instead in a one-stage revolution; (2) denial of the possibility or necessity of a permanent alliance between the proletariat and the peasantry in which the working class would retain hegemony because, according to Trotsky, the peasantry was reactionary and benighted; (3) the belief that revolution ought to be "pushed" in or exported to other countries, particularly western Europe, because (4) the productive forces in Russia were at too low a level to permit the construction of socialism in one country. Trotsky's distrust of the peasantry led him to advocate the export of revolution as a means of "saving" the Russian proletariat from certain doom. Lenin, on the contrary, asserted that socialism in one country was possible and consistent with the laws of capitalist development (V.I. Lenin, *Selected Works* (Moscow, 1970), Vol. 1, pp. 770-771). In practice, Trotsky's theory of permanent revolution was a justification for counter-revolutionary adventurism, factionalism and ultimately anti-Sovietism.

4. The Great Depression – The Reactionary Offensive

The market crash of late 1929 signaled the beginning of the deepest and longest economic crisis ever experienced by the world capitalist economy. The economies of the United States and Canada, just as the economies of Europe and elsewhere, were shaken to their very foundations. The class struggle intensified, reaching at times violent and bloody proportions. Repression became the rule in most capitalist countries as the ruling class sought to stifle the growing struggles of the increasingly militant and class-conscious workers.

1. The Economic and Political Crisis

Capitalist crises of relative overproduction have always been accompanied by high unemployment and consequently tremendous suffering for the working class. Joblessness in the 1930s meant either destitution and frequently starvation, or the humiliation of going on the welfare roles, of receiving charity. Most of Canada's hundreds of thousands of unemployed did not know when or where their next meal would come from or whether they would have a roof over their heads the next day.

The severity of the capitalist crisis in Canada can be illustrated with some statistics. Although unemployment figures were not kept before World War II, the bourgeois economist A.E. Safarian estimates that about one-fifth of the work force was unemployed in 1933 when the crisis reached its worse point.[1] By that year, personal disposable income was almost half that of 1929. The acute crisis of relative overproduction was at the heart of the lay-offs of hun-

dreds of thousands of workers. As most workers had no alternative source of income, a large portion of the domestic market virtually ceased to exist, thus exacerbating and then prolonging the crisis. After 1933, recovery was painfully slow. In 1937, personal disposable income still remained at substantially below the 1929 level.[2]

All economic indices remained below the 1929 level throughout the 1930s. Imports and exports declined sharply. Profits nose-dived, leading to a sharp fall in investments and a rapid rise in bankruptcies. Industrial production reflected the general state of the Canadian economy. In 1929, gross production in manufacturing amounted to 3.883 billion dollars, reached a low of 1.954 billion dollars in 1933 and recovered somewhat to 3.625 billion dollars by 1937.[3] Under these conditions, the 1930s witnessed the most extensive wave of corporate mergers up to that time.

The extent of the destitution of Canada's working people was indicated not only by the exceptionally high unemployment rate, but also by the phenomenal rise in the government's expenditures on relief and public welfare. Municipal finances were stretched to the limit and many municipalities in fact went bankrupt. In 1928, the last full year of prosperity, welfare expenditures constituted 1.2 per cent of the national income. In 1934, they constituted 8.4 per cent of the national income.

After 1934, the absolute amount of these expenditures rose continuously although by 1937 they had fallen as a percentage of the national income to 7.3 per cent.[4]

When Arthur Evans was jailed in 1934 for his union activities, his family found it impossible to keep up mortgage payments. Here, workers defy the sheriff's attempt to evict the Evans family.

These statistics can never fully convey the misery and suffering which afflicted millions of Canadians. Capitalism and its crisis not only deprived workers and farmers of the main, if not sole, source of income, thus forcing as many as a million people onto the welfare roles, it also sought to deprive them of what personal possessions they had. Seizure of people's goods, foreclosure of mortgages on farms and homes including eviction, were common and widespread practices during the Great Depression.

Canada's three levels of government showed no sympathy for the plight of victimized Canadians. In fact, they did as much as they could to foist the cost of the monopoly capitalist crisis onto the people. In its submission to the Rowell-Sirois Commission in 1939, the Communist Party drew attention to the fact that "1934 found the capitalists 18 per cent better off than they were in 1926 and only 12 per cent worse off than in 1929. The income of the mass of the people was however in 1934, 45 per cent below the 1926 level and 48 per cent below the 1929 level."[5] As the submission pointed out, the crisis favored the redistribution of the national income in favor of the capitalists and its prolongation assured that this trend would continue.

The Communist Party was the only political party which recognized that unemployment arose out of the very nature of the capitalist system. Ultimately, unemployment could only be eradicated by replacing the capitalist system of private ownership with the socialist system of social ownership. That socialism was actually capable of over-

coming unemployment and other economic and social consequences of capitalism was proven by the successes achieved by the Soviet Union in the 1920s and 1930s. While the world capitalist system suffered economic stagnation, industrial decline and political instability during the thirties, the socialist Soviet Union experienced rapid economic growth, industrial expansion and scored numerous advances on the social and political fronts.

In the conditions of the Great Depression, the Communist Party proposed a number of immediate measures to alleviate the worst effects of the crisis on the working people. It called on the federal government, which constitutionally controlled most of the important sources of government revenue, to set a minimum standard of living which would be uniform throughout Canada. To this end, the party demanded that the government assume responsibility for (1) relief and the introduction of unemployment insurance, (2) a national health insurance scheme, (3) the costs of education and a program to raise educational standards and making it universally accessible, (4) assistance to young workers and farmers so that they could have a good start in life, (5) labor legislation to include a fixed minimum wage for women and young workers, regulation of the maximum hours of work and days of rest and the setting of safety and sanitation standards with powers to inspect on these matters and (6) state-run crop insurance, minimum prices and rehabilitation for farmers.[6] The party proposed a substantial shift in the burden of taxation to reduce taxes on working people and increase those on corporations and the rich.[7]

While the Communist Party actively and consistently defended and advanced the interests of the working class and its allies, the bourgeoisie sought to contain the growing struggles of the workers. It moved to suppress the party which was playing a prominent role in the workers' struggles, and the working class movement as a whole.

In the general election of mid-1930, a millionaire reactionary by the name of R.B. Bennett became the new Prime Minister of Canada. With definite ideas about making the working class bear the brunt of the crisis, Bennett and his Tory colleagues were prepared to use the police and the courts to enforce unjust anti-democratic laws, commit acts of violence against the workers and sys-tematically undermine and violate human and democratic rights. In fact, during his tenure, the Tory Prime Minister acquired the well deserved name of "Iron Heel" Bennett. Capitalist profits and the preservation of the decaying social system he represented were the touchstones of and justification for his repressive policies. Under Bennett, politics in Canada shifted substantially to the right.

2. Estevan

After a year's lull, the Tory government made its move against the working class. In mid-August 1931, the Communist Party was outlawed and some of its leaders arrested. The government then extended its attack to the union movement with a "get tough" policy. The miners' strike near Estevan, Saskatchewan, provided Bennett with the opportunity to prove he meant business.

The oppressive and inhuman working and living conditions which had led to bitter and protracted strikes of coal miners in Nova Scotia and Alberta also prevailed in the coal mines of Bienfait near Estevan. Working conditions in the mines were bad in the extreme. What few regulations existed to compel the mine owners to observe certain inadequate minimum standards were virtually ignored. The company-owned store forced the miners to buy its goods at exorbitant prices on pain of losing their jobs. The company-owned homes of the workers and their families could have been better described as hovels. A district sanitation officer inspected 113 homes and variously described them as

M. Joe Forkin (1899-1962) (left) Winnipeg alderman from 1934 to 1951, re-elected in 1961-62. Sam Scarlett (1886-1940) (center) helped organize steelworkers throughout the 1930s in Hamilton, Toronto and Nova Scotia. In the late 1930s, he was chairman of the party in Toronto. Annie Buller (1895-1973) (right) was an organizer for the Industrial Union of Needle Trades Workers and the Workers' Unity League. She made substantial contributions to building the party press and to the theoretical development of the party.

The RCMP cordon off a street in Estevan to prevent the peaceful march of miners and their families.

cold, leaky, dirty, overcrowded and almost all of them in need of repair.[8]

The onset of the Great Depression exacerbated the destitution of the miners and their families.

As the Depression deepened, conditions worsened, and layoffs were frequent. Those who were laid off or fired now had to go on relief and endure further indignities and hardships.[9]

In order to compensate for the fall in coal prices (most commodity prices fell sharply during the twenties), the mine owners decided to recoup their lost profits by reducing the wages of the 600 miners by 10 to 15 per cent. The miners and their families thus found themselves literally on the brink of starvation. They had nowhere to turn but to organize a union and go on strike. That happened on September 8, 1931. They demanded recognition for their new union, the Mine Workers' Union of Canada and an increase in their wages.[10]

The miners' choice of the MWUC, an affiliate of the WUL was determined by the fact that the reformist-led unions refused to come to their assistance. The MWUC and the WUL were more than willing to provide the leadership, experience and resources at their command to help the miners in their unequal struggle against the employers. Several prominent Communists played leading roles in the organization of the union and the strike and its aftermath. Among them were Jim Sloan, the newly elected president of the MWUC, M. Joe Forkin, later a distinguished Winnipeg alderman for many years, Sam Scarlett, a former organizer of the IWW, and later, John Stokaluk and Annie Buller.

The companies replied to the miners' strike by threatening to bring in scab labor. On September 17, an attempt to open three mines with scab workers was defeated by a militant mass picket line of striking workers. On the pretext that the scabs needed police protection, the mine bosses asked for and received the assistance of the Royal Canadian Mounted Police (RCMP) who were to supplement the large number of "Specials" (private guards), already hired by the companies.[11] Little did the miners realize that the Bennett government intended to make them an example to the entire trade union movement: by sending in the RCMP, the government demonstrated that it would brook no defiance from workers.

In order to publicize the plight of the strikers and put pressure on the mine workers to come to terms with the union, the strike committee decided to stage a peaceful parade of miners and their families in nearby Estevan. But the RCMP, the mine owners and the town council had different ideas. With the tacit approval of the Bennett government they made plans to halt the stubborn miners once and for all. What followed was what A.E. Smith later characterized as a "police riot."[12]

This riot was clearly instigated by the police to justify the use of violence to break the strike.

The parade, consisting of some 63 trucks, containing the striking miners, their wives and children arrived in Estevan. The leading car carried a huge Union Jack. When opposite a point close to the city hall, a cordon of RCMP strung themselves across the street and proceeded to divert the parade from its route and turn it down a side street, in the meantime using their clubs and riding whips brutally on all they could reach. The first four cars broke through the line of police and proceeded on their way; the others however having to go down this street, came out on the same road as they had come in from Bienfait, and found their exit blocked by the rear of the parade. This was undoubtedly the trap laid by the police in which it was intended to hold up the parade and to incite an armed pogrom on unarmed men, women and children.[13]

Three workers were killed and 50 persons, including children, were injured. A police reign of terror was then instituted which resulted in the arrest of 16 persons including Sam Scarlett and Annie Buller. Annie Buller's crime was that she spoke to a mass meeting of miners as their invited guest on September 27, the day before the demonstration and the shooting deaths of the workers.

At the time of the strike, the workers' motives were savagely maligned by the bourgeois press. In addition, reports of the actual course of events leading to the Estevan tragedy were grossly distorted to justify the brutal police actions. To this day, the history of the bloody events of September 28 continues to be distorted and misrepresented by bourgeois rewriters of Canadian working class history.

The Canadian Labor Defense League (CLDL) quickly came to the aid of the victimized workers. A.E. Smith, General Secretary of the CLDL from 1929, personally attended their trials in Estevan and gave them every possible assistance. Nevertheless, the court handed out prison sentences from one month to two years. Sam Scarlett and Annie Buller received the longest sentences.

The issue did not rest here, however. The CLDL organized a mass protest campaign throughout the country around the demand for the release of the imprisoned unionists. Public opinion eventually forced the authorities to release Sam Scarlett and grant Annie Buller a new trial. At her second trial in March 1933, the police and the court strove to frame her on a charge of "unlawful rioting." They tried to evade the fact that she was not even in Estevan at the time of the police riot nor had she anything to do with organizing the parade. The police themselves admitted that her speech of the previous day was neither inflammatory nor cause for arrest.[14] "Outside agitators" did not cause either the strike or the riot, for as Annie Buller was to write 18 years later:

We proved that the strike was caused by bad conditions in which the men lived and worked; by the violation of the Mines Act by the operators; and by the low wages and short weight. We showed that the strike and parade were peaceful until the RCMP used force and violence resulting in the murder of three miners.[15]

Despite the exposure of the role played by the mine owners and the RCMP in staging the riot, she was nevertheless convicted and sentenced to a year in prison.

Although the miners failed to win union recognition, they did succeed in winning a number of other demands. The Mines Act was to be more strictly enforced; there would be no victimization or discrimination against strikers; the agreement achieved would be made retroactive to the day when work began again; and contract men would be employed on an eight-hour basis.[16] On the whole, it was a victory for the miners. The MWUC, the WUL and the CLDL

71

came out of the struggle with their prestige in the working class movement considerably enhanced.

3. The Canadian Labor Defense League and the Eight Communist Leaders

At the time Bennett launched his attack on the Estevan miners, the CLDL had already accumulated six years of experience in fighting for labor's rights. The CLDL was founded in Toronto in the summer of 1925.

Its objects are to provide legal, moral and financial aid to working class victims of capitalist courts and their dependents; to wage a struggle against deportation laws by means of which foreign-born workers who take an active part in the labor movement are removed or intimidated; to fight for the repeal of the obnoxious sedition laws and all anti-working class legislation.[17]

J.A. Young became the CLDL's first chairman; Malcolm Bruce, executive secretary; and later in the year, Florence Custance became General Secretary, a post she held until her death in 1929. Despite some good work in defense of the coal miners and other persecuted working class activists, the CLDL's first few years of existence were marked by relatively slow growth. The temporary economic boom of the 1920s and the accompanying alleviation of government repression against the working class movement seemed to make it less needed and thereby contributed to its initial difficulties. The 1927 convention of the Communist Party of Canada, however, decided to continue its support for the CLDL "inasmuch as the persecution of the workers by the capitalist class is certain to increase with the decay of the system. . . ."[18] And by the CLDL's first convention in October 1927, Florence Custance was able to inform the delegates that the organization had formed 52 branches with a total dues-paying membership of 3,000.[19]

Police repression against Communists and workers typical of the immediate post-war period revived in Toronto and then elsewhere in late 1928. This sparked what became known as the free speech fight against police efforts to prevent progressives from holding demonstrations and public meetings.

The free speech fight began soon after the newly appointed Chief of Police of Toronto, D.C. Draper, created the "Red Squad." At first, the Red Squad tried to prevent hall owners from allowing Communist meetings to be held on their premises. From there the Toronto police resorted to intimidation, threats, raids and on several occasions smashed demonstrations through brute force. Many demonstrators were arrested and some were savagely beaten and hospitalized. One issue of *The Worker* was seized even before it left the printshop. As A.E. Smith was to write in his autobiography:

The police had taken over the functions of parliament, the attorney-general, the judiciary, the jury. General Draper had decided to dispense with all of these.[20]

By 1930, there were almost daily reports in the pages of *The Worker* and other progressive newspapers of the growing frequency of police attacks.

Tom McEwen served on the Comintern's Anglo-American Secretariat in the 1930s. In 1945, he became editor of the Pacific Tribune, a post he held for more than 20 years.

From across the country came news of attacks on demonstrators and participants in party-sponsored meetings, of police brutality, arrests, imprisonment, deportations and threatened deportations. In the 12-month period ending in February 1931, there were 200 arrests, 130 of which had occurred since December.[21] This was just a prelude of what was to follow.

UTL, TF/MS COLL. 179/KENNY COLLECTION

In August 1931, the RCMP raided the offices of the Communist Party and the homes of party leaders. Nine Communists, including Tim Buck, party leader, and Tom McEwen, leader of the WUL, were arrested. This was done under the authority of one of the most repressive, anti-democratic laws ever to be placed on Canada's law books. Section 98 of the Criminal Code provided:

> Any association, organization, society or corporation, whose professed purpose or one of whose professed purposes is to bring about any governmental, industrial or economic change within Canada by use of force, violence or physical injury to person or property, or by threats of such injury or which teaches, advocates, advises or defends the use of force, violence, terrorism, or physical injury, in order to accomplish such change, or for any other purpose, or which shall by any means prosecute or pursue such purpose or professed purpose, or shall so teach, advocate, advise or defend, shall be an unlawful association.[22]

The government of course gave itself the power to determine what constituted the advocacy of governmental, industrial or economic change through the use of force and violence.

The intent of this all-encompassing section of the Criminal Code was revealed by the presiding judge at the trial of the Communist leaders. He informed the jury that sedition consisted of acts, words or writings which disturbed tranquility of the state or excited ill-will between classes.[23] In other words, the legislation sought to outlaw the class struggle. The Communist Party found itself at the top of the list of allegedly violent organizations, not because it advocated the use of force or violence, a charge it vigorously denied, but because it was organizing the workers and farmers in defense of their class interests.[24] As the party charged at the time, it was the bourgeois state which was really guilty of using force and violence to subvert democracy.[25]

The trial took place in November 1931. Eight Communists — Tim Buck, Tom McEwen, John Boychuk, Matthew Popovich, Malcolm Bruce, A.T. Hill, Sam Carr and Tom Cacic — were charged with being members and officers of an unlawful association and of being party to a seditious conspiracy.[26] The court had had to release the ninth person, Mike Golinsky on a legal technicality. W.H. Price, Ontario's Attorney-General, had neglected to include the YCL in the writ banning Communist organizations. Golinsky was a member of the YCL but not of the Communist Party.

The Communists charged under Section 98. Left to right: Matthew Popovich, Tom McEwen, Tom Hill, John Boychuk, Mike Golinsky (who was subsequently released on a legal technicality), Sam Carr, Tom Cacic and Tim Buck. Absent from the photo is Malcolm Bruce.

In order to obtain the desired convictions, the government had only to prove that the eight Communists were members of an unlawful association. It was not necessary to prove that the Communist Party advocated the use of force or violence although this false charge was used as the justification for banning it. It was clear from the beginning of the trial that the federal and Ontario governments were not as interested in punishing advocates of force and violence as they were in suppressing political dissent and the struggles of the working class. The trial after all, began only five weeks after the bloody events in Estevan.

The trial was a travesty of justice. With the exception of one person, all of the prosecution's witnesses were members of the RCMP, the Ontario Provincial Police and the Toronto municipal police.[27] The most notorious of the Crown's witnesses was a certain RCMP officer by the name of John Leopold. Under the alias of Jack Esselwein, he had infiltrated the OBU, the Society for the Collection of Medical Aid to Soviet Russia and later the Famine Relief Committee for Soviet Russia. He participated in the formation of the Regina branch of the Workers' Party in 1922 and was elected as a delegate to the party conventions of 1922, 1924 and 1925. While in Regina, he became president of the city's Trades and Labor Council. In the spring of 1927, he moved to Winnipeg and a few weeks later to Toronto. He was then exposed as a police agent and was summarily expelled from the party. The RCMP rewarded Leopold for services rendered by promoting him to the rank of sergeant.[28]

Leopold's appearance in the witness box as the government's chief witness caused quite a public sensation because it revealed the real extent of the RCMP's activities as political police. Canadians were generally unaware that the RCMP used such underhanded, secretive and undemocratic methods of operation. Historically speaking, however, the use of undercover agents was nothing new. The Crown's first witness, Frank W. Zaneth, the policeman who had produced the warrant to search Tim Buck's home, had also been an undercover agent during the Winnipeg General Strike.[29] Infiltration and surveillance of working class and progressive organizations were only a part of the RCMP's arsenal which included strikebreaking, police violence against workers, the subversion of elementary democratic rights and an entire array of illegal activities. The exposure of these sinister activities did not deter the RCMP or the federal government from allowing such practices to continue.

(Anti-labor repression has always been carried out by the RCMP. In 1946, Fred Rose was framed on dubious evidence obtained by the RCMP. And today, as the McDonald and Keable Commissions' investigations into the illegal activities of the RCMP revealed, the RCMP's anti-labor and anti-democratic functions are still being vigorously performed. The police are used to forcibly suppress and violate the fundamental human and democratic rights of the Canadian people. The employment of the police in this manner expresses not the strength but the weakness of monopoly rule which resorts to repressive measures to preserve the present system of capitalist exploitation and oppression.)

Following the parade of police witnesses at the trial, Tim Buck rose in his own defense — to take the offense. Capitalism was placed on trial by the Communist leader. His indictment pointed out that class struggle derived from the very nature of capitalism, from class society, which uses force to suppress the struggles of the working class for better living and working conditions. He explicitly rejected the prosecution's contention that the Communist Party of Canada advocated or taught force or violence.[30] In actual fact, force and violence were practised by the capitalist class and its state as demonstrated in Estevan.

Tim Buck also refuted the prosecution's attempt to equate strikes with force or violence. Communists participated in and organized strikes to defend the rights and interests of the workers by the means available to them and not in order to promote violence.

Communists have always carried on the strongest struggle against individual terror. And the implication — it comes from this mass of evidence submitted by the Crown — that because we are so active in strikes, because we organize demonstrations, therefore there is something violent about us or we are organizing violence — this inference falls completely to the ground if it is examined in conjunction with the whole body of the labor movement and the working class movement, and if it is examined in conjunction with how we have organized our strikes and campaigns.[31]

As Tim Buck noted in his conclusion, the very trial itself was indicative of the sharpness of the political situation, in which the increasing fear of the bourgeoisie led them to respond with increased repression.

To all intents and purposes, the trial of the eight Communist leaders was rigged by the police and the federal and Ontario governments. The eight were convicted on all counts. Seven were sentenced to five years in prison. The eighth, Tom Cacic, received a two-year term and was ordered deported to his native Yugoslavia which at that time was under a fascist government. Deportation in this case amounted to a death sentence, but fortunately friends arranged for his escape in England.[32]

On news of the arrests, the CLDL moved into action. As soon as the date of the trial was announced, it organized the election of a workers' jury to monitor the proceedings of the trial and bring in its own verdict. The workers' jury did not regard opposition to capitalist policies of mass starvation as a crime; it therefore declared the defendants not guilty.[33] This was no empty declaration. Quite to the contrary, it was a declaration of war against capitalist injustice and marked the beginning of one of the largest campaigns ever to be conducted in defense of democratic rights in Canada.

Five days after the conviction of the eight, the CLDL issued a call under A.E. Smith's signature to all democratically-minded organizations, as well as its own branches, to organize conferences for the repeal of Section 98. These conferences were to be as broadly based as possible. They were to mobilize petition campaigns, organize public meetings, combat deportations, demand the release of the eight Communist political prisoners and raise funds for the CLDL.[34] Through numerous statements, leaflets, pamphlets, petitions, meetings and demonstrations, the true facts of the circumstances surrounding the trial of the eight Communists came to be widely known by the Canadian public.

After the trial, the eight were released on 160,000 dollars bail pending a decision on their appeal to the Supreme Court of Ontario. In February 1932, the court dismissed the appeal on the spurious grounds that party publications were bristling with incitements to violence. As at the trial, the judge either deliberately or through blind class prejudice, misinterpreted party statements in such a way as to equate the class struggle and socialist revolution with the promotion of force and violence. Leopold's testimony was cited as corroborative evidence that the Communist Party intended to change Canada's economic and social order by forcible means.[35] In effect, the eight were convicted on the word of a single man, an RCMP infiltrator.

The eight Communist political prisoners were sent to Kingston penitentiary. During a prison riot in October 1932, shots were fired in an attempt to kill Tim Buck. Although the prison authorities tried to hush up the incident, it surfaced during the trial of one of the convicts accused of taking part in the riot. Tim Buck himself was sentenced to nine months for his alleged participation in the prison disturbances, but not before the presiding judge investigated and confirmed Tim Buck's contention that he was the victim of an assassination attempt.

The CLDL immediately took up the fight on Tim Buck's behalf and brought the matter to public attention. The government, which strove to suppress news of the incident, was forced to admit that shots had in fact been fired at the Communist Party leader. The admission was insufficient to satisfy the CLDL and public opinion.

The protest movement against the persecution of Communists continued to grow. At the first representative convention of the CLDL in July 1933, Beckie Buhay, the CLDL's organizational secretary, reported that the protest movement against Section 98 and for the release of the Communist political prisoners was now drawing hundreds of thousands of individuals from all sections of society including workers, farmers, the middle class and the churches into the fight for democratic rights.[36]

Since the beginning of the raids and arrests under Section 98 in 1931, the CLDL had distributed five million pieces of literature, nearly two million of which were issued in the first six months of 1933. Three pamphlets and a book on the case of the eight Com-

TORONTO STAR/UTL, TF/MS. COLL. 179/ KENNY COLLECTION

munists had reached a circulation of 60,000. Thousands of protest demonstrations, meetings, etc., had been staged. Hundreds of thousands of people from coast to coast had participated in united front conferences. In the first six months of 1933 alone, 400 demonstrations and mass meetings had taken place in defense of the rights of the Communist political prisoners. In the same period, three delegations with 300,000 endorsations had met with various government authorities.[37]

The trial of the eight Communist leaders inspired the production of *Eight Men Speak*, a play staged by the Workers' Theater of the Progressive Arts Club in Toronto. The first performance attracted a capacity crowd of 1,500; the next day, the police threatened to revoke

The CLDL contingent in the 1935 May Day demonstration in Vancouver.

the theater's license. The virtual banning of the play provoked the left-wing cultural movement to launch a political campaign in defense of working-class culture. Their efforts merged with the general campaign against Section 98.

This campaign began to have an effect on the reactionary Bennett government. As Beckie Buhay noted in her convention report:

The Minister of Justice grudgingly admitted that the CLDL had managed to build up a huge protest movement with even the churches committing themselves against Section 98.[38]

In November 1933, A.E. Smith led a delegation of 17 persons to Ottawa to meet with Prime Minister Bennett and present him with a petition bearing 459,000 signatures and demanding an investigation into the attempted murder of Tim Buck and the repeal of Section 98. Bennett reacted by declaring that there would be no repeal of Section 98 and that the remaining seven Communist political prisoners would not be released before the completion of their sentences.[39]

"Iron Heel" Bennett retaliated against the CLDL. Hoping to muzzle the growing tide of democratic sentiment, the federal and Ontario Tory governments collaborated in the indictment of the CLDL's leader, A.E. Smith, on a charge of seditious conspiracy. But Bennett badly miscalculated the changed political atmosphere in the country. Public indignation at the way the government had handled the attempted murder of Tim Buck and at the grossly undemocratic nature of the trial of the eight Communists was already at a very high level. Furthermore, the CLDL had developed a mass movement which encompassed not only Communists and militant workers but also other democratically-minded sections of other classes and social strata. By the end of 1933, the CLDL had grown to a membership of 43,000, a number far exceeding the total membership of the Communist Party.[40] And while the CLDL had achieved fame through its campaign against Section 98 and for the release of the eight Communist leaders and the victims of the Estevan events, it had also endeared itself to thousands of people by its defense of victims charged with much lesser offenses.

The CLDL undertook the defense of hundreds of Communists and militant

UTL, TF/MS. COLL. 179/KENNY COLLECTION

workers persecuted for their political and trade union activities. In 1932, 839 arrests led to over 200 convictions. And in the first six months of 1933, the CLDL convention report confirmed another 199 cases.[41] No case was too large or too small. Workers who faced 14 to 30 days in jail on such charges as participating in a demonstration or distributing literature, or who faced deportation because of their political beliefs and trade union activities in the immigrant community could always count on the consistent moral, legal and financial support of the CLDL. So when the Tory government and the courts sought to silence A.E. Smith, they only succeeded in arousing further storms of mass protest. About 4,000 demonstrators at Queen's Park in Toronto reminded the court that public opinion would not tolerate the muzzling of Tim Buck or the frame-up of A.E. Smith.[42]

The jury, reflecting public opinion, found A.E. Smith not guilty of the charge against him. This great victory for the working class and democratic movements gave the campaign against Section 98 and for the release of the seven remaining political prisoners added impetus.[43]

In June, the people of Ontario dumped the Tory government in the provincial elections. The Ontario voters had had enough of authoritarian rule and pro-monopoly economic and social policies.

The platform at the Maple Leaf Gardens rally celebrating Tim Buck's release. 1. Jacob Penner; 2. William Kashtan; 3. Pat Forkin; 4. Ewart Humphreys; 5. Bill Sydney; 6. Tim Buck; 7. Doba Okulevich; 8. Charlie Sims; 9. Sam Carr; 10. J.B. Salsberg; 11. Alice Buck; 12. A.E. Smith; 13. Izzie Minster; 14. John Boychuk; 15. Tom McEwen; 16. Beckie Buhay; 17. Bill Decker; 18. Charles Marriot; 19. Mike Buhay.

The mass welcome rally in Maple Leaf Gardens on December 2, 1934. About 17,000 people attended. Another 8,000 had to be turned away for lack of space.

Mitchell Hepburn and the Liberal Party which he headed came to power. Although the new government also pursued pro-monopoly policies, for its own reasons it supported the demand for the release of the seven imprisoned Communists. In July 1934, a month after Hepburn's electoral victory, five of the Communist political prisoners were released and by November the last two were freed as well.

Tim Buck's release was followed by a huge rally in Maple Leaf Gardens in Toronto with an overflow crowd of 17,000 supporters and sympathizers in attendance.[44] For the Communist Party it signified the coming of age of the Communist movement as a force to be reckoned with on the Canadian political scene. For the Bennett government, it was a severe setback.

The CLDL succeeded in mobilizing thousands of Canadians in militant struggle for basic democratic rights. This fight for democracy was complemented by the parallel fight conducted by workers, farmers and the unemployed against the devastation of the Depression on their lives.

---

1. A.E. Safarian, *The Canadian Economy in the Great Depression* (Toronto, 1970), p. 75.
2. Ibid., p. 86.
3. Ibid., p. 128.
4. N.W. Rowell and J. Sirois, *Report of the Royal Commission on Dominion-Provincial Relations* (Ottawa, 1940), Book 1, p. 162.
5. *Toward Democratic Unity for Canada* (Toronto, 1939), p. 31.
6. Ibid., pp. 42-58.
7. Ibid., p. 62.
8. L. Watson, *She Never Was Afraid* (Toronto, 1975), pp. 34-38.
9. Ibid., p. 39.
10. A.S. Buller, *Summary Report of Estevan Strike*, Archives CPC, p. 1.
11. Ibid., p. 2.
12. A.E. Smith, *All My Life* (Toronto, 1977), p. 121.
13. Buller, pp. 2-3.
14. Smith, p. 124; A.S. Buller, "The Estevan Massacre" in *National Affairs Monthly*, Vol. 6, No. 4, May, 1949, p. 170; and *Workers' Self-Defense in the Courts* (Toronto, 1933), pp. 20 and 26.
15. Buller, "The Estevan Massacre," p. 172.
16. Ibid., pp. 172-173.
17. *The Worker*, August 8, 1925.
18. *Report of the Proceedings of the Fifth Convention of the Communist Party of Canada, June 17-20, 1927*, p. 103.
19. *The Worker*, November 12, 1927.
20. Smith, p. 101.
21. *The Worker*, February 21, 1931.
22. *The King vs. Buck and Others* (Toronto, 1932), Judgement of the Court of Appeal of Ontario concerning the Communist Party in Ontario, published by direction of W.H. Price, Attorney-General of Ontario, p. 1.
23. O. Ryan, *The Story of the Trial of the Eight Communist Leaders* (Toronto, 1931), p. 5.
24. Communist Party of Canada, *Communism on Trial!* (Toronto, 1931), p. 23.
25. Ibid., p. 16.
26. *The King vs. Buck and Others*, p. 2; and Communist Party of Canada, *Section 98 Unlawful Association*, a reprint of Section 98, Archives CPC.
27. Ryan, p. 6.
28. E.C. Guillet, "Political Offenders, an Episode of Repression in Canada," copy from *Famous Canadian Trials*, Vol. 29, p. 30; J.L. Martin, *The Canadian Cossacks* (Vancouver, 1935), pp. 15-16; and *The Worker*, May 26, 1928.
29. L. and G. Brown, *An Unauthorized History of the RCMP* (Toronto, 1973), p. 44.

30. T. Buck, *An Indictment of Capitalism* (Toronto, no date), p. 66.
31. Ibid., p. 71.
32. Ryan, p. 27; and Smith, p. 148.
33. CLDL, *Not Guilty!* (Toronto, 1931), pp. 16-17; and *Declaration of the Workers' Jury,* November 14, 1931, Archives CPC.
34. A.E. Smith, "To all Workers' Rights and Anti-Deportation Conferences: To all Organizations of the Canadian Labor Defense League: To all Organizations in sympathy with the struggle for free speech," November 18, 1931, Archives CPC.
35. *The King vs. Buck and Others,* pp. 15-16.
36. *Report: First Representative National Convention,* July 14-17, 1933, p. 6.
37. Ibid.
38. Ibid.
39. Smith, *All My Life,* p. 165; and CLDL, *Mass Unity Wins!* (Toronto, 1934), p. 16.
40. *Mass Unity Wins!,* pp. 22-23.
41. *Report: First Representative National Convention,* p. 5.
42. *Mass Unity Wins!,* pp. 11-12.
43. Ibid., pp. 3 and 20.
44. Smith, *All My Life,* p. 180.

5. The Great Depression – Canadians Fight Back

With the Communist Party's active participation and leadership, mass movements of workers, farmers and the unemployed emerged to challenge those responsible for the economic crisis. The Worker's Unity League (WUL) defended the needs of both workers and unemployed; the Farmers' Unity League (FUL), the interests of the farmers; from the Hunger Marches initiated by the WUL grew the historic On to Ottawa Trek.

1. The Workers' Unity League

By 1929, when the Communist Party decided to turn the TUEL into an organizing body, life itself had forced the TUEL to acquire some experiences in this field.

In the spring of 1928, 4,000 auto workers in Oshawa struck General Motors and spontaneously set up their own industrial union.[1] The union joined the Toronto TLC during the strike on the condition that its industrial structure would be retained. The TLC, however, conspired to dismember the local by handing its membership to the Council's affiliated craft unions, thereby splintering the local's membership along craft lines. The strike itself was lost due to the craft mentality of the TLC toward the industrial unions.

The auto workers consequently pulled out of the TLC.[2] Under these circumstances, the TUEL decided to organize an auto workers' conference in November with the aim of establishing the Auto Workers' Industrial Union of Canada which would include locals from Windsor, Walkerville, Toronto and Oshawa. As the strike had been lost, the

new union's locals were forced to go underground, where they remained until the Committee for Industrial Organization came to Canada in 1937.

While the demands of the unorganized workers in the mass production industries were at the heart of the TUEL's change in orientation, the process was aided by the complacency and anti-communism of the TLC and the ACCL leadership. The TLC was consistently hostile to militant, industrial or Canadian-based unions. It refused to admit the LWIUC, the MWUC and even the reformist-led Canadian Brotherhood of Railway Employees. In addition, the TLC leadership persecuted its own left-wing minority movement. For example, Tim Buck was expelled from the International Association of Machinists because he was a Communist.[3] In cases where the left wing was especially strong, the craft unions resorted to whole-scale expulsions, sometimes of entire union locals. In the case of the ACCL, initial expectations ended in disappointment. The ACCL at first appeared ready and willing to organize the unorganized on the basis of militant industrial unionism. However, it backed off because, like the TLC, it was convinced that economic crisis was not conducive to union organizing.

In 1929, a strike at the National Steel Car Company in Hamilton, Ontario, led to the spontaneous formation of an industrial union. Rather than depend on the TLC or the ACCL to do the job, the TUEL assumed responsibility for consolidating the new union in the form of the National Steel Car Workers' Industrial Union. The new union won the strike. It was the forerunner of the

Top, these volleyball players were among hundreds of young people whose only access to recreational programs was provided by the Workers' Sports Association. The WSA, built by left-wing immigrant organizations and the Communist Party in the early 1930s, had clubs across the country. Bottom, Lil Ilomaki (née Himmelfarb) addressing a May Day rally in Hamilton, circa 1933.

WUL-affiliated Steel and Metal Workers of Canada.[4]

The new trade union orientation formalized at the 1929 party convention, occurred at a significant point in Canadian labor history. The TUEL was reorganized on the basis of democratic centralism.[5] A few months later, in January 1930, it became the Workers' Unity League with Tom McEwen as secretary.

The purpose of the WUL was not to divide the existing trade unions despite the rampant anti-communism of many in leadership. On the contrary, the struggle to convince the reformist unions of the need for militant industrial unions based on class struggle policies had to be continued. In this regard, the party made a distinction between the reformist leadership and the rank and file. The aim was to win the membership to militant policies. Communists in these unions had to struggle for trade union democracy, against the expulsion of militants and for the development of unity from below around specific issues.[6] Supporters of the WUL's policies in the TLC and the ACCL were members of Industrial Leagues. Their function was to fight for the immediate demands of the workers, expose the class collaborationism of the reformist leadership and contest union elections on a program of workers' demands.[7]

As a militant trade union center based on class struggle, the main purpose of the WUL was to organize the unorganized in the mass production industries. The WUL sought to organize the unorganized into powerful industrial unions under rank and file control, unions which could mobilize the workers for the defense and improvement of their living and working conditions and ultimately for the overthrow of the capitalist system.[8]

The WUL proved itself considerably more democratic than its two reformist rivals. The TLC allowed only AFL affiliates to join while the ACCL admitted only Canadian unions.[9] The WUL, on the other hand, accepted as members all wage workers "regardless of race, creed, color, sex, craft or political affiliations."[10] The only condition for membership was the endorsation of the program. While upholding the importance of an authoritative central leadership, the constitution emphasized the need for inner-union democracy based on the maximum initiative and activity of the entire membership. The WUL's 1931 conference declared that it was a revolutionary union center and a section of the RILU. Its second conference changed this formulation to correspond with its actual aims and the fraternal nature of its relationship to the RILU.

The WUL set itself the goal of recruiting independent unions into its ranks. When the LWIUC and the MWUC broke with the reformist ACCL in 1930, they decided to affiliate with the WUL. Formed and led by members of the disbanded TUEL, the IUNTW considered affiliation to the WUL as a logical step. In industries where unions did not exist, the WUL set up organizing committees to assume the task of organizing the unorganized. The Chesterfield Furniture Workers' Industrial Union was one of these. Concentrating mainly on the basic industries, the WUL also organized

(Top) In 1933, furniture workers in Stratford, Ontario, conducted a successful four-week strike against their employers. (Bottom) Stratford workers ridicule the government's attempt to intimidate them with tanks and militia.

ARCHIVES CPC/PAC/PA-125093

ARCHIVES CPC/PAC/PA-125089

workers in other sectors of the economy as well as the unemployed.

The WUL's first significant test had occurred in Estevan. The Estevan events were significant not only because they were the opening shot of a concerted government drive to destroy the labor movement, but also because they demonstrated that organized militant class struggle had the potential to beat back the monopoly attack on the living standards and rights of the workers. The slander campaign, harassment and violent repression which the bosses and the government used in Estevan were indicative of their attempts to destroy the WUL as a whole.

The barrage of invective and slander which it often met with in the columns of the capitalist press, coupled with similar allegations from so-called labor leaders, did not deter the WUL from pursuing the purpose it set out to accomplish. Moreover the WUL and its membership suffered extensively in the hands of capitalist governments.

Its national and district offices were raided and despoiled on several occasions; its books and technical apparatus seized and wantonly destroyed; its organizers and members imprisoned, clubbed, shot down, persecuted and beaten by the police, victims of vicious espionage and terror. Every form of repressive indignity was directed against the WUL.[11]

Bennett's attack on the Communist Party in 1931 was directed no less at the WUL. Tom McEwen, the WUL's national secretary, was among the eight Communists arrested under Section 98. The WUL was furthermore declared an illegal organization.

However, the intimidation did not overcome the working people's destitution or provide much-needed jobs. Consequently, the WUL enjoyed very wide appeal and its journal, *Unity,* flourished. The WUL rapidly became the most influential trade union center in Canada even though its total membership never exceeded that of the TLC or the ACCL. Whereas the reformist unions lost tens of thousands of members during the first half of the decade, the WUL achieved a membership of 40,000 in its first four years of existence.[12] From 1933 to 1936, the WUL led 90 per cent of the strikes in Canada. In 1933 alone, it led 181 of the 233 strikes which took place. Of this number, 111 were won.[13]

All the major strike struggles between 1930 and 1936 were led by the WUL. The next major strike after Estevan took place in Stratford, Ontario. There, the Chesterfield Furniture Workers' Industrial Union under the able leadership of Fred Collins conducted a bitter strike against several Stratford furniture companies. The bosses and the government tried to break the strike. Troops supported by street tanks and machine guns paraded through Stratford streets in an effort to intimidate the workers. But the unity of the workers and public opinion forced the companies and the provincial and municipal governments to concede defeat after four weeks. The strike created favorable conditions for the election of a pro-labor majority to city council a few days later.[14] It also had the long-term effect of discrediting the provincial and federal Tory governments.

In 1934, the miners of Flin Flon, Manitoba, joined the MWUC and went on strike. Led by Jim Coleman, Mabel Marlowe and William Ross, the workers were subjected to a most vicious anticommunist and anti-labor campaign of vilification from the company sponsored Anti-Communist League. The provincial government intervened on the side of the company by sending in the RCMP to break the strike. A number of miners and their leaders were arrested and some sent to prison. William Ross, future leader of the Communist Party in Manitoba, was sentenced to six months in prison on charges of unlawful assembly and intimidation.[15]

In early 1935, the miners of Corbin, British Columbia, walked off their jobs. Again the police were used as strikebreakers. In April, a demonstration of miners, their wives and their friends, was brutally attacked by the police. Two dozen demonstrators were arrested; some were heavily fined and given stiff prison terms.[16]

ARCHIVES CPC/PAC/PA-125053

Despite some setbacks, the overall results of the WUL's activities were positive. By its efforts, the WUL proved that it was both necessary and possible to organize and lead the workers against monopoly capitalist attacks on their economic well-being and democratic rights. It debunked the reformist myth which denied the working class' ability to fight back successfully or to become organized in conditions of economic crisis. The WUL proved that a united militant working class can be a powerful force for social change.

2. The Farmers' Unity League

Just as the orientation of the party's trade union work changed in 1929-30 to meet the changed conditions, so also there was a reorientation in the party's work among farmers.

In 1929, the sixth convention adopted a new agrarian program which paid a great deal of attention to the development of capitalism in the countryside as an objective force in the process of class differentiation among farmers. Canadian agriculture's growing dependence on the capitalist market had brought about a fundamental change in the orientation of Canadian agricultural production. Consequently, crises in the capitalist economy led to crises in Canadian agriculture.

In addition, the development of the productive forces in the rural economy encouraged specialization in farm production and the growth of larger farms, forcing the small farmers off the land. The farmers' deteriorating position was further aggravated by their dependence on monopolies in the agricultural industry — the railways, farm implement companies, food processing firms, grain companies and so on — who could "charge the farmer an extortionate rate for what they sell and pay a low price for what they buy."

This results in a vast number of the poorer farmers being forced to mortgage their land and buy their equipment on credit, for both of which they are charged a high rate of interest. This condition, coupled with ever-recurring agrarian crises drives the farmers into the arms of the banks, mortgage companies and implement companies, to whom they must pay toll of millions of dollars every year in interest, and fre-

Delegates to the October 1930 Agrarian Conference in Saskatoon which founded the Farmers' Unity League. Front Row, third from left, Jack Hudson, Ed Sarman, Leslie Morris, Walter Wiggins, J.M. Clarke. Back row, second from left, D. Prystash, second from right, Jack Kruger.

Leslie Morris and J.M. Clarke (1890-1972) holding copies of the Draft Agrarian Program which they wrote for the party in 1930. As National Secretary of the Lumber Workers' Industrial Union of Canada, J.M. Clarke was an important mover behind the founding of the One Big Union. However, when the OBU's divisive nature became clear, he joined the Communist Party. In 1927, he became editor of The Furrow, newspaper of the Farmers' Unity League. In 1931, he and William (Ol' Bill) Bennett went to India on behalf of the Red International of Labor Unions to help organize trade unions. On his return to Canada in 1934, he resumed his activity as a party and labor journalist.

quently leads either to their complete expropriation or to reduction to the status of tenants. This process causes further concentration of agrarian capital, ownership passing out of the hands of the poor stratum of farmers and into the hands of finance capital.[17]

The Communist Party's agrarian program concluded that the interests of the poor farmers and agricultural workers could not be advanced within the confines of the capitalist economy.[18] The poor farmers and rural workers therefore had a common interest in struggling with the industrial working class against capitalism.

In June 1930, Leslie Morris and J. M. Clarke made an important contribution to the elaboration of the party's agrarian program in preparation for the party-sponsored Agrarian Conference to be held in Saskatoon, Saskatchewan, in October 1930.[19] The Conference was convened "for the purpose of arriving at greater ideological clarity and to set in motion a militant farmers' movement in the West."[20] It adopted a program of immediate demands and a proposal to found a new left-wing farmers' organization, the Farmers' Unity League. *The Furrow*, newspaper of the dissolved PFEL, became the newspaper of the FUL.

In December, four western regional conferences, attended by a total of 500 farmers, were held to promote the new organization and its program. Organized into local action committees, the FUL "pledged to resist evictions and foreclosures, to fight for the cancellation of all farm debts and for an income of not less than 1,000 dollars per year for all poor families, this sum to be guaranteed by the State and raised by a heavy tax on the profits of those corporations which grow fat through robbing the farmers. In addition, free hospitals, schools, medical attention and social insurance are demanded."[21] With this program, the FUL mobilized farmers in militant struggle against the farm monopolies and anti-farmer policies of the federal government.

In October 1931, the FUL published a draft Farm Relief Bill which contained the immediate demands of the farmers.[22] Conducting a mass campaign in defense of the farmers' interests, the FUL collected the signatures of thousands of destitute farmers in support of the bill. With 11,654 signatures in hand, an FUL delegation led by Walter Wiggins, the secretary, and Fred Shunaman, the editor of *The Furrow*, met with Prime Minister Bennett and his cabinet.[23] After presenting the FUL's views, Fred Shunaman asked Bennett if he would make any statement on the petition. Bennett typically replied: "Not any!"[24] Such a reply compelled the FUL to step up its efforts.

The FUL employed many forms of struggle. It became actively involved in organizing struggles against evictions.[25] For example, a sheriff's sale would be transformed into a farce by organized bidding in which no neighbor would bid against another. The entire stock and equipment of a farm would be bought by neighboring farmers for a small sum after which it would be given back to its original owner.

The FUL also organized Hunger Marches of destitute farmers. On occasion, the FUL and the WUL organized joint demonstrations as a means of promoting labor-farmer unity and pub-

Participants in the joint demonstration of the unemployed, WUL and CLDL in Calgary in 1931.

ARCHIVES CPC/PAC/PA-125162

licizing their common interest in the struggle against the monopolies. Like many WUL demonstrations, the FUL's Hunger Marches were subjected to police repression. In December 1932, the police smashed a joint demonstration of workers and farmers in Edmonton resulting in the arrest of 41 persons, including FUL organizers.[26] As the FUL stepped up its activities in 1933 and 1934, police repression increased. Bennett was no more a friend of the farmers than he was a friend of the workers.

3. On to Ottawa

Though farmers fought to save their farms, and workers to save their jobs, there were hundreds of thousands who had neither farms nor jobs. From the beginning of the economic crisis, the Communist Party acted on the need to "undertake the struggle for Non-Contributory State Unemployment Insurance as the burning immediate demand of the Canadian working class."[27] In the first few months of the Depression, the party decided to organize the unemployed on its own initiative. This approach, which drew on the party's experiences of the early 1920s, lasted until the spring of 1930 when the Unemployed Councils created by the party merged with the National Unemployed Workers' Association, an affiliate of the WUL.

The WUL paid a great deal of attention to the problem of uniting the struggles of the unemployed with those of the employed.

This is of FUNDAMENTAL IMPORTANCE because the organization and struggle of the unemployed is not to be separated from but to be in the very center of the general struggle of the unions against speed-up, wage cuts and bad conditions.[28]

The WUL knew that high unemployment made it easier for the employers to force the workers to produce more, on penalty of being replaced by an unemployed person desperate for a job. Unity between the employed and the unemployed, on the other hand, would help undermine these efforts. Unity gave the unemployed the much needed support of organized labor in the struggle to realize their just demands.

To publicize their plight and demands, the organized unemployed frequently sent delegations to all three levels of government and staged numerous demonstrations. On March 6, 1930, for example, 20,000 unemployed workers in Montreal and 15,000 in Toronto held mass demonstrations to press their demands for jobs or unemployment insurance. Thousands of others participated in similar demonstrations in Edmonton, Winnipeg, Vancouver and Fort William (now Thunder Bay). The May Day demonstrations held a few weeks later proved to be the largest in Canada's history to that time. Approximately 80,000 workers from coast to coast took part.[29] Unemployment insurance was one of the main demands.

In conjunction with these activities, the WUL organized a Canada-wide petition campaign demanding noncontributory state unemployment insurance. On April 15, 1931, a WUL delegation headed by Tom McEwen presented Prime Minister Bennett with a petition bearing the signatures of 94,169 persons while a huge supporting demonstration gathered in Ottawa. In towns and cities across Canada, tens of thousands of workers staged mass demonstrations in solidarity with the WUL delegation. Bennett, to no one's surprise, rejected the WUL's demands.[30]

The militant actions of the unemployed raised the ire of the Canadian monopoly bourgeoisie. The police were frequently sent in to violently smash peaceful demonstrations and public meetings sponsored by the organized unemployed. Unemployed workers were often severely beaten; many were arrested. Some were deported, though many foreign-born workers were saved from deportation thanks to the efforts of the CLDL.

Police brutality against the unemployed at times extended to coldblooded murder. Urho Jaaska, a Finn, was beaten to death by police in Port Arthur for taking part in a demonstration demanding more relief. Nick Zynchuk, a Ukrainian, was shot in the back by a Montreal policeman because he entered a house where an eviction was taking place. Even Zynchuk's funeral procession of 20,000 people was broken up by the police. In Vancouver, demonstrations were subjected to systematic attacks by the police. Similar police violence was prevalent in Toronto where the struggle of the unemployed merged with the free speech fight. On May Day in 1932, 100,000 employed and unemployed workers participated in mass demonstrations across the country. The largest occurred in Hamilton where the police and firemen were mobilized in full force to make an unprovoked attack on its 20,000 participants. After a four-hour battle, 18 workers were arrested.[31]

Yet police repression failed to dampen either the spirit or the determina-

Delegates to the Workers' Economic Conference in Ottawa in 1932 lining up for food.

tion of the unemployed. By the end of 1932, unemployed organizations had sprung up in most major centers, in many smaller ones and in the relief camps.

From the tactic of combining mass demonstrations with delegations to governments to fight for the demands of the unemployed, there evolved the phenomenon known as the Hunger March. Unemployed from across the province would converge on the provincial capital while a delegation voiced their demands to the government. The first country-wide Hunger March took place in the summer of 1932. Unemployed workers from across Canada were to converge on Ottawa to attend a Workers' Economic Conference and present their demands to the Bennett government. The Workers' Economic Conference was intended to counter the Imperial Economic Conference with its imperialist aims. Bennett, as the latter's host, wanted to avoid the embarrassment of having so many unemployed in the capital. He therefore instructed the RCMP to lie in wait at major railway junctions and throw the workers off the trains. Nevertheless, about 8,000 unemployed managed to make their way past the RCMP blockade. Their demonstration was violently attacked by the police, resulting in 14 arrests and many injuries. Bennett again refused to consider their demands.[32]

Canada's ruling circles sought to meet the growing demands of the unemployed for jobs, unemployment insurance and adequate relief by herding the unemployed into "relief" camps. British Columbia's relief camps were typical of those in other provinces. The

ARCHIVES CPC/PAC/PA-124360

camps were usually located away from settled areas. Relief camp workers received the insulting sum of two dollars a day minus 85 cents for room and board for performing artificial, often unproductive jobs. In 1933, the camps came under the control of a joint federal-provincial commission which subsequently reduced the relief camp workers' wages. Later in the year, the camps were completely taken over by the federal government's Department of National Defense, which proceeded to reduce the workers' wages even further, to 20 cents a day and board.[33]

GLENBOW ARCHIVES, CALGARY, ALBERTA

The takeover by the Department of National Defense and the subsequent militarization of camp life earned the relief camps the reputation of being slave compounds. The *Relief Camp Worker,* newspaper of the WUL-affiliated Relief Camp Workers' Union (RCWU), carried numerous reports of deteriorating conditions in the camps and the efforts of the workers to improve their lot. For them, there was only one real solution to the steady erosion of their meager wages and severely limited rights — to organize into the RCWU. The union campaigned for better conditions, unemployment insurance, social insurance, adequate old age pensions and compensation for disability and sickness. It also organized conferences and conducted a number of strikes in support of these demands.

The Bennett government remained adamant in its refusal to meet the just demands of the relief camp workers. Government callousness led to a great deal of frustration. In early 1935, the WUL decided to assign Arthur H. Evans the task of leading the RCWU and organizing its struggles. A Communist with a great deal of experience in the IWW in the United States and the OBU in Canada, Arthur Evans had already shown himself to be a highly capable and effective organizer. So effective was he, that his organizing activities had landed him in prison on three separate occasions.

With Arthur Evans now its leader, the RCWU organized a conference of all relief camp workers to take place in Vancouver in April. Thousands converged on Vancouver; the camps were emptied in what amounted to a general strike of British Columbia relief camp workers. Over the next few days, a series of mass public meetings and mass demonstrations were held, enjoying wide public sympathy and support. On April 19, for example, the RCWU organized a mass meeting attended by more than 10,000 people, two-thirds of whom were Vancouver citizens. Working for the local reactionaries, the police attacked a peaceful demonstration which took place a few days later. On May Day, 15,000 demonstrators marched to Stanley Park where they were joined by 20,000 sympathizers. For another month, actions of this kind continued despite reactionary efforts to frustrate them.[34]

In late May, Arthur Evans proposed the organization of an On to Ottawa Trek as a means of forcing the Bennett government to act seriously on the demands of the relief camp strikers. Elected as leader of the Strike (On to Ottawa) Committee, he believed that although the Tories in Ottawa might be able to ignore a province-wide strike, they could hardly ignore a Canada-wide strike of relief camp workers, particularly if they were also converging on the country's capital. In early June, the main body of relief camp strikers began their trek to Ottawa.[35]

As the trek progressed eastward and the number of participants swelled, Bennett became increasingly alarmed. He had no desire to give his working class opponents another opportunity to strike a blow at his flagging popularity, but at the same time, he persisted in his refusal to make any concessions to the trekkers. Going over the head of the Saskatchewan government, Bennett ordered the RCMP to halt the trek in Regina.[36] Many interpreted the federal government's move as an attempt to intimidate the trekkers into abandoning their plans. The trekkers, however, remained undaunted as they realized that to turn back, when public opinion was solidly on their side, would mean certain defeat. On June 14, the trekkers arrived in Regina where they were greeted by 6,000 enthusiastic citizens.[37]

The Tory government then appeared to take a conciliatory approach. Two cabinet ministers negotiated an agreement with the Strike Committee whereby a delegation of eight trekkers headed by Arthur Evans would proceed to Ottawa at government expense to take up the demands of the trekkers. The main body of trekkers were to stay in Regina where they would be supplied with meals and shelter by the government.

The eight delegates of the trek met with the cabinet on June 22. But rather than listen to Arthur Evans' presentation on behalf of the relief camp workers, the Prime Minister launched into a vicious personal attack on the trek leader.

While negotiations were taking place in the capital, the Bennett government continued its preparations for an assault on the trekkers in Regina. The bourgeois press tried to whip up anti-communist hysteria in order to create an atmosphere in which violent police action could be justified. About 600 policemen, many bearing machine guns, were posted in and around the city. Meanwhile, a concentration camp for trekkers was being set up near Lumsden.[38]

(Top) The unemployed boarding a train in Calgary, Alberta, en route to Ottawa, June, 1935.
(Bottom) The police riot in Market Square, Regina, July 1, 1935.

Ontario trekkers taking a break on the way to Ottawa.

The trekkers' delegation returned to Regina on June 26. On the following day, the trekkers were denied food relief. The city was then cordoned off by the police and anyone who attempted to leave was subject to arrest. On June 29, the RCWU was declared an unlawful association under Section 98. On July 1, Canada's 68th anniversary, the government celebrated the occasion by ordering the police to break up a mass meeting of 3,000 people, of whom no more than four or five hundred were trekkers, which was being held at Market Square. RCMP officers and the city police charged into the peaceful crowd, clubbing unarmed men, women and children. A four-hour battle in the streets of Regina ensued in which about 100 people were hurt, a number of them shot by police. Over a hundred, including Arthur Evans, were arrested. One plainclothes city detective was beaten to death by his own fellow police officers.[39]

A wave of popular indignation and protest against the government's actions swept the country. Thousands joined in mass meetings and demonstrations.

In Winnipeg, unemployed who were to have joined the main trek as it proceeded eastward, set off for Ottawa on buses. Stopped at the Ontario border, the Winnipeg trekkers continued on foot to Kenora, where the presence of hundreds of RCMP officers signalled a potential violent confrontation. Not wanting a repeat of the Regina events, the trekkers negotiated with the Ontario government to ensure their peaceful return to Winnipeg. Some days later, 300 unemployed left Toronto for the capital. After walking the entire 250 miles to Ottawa, trekkers were finally able to present their demands to the Bennett government. The response was as usual negative.

In Ottawa, the parliamentary opposition vigorously condemned the Bennett government for its part in provoking the violence. Former Prime Minister King criticized the government for its excesses in its handling of the situation. J.S. Woodsworth, leader of the Co-operative Commonwealth Federation (CCF), accused the police of precipitating the riot. In Regina, a Citizens' Defense Committee was set up to counter the efforts of the government and the bourgeois press to slander the trekkers and blame them for the riot.[40] Many prominent personalities, including Saskatchewan CCF leader M.J. Coldwell and two Saskatchewan members of the Provincial Legislative Assembly, participated in this committee's efforts to have Arthur Evans and other political prisoners freed from detention. Within days after the Regina police riot, charges against half of those arrested were dropped due to widespread public indignation. Trekkers were allowed to receive food relief and return home. The mass campaign in Regina laid the groundwork for the election later in the year of a pro-labor city council including T. Gerry McManus, the local party leader.

However, the Bennett government intended to pursue charges against Arthur Evans and some others with a vengeance. Of the 117 who were arrested, 30 were committed for trial on a variety of charges ranging from vagrancy and assaulting police to membership in an unlawful association. Arthur Evans and six others were charged with being members of the RCWU.[41]

This action sparked a campaign to have all charges dropped and imprisoned trekkers released. Mass public unity soon brought about Arthur Evans' release on bail. In the fall, he conducted an exhausting tour across the country with the aim of exposing the Bennett government and obtaining the release of those still in jail.

The Hunger Marches, the On to Ottawa Trek, the activities of the WUL, the FUL and the CLDL were vivid expressions of popular rejection of Bennett's program of economic stagnation, sharply reduced living standards and political repression. Such rejection assumed massive proportions as workers, un-

employed and farmers sought alternative policies based on work and wages and guaranteed farm income. This sentiment helped bring about the resounding defeat of the Bennett government in the 1935 general election. The Liberals under the leadership of W.L.M. King gained 132 more seats than the Conservatives.

During the election campaign, King had been forced to respond to the massive working class pressure by promising to repeal Section 98 and abolish the relief camps. In June 1936, almost a year later, the relief camps were closed and Section 98 repealed. With this victory the RCWU was dissolved.[42]

The seemingly all-powerful "Iron Heel" Bennett was finally removed from the political scene. The militant policies and work of the WUL, the FUL and the Communist Party had shown that working people were capable of not only defending but also advancing their vital interests. Provided the working class was united in its struggle against exploitation and oppression, it could make real gains even under the harshest of conditions.

The Communist Party, meanwhile, emerged from this period firmly established in the minds of Canadian workers as an unshakable champion of the rights and interests of the working class, the farmers and the unemployed.

---

1. H. Murphy and B. Buhay, "The Automobile Industry and the Labour Movement" in *Canadian Labour Monthly,* No. 8, October, 1928, pp. 14-18.
2. *Automobile Workers' Conference,* November 3-4, 1928, Archives CPC.
3. O. Ryan, *Tim Buck: A Conscience for Canada* (Toronto, 1975), p. 109.
4. *Build the Industrial Union of Steel Car Workers,* Archives CPC; and *Trade Union*

Report, *Industrial Department, Communist Party of Canada,* June 1, 1930, Archives CPC, pp. 3-4.

5. *Report of the Sixth National Convention of the Communist Party of Canada,* May 31-June 7, 1929, p. 44.

6. *Resolutions of Enlarged Plenum of Communist Party of Canada,* February 1931, p. 29.

7. *Workers' Unity League: Policy — Tactics — Structure—Demands* (Toronto, 1932), p. 25.

8. *The Worker,* June 28, 1930; and CPC Industrial Department, *Perspectives and Tasks of the Workers' Unity League of Canada,* Archives CPC, p. 3.

9. Department of Labour, *Labour Organization in Canada (For the Calendar Year 1930)* (Ottawa, 1931), pp. 44 and 47.

10. *Constitution of the Workers' Unity League,* first national conference held in Montreal, August 5-7, 1931, p. 3; and T.A. McEwen, *The Forge Glows Red* (Toronto, 1974), reprint of constitution adopted by the second WUL conference in Toronto, September 9-12, 1933, p. 247.

11. *Final Statement of the WUL Executive Board to Those Trade Unionists Who Constituted Its Membership, and Who Have Now Merged within the Unions of the AFL,* June 18, 1936, Archives CPC, pp. 7-8.

12. Ibid., p. 6.

13. Ibid., p. 6; and McEwen, p. 157.

14. *Stratford Beacon-Herald,* November 3 and December 5, 1933.

15. M. Marlowe and W. Ross, *Demand Withdrawal of Charges against Flin Flon Arrested!,* Archives CPC.

16. Corbin Strike Committee, *Summary of Corbin Strike since January 20* (1935), Archives CPC.

17. J.M. Clarke, *Agrarian Program, Communist Party of Canada* (1929) Archives CPC, pp. 2-3; and also *Sixth Convention,* p. 50.

18. Clarke, p. 8; and *Sixth Convention,* p. 59.

19. L.T. Morris and J.M. Clarke, *Draft Agrarian Program of Communist Party of Canada,* June 1930, Archives CPC.

20. *Resolutions of Enlarged Plenum,* p. 35.

21. *The Worker,* December 20, 1930.

22. Ibid., October 10, 1931.

23. Ibid., March 19, 1932.

24. Ibid., March 26, 1932.

25. Ibid., May 17, 1932.

26. Ibid., January 7, 1933.

27. *Resolutions of Enlarged Plenum,* p. 25.

28. *The Worker,* May 31, 1930.

29. Ibid., March 15 and May 3, 1930.

30. Ibid., April 18, 1931.

31. Ibid., March 11 and 18, and May 7, 1932.

32. Ibid., July 30 and August 6, 1932.

33. J. Evans Sheils and B. Swankey, "Work and Wages!" (Vancouver, 1977), pp. 76-77.

34. Ibid., pp. 86-94.

35. Ibid., pp. 104-107.

36. Ibid., p. 114.

37. A.H. Evans, *Brief Outline of Events since Our Arrival in Regina* (1935), Archives CPC, pp. 2-3.

38. Ibid., p. 3.

39. Sheils and Swankey, pp. 163-164 and 170; Evans, p. 6; and *The Worker,* September 25, 1935.

40. *Toronto Daily Star,* July 3, 1935; and the Regina Citizens' Legal Defense Committee, *The Truth about the Relief Camp Strikers* (1935), Archives CPC.

41. Ibid.

42. Sheils and Swankey, pp. 180 and 227.

6. The Fight for Peace and Democracy

Bennett's defeat was the culmination of the fight against the reactionary offensive in the early thirties. Mass united action had determined the success of that struggle and gave momentum to the struggles of the later thirties. The working class regained the initiative. Conditions were becoming more favorable for deepening working class unity, the key to advance, particularly in the labor movement.

As conditions changed, so too did the relationship between the WUL and the reformist unions. The WUL's impressive record of achievements influenced many workers in the reformist unions. Even substantial sections of the TLC and the ACCL leadership were changing their attitudes. Canadian sections of the AFL-affiliated Internationals indicated that they were prepared to organize the unorganized into industrial unions around a program of militant struggle and that they wanted to set up a united Canadian trade union center.

The original reasons for founding the WUL receded into the background while the questions of organic unity, of merger came to the fore. Sensitive to the new attitude in the reformist unions and being conscious of the need for maximum unity, the WUL, during February 1935, raised the call for the full organizational unity of the Canadian trade union movement. This was to involve the merger of all parallel unions in a given industry into a single union and the creation of a single trade union center.[1]

Throughout the history of the WUL, the Communist Party played an active and determining role in its development and in the formulation of its policies. Communists had established the WUL in 1930 when it became clear that the existing unions would not accept the responsibilities of the new phase in the struggles of the working class. When the reformist unions indicated their intention of pursuing policies promoting the greater unity of the working class, the Communist Party was the first to call for the merger between the affiliates of the WUL and those of the TLC. The positions of the party with regard to the reformist labor unions changed as conditions and the attitudes of the reformist leadership changed. Yet the Communist Party did not waver from its goal — to promote and achieve genuine working class unity on the basis of militant policies.

The merger of the constituent unions of the WUL with their approximate counterparts in the TLC was accomplished within a year of the WUL's appeal. However, it was not yet possible to set up an entirely unified trade union center because the ACCL at this point persisted in its pursuit of anti-TLC policies.

1. The Committee for Industrial Organization

While the industrial unions of the WUL and the craft unions of the TLC were amalgamating in Canada, a split was developing inside the AFL in the USA which was later to have repercussions in the Canadian labor movement. Although the militant Trade Union Unity League had succeeded in convincing or influencing a substantial section of the AFL toward industrial unionism, the right-wing bureaucratic AFL leadership remained stubbornly opposed to indus-

Harvey Murphy (1906-1977) speaking to coal miners and their families on May Day 1936 in Blairmore, Alberta. In 1933, a left wing municipal council was elected which decided to rename the main street after Tim Buck.

UTL, TF, MS. COLL. 179, KENNY COLLECTION

trial unionism. In addition, the AFL leaders rejected the idea of organizing the unorganized in the mass production industries because they were convinced that workers could not be unionized in times of economic crisis. Their craft mentality caused them to be contemptuous of mass production workers whom they considered to be unworthy or incapable of union organization.

A substantial section of the AFL rejected this point of view. The most prominent leader of the dissident faction was John L. Lewis, who had learned from bitter experience the dire consequences of ignoring the workers' demands. To avoid a repetition of the disastrous events of the 1920s when a large portion of the union membership had defected, Lewis and some other social-reformist union leaders came to the conclusion that they had to accommodate themselves to the militant mood of the rank and file. After an unsuccessful attempt to persuade the AFL hierarchy to officially sponsor an organizational drive in the mass production industries, the Committee for Industrial Organization (CIO) was founded in November 1935, by a group of eight AFL affiliates.[2] Lewis became chairman of the new organization and then resigned as a vice-president of the AFL. The AFL leaders accused the new labor body of aiming to replace the existing unions. The CIO denied this charge of dual unionism, pointing out that its purpose was to promote the organization of the unorganized into industrial unions and not to encroach on the authority or membership of the existing unions.[3]

Despite pressure from the CIO and the membership of many AFL affiliated unions to support the CIO's organizational drive, the AFL executive council insisted that the industrial unions being set up, be divided up among the craft unions. It ordered the CIO to dissolve, an ultimatum which the CIO rejected. The CIO unions also declined to appear before an AFL trial committee.

Without consulting a convention of the AFL membership, the right-wing leadership decided to suspend the majority of the CIO unions. By this time, there were 12 CIO unions, composing over one-third of the AFL membership. The AFL edict was made effective in early September 1936. Over a million of the 3.4 million AFL members were thus deprived of a voice in the AFL.[4]

In the United States, the CIO grew very rapidly. By the end of 1937, it had a total of 38 affiliates. Some, most notably the Steel Workers' Organizing Committee (SWOC), were formed to pool the resources of several CIO unions. At the CIO conference of October 1937, the total membership stood at four million.[5]

Although the CIO proved that the workers in the mass production industries were more than ready and willing to be organized, the AFL bureaucrats still refused to have anything to do with industrial unionism. Instead, they persisted in their demand for the dissolution of the CIO. In February and May 1938, the AFL executive council revoked the charters of 9 of the 10 original CIO unions.[6] In November of the same year, the constituent convention of the Committee for Industrial Organization established a new trade union center called the Congress of Industrial Organizations (also CIO).

The CIO was established in Canada in the summer of 1936 when a group of Hamilton steelworkers, mostly Communists, invited the Amalgamated Association of Iron, Steel and Tin Workers (one of the unions which, with the UMWA and others, had formed the SWOC) to Hamilton to discuss union organizational questions. The invitation was accepted. The Hamilton committee of the Communist Party of Canada then decided to hold a general membership meeting at which they pledged to throw the weight of the party behind the campaign to organize Hamilton steelworkers into the Iron, Steel and Tin Workers union.[7]

Shortly afterward, a meeting took place between the representatives of the SWOC and those of the Communist Party, namely Stewart Smith, and Peter Boychuck.[8] It was agreed that the SWOC would provide the funds and take on staff organizers named by the Hamilton party organization. Consequently, most of the SWOC organizers in Hamilton were Communists, among them Harry Hunter and Harry Hamburgh. In Toronto, the only local of the General Steel Wares Workers' Union, originally founded by the WUL, also joined the Iron, Steel and Tin Workers union.[9] Richard Steele, its organizer and also a Communist, was put on the SWOC's full-time staff as the Toronto district organizer. In Sydney, Nova Scotia, George MacEachern organized steel-

A "sitdowner" in the Vancouver Post Office. On May 20, 1938, members of the Vancouver Unemployed Association occupied the Post Office, Art Gallery and Georgia Hotel in their campaign for government action to ease the desperate plight of the unemployed. With the aid of tear gas, whips and clubs, the RCMP drove out the last sitdowners some 30 days later. That evening, 30,000 people gathered at the ferry docks as a send-off for 100 jobless departing for Victoria to lobby the B.C. government.

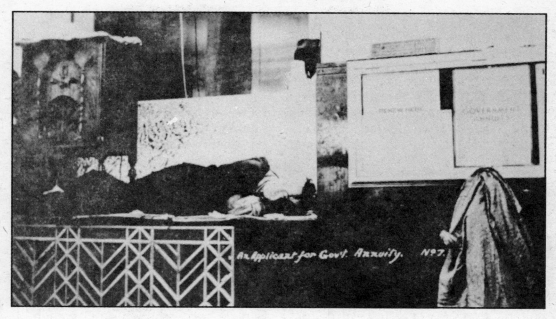

workers into the SWOC and was a founder of Local 1064 of the United Steel Workers of America, in which he subsequently held executive positions, including president.

While 1936 witnessed a split between the AFL and the CIO in the United States; in Canada, 1936 was a year preoccupied with the question of achieving and maintaining hard-won trade union unity. Support for industrial unionism came from both the membership and then the leadership of the AFL-affiliated unions of the TLC. In January, the convention of the Alberta Federation of Labor declared its support for industrial unionism.[10] In May, the Toronto TLC went on record "in favor of the industrial form of organization as a necessary step in the unionization of the unorganized workers in mass production industries; endorses the work of the CIO in this regard as a progressive step; supports it as an essential part of union democracy the right of a minority to continue its appeal to the broad masses of the membership, and refutes the contention that this work is not progressive and inevitably leads to dual unionism."[11] The resolution was adopted by a vote of 95 to 8, four months after the AFL had condemned the CIO and ordered its dissolution. The vote therefore constituted a bold and explicit rejection of the position taken by the the AFL leadership. Similar resolutions endorsing the CIO came from other district councils of the TLC during 1936.

While the TLC leadership was sensitive to the pressures of its membership and district councils, it declined to take an open position on the split in the labor movement in the USA, on the grounds that this was a matter outside of its jurisdiction. The 1937 TLC convention, where this question was discussed, had taken place only a week after the AFL had made its decision to suspend most of the CIO unions. A year later, the TLC convention voted to retain the status quo on CIO-AFL relations. On a more positive note, the resolution offered the TLC's good offices in healing the split between the AFL and the CIO.[12] The resolution's circumspection was dictated by events in both the TLC and the AFL.

In May of 1937, John Noble, an AFL organizer in Canada, visited Hamilton with orders from the AFL to revoke the Hamilton TLC's AFL charter. However, the district council voted 51 to 22 to retain the status of the existing body with the result that Noble and his cohorts set up a separate rival district council in Hamilton. This action did not go over well with the TLC which obliquely gave its support to the forces of industrial unionism by working for the reunification of the district council.[13]

The TLC thus found itself indirectly opposing the AFL's disruptive activities in Canada and its interference in the TLC's internal affairs. The TLC's *de facto* support for the CIO was in large part influenced by the widespread sentiment among Canadian workers in favor of working class unity. As the amalgamation of the unions of the WUL and the TLC proceeded, a pro-unity momentum was built up which carried over into the struggle to preserve unity between the CIO and the AFL unions in Canada. The leadership was impelled to adopt the principle of trade union unity not only in words, but also in practice.

Unity assisted organizational activity. As well, the successes achieved by the union movement in the United States, particularly the sit-in strikes which broke the resistance of the employers, inspired Canadian workers to join unions in ever increasing numbers. During 1936 and 1937, union membership increased 30 per cent, a phenomenal figure under normal circumstances, but one that paled compared to the increase in the USA where membership had more than doubled in the same period.

There were a number of factors affecting the different growth rates in the two countries. Firstly, Canadian unions did not have financial resources or organizers comparable to their U.S. counterparts. The CIO in Canada received little concrete assistance from the parent body. The organization of the CIO in Canada was essentially a Canadian affair. Secondly, the CIO unions in Canada had to contend with open government hostility in the two most populous and industrialized provinces, Ontario and Quebec. Both provincial governments were prepared to use various forms of coercion to prevent the CIO from establishing itself in Canada. Thirdly, Canadian unionists were deeply preoccupied with the struggle to maintain the unity of the TLC in the face of the AFL attack on the CIO. These difficulties, however, did not stop Communists and progressive trade unionists from continuing their efforts to organize the unorganized in the mass production industries.

In the struggle to achieve and preserve the unity of the trade union movement, Communists earned wide recognition from fellow workers as consistent and principled fighters. Communists rejected any narrow partisan interests that

A FAIR RETURN · FOR ALL FISHERMEN
FULL COMPENSATION COVERAGE

would stand in the way of achieving working class unity. They saw in the development of this unity new possibilities for expanding and strengthening the autonomy and independence of the trade union movement. Events since then have proven the soundness of this policy.

Communists were often elected to leading positions in many unions and TLC district councils. For example, after the Chesterfield Furniture Workers' Industrial Union merged with the Upholsterers' International Union, its former leader, Fred Collins, was elected to the TLC executive council. Sydney Sarkin, an organizer for the IUNTW and business agent for the cutters' local of the Amalgamated Clothing Workers' Union, was elected to the executive council of the Montreal TLC.[14] When the

Lumber Workers Industrial Union of Canada affiliated with the Carpenters Union and became the Lumber and Sawmill Workers Union, its Secretary, Bruce Magnuson, became the Secretary of the Port Arthur Trades and Labor Council.

Communists were also instrumental in organizing steelworkers. By the end of 1937, the SWOC could claim almost 9,000 members in Ontario and Nova Scotia. The SWOC was not the only CIO organization to be set up in Canada in this period. The Canadian Seamen's Union (CSU), the International Union of Mine, Mill and Smelter Workers (Mine-Mill), the International Woodworkers of America (IWA), the United Electrical, Radio and Machine Workers of America (UE) and many others established solid bases in their respective jurisdictions. By the end of 1937, the CIO unions, including the older established ones such as the UMWA, the Amalgamated Clothing Workers and the International Ladies' Garment Workers, had a total membership of 76,000.[15]

The most important struggle in the CIO's formative years, the struggle which forced the Canadian bourgeoisie to come to terms with the existence of the CIO, was the Oshawa auto workers' strike in April 1937. General Motors and the Liberal provincial government of Mitchell F. Hepburn did everything they could to break the strike and deny recognition to the United Auto Workers of America (UAW) as the bargaining agent for the Oshawa auto workers. Despite Hepburn's many underhanded manoeuvres, including red-baiting, the workers stood firm in their determination to win the fight. Popular support for the strikers grew rapidly. After 17 days, General Motors and Premier Hepburn were forced to concede defeat. This victory constituted a turning point for the CIO's organizational drive in Canada. Canadian workers began to join the CIO at an accelerated rate. The UAW's breakthrough meant that no company or government could stop the Canadian working class from opening up a new page in its history.

However, while the CIO was busy organizing the mass production industries, the AFL leadership pursued its anti-CIO policies and activities. In early 1938, the AFL formally expelled the unions of the CIO. This action put the TLC in a quandary. Most of its member unions belonged to the AFL Internationals, but the TLC wanted to maintain the unity within the TLC between the Canadian sections of the CIO and the AFL. The TLC therefore decided to pursue its efforts to reconcile the two groups in the United States.

The Communist Party fully supported the TLC's efforts. At its eighth convention in October 1937, the party pledged itself "to the cause of unity and urge all our members in craft and industrial unions, in the International unions as well as those who are members of the so-called National or Catholic unions, to work tirelessly together with all other workers in the trade union movement, for one united and democratic Canadian trade union movement within the Trades and Labor Congress; for the sovereignty of the congress as a mouthpiece of the Canadian trade union movement; for the maintenance of the congress as the parent body of all trades and labor councils and for the widest autonomy of all Canadian branches of International unions."[16]

In Canadian conditions, where national and international unions existed side by side, unity of the Canadian labor movement could not be achieved without sovereignty. The Canadian labor movement would otherwise be open to outside interference, specifically from the pro-imperialist reactionary AFL leadership. Sovereignty could not be achieved without unity, because only through a strong united trade union movement would Canadian workers be able to defend their particular interests.

In the unions, in the district councils and in the conventions of the TLC, Communists fought for a united, sovereign Canadian trade union movement capable of independent labor political action. Communists called not only for

During the late 1930s, Arthur Evans was the British Columbia organizer of the Mine, Mill and Smelter Workers' union. When he was organizing the miners of Trail, anti-labor goons unsuccessfully tried to scare him off by demolishing his truck.

unity within the TLC but also for unity between the TLC and other union centers. When several officials of the Vancouver Labor Council of the ACCL interpreted this to mean that the Communist Party supported the forcible liquidation of the ACCL, Tom McEwen refuted the charge by noting that the party opposed raiding and favored voluntary unity in action.[17] Unfortunately, elements of the anti-ACCL craft mentality lingered on in the TLC leadership and constituted an obstacle to the establishment of cooperation between the two union centers.

While many unionists were determined to preserve the unity of the TLC, the reactionary AFL leadership was equally determined to export its divisive policies to Canada. The AFL intended to provoke a split at the TLC's 1938 Niagara Falls convention where AFL fraternal delegate, J.J. Kehoe, attacked the CIO as a secessionist movement. Kehoe's remarks received a cool reception. In fact, even before Kehoe made his speech, R.J. Tallon, the TLC's secretary, articulated the delegates' pro-unity sentiment when he stated that the TLC was totally independent of the AFL (which was not quite accurate) and would not accept its dictation. The convention enthusiastically greeted the adoption of the resolution which instructed the TLC executive "to continue its efforts to maintain harmony within the international trade union movement in Canada. ..."[18] For the moment, it seemed that the unity forces had won a great victory.

The AFL leadership was very unhappy with the outcome of the TLC convention. A month later, in October, Green launched a vicious attack on the TLC at the AFL convention. W.G. Russell, the TLC's fraternal delegate to the convention, made a speech in which he made a fervent plea for unity in labor's ranks, a plea which was very well received by the AFL delegates. Green, however, followed Russell's speech with a demand for the expulsion of the CIO unions from the TLC. This demand amounted to crude interference in the internal affairs of the TLC.[19] Shortly afterward, the AFL decided to put heavy pressure on the TLC by threatening to use their control over the craft Internationals, which still formed the main basis of support for the TLC, to undermine and sabotage the TLC's unity and authority. The Canadian CIO affiliates were told to cut their ties with the U.S. parent unions, a demand with which they refused to comply. In February 1939, finally bowing to U.S. pressure, the TLC suspended the Canadian CIO unions. They were barred from attending the TLC's 1939 convention, which enabled the right wing to muster a majority in support of the CIO's expulsion.[20]

The intense preoccupation with the struggle to maintain the unity of the TLC as well as the determined efforts of the Ontario and Quebec governments to obstruct the unionization process, contributed to a temporary decline in union membership during the 1938-40 period. However, the struggle to achieve genuine trade union unity continued unabated. Under pressure from its membership to participate fully in the organizational drives of the late 1930s, the ACCL was compelled to set aside its prejudices against U.S. based unions. In fact, at its September 1940 convention, the ACCL voted to admit the CIO unions expelled from the TLC. The new union center named itself the Canadian Congress of Labor (CCL). The Communists hailed the merger as a step forward in the long struggle to achieve Canadian labor unity.

The fight for unity in the labor movement, as in the working class and democratic movement, is a dominant theme of the work of the Communist Party. The reactionary offensive of the 1930s in Canada and internationally, gave this fight an added urgency.

2. The United Front

Canada's experiences with economic stagnation, climbing unemployment, savage wage cuts, social destitution and reactionary anti-labor, pro-monopoly policies were features shared with other capitalist countries. In some countries, the monopoly bourgeoisie resorted to fascism and militarism to stop the working class movement and suppress its struggles. Military aggression was another aspect of fascist policy. It was a means of asserting the interests of the monopolies of the fascist country at the expense of other countries.

For the imperialists, the Soviet Union was a threat to the capitalist domination of the entire world. The example of socialism evoked considerable anxiety in the imperialist circles because they feared that their own workers might opt for socialism. The cornerstone of imperialist policy remained, and remains, the destruction of the USSR.

In this context, unity of the working class was essential, unity first and foremost between the two main trends in the working class — revolutionary and reformist. This question occupied the deliberations of the world communist movement.

At the sixth congress of the Communist International in 1928, the delegates concluded that the dominant tendency in the foreign policy of the imperialist states was their preparations for war against the Soviet Union. Imperialism's fear and hatred of socialism increased as the USSR's socialist construction made great strides.[21]

The congress also took up the questions of the communist attitude toward fascism and social democracy. The relative economic and political stability of the mid-1920s had temporarily reinforced the dominance of social-democratic parties in most European countries. On the other hand, although as yet a relatively isolated phenomenon, fascism had begun to manifest itself. In 1922, Benito Mussolini seized power in a military coup in Italy and imposed a regime which systematically and violently sought to destroy the Italian working class and democratic movements. The right-wing leadership of the social-democratic parties were blind to the danger presented by the rise of fascism.

In contrast, the Comintern understood that fascism, although demagogically duping the petty and middle bourgeoisie, supported the aggressive policies of the big bourgeoisie. However, the tendency to underestimate the danger persisted. As the betrayal of the social-democratic leadership during and after the world war was still fresh in the minds of many Communists, the sixth Comintern congress called for a stepped-up struggle against social democracy. Social democracy was characterized by the 11th ECCI plenum as the bulwark of the bourgeoisie, as social-fascism, because its leaders supported the workers in words but the bourgeoisie in deeds, including under certain circumstances, its fascist variety.[22] This formulation gave rise to sectarianism in the world communist movement.

The social-fascism formula prevented the Communists from taking timely notice of the fact that with the onset of fascism the social democrats, with the exception of their Right leaders and the right-wing groups, were capable of taking part in the anti-fascist struggle.[23]

In other words, the social-fascism formulation obstructed cooperation between Communist and social-democratic workers at a time when unity was even more urgent.

The first half of the 1930s was a period marked by an increase in the number and scale of military conflicts or the threat of military conflicts as a direct consequence of the expansionist ambitions of the fascist states.

In Japan, the military took power and immediately proceeded to realize its long restrained ambitions in Asia. In 1931, Japan began a long bloody war against China by conquering the northern mineral-rich province of Manchuria. In 1933, Adolph Hitler came to power in Germany and began what was to become one of the most barbaric regimes in human history. Meanwhile, Mussolini dreamed of resurrecting the Roman Empire. In 1935, fascist Italy invaded Ethiopia, with the aim of annexing that country.

While the imperialist countries failed to do anything more than verbally condemn fascist military aggression, the Soviet Union stood out as the only state to consistently oppose fascist ambitions and actively seek the formation of an anti-fascist alliance.

Fascism's aggressive foreign policy was accompanied by mass repression at home, not only against Communists but also against social democrats and the working class and democratic movements as a whole. Social democrats learned from experience that fascism would stop at nothing to destroy the hard-won gains of the working class. In bourgeois-democratic countries, social democrats as well as Communists found themselves the targets of reactionary, anti-labor policies. Fascist gangs with open sympathies for Nazi Germany and fascist Italy became very active.

In Canada, the experience of ultra-conservative federal and provincial governments had taught both Communists and social-reformists much. If the interests and rights of the working class and its allies were to be properly defended against reactionary and fascist attacks, if the shift toward the far right was to be curbed and beaten back, it would be necessary to unite their efforts. The rise of fascism therefore necessitated a change in strategy and tactics.

In the case of the Communist Party, it became necessary to combat left-sectarianism; in the case of social democracy, it meant the strengthening of the left wing.

The Comintern re-examined its strategy and tactics in 1934, in order to take into account the new political situation and the experiences of the Communist Parties. In Canada, for example, Communists and social-reformists in the TLC were moving toward unity and cooperation within the Canadian trade union movement. Similar trends were occurring in other capitalist countries as well. The seventh congress, which took place in the summer of 1935, confirmed the Comintern's new orientation. The change involved more than the question of simply overcoming sectarianism; Communists had to build a united workers' and popular front in the struggle against fascism and reaction. The historic significance of the seventh congress is precisely this orientation on the united front.[24]

The detailed report on the struggle for the united front and against war and fascism was delivered by Georgi Dimitrov, General Secretary of the Comintern. Dimitrov rejected equating fascist with bourgeois-democratic methods of rule, as this led to the underestimation of the fascist danger. He defined fascism as *"the open terrorist dictatorship of the most reactionary, most chauvinistic and most imperialist elements of finance capital."*[25] It is a form of the class domination of the bourgeoisie. Although fascism enjoyed a mass base in both Germany and Italy in the thirties because of its demagogic appeals to the petty-bourgeoisie, the middle classes and the backward elements in society; its support for the policies of the monopoly bourgeoisie always brings it into conflict with these classes and social strata. Ferocious as it is, fascism is also quite unstable. For objectively speaking, the interests of monopoly capital inevitably come into conflict with the nonmonopoly classes and social strata.

As outlined by Dimitrov, the way to prevent fascism from coming to power or, if already in power, to overthrow it, would be the formation of a united front to establish unity of action of the workers. Such unity on a national and an international scale would be a powerful weapon in the struggle against fascism and for the interests of the working class.[26] The united front of the workers would consist of Communists and social democrats around a common antifascist program. It would be able to exert considerable influence on Catholic and unorganized workers and even on backward elements who had become temporary victims of fascist demagogy. On the basis of a proletarian united front, a broad people's anti-fascist front could be formed. This front would incorporate the working class, peasantry, petty-bourgeoisie, intellectuals and others whose interests were fundamentally opposed to the selfish interests of monopoly capital.

Dimitrov refuted right-wing social-democratic allegations that the united front was not decisive for the struggle against fascism and its defeat. He countered allegations that Communists would use the united front to further their own particular purposes. He pointed out that the growth of fascism's influence was objectively aided by the divisive class-collaborationist policies of the right-wing social-democratic leaders. Furthermore, the united front would be a voluntary and equal alliance whose members would have as their common aim, the fight against fascism and reaction, in the interests of the working class and its allies. The government of the united or the popular front would take measures against fascism and its political and economic base — monopoly capital. It would be fundamentally different from a social-democratic government because the latter was "an instrument of class collaboration with the bourgeoisie in the interest of the preservation of the capitalist order...."[27] On the other hand, the united or popular front government could be a solid basis for the transition to socialism. In or out of government, the united front would not bury the separate organizational and ideological identities of its participants. It would exist to defend the interests of the working masses against the reactionary policies of the monopolies.

Dimitrov's report to the seventh congress of the Communist International was an invaluable contribution to the struggles of Canadian Communists and the world communist movement against war and fascism. Although fascism was defeated in the Second World War, this did not eliminate the reactionary forces that supported it and therefore did not eliminate the dangers of world war and reaction, up to and including fascism. Despite its various forms, monopoly capitalism remains reactionary all along the line. It still seeks to ensure national and international domination although its ability to do so is limited by the struggles of the working class, the national liberation movements and by the existence of a powerful world socialist system headed by the Soviet Union. The concepts of the united front and the popular front, as outlined by Dimitrov, were to change their forms while retaining their essential anti-monopoly content. Dimitrov's contribution to Marxist-Leninist theory retains its validity to this day.

3. A Canadian People's Front

The ninth plenum of the Communist Party of Canada in November 1935, hailed the seventh congress of the Comintern as a great historical event. Stewart Smith, the party's delegate to the Comintern congress, delivered a report on its results and decisions. The plenum evaluated the congress decisions in the light of Canadian experience. The political situation in Canada and around the world had altered substantially and therefore required a new orientation in the strategy and tactics of the communist movement. In Canada, this new direction had actually begun to take place in late 1934.

At that time, a number of social-reformist leaders, particularly in the TLC and the ACCL, indicated their willingness to struggle against the drive to the right, against the threat of war and fascism and for the unity of the working class around its immediate demands, including the organization of the unorganized into the industrial unions. Under these circumstances, the Communist Party was obliged to reappraise its social-fascism formulation, a concept which was coming into sharp contradiction with the possibilities of working class unity. These changes in the Communist Party's attitude were reflected in the WUL, leading to the successful mergers with TLC affiliates during 1935-36.

Prior to the party's reorientation, a rather strong element of sectarianism had crept into the party's thinking, as a response to the stubborn opposition of social-reformism to the growing militancy of the period. Although the Communist Party was far from sectarian in terms of its slogans and the support it enjoyed in the working class movement, there was a tendency to react subjectively to the poisonous anti-communism of social-reformist leaders. Some of the hostility experienced by Communists was returned in kind. For example, a little over three months after the formation of the WUL, its provisional executive sent a letter to the unity conference of Alberta miners calling for, among other things, "the systematic breaking up of the reactionary A.F. of L. Unions. . . ."[28] Fortunately, the danger to working class unity inherent in the pursuit of such a policy was quickly perceived and never acted upon.

A more important manifestation of sectarianism was found in the party's attitude toward and relations with the social-reformist CCF which had been founded in 1933. The following February, Stewart Smith published a book under the name G. Pierce in which he characterized the CCF as a social-fascist party, as the twin of fascism. He denied that there was any real distinction between bourgeois democracy and fascism as both were dictatorships of the capitalist class. As monopoly capital was tending toward fascism and as there were elements of fascization apparent in the Canadian state under "Iron Heel" Bennett, it therefore seemed to follow that class collaboration in a capitalist country amounted to class collaboration with fascism.[29] A similar sentiment was officially expressed by the party's seventh convention in July 1934. The seventh convention characterized social-reformism as social-fascism, as "the main social support of the bourgeoisie, assisting finance capital in its attacks upon the masses, in fascization and in preparations for a new war."[30] This concept had dangerous implications for the struggle for working class unity.

Despite this, there were elements of a change in the party's attitude. There was also a growing realization that a clear distinction had to be made between the social-reformist membership and the social-reformist leaders. The convention resolution on "The Present Situation and the Tasks of the Communist Party of Canada" called on the party membership to conduct a persistent struggle to realize the united front with the workers and farmers of social-reformist organizations. This change sought to exempt at least the main body of social-reformists from the sweeping characterization of social-reformism as social-fascism.

The same resolution criticized both right and left deviations committed by Communists in united front work. The right deviation tended to hide the party for the sake of formal unity. The left deviation took a mechanical and formalistic approach to the question of building the workers' united front; in practice rejecting the united front and shirking work among the masses in the fight for their immediate demands.[31]

Given the changes in the Canadian and world situation and in the context of the seventh Comintern congress, the ninth plenum of the Communist Party of Canada removed the erroneous concept of social-fascism from the party program. However, hangovers of this sectarian idea lingered on in the minds of some Communists for many years afterward. Nevertheless, the party's political line was corrected to more closely correspond with the need for working class unity.

The ninth plenum re-examined the Communist Party's relations with the CCF. Reversing his previous position of having nothing to do with the CCF, Stewart Smith then maintained that the CCF had the potential of becoming a federated party of the working people because its federative structure permitted the affiliation of entire organizations. The Communist Party endorsed this position. Unity could be achieved around such immediate demands as unemployment insurance, higher prices for the farmers, a system of steeply graduated income tax to force the rich to pay the costs of the economic crisis, the repeal of Section 98 and the defense of the democratic rights of the people against fascism and reaction. These were demands which the CCF supported.[32]

Relations between the CCF and the Communist Party were complex and contradictory. Usually the CCF leadership opposed cooperation with Communists, although on rare occasions they did work together unofficially on certain specific issues. The left wing

Left, Jacob Penner (1885-1965), Winnipeg alderman from 1933 to 1961. Right, Andrew Bileski, Winnipeg school trustee from 1933 to 1940 and from 1961 to 1965.

ARCHIVES CPC/PAC/PA-125066

ARCHIVES CPC/PAC/PA-125090

was more sympathetic and pressed for closer cooperation between the two parties; sometimes a working relationship was actually established. But more often than not, the right wing quashed such attempts to achieve unity of action around immediate demands at the grass roots level.

In early 1935, Sam Carr wrote to the CCF on behalf of the Communist Party proposing the formation of an alliance in the forthcoming federal elections. The idea was rejected. On the other hand, the CCF and the Communist Party established a joint defense committee for the striking workers of Corbin. During the On to Ottawa Trek, many CCFers, including M.J. Coldwell, pledged their support for the trekkers' efforts.[33] Woodsworth himself did excellent work in the House of Commons in defense of the trekkers in the wake of the Regina police riot, despite the Bennett government's attempt to red-bait him. Yet these remained relatively isolated cases.

In August 1935, *The Worker* felt obliged to point out that prohibitions in the CCF constitution had blocked several attempts at unity of action. The Communist Party wrote again to the CCF proposing the establishment of an electoral alliance, but, in a letter signed by Coldwell, was once again rejected by the CCF leadership.[34]

Persistent hard work by Communists to achieve united action with the CCF and other social-reformist organizations in the electoral sphere did eventually bear some fruit. In Winnipeg, the municipal candidates of the Communist Party and the Independent Labor Party agreed to support each other. In Sudbury, the CCF and the Communist Party held a joint conference endorsing a common platform for the Sudbury municipal elections. Similar alliances were formed in Regina and a number of other cities and towns. Where electoral alliances were established, labor candidates won or did quite well. In Winnipeg, for example, Communists Jacob Penner and Andrew Bileski were elected alderman and school trustee respectively along with a number of candidates of the Independent Labor Party. Big gains were

114

achieved in Toronto where the CCF and the Communist Party conducted a joint campaign. Two CCFers were elected to the school board while other labor candidates registered big increases in the pro-labor vote.[35]

Yet despite the demonstrated advantages of an electoral alliance between social-reformists and Communists during the municipal elections of late 1935 and early 1936, the CCF leadership headed by Woodsworth still refused to entertain the idea of a more formal electoral alliance between the two parties. In April 1936, the CCF leadership's anti-unity position received a boost at the Ontario CCF convention which voted to ban cooperation with the Communist Party.[36] Many of those who defied the ban were subsequently expelled.

Without doubt, these expulsions demonstrated that the CCF leadership had every intention of sabotaging unity around the burning issues of the day. At the same time, the successes scored by the Communist Party in achieving joint actions with the left and center elements of the CCF confirmed the validity of the party's tactical changes aimed at promoting unity in action with social-reformists. The Communist Party's 10th plenum noted that the divisive and disruptive policies of the right-wing CCF leadership were polarizing the CCF membership. In his report to the party plenum, Tim Buck declared that Communists could not remain disinterested observers of the deep crisis within the CCF.[37] At stake was whether or not the CCF would work for working class and people's unity.

Despite the measures taken by the CCF leadership, the left-wing elements remained undeterred. The provincial convention of the CCF in British Columbia adopted resolutions denouncing the red-baiting tactics of some CCF leaders and calling for the participation of all labor organizations, including the Communist Party, in a proposed unemployment conference. The Alberta and Saskatchewan CCF conventions passed resolutions calling for either the affiliation of the Communist Party to the CCF or at least united action between the two parties.[38]

During the CCF's third convention, Woodsworth vigorously opposed a Communist Party proposal before the delegates calling for the formation of a Farmer-Labor Party. The appeal was rejected by the convention which voted not to ally itself with any political group. This decision effectively closed the door to formal united action on immediate issues such as the defense of civil liberties, the defense of the unemployed, joint participation in labor demonstrations and peace activities.[39]

The Communist Party's 11th CC plenum in February 1937, paid considerable attention to the ebb and flow of relations with the CCF. Tim Buck reported that although the CCF leadership was resisting the formation of a united front, sentiment within the CCF favoring united action was growing stronger and stronger.

The Communist Party's main task was to put all its energies into developing a united front of the working class and a people's front of all progressive forces into a federated party of the working people. As far as the Communist Party was concerned, the CCF had the potential, because of its organizational structure, of drawing all the progressive forces into one uniform channel for effective action in a united mass movement. The strengthening of the left in the CCF would open up the possibility of transforming it into a genuine broadly-based party of the working class and its allies. Urging the CCF to allow all progressive forces to affiliate, Tim Buck attempted to allay the fears of the CCF leadership concerning the Communist Party's intentions by asserting that "we have at no time proposed that the CCF should liquidate its individual membership branches, or that other organizations should take possession of the CCF."[40]

However, the right wing of the CCF would not accept any form of the united front, be it the affiliation of the Communist Party to the CCF, or an alliance between the two parties, or the creation of a Farmer-Labor Party. When Premier Maurice Duplessis of Quebec and Premier Mitchell Hepburn of Ontario formed a reactionary anti-labor axis, a new situation was created. However, the CCF leadership still refused to work with Communists against the increasing attacks of the ultra-conservative provincial governments on trade union and democratic rights.

In the party's struggle to build the united front, a great deal of attention was given to the question of building the Communist Party as an independent, revolutionary party of the working class. Although the illegality imposed by Section 98 had made party work extremely difficult, it did not prevent or discourage workers from joining the party's ranks. The ninth plenum, which coincided with a very high level in the class strug-

gle in Canada and the defeat of the Bennett government as a direct result of that struggle, registered a membership of 9,000 as compared to over 3,000 in 1927 just before the beginning of the free speech fight.[41] Two years later, at the eighth convention in October 1937, the party could boast a membership of 15,000.

This large influx of new inexperienced members did cause some problems as it strained the party's resources to the utmost. The educational work and inner club life of the party began to suffer. The party did not have the funds or cadre necessary to immediately overcome these weaknesses.[42]

The growing popularity and influence of the Communist Party in the working class and democratic movements also found expression in the growth of the party's electoral support, particularly at the municipal level.[43] In 1934, M. Joe Forkin joined Jacob Penner as a Winnipeg alderman. W.C. Ross was elected in 1937 to the school board and was followed by Joe Zuken in 1941. Joe Zuken held the office for 20 years, until his election to city council. In the Manitoba provincial election of July 1936, James Litterick, who had succeeded the imprisoned Tom McEwen as head of the WUL, became the first Communist ever to be elected to a provincial legislature. W.A. Kardash, a veteran of the fight for Spanish democracy, replaced him in 1941.[44]

In Toronto, the Communist Party made its first breakthrough in 1936, with the election of Stewart Smith and John Weir as alderman and school

Left, *William A. Kardash, a member of the Manitoba Legislative Assembly from 1941 to 1958. Right, John Weir, prominent in the progressive Ukrainian-Canadian community, many times editor of party papers.*

trustee respectively. Salsberg narrowly missed election as alderman but succeeded in the following year. Tim Buck obtained 32,000 votes in his bid for a seat on the Board of Control. In other Ontario centers in 1936, Ewart Humphreys was elected deputy reeve in York Township; James Wilson in Scarborough, Ellis Blair and Percy Laurin in Cornwall were elected to their respective city councils; Reginald Morris and Olive J. Whyte were re-elected in Windsor.[45] In subsequent years, many of these and other Communists were elected and re-elected.

These successes were accompanied by a rapid growth in the circulation of the Communist press. In August 1934, *The Worker* began publishing twice weekly. On May 1, 1936, it changed its name to the *Daily Clarion,* publishing every day except Sunday. This was further indisputable proof that the Communist Party's roots were deepening in the Canadian working class.

As the Communist Party's influence grew, so did its ability to help build a people's front. By 1937, this fight for principled unity had gained some ground. In Alberta, a large measure of agreement was reached among the Communist Party, the CCF and the Social Credit movement (which at that time contained a strong populist element in its program), the labor unions and the United Farmers of Alberta.[46] At the local level, alliances on specific issues were successfully formed in many parts of the country.

A vital task was to unite youth in action against fascism, the threat of war and for youth rights. Working with other organizations, the Young Communist League played a key role in establishing the Canadian Youth Congress, made up of representatives from a wide variety of youth organizations. Never before had there been a youth movement with such widespread influence. For the first time, youth in English and French Canada were united under the banner of the Congress. In 1936, the Congress adopted the Declaration of Rights of Canadian Youth and a draft Canadian Youth Act;

the Congress movement moved into action in local areas throughout the country. The special problems of youth were brought to the attention of all Canada and of parliament. As a united front, the Youth Congress was also a major breakthrough in the crucial work to develop anti-fascist sentiment among youth.

Nowhere was the need for a united front against fascism and repression more necessary than in Quebec.

4. The Fight against Duplessis

The conditions of French Canadian workers were no better and usually worse than those of their English-speaking brothers and sisters. The Great Depression brought more than its share of misery and unemployment to French Canada. Efforts by the workers to improve conditions were usually met with repression. Nationalist, anti-communist demagogy was widely employed in order to dupe French Canadian workers into supporting reactionary policies and to prevent their being attracted to progressive policies. Working hand in hand with the reactionary bourgeois nationalists was the hierarchy of the Roman Catholic Church, which regularly used the pulpit as a forum for the propagation of anti-communist and nationalist views. The right-wing Union Nationale came to power under this cover of religion and nationalism.

In August 1936, Maurice Duplessis' Union Nationale swept into office on a wave of popular discontent with the Liberal government of Louis A. Taschereau. Like Bennett and the reactionary provincial governments of English-speaking Canada, Taschereau

had openly sided with the monopolies against the workers. His government, for example, had resorted to violence and arrests in order to crush the Noranda miners' strike in 1934. Twenty Finnish, Ukrainian and Yugoslavian workers were charged with "rioting," each receiving a two-year prison term plus a deportation order. Two other workers received lesser sentences for "unlawful assembly" and "sedition." Jeanne Corbin, the strike's WUL organizer, and another worker received three years and six months respectively for "seditious utterances." In an effort to divide the strikers, the sentences imposed on immigrant workers contrasted sharply with the treatment of Anglo-Saxon and French Canadian miners, who received only suspended sentences.[47]

The Communist Party was quite aware of the true nature of the Union Nationale even before it came to power. The party drew attention to the fact that the Union Nationale enjoyed the support of openly reactionary groups, including the Tories, the Corporation des Chambres Economiques, the Patriot Youth (Jeunesse Patriotes) whose leader was a known sympathizer of Mussolini, and the People's Social School. Paul Gouin, confidant of Duplessis, was known to have favorably mentioned Mussolini in the context of supporting "strong government." He declared himself in favor of a "social-Christian order" modelled on Austrian fascism. It was clear that the Union Nationale had fascist tendencies and therefore constituted a serious threat to the Quebec working class. To combat this danger, the Communist Party pro-

Secretary of the CLDL in Timmins in the early 1930s, Jeanne Corbin (1908-1944) was also a WUL organizer of bushworkers and miners in northeastern Ontario and the adjacent areas of Quebec. A leader of the miners' strike in Noranda, Quebec, she was sentenced to three years imprisonment. While in prison, she contracted tuberculosis and died at the young age of 36.

posed the establishment of a progressive coalition.[48]

In December 1935 or January 1936, the Communist Party helped to set up the Popular Front for the Immediate Needs of the Unemployed. Although the Popular Front at first lacked organizational strength, it was able to make significant steps toward organizing the struggles of French Canadian workers in unity with their fellow workers in English-speaking Canada. In the new organization's opinion, the main prerequisite for building its strength lay in the unionization of Quebec's workers.

ARCHIVES CPC/PAC/PA-125104

A few months before Duplessis' electoral victory, Lucien Dufour, the president of the Popular Front, was able to report that 56 organizations were actively involved in unemployed struggles throughout Quebec.[49]

Duplessis' accession to power encouraged Quebec fascist groups to step up their anti-communist and anti-Semitic activities. For example, *Le Patriote* referred to Jews as the "sons of Satan" and exhorted its readers to "never buy from the Jews" because "they are dangerous," "immoral and corruptors."[50] In October 1936, fascist thugs smashed the windows of Communist Party bookstores and carried out similar actions against the offices of *Clarté,* the party's French language newspaper. A few days later, a squad of 300 fascist students from the University of Montreal intimidated the mayor of the Montreal suburb of Westmount into

banning a meeting at which representatives of the Spanish Republic were scheduled to speak. Duplessis lauded these actions.[51]

The Quebec government then began to move against the Communist Party. In the spring of 1937, Duplessis proposed outlawing the party. A few days later, the Quebec Legislative Assembly passed an "act to protect Quebec against communist propaganda" which prohibited landlords from allowing their premises to be used by Communists. It was rushed through all three legislative readings and the committee-as-a-whole in only one afternoon. The law was made retroactive by 12 months. It explicitly stated that the onus of proof that premises had not been used for Communist meetings or the distribution of Communist literature lay with the owner. Duplessis, who was Attorney-General as well as Premier, had the power to padlock any premises. The bill, which soon became known as the Padlock Law, did not define "communism," and left its definition to Duplessis' discretion. It was a law designed for use against labor and other progressive organizations.[52] That was exactly what happened. Although the Communist Party was not banned as such, the fact that it was not allowed to disseminate its ideas in any form amounted to a *de facto* ban.

Duplessis and the reactionary circles he represented were motivated in their actions by fear of the increasing strength of the industrial union movement and the Communist Party which played a prominent role in its growth. The party's influence among French Canadian workers, especially the unemployed, was increasing rapidly. Between the 1934 convention and the eighth plenum a year later, the party's French Canadian membership registered considerable growth. The party in Quebec, particularly in Montreal, was transformed from a party in which the majority were English-speaking to one in which 60 per cent were French Canadians.[53]

Equally disquieting to the Duplessis regime was the high level of militancy of the workers' and unemployed movements. Progressives led the Montreal TLC. As if to confirm Duplessis' worst fears, 6,000 Montreal members of the International Ladies' Garment Workers, 5,000 of them French Canadians, went on strike in April 1937. Despite a back-to-work order and the arrest of the strike leaders, Duplessis was forced to concede defeat in early May. The adoption of a law doing away with the principle of collective bargaining and the formation of a special provincial police squad to "investigate" labor disputes later in the month, did not discourage the 7,000 members of the National Catholic Textile Federation from conducting a strike or from moving toward closer cooperation with the textile unions of the TLC.[54]

In November, Duplessis banned *Clarté* and initiated a wave of raids and padlockings directed against the Communist Party. The home of Jean Perron, editor of *Clarté*, was raided. Bookstores and printshops were padlocked. The Montreal bureau of the *Daily Clarion* was raided and all books and materials confiscated. All these actions were taken under Duplessis' direct orders. He also confidently announced that he would not recognize any CIO affiliates as *bona fide* unions.

Communists, trade unionists, members of the CCF and other progressive activists denounced the repression. Prominent unionists saw a direct link between the anti-communist padlockings and the government's intense anti-labor activities.[55] Despite wide-scale public criticism, Duplessis ordered more trials and padlockings. Toward the end of November, the homes of two leaders of the Montreal butchers' strike were raided. The Montreal TLC characterized this as an attempt to smash the strike. The *Daily Clarion's* Montreal offices were raided once again and all books, papers and legal documents were seized. In December, at least two shipments of the *Daily Clarion* were confiscated. Communists were forced to distribute their newspapers by clandestine means. From mid-November 1937 to mid-January 1938, more than 40 raids were carried out by the police on Quebec homes. Late in January, the first arrests under the Padlock Law were made as the Duplessis government stepped up its efforts to suppress the Communist Party and the labor movement.[56]

While trampling on the democratic rights of the Quebec working class movement, Duplessis gave tacit approval to and received support from Quebec fascist groups. In fact, fascists in Quebec had full freedom to distribute their Nazi-inspired, anti-Semitic, anti-communist hate literature. The largest of the fascist groups was the

National Social Christian Party led by Adrien Arcand. He was editor of *l'Illustration Nouvelle* and he and his party had known links with Nazi Germany. Another fascist party was the Autonomist Party whose leader, Paul Bouchard, was also editor of the newspaper, *La Nation*. His party had connections with fascist Italy. As in other countries, the fascist groups in Quebec and, for that matter, in the rest of Canada, were financed by big business interests. In Quebec, some cabinet ministers were members of the secret Knights of Jacques Cartier which centralized the work of the various fascist groups.[57]

As part of his attempt to move politics to the far right, Duplessis set up a reactionary alliance with Premier Hepburn of Ontario. The Communist Party's 11th plenum which met in June 1938, drew attention to the significance of this alliance for the most reactionary circles of big capital in Canada.

Thus the alliance between Hepburn and Duplessis represents the successful achievement of a national center, around which the reactionary forces can be mobilized and which, immediately (after) it was achieved, represented what might be called the dominant section of Canada's economic life. It is a new and dangerous factor.[58]

The aim of the alliance was to carry through the political program of the most reactionary forces of monopoly capital, the suppression of the working class movement. In Quebec, the Communist Party's main task in combating this policy was to fight energetically for trade union unity, not only between Communists and social-reformists and between the TLC and the CIO, but also between these unions and the Catholic syndicates. While participating in the wage struggles of the French Canadian working class, it was also necessary to rally democratic public opinion against the fascist-inspired repressive measures of the Duplessis government.

The specific conditions in Quebec demanded a struggle on two levels. One level was the struggle of the working class around wages and the need to defend the most fundamental rights of the workers against reactionary attacks. The second, parallel wtih this struggle, was the urgent need to mobilize democratic public opinion against fascism, from which Duplessis drew his inspiration. In this, the Communist Party drew heavily on the lessons of the seventh Comintern congress. Fascism was rearing its head both abroad and in Canada; the task facing Communists was to build unity in the working class and democratic movements to withstand and defeat the onslaught of fascism.

5. The Threat of a New World War and the Fight for Spanish Democracy

Throughout the 1930s, the Communist Party was the only political party in Canada to recognize that fascism and the danger of world war were very closely linked. In 1934, the seventh convention had tied the growth of fascism and the danger of war to the reactionary offensive in Canada itself. All three phenomena were manifestations of finance capital's desperation to preserve its class dictatorship.[59]

In this political context, the party decided to help found the Canadian

A group of delegates to the Youth Conference against War and Fascism which took place in Montreal in 1934, presenting a protest to the German Consul against Hitler's aggressive policies.

League against War and Fascism. Membership was open to all those who opposed fascism and war. A wide spectrum of beliefs was represented. Trade unionists, CCFers, Communists, representatives of many churches and synagogues and others, all participated in the new body's work. Its first congress was held on October 6-7, 1934, and was attended by 305 official delegates, representing 211 organizations with a total membership of 377,000, and 415 observers.[60] The congress declared that war and fascism marched hand in hand and threatened world peace. The aim of the new organization was to create the "broadest united front, irrespective of political, religious or national differences" in order "to stem the advance of this two-fold menace."[61]

International events moved quickly in 1936. Militarist Japan extended its conquest of China and threatened Mongolia and the USSR. Fascist Italy consolidated its subjugation of Ethiopia and expressed its contempt for world public opinion by withdrawing from the League of Nations.

While fascism made these advances, it also suffered setbacks. In Spain and France popular front governments of which Communists were a part, were

Canadian, U.S. and Cuban delegates attending the World Youth Congress in Geneva, 1936. William Kashtan and Roy Davis are the second and third from the left respectively.

elected. But Mussolini and Hitler were determined to undermine and destroy these victories of the democratic forces. While their ability to influence developments in France was limited, they paid special attention to reversing the progressive advance in Spain by giving General Franco's fascist armed forces extensive military and diplomatic support.

In July 1936, the fascists started an insurrection against the legally elected and constituted government of Spain. Great Britain and France reacted by imposing an arms embargo on Spain. The Soviet Union, Britain, France and other countries, including the fascist powers, joined in a pact which stipulated non-intervention in the Spanish conflict.

However, it soon became apparent that the fascist powers — Germany, Italy and Portugal — were deliberately ignoring the agreement and were pouring men and arms into Franco's rebel armed forces. Great Britain, France and their allies continued the arms embargo on Spain as if the non-intervention pact was still effectively functioning. The USSR, on the other hand, refused to be a party to a false neutrality and consequently abandoned the agreement in early October. The Soviet Union and the world communist movement realized that a fascist victory in Spain would bring the world to the brink of war.

To ascertain what Canadian anti-fascists could do for Spain's beleaguered democratic government, A.A.

MacLeod, chairman of the Canadian League against War and Fascism, travelled to Madrid in September 1936 to confer with the Spanish president, Manuel Azana. While there, he sent back to Canada, Azana's request for a hospital unit with portable operating equipment. A committee of prominent members of the Communist Party, the CCF and other groups was promptly set up to raise the necessary funds. Tim Buck, who was also in Spain at the time, requested the postponement of the party's scheduled convention until the following year because of the urgency of the situation in Spain and the need for Canadian Communists to devote their energy and resources to supporting the Spanish government.[62] Meanwhile, William Kashtan and Roy Davis, who had been attending the World Youth Congress in Geneva, spent 10 days in Spain to obtain first-hand information exposing fascist machinations in Spain and the failure of the non-intervention pact. While in Spain, William Kashtan was made an honorary member of the Young Guard of the Spanish people's militia, the first Canadian to be so honored.[63] On their return, they drew attention to the fact that British and French "neutrality" was working in favor of the fascist forces.[64]

On the return of A.A. MacLeod, William Kashtan and Roy Davis to Canada in October (Tim Buck stayed in Spain until November), arrangements were made for representatives of the Spanish Popular Front government to tour a number of Canadian cities including Hamilton, Ottawa and Winnipeg. Thousands packed the meetings and listened intently to the Spanish representatives speak on the situation in Spain and the need for solidarity with their struggle against fascism and to save democracy. In Toronto, for example, 11,000 attended; at this meeting it was reported that sufficient funds had been raised to send a medical unit headed by Doctor Norman Bethune to Spain.

The Communist Party and the Canadian Committee to Aid Spanish Democracy (CCASD), which the party helped to create, stepped up their activities in the months following the tour of the Popular Front representatives. In December, A.E. Smith went on a lengthy tour of western Canada during which he addressed 33 meetings attended by a total of 13,000 people. In these meetings, hatred for fascism and enthusiasm for the just cause of Spanish democracy was running so high that many asked how they could volunteer to fight in Spain. Clearly, progressive sentiment strongly favored a Canadian military contribution on the side of the Popular Front government. Shortly after A.E. Smith's tour, the Communist Party of Canada decided to actively recruit volunteers for Spain. In January 1937, the first organized group of five Canadians left for Spain to fight fascism.[65]

The Canadian government's official position on the Spanish civil war was to tail British foreign policy. In order to maintain Canada's "neutrality," the King Liberal government introduced legislation to amend the Foreign Enlistment Act. The amendments prohibited Canadians from fighting not only against, but also for a friendly government.[66] They were specifically designed to prevent the recruitment of Canadian volunteers to fight on the side of Spanish democracy — this despite the

Top left, Norman Bethune (1890-1939), Bachelor of Medicine, University of Toronto. Top right, Dr. Bethune with a Chinese soldier in the Chinese interior, where he had gone to assist the people of China against the Japanese invaders — and, where he died in November 1939. Bottom, Dr. Bethune helping refugees into a truck near El Rabita, Spain, on the seventh day of the retreat from Malaga, 1937.

Left, soldiers in the Mackenzie-Papineau Battalion. Right, Adrian van der Brugge (1904-1937).

fact that Nazi Germany and fascist Italy were openly aiding the Spanish fascists in flagrant violation of the non-intervention pact. In defiance of the government, Canadians volunteered for Spain in increasing numbers.

At first, Canadian volunteers fought mainly in the ranks of the Lincoln and Washington battalions of the XVth International Brigade; in the first few months of Canadian participation in the civil war, their number did not justify the creation of a separate battalion. It was at this time that the first battles in which the Canadians participated were fought at Jarama, claiming the life of St. Catharines party secretary Adrian van der Brugge.[67]

By May, 500 Canadians were fighting in Spain and their request for a separate Canadian company was granted.[68] The Canadian battalion was named after two famous Canadian radical democrats, William Lyon Mackenzie and Louis-Joseph Papineau.[69] On July 1, 1937, on Canada's 70th anniversary of Confederation and 100 years after the Rebellion of 1837, the Mackenzie-Papineau Battalion

was officially founded.[70] The party sent William Kashtan to Spain to organize the battalion, as well as to bring Norman Bethune back to Canada and gather materials for a Canadian lecture series.

Also in 1937, a support organization for the Mac-Paps was created in Canada, the Friends of the Mackenzie-Papineau Battalion, whose work complemented the activities of the CCASD.

We have realized, too, that news of casualties in the battalion should be received by some responsible body and appropriately published and commemorated. Arrangements will be made at once to have the undersigned committee act as a center for information about the Canadian battalion.[71]

Supporting the Mac-Paps and sustaining the solidarity movement in Canada required extensive fundraising. In the 13 months ending on June 30, 1938, goods valued at more than 50,000 dollars had been sent to Spain. In addition, the Friends of the Mac-Paps collected over 23,500 dollars in donations, of which 11,560 dollars was sent to Spain. When one considers the fact that the dollar was worth several times more then, it was an impressive amount of money. The remaining donations were spent on tours, publicity and meetings, administrative costs and the rehabilitation of returned veterans.[72] While not as spectacular as the exploits of the Mac-Paps in Spain, the work of the solidarity movement in Canada was vital to their fight against fascism.

Non-communist progressives, especially in the TLC and the CCF, played a very important role in the various bodies working in support of democratic Spain. CCF members of Parliament such as T.C. Douglas, contributed invaluable assistance to the cause by exposing Canada's fake neutrality and opposing the amendments to the Foreign Enlistment Act.[73] Nevertheless, Communists played the leading role in the solidarity movement and made up the active core of the membership. The CCASD, the Canadian Medical Mission to Aid Spanish Democracy, the Friends of the Mac-Paps and the Mac-Pap Battalion itself had prominent Communists in their leadership. David Goldstick, for example, was treasurer of both the CCASD and the Canadian League against War and Fascism. Fred Collins, Harvey Murphy (a prominent union organizer in both the WUL and the CIO and a leader of the struggles of the unemployed in Ontario in the last half of the thirties), Richard Steele, Paul Phillips and others, were all members of the Friends of the Mac-Paps. When Bob Thompson, the U.S. commander of the Mac-Paps fell ill in the summer of 1937, a former reporter of *The Worker*, Edward Cecil-Smith, became the battalion's new commander, a post he held until demobilization.[74] Communists constituted the main core of the recruits who fought

— and died — in Spain. In fact, the party lost a large section of its cadre in Spain.

The Mac-Paps were motivated by the highest political ideals. They were men who understood that fascism's victory in Spain would almost certainly lead to a world war. William Kardash, for example, wrote that the fight for democratic Spain "was of great concern to the people of my country, and that the greatest service I could render it, was to go to Spain and defeat fascism."[75] It testified to the depth of the democratic and political convictions of Canadian Communists and progressives that "excepting France, no other country provided so great a number of volunteer soldiers in proportion to its population as did Canada: 1,200 out of 12,000,000"[76] The Mac-Paps fought heroically in battles at Jarama, Brunete, Quinto, Belchite, Fuentes de Ebro, Teruel, the Retreats and the Ebro. They earned the nickname "The Fighting Canucks" and won recognition in the XVth Brigade as "The Model Battalion."[77]

But the efforts of the Spanish people and the International Brigades met growing difficulties. Nazi Germany and fascist Italy were sending men and arms into the war against the Spanish government on a massive scale. The imperialist states persisted in their policy of "neutrality" and appeasement of the fascist powers. These policies enabled the fascists to effectively blockade Spain and prevent much needed medical and military supplies from reaching the loyalist forces. By the end of 1938, the military situation in Spain had deteriorated badly for the democratic forces. The Spanish government, recognizing that defeat was

Top, a meeting in Vernon, British Columbia, in solidarity with democratic Spain, July 1937. Bottom, ambulance contributed by the Communist Party in solidarity with Spain.

GLENBOW ARCHIVES, CALGARY, ALBERTA 3634-17

inevitable, ordered the demobilization of the International Brigades and their return home.

In early 1939, the Mac-Paps came back to Canada. Of the 1,239 Canadian volunteers who went to Spain, over a third never saw their country again.[78] They died for democracy.

The importance of the Canadian rehabilitation fund grew rapidly as the Spanish civil war drew to a close. Sick and wounded veterans had to be cared for. Veterans needed support while they looked for jobs and readjusted to life in Canada. Consequently, the Friends of the Mac-Paps had to intensify its fund-raising efforts. Beckie Buhay and William Kardash, for example, went on a tour of 27 cities and towns and spoke to 40 meetings during which they raised 4,500 dollars. Indeed, in the first three months of 1939, the Friends of the Mac-Paps succeeded in raising the remarkable sum of almost 22,000 dollars, or almost as much as in its first 13 months of existence.[79]

During the entire course of the war, the Canadian government and the mass media downplayed or ignored the efforts of progressive Canadians to aid Spanish democracy. From the standpoint of bourgeois history, the Mac-Paps and their supporters sank into oblivion. For the working class, it was one of the most unforgettable and glorious chapters in its rich history of international solidarity in struggle against exploitation and oppression. The Communist Party of Canada was the motive force in making that history.

Emboldened by their success in Spain and the refusal of the imperialist powers to guarantee genuine neutrality in the Spanish civil war, the fascist powers not only tipped the balance of forces in Spain in their favor, but were convinced that Britain and France would not stand in the way of further fascist military adventures. The Soviet Union was the only country to consistently oppose the aggressive actions and expansionist ambitions of the fascists.

While pursuing its expansionist ambitions in the capitalist world, fascism — and no less the other imperialist powers — also sought to subvert socialism in the USSR. For this purpose it utilized Trotskyists and right-opportunists. In 1936, 16 followers of Trotsky and Zinoviev were placed on trial in the Soviet Union for treason, terrorism and other equally serious charges. During the course of the trial, the defendants admitted their links with both the German Gestapo, and Trotsky who, they said, gave them a directive to organize a campaign of terror against the leaders of the CPSU.[80] Two years later, 21 other members of the anti-Soviet "Bloc of Rights and Trotskyites" were charged with similar crimes. Tim Buck and R. Page Arnot, a member of the Communist Party of Great Britain, witnessed the proceedings. They reported that the defendants confessed to ties with Trotsky and the Nazi German government.[81] Some of them were also connected to the secret services of the Japanese, British and Polish governments.[82]

Fascism was becoming more aggressive and more flagrant in its preparations for world conquest. In late 1936, Japan entered into an alliance with Nazi Germany. In the summer of 1937, Japanese militarism extended its conquest of China. In September 1938,

Top, at the 1938 May Day parade in Vancouver, YCL members selling the YCL newspaper, The New Advance. From left to right: unidentified, unidentified, Sadie Bisgold (kneeling), "Slats" McLaren, Surah Roseman, unidentified, Bill Turner. Bottom, part of the vast crowd which greeted returning veterans of the Mackenzie-Papineau Battalion on their arrival at Windsor Station in Montreal, 1939.

Neville Chamberlain of Great Britain and Edouard Daladier of France signed the Munich agreement with Hitler, which handed the Sudetenland over to the Nazis against the will of the people and government of Czechoslovakia. From the standpoint of the imperialist countries, this agreement had the objective of appeasing Hitler and directing his aggressive ambitions toward the USSR. It made world war virtually inevitable. In March 1939, Nazi Germany absorbed the Czech section of the country and turned Slovakia into a puppet state. Immediately afterward, Hitler made territorial claims on Lithuania and Poland, while Mussolini occupied Albania.

With the USSR isolated by the hostility of both the fascist and the other imperialist powers; with Great Britain, France and their allies prepared to appease and support Germany in the mistaken belief that fascism could be turned against the Soviet Union alone, the stage was set for the bloodiest war in human history, a war which was to exact a toll of tens of millions of lives.

---

1. *Final Statement of the WUL Executive Board to Those Trade Unionists Who Constituted Its Membership, and Who Have Now Merged within the Unions of the AFL,* June 18, 1936, Archives CPC, p. 9.
2. CIO, *Industrial Unionism* (Washington, 1935), pp. 7-8.
3. Department of Labour, *Labour Organization in Canada (For the Calendar Year 1936)* (Ottawa, 1937), p. 162.
4. Ibid., pp. 162-165.
5. Ibid., p. 175.
6. Department of Labour, *Labour Organization in Canada (For the Calendar Year 1938)* (Ottawa, 1939), pp. 30-31.
7. *Daily Clarion,* June 26 and 30, 1936.
8. Interview with Peter Boychuck Sr., October 31, 1977.
9. *Daily Clarion,* January 7, 1936.
10. *The Worker,* January 23, 1936.
11. *Labour Organization in Canada 1936,* p. 161.
12. *Daily Clarion,* September 18, 1937.
13. Department of Labour, *Labour Organization in Canada (For the Calendar Year 1937)* (Ottawa, 1938), pp. 178-179.
14. *Daily Clarion,* June 29, 1937; and February 5, 1938.
15. *Labour Organization in Canada 1937,* p. 181.
16. *We Propose . . .,* resolutions of the eighth convention of the CPC, October 8-12, 1937, p. 12.
17. *Daily Clarion,* July 6, 1936.
18. *Labour Organization in Canada 1938,* p. 24; and also *Daily Clarion,* September 16, 1938.
19. *Daily Clarion,* October 7, 1938.
20. Department of Labour, *Labour Organization in Canada (For the Calendar Year 1941)* (Ottawa, 1943), p. 13.
21. Institute of Marxism-Leninism, Central Committee of the CPSU, *Outline History of the Communist International* (Moscow, 1971), pp. 273-274.
22. *Outline History of the Communist International,* p. 274; and *International Press Correspondence,* Vol. 11, No. 22, April 27, 1931, p. 414.
23. *Outline History of the Communist International,* p. 312.
24. Ibid., p. 355.
25. G. Dimitrov, *The United Front against War and Fascism* (New York, 1936), p. 8.
26. Ibid., p. 29.
27. Ibid., p. 71.
28. Letter of the Provisional Executive of the WUL to the convention of the MWUC, April 14, 1930. Archives CPC, p. 5.
29. S. Smith (using alias G. Pierce), *Socialism and the CCF* (Montreal, 1934), pp. 142-143 and 162.

30. *The Way to Socialism* (Montreal, 1934), seventh convention of the CPC, July 23-28, 1934, p. 31.
31. Ibid., pp. 45-46.
32. *Toward a Canadian People's Front*, ninth CC plenum of the CPC, November 1935, pp. 21-23.
33. *The Worker*, April 30 and June 18, 1935.
34. Ibid., August 6 and 24, 1935.
35. Ibid., November 23 and 26, 1935; and January 4, 1936.
36. Ibid., March 28 and April 14, 1936.
37. T. Buck, *What We Propose* (Toronto, 1936), pp. 45-46.
38. *Daily Clarion*, July 15 and 17, 1936.
39. Ibid., August 4 and 6, 1936.
40. T. Buck, *The Road Ahead* (Toronto, 1937), pp. 27-28.
41. *Toward a Canadian People's Front*, p. 104.
42. *A Democratic Front for Canada*, 13th session of the Dominion Executive of the CPC, June 3-6, 1938, p. 47.
43. *The Worker*, December 22, 1934.
44. M. Kardash, *50 Years of the Communist Party in Manitoba* (Winnipeg, 1971), p. 12.
45. *Daily Clarion*, December 8, 1937.
46. T. Buck, *The People vs. Monopoly* (Toronto, 1937), p. 35.
47. *The Worker*, December 1, 5 and 8, 1934.
48. Ibid., January 14, 1936.
49. *Daily Clarion*, May 16 and July 15, 1936.
50. *The Worker*, October 12, 1935.
51. *Daily Clarion*, October 14 and 24, 1936.
52. Ibid., March 16 and 20, 1937.
53. "Lessons and Experiences of French Work" in *Review*, Vol. 3, No. 7, August, 1935, p. 19.
54. *Daily Clarion*, April 16, May 7 and 12, and August 10, 1937.
55. Ibid., November 10, 11, 12 and 17, 1937.
56. Ibid., November 23, 25 and 26, December 1 and 2, 1937; January 22 and 24, 1938.
57. F. Rose, *Fascism over Canada* (Toronto, 1938), pp. 7-11, 14-19 and 40; *Daily Clarion*, November 17, 1937.
58. *A Democratic Front for Canada*, p. 15.
59. *The Way to Socialism*, p. 16.
60. *Report: first Canadian congress against war and fascism* (Toronto, 1934), p. 22.
61. Ibid., p. 21.
62. *Daily Clarion*, September 22 and October 5, 1936.
63. Ibid., October 3, 1936.
64. R. Davis and W. Kashtan, *War in Spain* (Toronto, 1936), p. 14.
65. *Daily Clarion*, November 25 and December 30, 1936; and January 28, 1937.
66. Ibid., January 9 and March 23, 1937.
67. Ibid., May 13, 1937.
68. Ibid., May 21, 1937.
69. W. Kashtan, letter to the Canadian Broadcasting Corporation, September 19, 1977, reprinted in *Canadian Tribune*, September 26, 1977.
70. *Daily Clarion*, July 19, 1938.
71. Ibid., May 22, 1937.
72. Ibid., July 19, 1938.
73. Ibid., January 18, 1937.
74. Ibid., July 19, 1938.
75. W. Kardash, *I Fought for Canada in Spain* (Toronto, 1938), p. 5.
76. V. Hoar, *The Mackenzie-Papineau Battalion* (1969), p. 1.
77. T. Buck, "Soldiers of Democracy" in *The Marxist Quarterly*, No. 18, summer 1966, p. 26.
78. Friends of the Mackenzie-Papineau Battalion, *National Committee Report on Activities from Jan. 1 to March 31, 1939*, Archives CPC, p. 3.
79. Ibid., pp. 5-6 and 9.
80. *Daily Clarion*, August 20, 1936.
81. R.P. Arnot and T. Buck, *Fascist Agents Exposed* (London, 1938), pp. 16-17.
82. *Report of the Proceedings in the Case of the Anti-Soviet 'Bloc of Rights and Trotskyites'* (Moscow, 1938), p. 796.

7. The War Years

1. From Imperialist War, to Anti-Fascist War

From the time Hitler came to power, the Soviet Union sought to establish an effective system of collective security with the object of preserving peace and warding off aggression. This policy included attempts to form mutual assistance pacts with countries threatened by aggression. As late as July and August 1939, negotiations continued between the USSR, Britain and France, but they remained deadlocked because the ruling élites of Britain and France were constantly sabotaging the conclusion of a multilateral mutual assistance pact.[1] Britain in particular entertained hopes of pitting Nazi Germany against the socialist USSR or of creating an imperialist anti-Soviet front.

However, serious inter-imperialist differences existed between Britain and Nazi Germany, differences which facilitated the efforts of the USSR to impede the formation of an anti-Soviet front. When offered a non-aggression pact by Hitler, the Soviet government seized the opportunity to buy time. It wanted to avoid a war on two fronts with Nazi Germany and fascist Japan and needed time to prepare its defenses for a war it knew would come. Despite signing the non-aggression pact with Hitler, the Soviet government had no illusions that, in the final analysis, Germany would not hold back from a war against the Soviet Union.

Bourgeois governments and mass media hypocritically greeted the announcement of the Soviet-German agreement as a betrayal — a slander bourgeois historians have maintained ever since.[2] I. Avakumovic, for example, asserts that the USSR and Nazi Germany signed a treaty of non-aggression and friendship.[3] In fact, the two countries agreed only to refrain from attacking each other or from participating in a conflict between one of them and a third country. This was a far cry from a "friendship" treaty, an alliance or a mutual assistance pact such as the USSR sought to conclude with Britain and France. The Soviet-German non-aggression pact was signed precisely because Britain and France had effectively scuttled their talks with the Soviet government in line with their policy of bringing about a Soviet-German war. The non-aggression pact was a defensive measure aimed at preventing the isolation of the Soviet Union and making it the target of an imperialist war. When war broke out between the fascist powers and the bourgeois democracies, the Soviet Union maintained a position of neutrality since both imperialist war blocs were intent on destroying the Soviet Union.

Three days after the announcement of the Soviet-German pact, the Dominion (Central) Committee of the Communist Party of Canada issued a statement placing the blame for this turn of events on Britain. Still pursuing its unprincipled policy of appeasing Hitler, Britain allowed the free city of Danzig (now Gdansk, Poland) to be taken over by Nazi Germany. The aim was to gain access to the USSR's western borders as part of Hitler's plan to attack the USSR.

That is why the British Tories, for all their loud talk, are refusing to sign a water-proof pact with

Florence Theodore (1889-1977), party leader in Saskatchewan from 1942 to 1945, was the first woman to be elected a provincial leader of the Communist Party.

the USSR. That is why they have sacrificed seven peaceful and friendly countries.[4]

The strategy of the imperialist bourgeoisie of Great Britain, France, Canada and other capitalist countries backfired. They had hoped to achieve some sort of anti-Soviet understanding with Hitler, but Nazi Germany invaded their ally, Poland. Britain and France had no choice but to declare war against Nazi Germany the day after the invasion of Poland began. Canada declared war on Nazi Germany a week later. Britain and France avoided open military conflict in the hope of persuading Hitler to direct his attention to the Soviet Union. It was in fact a "phoney war," an armed standoff during which a great deal of anti-Soviet manoeuvring was taking place.

The outbreak of war between the fascist powers and the bourgeois democracies (with the early exception of the United States) led to some confusion in the communist movement in Canada. Initially the Communist Party did not know what to make of Britain's declaration of war because, for years, British foreign policy had been based on the appeasement of Hitler and on making an anti-Soviet, anti-socialist alliance with Nazi Germany. Now the party was faced with a situation in which Britain declared war on Hitler shortly after it had refused to make an anti-Nazi alliance with the Soviet Union, thus depriving itself of a

ARCHIVES CP/C/PAC

potentially powerful ally. The situation was further complicated by the "phoney war" and the fact that Britain still supported the fascist Mannerheim government in Finland, a Nazi German ally, in its war against the Soviet Union.[5]

Throughout the 1930s, the world communist movement had worked to build a strong anti-fascist alliance as had the Communist Party of Canada. Fascism was the main threat to peace, democracy and socialism, a fact which did not change with the outbreak of the war. From this standpoint, many party members initially considered the declaration of war against Hitler as laudable. As the party still regarded the fight against fascism as its central task but was at the same time wary of Britain's motives in declaring war on Hitler, it was understandable that its first position was to call for a fight on two fronts as explained by Tim Buck in the *Clarion*.

Our immediate tasks are clear. In collaboration with anti-fascist forces everywhere and in the interests of the international working class, we will strive to combine with the military defeat of Hitler in the field of battle, the political defeat of his reactionary friends at home, the turning of this war into a just anti-fascist war and the conclusion of an early democratic peace.[6]

Nevertheless, the Communist Party of Canada had a great deal of difficulty in reconciling the anti-Hitler and the anti-Soviet aspects of the foreign policies of Britain and France. Considerable debate

Left, R. George MacEachern and right, Beckie Buhay.

therefore took place in the party on how to explain this apparent contradiction. Arguments were advanced that inter-imperialist rivalries had come to the fore and had resulted in the war. This theory at least seemed to explain why there were two warring blocs of imperialist powers, the bourgeois democracies and the fascist states.

When military hostilities finally broke out, bringing the period of the "phoney war" to an end, the party came to the conclusion that what was taking place was an inter-imperialist war.

The party's characterization of the initial stage of World War II paralleled Lenin's characterization of World War I. In many ways, such a characterization seemed to be justified because the two blocs of imperialist countries were at war in the apparent hope of gaining plunder and territories at each other's expense. The experience of World War I had demonstrated that in a war between imperialist countries, the monopoly capitalist bourgeoisie made scandalous profits while the burden of the war in terms of lives and livelihood was borne by the workers and farmers.[7]

The Communist Party of Canada's policy of the fight on two fronts was discarded with the beginning of the hot war, in favor of neutrality between the two belligerent blocs. Initially, this was a correct position given the fact that both imperialist military blocs were equally hostile to peace, socialism and the Soviet Union. However, as the hot war progressed, its character began to change from an inter-imperialist conflict into an anti-fascist national liberation war, particularly in the countries occupied by Hitler fascism. This transformation of the war's character came about as the Communist Parties of Europe and other patriotic forces took the lead in organizing partisan resistance movements. Canadian Communists were slow in taking note of the changes in the war's development.

While debates were taking place in the party on the characterization of the war, the Canadian government initiated anti-communist measures and launched an intensive anti-Soviet propaganda campaign which claimed that the USSR had "betrayed" Britain and France by signing a non-aggression pact with Hitler. The government sought to convince Canadians that the Communist Party's policy of neutrality amounted to treason. Accordingly, this propaganda claimed that it was necessary to suppress the party as a danger to Canada's national security.

2. Illegality and Internment

The declaration of war against Nazi Germany served as a pretext for the enactment of the War Measures Act by Parliament in September 1939. Among its provisions, the Act abolished the right of release and permitted the indiscriminate search of homes, premises and persons. It gave the Secretary of State full control over the press, freedom of speech, and so on. The Minister of Justice could order the detention without trial for five years of any person on mere suspicion of "acting in a manner prejudicial to the public safety." The Cabinet was empowered to substitute law by Parliament, with Orders-in-Council, which under the terms of the War Measures Act were known as Defence of Canada Regulations. Within the space of four months, 64 such ministerial fiats were adopted by the Cabinet.[8] Each Defence of Canada Regulation had the force of law immediately on its enactment. The constitutional and democratic rights of the Canadian people were suspended. They were replaced by a virtual Cabinet dictatorship.

The War Measures Act was supposed to aid Canada's war effort against Nazi Germany. In practice, the War Measures Act was used as an instrument to suppress the Communist, progressive and labor movements — the King government's aim for several years. The Regulations had been in preparation from as early as March 1938, a time when archreactionaries like Hepburn and Duplessis were pressuring Ottawa to ban both the Communist Party and the CIO, a time when the Canadian government was following Britain's lead, appeasing the fascist powers and encouraging Hitler to direct his military ambitions toward the Soviet Union.[9] Thus, from the start, the Defence of Canada Regulations were consciously intended to be anticommunist and anti-labor; they were not originally intended to be anti-fascist or to defend Canada from outside threats.

The first set of Defence of Canada Regulations was published in September 1939. In November, the *Clarion* (which had been transformed into a series of regional weeklies a few months earlier because it was financially impossible for the party to maintain a daily newspaper) and *Clarté* were banned.

In order to disseminate its ideas, the Communist Party produced illegal mimeographed editions of the *Clarion* and a magazine called *Monthly Review*. At the same time, the party established a legal newspaper with no formal connection to the party and whose immediate purpose was to fight for democratic rights. The *Canadian Tribune*, whose editorial board also included noncommunist progressives, began publication on January 20, 1940, as "a journal of democratic opinion," a function that became even more important after the

Tim Buck and J.L. Cohen (1898-1950), prominent lawyer in defense of democratic rights, discussing plans for the campaign against internment.

formal proscription of the party a few months later.

The infamous War Measures Act was used against Communists and non-communists alike. According to the Canadian Civil Liberties Union, 64 persons had been arrested by the end of February 1940. Nineteen of them received prison terms ranging from one month to two years while the rest were fined from one to 500 dollars.[10] The social-reformist C. H. Millard, a CIO organizer and a leader of the UAW, was charged with uttering words which allegedly contravened the Regulations.[11] The charge against Millard was a clear indication that the government intended to suppress any expression of opinion emanating from the working, class.

On June 6, 1940, a wave of repression against the left began. The Communist Party and 15 other progressive organizations including the YCL, the CLDL, the Finnish Organization of Canada and the Ukrainian Labor-Farmer Temple Association, were proscribed and all their properties confiscated. In the case of the Ukrainian organization, some of its halls were sold to ultra-rightist Ukrainians. The government conveniently ignored the fact that Britain, Hitler's main target until the Nazi invasion of the USSR, had seen no cause to ban the Communist Party of Great Britain. The fact was, Canada had the dubious distinction of being the only bourgeois democracy in the anti-fascist grand alliance to ban its Communist Party at any point in the war.[12] In all, 250 Communists were interned from 1940 to 1942.

The federal government's treatment of

its political prisoners was far from humane. Soon after the June 1940 raids on the homes of party members, the wives of a number of the arrested men complained that the police descended on their victims as though they were notorious criminals. All the property of the arrested was confiscated and made inaccessible to their families. While their wives and families faced destitution, Canada's political prisoners were placed in concentration camps. They were given no trials nor were any charges laid. While interned, the political prisoners' mail was heavily censored. They were not permitted to receive visitors or news of the outside world.[13] Only the government's racist treatment of Canadians of Japanese descent was worse. They were deported to the interior of British Columbia. Their property was seized and has never been returned.

With the Communist Party driven underground, many of its leaders and cadre were either interned or forced into hiding or exile. It was a situation which gave Stewart Smith (a member of the CEC hiding in Montreal who had differences with the party going back to the 1920s), the opportunity to take over the leadership and impose his own particular ideas as party policy.

Smith was one of those who mechanically drew a direct parallel between World War I and World War II. As far as he was concerned, there was no qualitative difference between the two wars. He saw the second war as a straightforward inter-imperialist conflict of the same character as the war of 1914-18. As the working class therefore had absolutely no stake in supporting either bloc of bel-

ligerents, it followed that the working class was confronted *by exactly the same tasks* as 25 years earlier.

The Canadian working class and our party face the task of transforming the war into civil war against the bourgeoisie, into a victorious Socialist revolution to build a peaceful, happy and Socialist Canada.[14]

No conditions existed to justify this erroneous approach; further, the character of the war was becoming more obviously anti-fascist. Such a slogan was therefore dangerously adventuristic. In fact, it played into the hands of reactionaries who wanted to use extreme methods to suppress the Communist Party. For example, A. G. Slaght, Conservative Member of Parliament for Parry Sound, Ontario, demanded no-

THEY FOUGHT FOR LABOR ————

NOW INTERNED!

Price 5c

Foreword by Mrs. Dorise W. Nielsen, M.P.

thing less than the death penalty for Communists.

Sabotage, espionage and fifth column activities reek with treachery...Let the parliament of Canada issue solemn warning by creating this death penalty against any of those hidden subversive elements that are within our bosom today...In other words, let us get tough, and let us make it known to criminally-minded people in Canada that they can expect no mercy.[15]

In defiance of such demands and despite the imposition of the War Measures Act, there developed in Canada a movement to have the internees released and the ban on the Communist Party lifted. At first, this democratic protest movement against the first wave of arrests was led by the CLDL headed by A.E. Smith. However, the government, anticipating that the CLDL might succeed in organizing a campaign on the scale of that which helped bring down the Bennett government in 1935, moved to forestall this possibility by having the CLDL banned at the same time as the Communist Party. But the government's attempt to stifle democratic opposition failed. The banned CLDL was quickly replaced by a new organization, the National Council of Democratic Rights, headed by A.E. Smith as General Secretary and Beckie Buhay as Executive Secretary.

The bourgeois press attempted to justify the anti-communist repression by claiming that changes in the Communist Party's policies came about solely as a consequence of its "loyalty to Moscow." In a pamphlet directed toward refuting these charges, A. E. Smith pointed out that the bourgeois press was in effect falsifying history out of class hatred for socialism and the Communist Party. Communists had for years advocated the formation of an anti-fascist military alliance as the best means of curbing Hitler's drive for world domination. Instead, the imperialist countries, Canada included, had encouraged Hitler to turn on the Soviet Union and had pursued a policy of appeasement to achieve this aim. True loyalty could only be demonstrated by *consistent* opposition to fascist aggression. The Communist Party was the only party in Canada that was so distinguished.[16]

The implementation of the War Measures Act had temporarily put an end to most of the party's electoral activities. Those Communists who had been elected to public office had been interned or forced to go into hiding. By making the Communist Party illegal, the Canadian government effectively deprived thousands of Canadian voters the right to be represented by the people they had freely and democratically elected. Despite severe government repression, communist electoral activities quickly resumed. The Communist Party achieved major successes.

In the March 1940 federal election, Dorise W. Nielsen, a candidate in the Saskatchewan riding of North Battleford, acquired the distinction of being the first member of the Communist Party of Canada to be elected to the House of Commons. She was elected as the representative of the "Unity platform" which consisted of Communists and disaffected members of other parties, including the CCF, whose aim was to defeat the unpopular Liberal incumbent. She was their popular choice. She also achieved the notable distinction of

Left to right: Tim Buck, John Weir, Annie Buller, Dorise Nielsen.

Left to right: Tim Buck, John Weir, Annie Buller, Dorise Nielsen.

being the only woman to win a seat in those elections.

Dorise Nielsen made a substantial contribution in Parliament to the struggle for women's rights. In her first speech to the House of Commons, she observed that it was a sad reflection on the condition and equality of women in Canada that "while over fifty per cent of the voters are women, we can have only one representative of our sex in the House."[17] During her term of office, she became an effective voice in the fight for the interests of the working people. She gave very strong support to the introduction of unemployment insurance and, during the early phase of the world war, opposed conscription. She frequently lambasted the government for its anti-democratic practices, especially the banning of progressive organizations and the internment of anti-fascists.

Dorise Nielsen's election to the House of Commons was followed by the election of W. A. Kardash to the Manitoba Legislative Assembly in 1941.

The Nazi invasion of the Soviet Union on June 22, 1941, once again demanded a re-evaluation of the Communist Party's attitude toward the war. The character of the war was now clear; it was a just anti-fascist war. In July, the party's leadership issued a statement which called on the labor movement and all progressive forces in Canada to unite their efforts in support of every measure of the King government to step up the war against fascism and render effective aid

140

The 1942 leadership of the Communist Party. Front row, left to right: Henri Gagnon, Fred Rose, Tim Buck, Emery Samuel, Sam Lipschitz. Back row, left to right, Gus Sundqvist, William Kashtan, Evariste Dubé, Jim Litterick, Sam Carr, Willie Fortin, Stewart Smith and Stanley Ryerson.

to the Soviet Union. It called for the formation of a National Front which would cut across class and party lines in the common struggle against fascism. Such unity, the statement urged, could be enhanced by the restoration of democratic rights. It called on the federal government to grant full rights to the trade union movement on the principle of collective bargaining and ensure the equal participation of the workers in the organization of Canada's war effort.[18]

Given the need for all-out unity on the home front, the Communist Party conference of February 1942 backed the King government in its contribution to the war.

The Communist Party supports this war effort, and exerts every effort to strengthen and acceler-

ate it, and to contribute towards the development of firmer and wider national unity for total war effort.[19]

But at the same time, the party conference castigated the government for being too slow and hesitant in increasing Canada's contribution to the war by introducing conscription for military service overseas. King was reluctant to take this action for fear of alienating the Liberal Party's strong base of support in French Canada, which had a long tradition of preparedness to fight for its own soil but not for what it perceived to be Britain's wars.[20]

The Communist Party was quite aware of this anti-imperialist aspect of French Canada's anti-war sentiment. However, the party was compelled to

decide that under the circumstances the war against fascism was primary. The February 1942 party conference concluded that what was needed was a political offensive in Quebec which would isolate the pro-Axis elements and win over the French Canadian masses to the necessity of defeating Hitler. To achieve this, the government would have to take unequivocal measures to solve the long-standing grievances of the French Canadian people.[21]

Those Communists who were not interned or forced underground had to find a public form through which they could combine the fight for all-out unity on the home-front war effort with the continuing struggle for the restoration of democratic rights — the two main tasks of the party at that time.

In late 1941 or early 1942, the Tim Buck Plebiscite Committee was set up with this general aim in view, and with the immediate objective of supporting a "yes" vote in the 1942 government referendum on conscription. However, further growth required a change in name and organizational form to accurately reflect the party's tasks. In the summer of 1942, the Dominion Communist-Labor Total War Committee was established to carry on the party's activities.

The Total War Committee called on

ARCHIVES CPC/PAC/PA-124392

the labor and progressive movements to pressure the King government to introduce conscription and step up its contribution to the anti-fascist war.[22] Pledging to oppose strikes for the duration of the war but condemning policies which provoked strikes, the Total War Committee demanded the revision of the federal government's labor policies with respect to wages, collective bargaining, labor-management relations and the labor movement's participation in the war effort. Government labor policies had hitherto led to frustration, strikes and lockouts at a time when Canada could least afford them. The King government's failure to change its labor policies consequently undermined Canada's war effort.[23]

Despite the party's support of the war effort, the federal government still treat-ed the Communist Party as its worst domestic enemy.[24] The government remained reluctant to rescind its anti-communist measures. In 1942, it was in the incongruous position of persecuting Canadian anti-fascists while simultaneously tolerating the activities of fascist and pro-Nazi elements.[25] Canada's government found it increasingly difficult to justify its suppression of the Communist Party on the grounds of its political beliefs.

The National Council of Democratic Rights organized and led a mass campaign to force the government to release its anti-fascist political prisoners and lift the ban on the Communist Party and other progressive organizations. The National Council of Democratic Rights demonstrated to the Canadian people that the government had no genuine

143

Demonstration demanding the release of C.S. Jackson and other interned union leaders.

basis for detaining and persecuting Communists. Once the party had placed itself in favor of all-out war against Hitler and in the forefront of the battle of production for the just anti-fascist war, whatever pretext the government had for suppressing the party vanished.[26] The government's repressive laws were revealed for what they were — anti-democratic measures designed to suppress political dissent, specifically, the opinions of the revolutionary party of the working class, the Communist Party.[27]

The campaign to free the internees and lift the ban on the party developed into a mass movement which brought heavy pressure to bear on the King government. Citizens of all walks of life, including provincial premiers, the churches, the vast majority of the labor unions and even, belatedly, some bourgeois editorial writers, came to the support of the imprisoned anti-fascists.

The great mass movement of the Canadian

people finally brought about the release of the anti-fascists ... Hundreds of thousands of citizens by mass meetings, wires, have repeatedly declared their opinions in favor of lifting the Communist ban. Dozens of reputed newspapers have carried large advertisements signed by noteworthy citizens ... [28]

As public indignation grew, the King government was compelled to release the anti-fascist political prisoners. What had begun as a trickle in late 1940, became a flood in 1942. The King government withdrew the Orders-in-Council which had authorized their imprisonment in the first place.

Those who had escaped capture were finally able to come out of hiding or exile. For many internees and fugitives, it was the first time they were to see their wives and children in three years.[29] Many internees then joined the armed forces to fight fascism, while others joined the reserves. Over 60 Communists, most of Yugoslav, Bulgarian and Hungarian descent, served with distinction behind the fascist lines.

3. Formation of the Labor-Progressive Party

The rapidly changing political conditions in Canada had compelled Communists to adjust their tactics and forms of struggle; the Communist Party was obliged to combine illegal with legal forms of work. The government refused to lift its ban on the party as such, although being a Communist was legal. Taking into account the political situation and the need for an open political party for Communists, the party leadership decided that it would be best to form a new party with a different name — the Labor-Progressive Party (LPP) — but with the same political objectives.

The preparations for forming the new party facilitated Communist electoral work which had once again become possible after the release of the internees. On August 4, 1943, 17 days before the LPP's constituent convention, J. B. Salsberg and A.A. MacLeod were elected to the Ontario Legislative Assembly from Toronto ridings. A few days later, Fred Rose won a by-election in the federal riding of Montreal-Cartier. Successes at the federal and provincial levels were quickly followed by successes in municipal elections across the country. Already influential in the labor movement, Communists were becoming a force to be reckoned with in Canada's legislative institutions.

In this situation of growing Communist influence, the constituent convention of the Labor-Progressive Party was convened on August 21-22, 1943. The main issue facing the delegates was of course the anti-fascist war. For two years, the Soviet Union had borne the brunt of the bloody war against Hitler, at the irretrievable cost of millions of lives and untold amounts of property. A second, western front was badly needed to draw off sections of the Nazi war machine and thus relieve pressure on the Soviet Army and the partisan forces. The Communist-Labor Total War Committee had demanded the opening of a western front as early as 1942.[30] However, some reactionary elements in the bourgeois democracies allowed their anti-Soviet prejudice to override their military obligations to their socialist ally.[31] The bourgeois democracies asserted that they were too weak militarily to launch such an invasion of western Europe. As the Soviet Union's allies were still stalling on this question, the LPP's constituent convention, in its manifesto to the Canadian people, repeated the demand for the opening of the second front.[32] This call continued until the invasion of Normandy in 1944.

The delegates also drew attention to the need to prepare for the post-war years so that production levels achieved during the war could be maintained to the benefit of Canadian working people. This could be done through various measures designed to raise the living standards of Canadians through higher purchasing power, economic and social equality for Quebec and so on.[33] This theme was further developed several months later at the National Committee (NC) meeting in February 1944. Tim Buck pointed out that during the war, Canadian living standards had risen; but that there was a danger of unemployment and economic recession if the level of production was not maintained into peace time. A high level of production

A dinner in September 1943 in Montreal to celebrate the election of Fred Rose to Parliament.

ARCHIVES CPC/PAC/PA-125167

and full employment was possible provided the government initiated and undertook the modernization and reconstruction of Canada's economy. The resources that were put into the war could be used to abolish slums and build homes, hospitals, schools, libraries and recreational facilities for Canadians. Other funds could be used to rebuild and extend Canada's economic infrastructure and develop Canada's natural resources.[34]

The LPP realized that the successful implementation of a new economic policy for Canada in the post-war period was closely connected with continued cooperation between Canada and the USSR. Peaceful reconstruction in the interests of Canada's working people was not possible without peaceful relations and cooperation with the Soviet Union.[35] At that point, cooperation did not seem impossible. In late 1943, the leaders of the three main anti-fascist powers — the Soviet Union, the United States and Great Britain — agreed at the Tehran summit that, in addition to opening the western front in France, they would con-

tinue their cooperation on questions of world peace into the post-war period.*

On the home front, the anti-fascist al-

---

*The Tehran Conference was followed by two further summit meetings involving these three countries. The Yalta Conference in February 1945 drew up terms for Germany's unconditional surrender and accepted a program submitted by the Soviet Union for Germany's military, economic and political disarmament. The program provided for the destruction of German militarism and fascism and for guarantees against leaving Germany any chance to make war in the future. The Yalta Conference undertook to set up democratic regimes in the liberated European countries and afford them military aid. It was also decided to establish the United Nations.

The Potsdam Conference took place in July 1945. The Conference proclaimed its aims to be the demilitarization, denazification and democratization of Germany. Germany's eastern borders were settled. Germany was divided into four occupied zones (Soviet, U.S., British and French). To demonstrate its good-will and desire to cooperate with its Western allies, the Soviet Union permitted the partitioning of Berlin, which was wholly within Soviet-occupied Germany, into four sectors as well.

The imperialist powers proceeded to violate most of these agreements as part of their cold war plots.

liance between the working class and the bourgeoisie would cease to be a correct tactic with the end of the war, as its aim would have been achieved — the complete military defeat of fascism. But some Communists misinterpreted this temporary tactic to mean permanent, post-war class collaboration. A political deviation along this line developed in the communist movement in North America.

4. Browderism

Earl Browder was for many years General Secretary of the Communist Party of America. When the USA declared war on the fascist powers, this party "correctly called for national unity of the anti-Hitler forces to prosecute the war."[36] But Browder gave this call an opportunistic interpretation. For him, national unity meant the subordination of the independent interests of the working class to the monopoly bourgeoisie. He extended the nature of inter-state relations to domestic class relations. To buttress his position, Browder claimed that capitalism had become "organized" because maximum war production had required a centralized government administration to plan, direct and control the entire economy. U.S. capitalism, according to his theory, had demonstrated its ability to carry on planned production and therefore overcome its contradictions.

The heart of Browder's opportunist ideas was the traditional 'American exceptionalism,' the illusion that the capitalist system in this country is basically different in that it is not subject to the laws of growth and decay that govern capitalism in other countries.[37]

Temporary class cooperation necessary during the war was thus converted into class collaboration for the period after the war. Class struggle had no place in "organized" capitalism. U.S. national unity required acceptance of the monopoly bourgeois two-party system which of course meant the exclusion of the Communist Party from the political process. In May 1944, the Communist Party of America was formally dissolved and was replaced by a loosely organized class-collaborationist body called the Communist Political Association. (By June 1945 the revisionist trend had been defeated, and the party was reconstituted as the Communist Party of the United States of America.)

In Canada, the Communist Party gave critical support to the King government during the war. In the context of international cooperation between countries with differing social systems, the party decided that the struggle to defeat fascism required a coalition between labor and capital, or at least certain sections of capital, at home.

The only Dominion government, that can be elected, which will carry through policies of cooperation in mutual aid abroad and full employment with far-reaching social reforms at home is *a government representing a partnership of Labor and that section of the capitalist class which is willing to support policies based on the principle enunciated in the joint declaration issued at Tehran.*[38]

Thus unlike Browder, the Labor-Progressive Party regarded cooperation between the working class and some sections of the bourgeoisie as a means to a very definite end — the defeat of fascism and the securing of world peace after the war. Such a class alliance was therefore

Labor Youth Federation school in Port Hope, Ontario, September 1944. Left to right: Ruth Ross, Bill Sydney (teacher), Betty Griffin (kneeling), unidentified and Ann Lew.

a *tactical* question and not an end in itself. Although Browderism as an ideology was never accepted by the LPP, elements of Browderism did exist in the party. However, the LPP's mistakes arose from a different source. What influence Browderism had, stemmed from a certain degree of subjectivism which had crept into the party with respect to its relations with the social-reformist CCF.

Since the CCF's formation in 1933, its right-wing leadership had done everything possible to block cooperation with the Communist Party. This policy continued during the war against Hitler even though the international situation urgently demanded the highest possible degree of unity of the labor and progressive movements. Consistent with its anti-unity policy, the CCF leadership rejected any cooperation with Communists in the August 1943 Ontario provincial election. The LPP felt that if cooperation between the two parties, the

trade unions and farm groups had been achieved, a majority of labor and farmer members could have been elected to the Legislative Assembly.[39] Instead, the 34 elected CCF candidates (two Communists were also elected) had to be satisfied with being the Official Opposition, a role they lost in the 1945 provincial election.

The LPP reacted subjectively to this and other incidents. Preparations for the 1945 federal election brought the matter to a head. The CCF's policy of rejecting cooperation in the fight to prevent the election of a reactionary Tory government played into the hands of the Tories.[40] Motivated by the desire to forestall a possible Tory victory, and in opposition to the CCF's irresponsible hope that deteriorating conditions would benefit the CCF, the LPP advanced the slogan for a Liberal-Labor coalition, by-passing the CCF. Under this banner, Alex Parent, president of UAW Local 195 and a Communist, was elected to the Ontario provincial legislature from a Windsor riding.

The LPP soon recognized that this slogan was a mistake, as was indicated by the National Committee (NC) plenum of August 1945. In his report, Tim Buck noted that the Liberal-Labor slogan reflected the party's subjective reactions to its relationship with the CCF, "rather than a study of the objective factors of the partnership of political forces in Canada."[41]

The Liberal-Labor slogan gave left-sectarian elements the chance to launch an attack on the party. At the August 1945 NC plenum, Fergus McKean, who had been provincial leader of the LPP in British Columbia until just prior to the

Left, William "Ol' Bill" Bennett (1881-1949) was a prominent journalist, trade unionist and a founder of the Communist Party in British Columbia. Right, Nigel Morgan (1913-1978), provincial leader of the Communist Party in British Columbia from 1945 to 1977.

ARCHIVES CPC/PAC/PA-125074

ARCHIVES CPC/PAC/PA-125057

meeting accused the party leadership of advocating Browderism. The NC, which was already self-critical for flirting with some aspects of Browder's opportunist theory, emphatically rejected McKean's charges. In a lengthy reply to McKean's speech, Sam Carr showed that McKean did not clearly understand Browder's revisionism. Browder had transformed cooperation between the working class and the bourgeoisie *under certain circumstances* (e.g., in the just anti-fascist war against Hitler) into a permanent cooperation or rather collaboration with the bourgeoisie in all circumstances.[42] In other words, Browder turned a temporary tactical alliance between two essentially irreconcilable classes into a change in strategy.

McKean's opposition to the party was obvious even before the NC plenum took place. In July, he was suspended for false accusations made against the party leadership including the slander that it consisted of *agents provocateurs.* He then began to organize an opposition group within the LPP against the pro-

vincial leadership. In September, he was expelled from the party.[43] Nigel Morgan, a worker who had risen to leading posts in the IWA and the British Columbia Federation of Labor (BCFL), became provincial leader of the LPP in British Columbia. In the autumn of 1945, McKean set up his own "Communist Party of Canada." McKean's rump group wielded little influence and soon sank into oblivion.[44]

The LPP's experiences with elements of Browderism and left-sectarianism helped to clarify the party's attitude toward the CCF. The tactic of the Liberal-Labor coalition, which was short-sighted and widely misunderstood, was dropped and the struggle to achieve unity between Communists and social-reformists was resumed. At the same time, the LPP realized that the achievement of cooperation between Communists and the CCF was not just a tactical question but also a long-range historical struggle.

The essence of the fight for Communist-

Socialist unity is the fight for Marxist policies. There will be no Communist-Socialist unity except as the Communist movement grows strong. There will be no LPP-CCF unity in Canada except as our party strengthens the fight for Marxist policies in the ranks of the working class and wins large masses of workers to the understanding that the unity of Communists and Socialists is an essential factor in the fight for socialism.[45]

The NC also paid a great deal of attention to the need to raise the theoretical level of the party. Only by a consistent struggle against revisionism and tendencies toward revisionism could the party develop a correct line.[46]

The war years were exceptionally eventful years for Communists. Initially, the party was confronted with severe government repression. It was proscribed and many of its leaders and members were interned, exiled or driven underground. Later, the party had to contend with elements of Browderism and left-sectarianism. Despite these trials, the party overcame both sets of difficulties. Through the formation of the LPP, Communists found a form in which to conduct their principled struggle for anti-fascist unity in Canada. Canadian Communists played a substantial role in enhancing Canada's contribution, as a member of the Grand Alliance, to the defeat of Hitler.

The fall of Berlin to the Soviet Army on May 8, 1945, signalled the final defeat of Nazism. It was a historic victory, but won at tremendous cost. Millions of lives had been sacrificed to stop the brutality and horrors of fascism.

---

1. *The Clarion*, July 8, 1939.
2. Ibid., September 2, 1939.
3. I. Avakumovic, *The Communist Party in Canada* (Toronto, 1975), p. 139.
4. *The Clarion*, August 26, 1939.
5. T. Buck, *The Truth about Finland* (Winnipeg, 1939), p. 4.
6. *The Clarion*, September 16, 1939.
7. J. B. Salsberg, *The War Situation and Canadian Labor* (Toronto, 1940), pp. 6-8.
8. A. E. Smith, *On Guard for Civil Liberty* (no date), pp. 6-12.
9. *Canadian Tribune*, January 20, 1940.
10. Ibid., February 24, 1940.
11. Ibid., January 20, 1940.
12. A. E. Smith and B. Buhay, *The Great Issue, Democracy* (Toronto, 1942), p. 3.
13. D.W. Nielsen et al, *They fought for Labor — Now Interned!* (Winnipeg, no date), p. 21.
14. S. Smith, "Our Tasks" in *Monthly Review*, March 1940, p. 24.
15. *Dominion of Canada Official Report of Debate, House of Commons* (Ottawa, 1940), Vol. 1, p. 714.
16. A. E. Smith, *Should the Communist Party Be Illegal?* (Toronto, 1942), pp. 7-9.
17. D. W. Nielsen, *Democracy Must Live!* (Toronto, 1940), p. 9.
18. T. Buck, *A National Front for Victory* (1941), pp. 9-13.
19. *Resolution of the National Party Conference* (1942), p. 7.
20. A. E. Smith, *Remove the Ban!* (Toronto, 1942), pp. 9-10; and T. Buck, *The Way Forward to Total-War* (Toronto, 1942), pp. 8-9.
21. *Resolution of the National Party Conference*, p. 15; and Buck, *The Way Forward to Total-War!*, pp. 10-11.
22. T. Buck, *Organize Canada for Total War!* (no date), p. 15.
23. T. Buck, *Canada in the Coming Offensive* (Toronto, 1943), p. 15; and T. Buck, *A Labor Policy for Victory* (Toronto, 1943), p. 3.
24. National Council for Democratic Rights, *1939-1942 Interned & Imprisoned Anti-Fascists Now Released* (Toronto, 1942), p. iv; A.E. Smith, *All My Life* (Toronto, 1977),

pp. 202-204; and A.E. Smith, *Should the Communist Party Be Illegal?*, p. 15.

25. F. Rose, *Hitler's Fifth Column in Quebec* (Toronto, 1942), pp. 9-12.
26. A.E. Smith, *Remove the Ban!*, p. 5.
27. A.E. Smith, *Communist Illegality and the New Minister of Justice* (Toronto, 1942), pp. 15-16.
28. *1939-1942 Interned & Imprisoned Anti-Fascists Now Released*, p. 1.
29. *Toronto Daily Star*, October 7, 1942.
30. Buck, *Organize Canada for Total War!* p. 9.
31. T. Buck, *Victory through Unity* (Toronto, 1943), p. 5.
32. *Resolutions of the Labor-Progressive Party* (Toronto, 1943), pp. 1-2.
33. Ibid., p. 3.
34. T. Buck, *Canada's Choice: Unity or Chaos* (Toronto, 1944), pp. 23-24.
35. Ibid., pp. 14-15.
36. W.Z. Foster, *History of the Communist Party of the United States* (New York, 1952), p. 415.
37. Ibid., p. 425.
38. T. Buck, *What Kind of Government?* (Toronto, 1944), p. 9.
39. Buck, *Victory through Unity*, pp. 32-33.
40. Buck, *What Kind of Government?*, pp. 12-13; and *The LPP and Post-War Canada* (Toronto, 1945), p. 19.
41. *The LPP and Post-War Canada*, p. 18.
42. Ibid., p. 43.
43. C. Stewart et al, *Report of the Review Commission Concerning Fergus McKean's Conspiracy against the Labor-Progressive Party*, September 14, 1945, Archives CPC.
44. Provisional Executive Committee of the Communist Party of Canada, *What the Communist Party Stands For* (no date), Archives CPC.
45. *The LPP and Post-War Canada*, p. 22.
46. Ibid., p. 29.

8. The Cold War

Great changes swept the world in the wake of the war. A number of countries of Europe and Asia broke away from the capitalist system, laying the basis of a world socialist system. An upsurge of the national liberation movement in the colonial countries culminated in the achievement of political independence of several states. These victories signalled a new, second stage of the general crisis of capitalism which was further characterized by the growing instability of the capitalist economy. The sharpening of the internal contradictions of capitalism speeded up the transformation of monopoly capitalism into state-monopoly capitalism. The intervention of the bourgeois state in regulating the economy became a permanent feature of the imperialist world.

Even as the USSR and the bourgeois democracies fought side by side against fascism, imperialism never veered from a consistently hostile attitude toward socialism. As the allied armies closed in on Nazi Germany, British imperialism invaded Greece, not to expel the Nazis but to prevent a victory of the liberation forces, particularly the Communists, and to restore the reactionary monarchy. The *Canadian Tribune* of January 13, 1945, charged that British collaboration with the very elements that had worked with the Nazis showed "there are still elements of Munich in our midst. . . ."

Even before the war ended, the U.S. and British governments were planning to replace their Tehran policy of peace and cooperation with the Soviet Union with what later came to be known as "atomic bomb diplomacy."

Fearful of the great advances made by the Communist and national liberation movements whose programs clearly coincided with the interests of the vast majority of the world's peoples, imperialism placed before itself two main tasks. On the international front, it intended to "contain" socialism and suppress the growing movement for national and social liberation. Known as the Truman Doctrine, this was to be accomplished through economic, political and military means. Domestically, the imperialist bourgeoisie sought to bring the working class movement under its political and ideological control. Fierce anti-communism and anti-Sovietism were combined with use of right-wing reformism in the labor movement.

U.S. imperialism began a general offensive against socialism and the national liberation movement.[1] The United States had the monopoly on the atomic bomb in 1945 and with it intended to establish world hegemony. The horror of the nuclear bomb shocked the world. In August 1945, two atomic bombs were dropped on Hiroshima and Nagasaki, killing 280,000 people, at a time when Japan was on the point of surrendering. The terrifying experiment staged by U.S. imperialism unleashed the policy of nuclear blackmail on the people of the world, in the first place on the Soviet Union.

After the war, the most bellicose imperialist circles even put forward the idea of launching a nuclear war against the Soviet Union.[2] However, to start such a war would have had dire political consequences at home because public opinion still regarded the USSR as an ally. Imperialism had to find a way around this obstacle; it had to destroy the public notion of the USSR as a friend.

In the spring of 1946, Winston Churchill made his infamous speech in Fulton, Missouri, calling for war preparations against the USSR. But once again, imperialism was forced to restrain itself. In 1947, the Soviet Union also developed an atomic bomb. U.S. imperialism rejected and sabotaged Soviet attempts to reach agreements on disarmament and the prohibition of the atomic bomb. The world was now faced with the prospect of an imperialist-inspired nuclear war which could result in the annihilation of mankind, a sobering thought even for substantial sections of the imperialist bourgeoisie.

A number of European countries were led by progressive governments in which Communists played a prominent role. For imperialism, this was an intolerable situation because they were carrying out fundamental economic and social transformations which undermined the basis of monopoly capitalism and laid the basis for the construction of socialism. Imperialism yearned to intervene militarily in eastern Europe. In 1948, the U.S. Secretary of State, J.F. Byrnes, devised a plan to drive the Soviet Army out of eastern Germany through armed force. However, fear of Soviet military strength, which had been amply proven in the war against Hitler, and vocal public opinion dissuaded the USA from implementing these plans.[3]

Nevertheless, imperialism did not cease its efforts to subvert the progressive regimes in these countries, as it had successfully done in France and Italy. To bribe the progressive movements to leave their chosen path of socialist development and to preserve the capitalist economic order in western Europe, the USA introduced the Marshall Plan.

Ostensibly, the Marshall Plan was designed to rebuild the war-torn economies of *all* the countries of Europe. Economic aid was even formally offered to the Soviet Union. In actual fact, funds would not be given unless certain U.S. conditions were met, the most important being the opening of the European economies to the penetration of U.S. capital, the abandonment of nationalization and the exclusion of Communists from government. Italy and France were refused assistance until the Communists were ousted from the government coalition. Aid to Hungary was cut off because the USA disapproved of the government's policies. During the hearings on aid to Greece and Turkey in the U.S. Congress, spokesmen for the administration made it quite clear that the Marshall Plan was determined by U.S. strategic requirements.[4]

U.S. economic policies for Europe were buttressed by war preparations, military provocations and the violation of agreements made by the Allies at Tehran, Yalta and Potsdam.

The Yalta and Potsdam agreements provided for the administration of occupied Germany by the Soviet Union, the United States, Great Britain and France. They also called for denazification, demilitarization, reparations to the devastated countries of eastern Europe and the establishment of a unified, democratic Germany. But the imperialist powers refused to accept the dismantlement of Germany's war industries and four-power control of the

Ruhr.[5] In September 1949, the Federal Republic of Germany (West Germany, or FRG) was formally established through the merger of the three western zones. In response to these Western violations of the Yalta and Potsdam agreements, measures were taken in the Soviet zone which culminated in the creation of the German Democratic Republic (GDR) in October 1949.

Imperialist military adventures were marked by varying degrees of success. U.S. assistance to Great Britain helped that country crush insurgents in Greece and Malaya. On the other hand, U.S. military assistance to the Guomindang could not stop the Chinese liberation forces from achieving victory in 1949. Britain was forced to concede independence to India and Pakistan, but not before leaving these countries with a legacy of national and religious strife. France and the Netherlands attempted to restore their imperial hegemony over Vietnam and Indonesia respectively but were defeated.

This inability to preserve imperialist empires brought about the organization of new forms to halt the decline of the capitalist system. The North Atlantic Treaty Organization (NATO) was formed in 1949. Its sole aim was to "contain communism" and re-establish world imperialist domination. While claiming to be a pact dedicated to the preservation of world peace, in actual fact it was a pact for war.[6]

Imperialism's attack on world peace and socialism in the post-war period was heralded by an appropriate ideological attack. Imperialism was obliged to conceal its violations of war-time agreements reached with the USSR under a torrent of anti-Soviet lies and slanders.

Imperialism maintains its power through an array of devices, not least of which is imperialist ideology. That ideology is anti-communism, at the core of which is anti-Sovietism. Serving selfish class aims, it conceals and justifies the profit-hungry imperialist oppression and exploitation of the working class and the peoples under colonial and neo-colonial rule. It serves as a tool to deflect the minds of the working people from the truth of socialism as a genuine democratic alternative to capitalism.

In this context, Canada had the dubious distinction of being the country where imperialism launched its anti-Soviet ideological offensive; the attack marked the beginning of the cold war, a period marked by military conflicts, threats of nuclear war and the imperialist policy of "containment" and "brinkmanship."

1. The Cold War in Canada

In early 1946, a widely known and notorious U.S. columnist and radio commentator by the name of Drew Pearson "revealed" the existence of a Soviet spy ring in Canada. His allegations were given immediate and unquestioned credence and publicity in the bourgeois mass media as if they were indisputable facts. The *Canadian Tribune* branded Pearson's allegations as an attempt to foment anti-Soviet hysteria and sabotage post-war cooperation between the USSR and its war-time Western allies.[7] In February, the federal government appointed a Royal Commission headed by R. Taschereau and R.L. Kellock to inves-

Fred Rose, Member of Parliament for Montreal-Cartier.

PAC/PA-47655

tigate "all facts relating to and the circumstances surrounding the communication by such public officials and other persons of trust of such secret and confidential information to the agents of a Foreign Power."[8]

The real purpose of the Royal Commission was to poison the atmosphere of friendly relations between Canada and the USSR built up during the anti-fascist war, open up the cold war internationally and justify the start of a vicious campaign of propaganda and persecution of Communists and other progressive and peace forces. With the help of the Taschereau-Kellock Commission, the bourgeois mass media orchestrated a "spy" scare which would allow reactionary monopoly circles to proceed with plans to "roll back" socialism and reassert their domination of the world.

Twenty Canadians were arrested and held incommunicado for a month. Among those arrested were Sam Carr, organizational secretary of the LPP, and Fred Rose, the LPP's only Member of Parliament. Tim Buck charged that the arrests were intended for provocative propaganda and were significant because they were a signal for a *prepared* anti-Soviet slander campaign.[9]

Charges of imparting confidential information to a foreign power were laid under the sweeping and profoundly anti-democratic provisions of the Official Secrets Act. This Act was a very useful tool for creating a cold war atmosphere in Canada. It presumed guilt unless innocence was proven. It required no proof of any act prejudicial to the "interests and safety of the state" because only the *appearance* of "reasonable suspicion" of such an act was sufficient to be deemed contrary to the law. So fundamentally reactionary was the Act that even the *Toronto Daily Star* felt obliged to comment that it limited democratic practices.[10]

The Taschereau-Kellock Commission wasted no time in investigating the alleged Soviet espionage ring in Canada. Its entire case rested on the testimony of a single man, a man who hides his face in a paper bag, and who some 35 years later is still trotted out to give "evidence." Igor Gouzenko, a cipher clerk in the Soviet embassy, chose to betray his country in exchange for "the good life" in Canada at the expense of the Canadian people. His defection was enthusiastically facilitated by the anti-labor anti-Soviet RCMP. Gouzenko's "evidence" proved to be tenuous at best. At one point in its report, the Commission was compelled to confess that it was impossible to obtain direct evidence on many points.

We realized that the admission of hearsay or secondary evidence might mean that conclusions would be come to about certain individuals which, while entirely sound and incontrovertible, might not be possible of proof in subsequent proceedings where the stricter rules of evidence were applied. But, after full consideration, we had no hesitation in deciding that all evidence available, direct, hearsay and secondary, should be considered by the Commission. In fact, *if this were not done, it was doubtful whether the purposes of the Commission could be achieved* [author's emphasis].[11]

The Commission's report went on to say that from the standpoint of the strict rules of evidence, not all of the documents produced by Gouzenko were by themselves admissible. In other words, Gouzenko's documents, testimony and "evidence" were of no legal use in a normal court. As if to confirm this confession, one of the accused, Dr. David Shugar, was acquitted in a court of law because of lack of evidence, even as the Commission's hearings took place.[12] Yet the Commission was to conclude that the accused were agents of a foreign power, a conclusion whose timing prejudiced the fairness of their upcoming trials.

According to the Taschereau-Kellock Commission's report, Gouzenko approached the RCMP with embassy documents in September 1945.[13] Yet it was not until February 1946, that the alleged spy ring was revealed. Why such a long interval? Given the Commission's confession that Gouzenko's documents would not normally be admissible in a court of law, the hiatus between his defection and his "revelations" could only be explained by the need for time to organize the "evidence." As the Emergency Committee for Civil Rights later charged, the RCMP had to go over the documents with Gouzenko first. This claim implied that the "evidence" was so tenuous that the

closest coordination between Gouzenko and the RCMP was required.

Expressing their admiration for the RCMP's dirty work, the members of the Royal Commission singled out the notorious John Leopold for special praise. Leopold, it will be recalled, was the undercover agent whose testimony led to the frame-up and conviction of the eight Communist leaders in 1931. An experienced expert in perverting the truth and violating basic democratic rights, he was in immediate charge of the staff and RCMP personnel who assisted the Commission.[14]

Canada's political police had a special interest in doing what Fred Rose called "a job on me" because, in speeches, articles and pamphlets, he had exposed their profoundly anti-democratic practices. In the late 1930s, for example, he wrote a pamphlet entitled *Spying on Labor* in which he proved that the RCMP made use of espionage and informers to disrupt the labor movement.[15] Fred Rose was an obstacle to the unrestricted anti-labor, anti-communist activities of the RCMP — he had to be removed.

By the end of May 1947, nine of the accused had been acquitted in court due to lack of evidence.[16] However, because Fred Rose and Sam Carr were prominent leaders of the LPP, the bourgeois court had little trouble in capitulating to the pressure of anti-communist hysteria being promoted by the hearings of the Royal Commission, the activities of the RCMP and the propaganda of the bourgeois media. Although Gouzenko's "evidence" against the two Communist leaders was considerably weaker than that used against some of the acquitted, both were sentenced to six years in pris-

Vigil for Ethel and Julius Rosenberg in front of the U.S. consulate in Toronto, January 1953.

CANADIAN TRIBUNE/PAC/PA-93669

on — Fred Rose for espionage and Sam Carr for a passport violation. Fred Rose was then stripped of his seat in Parliament.

Internationally, the Fred Rose case was followed by similar trials and persecution in other imperialist countries most notably the USA, Great Britain and Australia. In the United States, Julius and Ethel Rosenberg were falsely charged with espionage and sentenced to death. On the night before the scheduled execution on June 19, 1953, all-night vigils outside U.S. embassies in Canada and throughout the world pressed for a last minute reprieve. News of the execution shocked the world. Imperialism would stop at nothing in the calculated plan to fan the cold war.

2. In Defense of Labor Unity

From the time of the Gouzenko affair, every possible method was employed to isolate Canada's Communists both politically and ideologically. In the labor movement, the monopoly bourgeoisie intervened both directly and through right-wing social-reformism, to reduce, if not eliminate, communist influence in the unions. This intervention was part of a new offensive launched by monopoly to take back some of the concessions that had been wrung from the companies by the trade unions.

The strike movement developed quickly in response to the employers' attacks on the labor movement's war-

Top left, part of the car barricade erected against the Ford Motor Company in Windsor by striking auto workers, September 1945. Top right, demonstration in Victoria, British Columbia, supporting the June 1946 province-wide strike of the IWA in British Columbia. Bottom, in July 1946, Stelco workers in Hamilton seal off the plant with pickets.

ARCHIVES CPC/PAC/PA-124359

ARCHIVES CPC/PAC/PA-124970

UNITED STEELWORKERS/PAC/PA-120521

Top left, strikers at the main gate of Noranda Mines in Rouyn, Quebec, 1947. Top right, bush-workers on strike in Cochrane, Ontario. Bottom, Timmins workers celebrate the triumphant return of Bruce Magnuson (on shoulders) from negotiations in Toronto where he and the other members of the negotiating committee won a successful settlement of the 1946 bushworkers' strike.

time gains. In 1944, less than 500,000 working days had been lost through strikes, but in 1945, this figure tripled due largely to strikes occurring in the second half of the year. In September 1945, Ford Motor Company reneged on its war-time commitment to recognize the UAW as the bargaining agent for Local 200 in Windsor. Despite the attempts of the federal and provincial governments to intimidate the workers, they staged a successful strike.[17] The working class had served notice that the monopolies would not be allowed to restore the old order of complete employer domination.

In 1946, the number of working days lost through strikes tripled yet again to 4,500,000.[18] In May and June, the 37,000 members of the IWA in British Columbia won major concessions in their strike against the big lumber companies. In June, 6,000 Quebec members of the United Textile Workers of America conducted a bitter and protracted struggle which saw the Duplessis government employ the police and the courts to break the strike. In the same month, the CSU won the eight-hour day for its Great Lakes seamen. In July, 15,000 steelworkers in Hamilton, Sault Ste. Marie and Sydney joined 35,000 other workers in the rubber, textile, auto, mining and electrical industries already on strike. In northern and northwestern Ontario, 12,000 members of the Lumber and Sawmill Workers' Union carried out a successful strike and won higher wages, vastly improved camp conditions and a province-wide contract from the Ontario Forest Industries Association representing 18 pulp and paper companies.[19]

The strike struggles of 1945-47, conducted around demands for more wages, union recognition and the 40-hour work week, defeated the war-time wage freeze. Concessions by the capitalist class were made also in the context of an economic upturn. Union membership grew rapidly. The trade union movement became a decisive force in Canada's economic, political and social life.

Concessions on economic demands however, were combined with an ideological and political attack on the labor movement. The monopoly bourgeoisie and right-wing social-reformism joined hands to roll back the tide of working class struggle. Monopoly initiated a virulent anti-Soviet and anti-communist campaign while right-wing CCF and union leaders such as David Lewis and C.H. Millard moved against the Communists in the labor movement.[20]

In January 1945, the CCF took advantage of its majority on the CCL's Political Action Committee to turn it into a CCF vehicle. The LPP criticized the move on the grounds that it narrowed down the Committee's political base of support. The *Canadian Tribune,* too, criticized the CCF for turning the Political Action Committee into a partisan instrument of CCF electioneering and for striving to seize political hegemony over organized workers. This CCF manoeuvre was followed by a purge of some prominent CCF members who opposed the leadership's positions.[21] The positions in question included support for the foreign policy of Canadian and U.S. imperialism and the rejection of repeated

160

appeals for labor and democratic unity in the fight for social progress.[22]

At the 1946 conventions of the CCL and TLC, the CCF right wing intensified its anti-communist crusade by proposing a resolution prohibiting Communists from holding union office. Both conventions, expressing the militant and democratic spirit of the workers at that time, firmly rebuffed this move. Despite this defeat, the CCF right wing managed to regain some ground when both conventions rejected a resolution calling for a non-partisan Political Action Committee.[23]

The CCL executive, dominated as it was by right-wing social-reformists, sought to turn the 1947 convention in a cold war direction. Bourgeois anti-Soviet and anti-communist propaganda was freely used in an effort to poison the atmosphere at the convention. Twenty-four resolutions, all denouncing the Truman Doctrine, Dutch imperialism in Indonesia and calling for friendship and trade with the USSR, were replaced by an executive resolution in line with CCL President Mosher's public statements condemning "militant Russian communistic imperialism assisted by its fifth columns in all countries."[24] It was language borrowed directly from the Chamber of Commerce and other reactionary employer organizations. Despite the vigorous opposition of the left wing, the convention upheld the executive resolution. Another resolution condemning red-baiting was then replaced by the executive with a resolution of its own. Mosher ignored charges from the floor that he was acting unconstitutionally. Confused by the intent of the substitute resolution and swayed to some extent by the anti-communist tirades of the CCL executive, the delegates voted to "condemn and denounce both Communist and Capitalist attempts to stifle the freedom of the workers."[25] It was a deplorable act of political discrimination which effectively toed the line of the employers and the government.

The anti-communist manoeuvres of the right-wing leadership of the CCF and the labor movement extended beyond anti-communist resolutions rammed through conventions. Beginning in 1946, some CCL leaders sponsored raids on left-led unions. Edward Cluney of the CCL-affiliated Textile Workers Union of America, for example, frankly justified his union's raid on the militant TLC-affiliated United Textile Workers of America on the grounds that "Communism and trade unionism are not compatible."[26] In actual fact, it was Cluney's actions and attitude which were not compatible with the best traditions of the working class. He and others chose to ignore 25 years of history during which Communists had been in the vanguard of the organization of the modern industrial union movement in Canada. Communists fought consistently on behalf of the workers' interests for wage increases, union rights, the 40-hour work week, unemployment insurance and comprehensive social security schemes. Disruption and raiding were no substitutes for working class unity and the organization of the unorganized. Cluney reflected the anti-communist and class-collaborationist policies of the CCL and CCF leadership.

Unable to fully manipulate the democratically-elected delegate convention, the right-wing leaders took to

When the British Columbia Federation of Labor was refounded by the CCL in 1944, its first convention elected an executive of four members. From left to right: Harold Pritchett (secretary-treasurer), Alex McKenzie (second vice-president), Daniel O'Brien (president), Harvey Murphy (first vice-president) and CCL organizer for British Columbia Alex McAuslane.

intrigue behind the scenes to isolate the Communists from their fellow workers. In August 1948, the CCL executive suspended Mine-Mill because it criticized Mosher's retreat on the railway workers' wage demands. The United Steel Workers of America (USWA), one of the first unions to adopt the anti-communist clause in its constitution, conducted an unsuccessful raid on a Mine-Mill local in Toronto. But the immediate aim of the Mine-Mill suspension was to facilitate the CCL's drive to oust the Communists from the leadership of the British Columbia Federation of Labor (BCFL). Harold Pritchett, for example, was first vice-president of the British Columbia District of the IWA and secretary-treasurer of the BCFL; Harvey Murphy of Mine-Mill was BCFL vice-president.

The arbitrary suspension of Mine-Mill from the CCL and thus from the BCFL automatically resulted in Harvey Murphy's removal from his BCFL post. The BCFL membership was not allowed to participate in the decision but expressed its disapproval at the 1948 convention by unanimously demanding Mine-Mill's re-instatement and refusing to support any single party. Despite this, the divisive forces led by William Mahoney, the CCL's Western Director, succeeded in making important gains on the BCFL executive.[27] In 1949, the CCL executive expelled Mine-Mill without allowing the union the opportunity to make an appeal to a delegates' convention.

The British Columbia District of the IWA under the presidency of Ernest

Dalskog, a Communist, was also under attack. Mahoney, whose unofficial task was to rid the British Columbia labor movement of its Communist leadership, conspired with right-wing elements within the IWA to undermine the union's leadership. The IWA's international leadership was more than happy to collaborate with the CCL in bringing the militant district under right-wing control.[28] The International clearly intended to curb the district's autonomy. It fired the district's membership-approved organizers, made false charges relating to the expenditure of union funds, attacked the district in the midst of its wage negotiations with the employers thus undermining the union's bargaining power, and suspended the Canadian officers for refusing to abide by U.S. labor laws. Under these circumstances, the District Council voted to disaffiliate its 30,000 members from the International and establish the Woodworkers' Industrial Union of Canada.[29]

That decision, supported by the British Columbia provincial committee of the LPP, turned out to be a serious mistake. Although the active union membership supported the leadership which included Communists, as indicated by their consistent election of the left to the district's top posts, many workers were unwilling to break with the International. The new union soon collapsed as those few locals that had broken away from the IWA returned to the fold. The district's left leadership had made a grave tactical blunder which facilitated the right wing's drive to isolate the Communists from the workers and bring the union under class-collaborationist control. The lesson

learned in this experience made it possible to avoid similar mistakes.

The removal of Mine-Mill and the change in leadership of the British Columbia District of the IWA seriously depleted the left wing of the CCL. Its 1948 convention was a witch-hunt unparalleled in Canadian labor history. The CCL executive took open cold war positions on domestic and international questions. The right wing won elections to the CCL executive by large majorities although it was not yet confident enough to stake its reputation on the outcome of a vote barring Communists from holding office.[30] That came a year later.

These developments significantly strengthened the right wing in its long-standing feud with the militant UE. During the first half of the 1940s, UE had commanded enormous respect and admiration from Canadian workers for its principled policies, organizational and fighting abilities. Its left-wing leadership headed by C.S. Jackson, included Communists such as George Harris, Ross Russell and Jean Paré (also a member of the executive of the Montreal Labor Council) who were secretary-treasurer, director of organization and vice-president respectively. A number of the union's staff representatives were also party members. When Dick Steele and Harry Hunter were fired by the SWOC in 1940 because of their membership in the Communist Party, the UE utilized their wealth of organizational talent and experience to organize workers in the electrical industry. In UE, many Communists gained the reputation of being capable, reliable leaders and organizers who fought for the interests of the workers to the best of their abilities.

The leadership of the CCL and the CCF were anxious to rid the CCL of UE. On several occasions, the CCL executive suspended or threatened to suspend UE on various technicalities or for its biting criticisms of the right-wing's class-collaborationist policies. At the 1948 CCL convention, UE found itself relatively isolated. Mosher and secretary-treasurer Pat Conroy openly declared their intention of "cleaning out the Communists" from the CCL and of throwing out UE. But it was not until the fall of 1949, when the anti-communist hysteria was nearing its peak, that the CCL executive felt confident enough to take the question of UE's expulsion to a convention. In addition to formalizing the expulsions of UE and Mine-Mill, the convention chartered the breakaway International Union of Electrical, Radio and Machine Workers of America (IUE) to take over UE's jurisdiction and voted to bar Communists from holding CCL offices.[31] Mine-Mill was already under attack from the USWA, which had acquired jurisdiction over mine workers from the CCL. A virtual open season of raiding was declared on both UE and Mine-Mill.

The right-wing's attempt to take over the TLC proved to be a more difficult proposition. Under the center-left presidency of Percy Bengough, the TLC supported working class unity, Canadian autonomy and the organization of the

ARCHIVES CPC/PAC/PA-124412

unorganized in the mass production industries. It demonstrated that policy in its almost consistent support for the CSU's struggles against the combined might of the shipping companies, the government and the right wing of the labor movement including some gangster elements.

From the beginning, the CSU's drive to organize Canada's seamen had met with the hatred and fierce resistance of the shipping companies. Founded in 1936 and chartered by the TLC, the CSU conducted major strikes in 1937 and 1940 which forced the companies to concede to the workers' demands.

Communists played a leading role in these and subsequent struggles. T.G. McManus, for example, was treasurer of the union until 1947, at which time he became president. Previously, he had been the Saskatchewan leader of the Communist Party and had been elected to the Regina city council in 1935. Dewar Ferguson was one of three vice-presidents. Founder of the union in Toronto, he was a Toronto alderman for a one-year term in 1946.

In the spring of 1947, the notorious assault on the CSU — and indirectly on the independence of the TLC — began. The CSU's president, J.A. Sullivan, with the prior knowledge of the RCMP, defected from the union and publicly launched a hysterical anti-communist tirade against his former colleagues. He immediately set about organizing a scab group under the name of the Canadian

Top, RCMP officers attacking striking members of the Canadian Seamen's Union in Toronto, *c. 1948. Bottom, demonstration in Toronto in solidarity with striking members of the CSU, c. 1948.*

Lake Seamen's Union which later in the year joined the Seafarers' International Union (SIU), a union dominated by gangster elements. His defection was the signal to the shipping companies that the time was ripe to smash the militant union. As a consequence of his defection and anti-union activities, Sullivan was expelled from the LPP.

For two years, the SIU, the shipping companies, the RCMP and the government used all the means at their disposal, including violence, to break the CSU. The seamen and their union were systematically subjected to police harassment and intimidation, arrests and imprisonment, beatings, shootings and uninterrupted contract violations. The companies even used the Canada Shipping Act in such a way as to interpret the strike weapon as an act of desertion.[32]

The TLC and its leadership supported the CSU during most of these bitter battles. The 1947 convention of the TLC, for example, endorsed a resolution charging the SIU with dual unionism, rendering it ineligible for membership in the TLC. A great deal of material and moral support was given to the CSU by the TLC during 1947 and 1948. For the TLC, the real issue was not communism, but the right of workers to belong to the union of their choice. However, the right-wing forces within the TLC, supported by the parent bodies of the Internationals, were intent on getting rid of the CSU and forcing the TLC to take anti-communist and pro-imperialist positions. The 1948 TLC convention witnessed a deep split between the center-left leadership of Percy Bengough, and the right-wing forces led by Frank Hall, vice-president of the

Brotherhood of Railway and Steamship Clerks. The right wing lost in 1948 — but only temporarily. Hall's union was briefly suspended for supporting the affiliation of the company-dominated Canadian Lake Seamen's Union to the gangster-ridden SIU. Sworn statements by former SIU officers later revealed that Hall was connected with the RCMP, the federal government and the shipping companies.[33]

The failure of the right-wing forces to alter the TLC's policies brought the AFL into the fray. In the summer of 1949, the AFL delivered an ultimatum to the TLC to expel the CSU. Communists fully understood the significance of the AFL's latest act of interference in the internal affairs of the Canadian labor movement. Dewar Ferguson observed that the AFL ultimatum went beyond the CSU "and extends to an American demand on the TLC for the surrender of the autonomous rights and independence of the Congress."[34] It was tantamount to a demand that the TLC subordinate itself to the policies and interests of U.S. imperialism. The Bengough leadership was unable to withstand the pressure of the combined forces of the AFL, the leadership of the CCF, the right wing within the TLC and the anti-communist propaganda carried out by the monopolies. The TLC finally capitulated. By the end of the year, the shipping companies had signed contracts with the SIU, thereby effectively destroying the CSU.

With UE, Mine-Mill and the CSU outside the main current of the Canadian labor movement, right-wing social-reformism achieved its domination over Canada's organized workers. The TLC

After the war, prices skyrocketed. The LPP supported "Roll Back Prices" actions by the Housewives' Consumer Association. This protest in Windsor was part of a country-wide campaign which culminated in the presentation to the federal government of a petition backed by over three-quarters of a million people.

ARCHIVES CPC/PAC/PA-124366

leadership backed down and accepted social-reformist policies — at first reluctantly, but later willingly.

Similar developments occurred in the UAW where the LPP had enjoyed a great deal of influence. Among the prominent Communists in that union were Gordon Lambert in St. Catharines, Jock Turner and Lloyd Peel in Oshawa, Alex Parent, Jack Taylor (secretary-treasurer of Local 195), Roy England (president of Local 200), Cyril Prince and Mike Kennedy (alderman in 1946 and 1947) in Windsor. Up to the end of 1948, progressives in the UAW had consistently supported the positions of the militant unions. This ended when many of the left were unseated by the right-wing leadership of the UAW.

The task of bringing the labor move-

ment under right-wing control was further facilitated by the Korean War, which provided the excuse for completing the purge of Communists.

Throughout this difficult period, the LPP pursued policies which defended the unity and interests of the Canadian working class. The party's second convention in 1946 drew attention to Canadian monopoly capitalism's determined effort to enforce its anti-working-class program. Even at this stage of the orchestrated anti-communist campaign, the LPP convention emphasized the urgency of achieving working class unity, and unity between labor and other Canadian working people. For this, the LPP warned, united trade union action was absolutely necessary. Dividing the workers in their struggle against a powerful foe in effect meant rendering a great service to the monopoly capitalist bourgeoisie.[35]

The LPP drew attention at this time to the particular effect of the post-war period on women. During the war, women had taken over jobs which previously had been reserved for men, so that men could be freed to fight fascism.

The war had no sooner ended than efforts were made to drive women back to the kitchen. Married women were driven out of the civil service. Women in higher paid specialized jobs at pay almost equal with that of men, were forced into the less skilled industries and into sweat-shop occupations.[36]

This attempt to drive women out of the work force was, in the long term, unsuccessful. But it did succeed in forcing women into lower-paying and inferior jobs.

Economic discrimination was reinforced with social discrimination. Access to higher education and the professions remained severely limited, preventing women's further social advancement. The LPP called for an end to discrimination against women while noting that women's complete emancipation can only be achieved with the victory of socialism.

Despite attacks against it, the LPP never wavered from its positions. Communists fought vigorously against attempts to isolate the LPP from the working class, divide the workers and bring them under the influence of bourgeois ideology. The LPP's third convention in February 1949 focused on bourgeois and class-collaborationist policies which threatened to seriously set back the development of the labor movement. The convention advanced a program around which working class unity and

social progress could be restored.[37] But as events later in the year demonstrated, right-wing social-reformism had no intention of pursuing such policies. It continued to perform its proclaimed task of purging Communists from the unions, often with the direct assistance of the reactionary labor bureaucrats in the AFL and the CIO, destroying the left wing through red-baiting and administrative methods.

3. Keep Canada Independent

Red-baiting was not of course confined to the labor movement; it became the chief electoral tactic of the Tories and Liberals as well as the CCF. A particularly savage anti-communist campaign during the Toronto municipal elections in January 1947, contributed to the defeat of Controller Stewart Smith, and Alderman Dewar Ferguson who had both been elected the year before. However, as the campaign to isolate the Communists was still in its early stages, it was unable to prevent the election of Norman Freed and Charles Sims as aldermen and Elizabeth Morton, Hazel Wigdor, Edna Ryerson and John Boyd as school trustees. It would take years of intense anti-communist hysteria and capitalist prosperity before the conditions necessary for the almost complete purge of Communists from public office were created.[38]

As the new decade approached, the monopoly bourgeoisie intensified its efforts to saturate the minds of the Canadian people with its anti-communist and anti-Soviet hate campaign. In 1947, the Canadian Chamber of Commerce, one of the main voices of business in

Canada, published a pamphlet for mass consumption which accused Communists of being revolutionary agents of a foreign power whose loyalty was to an imported ideology. Communists were alleged to be intent on destroying Canada's way of life with lies, strife and bloodshed.[39] The *Vancouver Daily Province* issued a leaflet claiming that every twist and turn of the LPP was "dictated by the political expediency of the moment, as conceived in the Kremlin."[40] The abbé Gérard Dion called for the intensified use of the Padlock Law in Quebec, even though Duplessis had already anticipated this advice.[41] John Hladun, a renegade from the party in the mid-1930s and by this time a self-styled expert on communism, accused the Minister of External Affairs and future Prime Minister, L.B. Pearson, of being too soft on communism.[42] Fantastic as these assertions were, they became part and parcel of the reactionary arsenal of anti-communist and anti-Soviet propaganda in use not only in Canada but throughout the world. These crude bourgeois prejudices, lies and distortions were treated as absolute truth and were disseminated as such by the mass media, in the schools, churches, Parliament and wherever a forum for anti-communism was presented. In time, this propaganda took hold.

Nowhere in Canada was anti-communism more intense than in Quebec. Although French Canada's anti-fascist sentiment had helped defeat the Union Nationale in 1940, during the war the King government had pursued policies which contributed to a resurgence of nationalist sentiment in French Canada. Nothing was done to convince French Canada that it had a stake in the anti-fascist war. Conscription was forced on Quebec and the ensuing battle swung popular opinion back to Duplessis. In 1944, the Union Nationale returned to power on a program of provincial autonomy.

At first Duplessis was restrained in his dealings with the labor and progressive movements. The international and domestic situation was such that he did not dare take on the working class directly. It was not until after the Gouzenko spy affair and the about-face in the federal government's attitude toward the Soviet Union and world peace that Duplessis felt free to attack the working class movement in Quebec. In 1946 and 1947, his government used the police and courts to crush the textile workers' strike led by the United Textile Workers of America in Valleyfield and Lachute. He showed no mercy whatsoever in brutally smashing the 1949 Asbestos strike, even though the workers belonged to a Catholic union and enjoyed the support of a substantial segment of the Catholic Church.[43]

Duplessis had a particularly intense hatred for the LPP which he regarded as the source of Quebec's problems. His main instrument against the party was the Padlock Law. In February 1948, Duplessis sent the police against *Combat*, a French-language Communist newspaper established in November 1946 under the editorship of Pierre Gélinas. Everything from subscription lists to furniture was seized. The office doors were padlocked. From there, the Duplessis government extended its attack to include a book shop, the United Jewish People's Order, the Association

Barred from the Carpenters' Hall on St. Lawrence Boulevard in Montreal by the Padlock Law, the Quebec LPP organized this peace rally on the street instead, March 1949.

of United Ukrainian Canadians, the National Federation of Labor Youth and the *Canadian Tribune*.[44] In early 1949, Duplessis introduced a new labor code barring Communists or their sympathizers from holding union office in Quebec.[45] All these violations of democratic rights were justified on the grounds that communism represented an ideology alien to the culture and traditions of French Canadian society.

The ideological war against communism was accompanied by closer economic and military ties between Canada and the USA. During the 1930s and 1940s, U.S. monopoly capital accelerated its takeover of key branches of the Canadian economy. In fact, by the end of the war, the economies of the two countries had become very closely integrated. U.S. imperialism had definitely become the dominant economic force in Canada.

The foreign policy of Canada was reoriented along lines that more closely suited U.S. imperialism. This had become obvious during the "spy" scare. The *Canadian Tribune* had pointed out at the time that the crisis in relations between Canada and the USSR was planned in Washington and London.[46]

That Canada was a willing tool in the plot to undermine world peace and ensure the world domination of U.S. imperialism was critically noted in the main resolution of the 1946 LPP convention. By aligning Canada to the Anglo-U.S. war bloc, the Canadian monopoly bourgeoisie jeopardized Canada's security, thus sacrificing the interests of the Canadian people.[47] In July 1946, the LPP's estimation of the political situation was confirmed by none other than Prime Minister King himself, who admitted in the House of Commons that negotiations were under way between Ottawa and Washington to build a chain of atomic bomb launching bases. In December, the *Canadian Tribune* revealed that these negotiations also involved the creation of a military pact (NATO).[48]

The decision to integrate Canada into U.S. imperialism's plans for world domination arose out of the belief that Canadian monopolies would benefit thereby in the form of greater profits. Moreover, this integration would "protect" Canada against the alleged Soviet threat. The Truman Doctrine of U.S. military expansionism coupled with the Marshall Plan, impelled Canada's monopoly ruling class to *consciously* extend the subordination of Canadian economic life to U.S. interests. Toward the end of 1947, the Minister of Finance, D.C. Abbott, announced the government's intention of selling out more of Canada's severely eroded independence.

The Abbott Plan's immediate aim was to reduce Canadian consumption of imported fresh fruits and vegetables and manufactured goods in order to halt the drain on Canada's U.S. dollar reserves. This aspect of the Plan entailed substantially higher prices and the lowering of Canadian living standards. Its long-term aim was to stimulate U.S. investment in certain key areas of the Canadian economy, leading to the acceleration of the process of economic integration with the United States and subordinating Canada even more to the interests of U.S. imperialism. As Tim Buck wrote:

If the policy now being developed is persisted in we, as a nation, will pass into servitude to the United States through economic colonialism and Canada will be inextricably enmeshed in the war plans of U.S. imperialism regardless of the people's will.[49]

In a very real sense, the Abbott Plan was a Canadian version of the Marshall Plan. It facilitated and accelerated a tendency that was already clearly discernible in Canada's economic development — the growing penetration into and control of key sectors of the Canadian economy by U.S. monopolies and transnationals.

The introduction of the Abbott Plan indicated that Canada was in the throes of what the NC plenum of January 1948, characterized as "the crisis of national policy." While prices rose rapidly, wages failed to compensate. Given these conditions, the NC estimated that an economic crisis was definitely brewing.[50] As the 1940s drew to a close, its estimation of the economic situation appeared to be confirmed as inflation increased at an even faster rate in relation to wages; unemployment crept upward and production slowed down.

To forestall the coming crisis, Canada and other imperialist countries were compelled to rely more heavily on the state sector and state regulation to prop up the sagging economy. Ominously, imperialism also contemplated using war as a means of sustaining the capitalist economy in much the same way as World War II had ended the Great Depression.[51] This policy was manifested in the growing militarization of the economy.

The January 1948 plenum of the LPP placed before the party membership and

The National Federation of Labor Youth (NFLY) "on strike" against the eight-cent chocolate bar, Montreal, 1947. The campaign to save the five-cent bar was successful, at least temporarily.

the Canadian people the slogan "Keep Canada Independent." It called for labor unity as "the basic and continuing need of the working class in its struggle for democratic social progress."[52] It called for the building of a broad coalition of democratic forces that would include progressive political parties, the labor movement and farm organizations, as a step that would advance the fight for Canadian independence. If elected, the coalition would develop Canadian production by reducing the country's dependence on the United States, developing Canadian manufacturing based on its natural resources and developing trade with other countries including the socialist community. Key sectors of the economy would be nationalized. The NC also proposed a number of immediate measures designed to prevent the coming economic crisis in a way that served the interests of the Canadian people.[53]

The LPP realized that questions of peace and Canadian independence were very closely intertwined. The resolution of the February 1950 NC meeting drew attention to the fact that Canada had tied itself to the war-mongering ambitions of U.S. imperialism and the aggressive NATO alliance. In effect, the policies of the government of Prime Minister Louis St. Laurent were the policies of U.S. imperialism. But in a nuclear war between the USA and the USSR, Canada would be caught in the middle of a holocaust. The resolution drew the conclusion that the "fight against the economic crisis and the fight for peace and independence are inseparable."[54] The government's subservience to the dangerous course pursued by U.S. imperialism was profoundly anti-Canadian. As the only political party in Canada to understand the significance of the connection between the fight for peace and the struggle for Canadian independence, the LPP bore a particular responsibility to ensure that the Canadian working class and people took up the struggle against the aggressive imperial designs of monopoly capitalism.

Thus the 1940s ended with an all-out political and ideological offensive against the LPP and the labor movement in progress. Cooperation between states with differing social systems which had reached its peak during the war against fascism was by then just a memory. The threat of an imperialist-inspired nuclear war hung over the world. Domestically, the anti-Soviet and anti-communist campaign continued unabated. In these conditions, the LPP pursued its fight for world peace, Canadian independence and social progress with all its strength.

1. T. Buck, "Atomic Diplomacy": A Threat to World Peace! (Toronto, 1945), p. 24.
2. Canadian Tribune, November 3, 1945.
3. C. Marzani, We Can Be Friends (New York, 1952), pp. 295 and 298.
4. Canadian Tribune, June 1, 1947.
5. L.T. Morris, Peace Is in Your Hands (Toronto, 1949), pp. 8-10.
6. T. Buck, Suicide Pact (Toronto, 1949), p. 2.
7. Canadian Tribune, February 16, 1946.
8. R. Taschereau and R.L. Kellock, The Report of the Royal Commission (Ottawa, 1946), p. 7.
9. Canadian Tribune, March 23, 1946.
10. Ibid., April 6, 1946.
11. Taschereau and Kellock, p. 682.
12. Canadian Tribune, May 4, 1946.
13. Taschereau and Kellock, p. 637.
14. Canadian Tribune, August 24, 1946.
15. F. Rose, untitled notes on the legal status of the Royal Commission (no date), Archives CPC, p. 11.
16. Canadian Tribune, May 28, 1947.
17. L.T. Morris, The Big Ford Strike (Toronto, 1947).
18. Canada Year Book 1952-53 (Ottawa, 1953), p. 734.
19. Canadian Tribune, June 8 and 29, July 20 and October 5, 1946.
20. G. Horowitz, Canadian Labour in Politics (Toronto, 1968), pp. 120-123.
21. Canadian Tribune, January 27, February 3 and May 19, 1945.
22. For Peace, Progress, Socialism (Toronto, 1946), p. 59.
23. Canadian Tribune, October 5, 1946.
24. Ibid., October 8, 1947.
25. Ibid., October 9, 1947.
26. Ibid., June 10, 1947.
27. Ibid., September 11, 1948.
28. I.M. Abella, Nationalism, Communism, and Canadian Labour (Toronto, 1973), pp. 130-131.
29. Canadian Tribune, October 11, 1948.
30. Ibid., October 25, 1948.
31. Abella, pp. 149 and 154.
32. Canadian Tribune, March 22 and May 28, 1947; September 11, 1948.
33. Ibid., September 20 and October 25, 1948; May 23, 1949.
34. Ibid., June 6, 1949.
35. For Peace, Progress, Socialism, pp. 63-64.
36. B. Buhay, "The Struggle for Women's Rights" in National Affairs Monthly, Vol. 5, No. 2, February 1948, p. 102.
37. "Resolutions" in National Affairs Monthly, Vol. 6, No. 2, March 1949, pp. 104-105.
38. Canadian Tribune, January 11, 1947.
39. Canadian Chamber of Commerce, The Communist Threat to Canada (Montreal, 1947), p. 5.
40. Reproduced from the Vancouver Daily Province, Communism in British Columbia (Vancouver, no date), p. 6.

41. G. Dion, *Le Communisme dans la province de Québec* (Québec, 1949), p. 20.

42. J. Hladun, *Iron Curtain over Canada?* (Toronto, no date).

43. P. Normandin, *The Padlock Law Threatens You* (Montreal, no date), pp. 10-11.

44. T.C. Roberts, *The Story of the Padlock Law* (Toronto, no date), pp. 14-15.

45. *Canadian Tribune*, January 31, 1949.

46. *Canadian Tribune*, March 2, 1946.

47. *For Peace, Progress, Socialism*, pp. 13-14.

48. *Canadian Tribune*, July 13 and December 7, 1946.

49. T. Buck, "The Abbott Plan: Step to Economic Colonialism" in *National Affairs Monthly*, Vol. 4, No. 11, December 1947.

50. T. Buck, *Keep Canada Independent* (Toronto, 1948), p. 3.

51. W. Kashtan, *You and the Depression* (Toronto, 1949), pp. 6 and 15.

52. Buck, *Keep Canada Independent*, p. 12.

53. Ibid., pp. 14-16.

54. "Unity for Peace and Canadian Independence" in *National Affairs Monthly*, Vol. 7, No. 3, March 1950, p. 13.

9. We Fight for Canada

In its attempts to stem the growing tide of national and social liberation, U.S. imperialism at first relied on nuclear blackmail of the USSR. Unable to prevent revolutionary change, it next resorted to open military intervention. Although failing to achieve all its aims in Korea during the 1950-53 war, the United States continued its policy of interference in the internal affairs of other countries.

1. Against the Threat of Nuclear War

The Canadian monopoly bourgeoisie responded to the U.S. offensive by tying its foreign policy more firmly to that of U.S. imperialism. In these conditions, the LPP defined its main task as the fight for peace and Canadian independence from U.S. domination. The party carried this fight into elections, the trade unions and the struggle for labor and democratic rights. However, during this period, the party was severely hampered by the rampant anti-communism of the day.

Anti-communism flourished in conditions of the partial economic and political stabilization of capitalism. Participation in World War II had stimulated Canadian economic expansion and helped pull Canada out of the Great Depression. During and after the war, the Canadian bourgeois state became directly and extensively involved in the economic life of the country. State intervention and regulation, as well as the growing international demand for Canadian raw material exports were factors in forestalling the economic crisis predicted by the 1949 LPP convention.

Monopoly encouraged the increased application of Keynesian economic policies. Canadian corporations were, for the most part, willing partners in the evolution of monopoly capitalism into state-monopoly capitalism.

Given favorable economic conditions, the working class was able to make important gains in real wages and benefits despite the ebb of strike activity. Strikes were few because the monopolies in most instances conceded to the workers' demands in order to ensure the uninterrupted flow of profits. At the same time, the rise of the workers' living standards contributed to economic prosperity by expanding the domestic market.

Illusions fostered by monopoly about capitalism's ability to avoid economic crises and meet workers' demands had a receptive audience. And when the recession of 1953 proved to be so mild that it, too, could be considered a year of prosperity, bourgeois economists claimed that this was proof of the validity of their theories. That the gains of the working class resulted from long years of hard class struggles was of course conveniently forgotten. Indeed, the material gains of the working class at this time partially contributed to imperialism's respite from serious economic crises.

Economic and industrial expansion, low unemployment, low inflation and real increases in living standards also created fertile ground for the illusion accepted by many workers that they were part of a massive and growing middle class whose interests would be threatened by socialism. Capitalism's estimation of itself appeared to be valid,

Rally at Queen's Park, Toronto, against the U.S. imperialist war in Korea, 1951.

lending credence to the crude propaganda of the cold war against the socialist countries. Imperialism justified its interference in the internal affairs of other countries on the grounds that it was protecting them from communism. Propaganda on this theme was so intense and so persistent that many people fell victim to the lies, distortions and misconceptions that were regularly churned out by the CIA and the U.S. State Department. Imperialist propaganda managed to break the link in many people's minds between monopoly's foreign policy of subverting anti-

imperialist states and its domestic policy of subverting labor and democratic rights.

The Korean war was seven months old when the LPP's fourth convention was held in January 1951. The convention adopted a resolution drawing attention to the fact that the newly created system of socialist countries led by the Soviet Union stood for peaceful coexistence and peaceful competition between the two opposing social systems.[2] In contrast, U.S. imperialism's aim was world domination, and if possible, a war to exterminate the world socialist system. From the war preparations of the late 1940s, the U.S. had moved to armed aggression, posing the threat of a third world war.

The establishment of the People's Republic of China (PRC) in October 1949, had been a severe blow to U.S. power and prestige in Asia. Given this experience, U.S. imperialism was determined to prevent a similar occurrence in Korea where the liberation forces led by the Communists enjoyed very wide support. While a revolutionary government was set up in the north of the country, the United States intervened in the south to install a reactionary military dictatorship. To forestall the Korean people's movement for the unification of Korea, the pro-imperialist government in south Korea, with the active connivance and support of the United States, launched an invasion of the north. The armed forces of the Democratic People's Republic of Korea (DPRK) repelled the aggressors in a matter of a few hours.[2] Falsifying the actual course of events, the U.S. government accused the DPRK of aggression. Under the mantle of the United Nations, it launched a war of aggression against north Korea.

Under Prime Minister Louis St. Laurent, the government pursued a policy of subordinating Canada's economic, political and military independence to U.S. war aims. Canada's support for U.S. military aggression in Korea included a contingent of the Canadian armed forces. From the outset, the LPP demanded the withdrawal of Canadian military forces from Korea and wholeheartedly supported the organized peace movement headed by the recently established Canadian Peace Congress.[3]

The NC adopted a resolution in late 1950 which condemned Canadian subservience to U.S. imperialism's aggressive plans in Korea and elsewhere.

The Korean war lasted three years. Throughout its course, the LPP remained adamantly opposed to imperialist attempts to subjugate Korea. President Harry S. Truman's threat to use atomic bombs against Korea further undermined the world's fragile peace. As its contribution to the struggle for a secure world and stable peace, the LPP demanded the prohibition of the atomic bomb and all other weapons of mass destruction.[4]

The LPP paid much attention to the question of nuclear disarmament. As early as July 1946, Canadian Communists advanced the slogan "Ban the Bomb!" while exposing the King government's complicity in U.S. plans to build atomic launching bases on Canadian territory.[5] The LPP was deeply involved in the Ban the Bomb petition campaign organized by the Canadian Peace Congress. About 200,000 names were gathered during the first half of 1950.[6] The Canadian Peace Congress, with the full participation of the LPP, also led the campaign in Canada around the first Stockholm Appeal, which demanded the unconditional prohibition of atomic weapons. Initiated in the spring of 1950 by the World Committee of the Defenders of Peace, the Stockholm Appeal campaign highlighted the early activities of the World Peace Council, founded in November 1950. By the end of 1951, almost 300,000 signatures and endorsations had been collected in Canada.[7] They became part of the 500

Top left, Stockholm Appeal float, summer 1950. Top right, Hazel Wigdor, Toronto school trustee in 1946 and 1947, and husband John, collecting signatures for Stockholm Appeal. Bottom, demonstrators at the U.S. consulate, Toronto, protest the U.S. invasion of Guatemala in June 1954. A democratically-elected government was overthrown and a military dictatorship imposed.

CANADIAN TRIBUNE/PAC/PA-93768

CANADIAN TRIBUNE/PAC/PA-93530

ARCHIVES CPC/PAC/PA-124382

million gathered worldwide. The tremendous response to the Stockholm Appeal played a significant role in preventing the United States from using the atomic bomb against Korea.

Reporting to the 1951 LPP convention on the results of the second congress of the World Peace Council which he had attended as a delegate, Leslie Morris noted that the vast majority of the peoples of the world wanted and had a vital interest in world peace and disarmament. The most urgent tasks of the peace movement were the cessation of hostilities in Korea, independence for the colonial countries and nuclear disarmament. The ultimate aim of the peace movement was complete and general disarmament and the use of funds thereby saved for peaceful purposes for the advancement of the welfare of the peoples.[8]

The LPP demanded Canada's withdrawal from all war alliances, including NATO, and the realization of a genuine peace pact between the great powers.[9] The party publicized the fact that the Soviet Union and other socialist countries made every effort to secure a political settlement that would give the world lasting peace, a settlement spelling out the creation of a system of collective security. At the 1954 Berlin conference of Soviet, U.S., British and French foreign ministers, the Soviet Union submitted the draft of a European treaty on collective security.

The Soviet proposal was rejected; the Western powers were, at the time, concentrating on speeding up the militarization of the FRG. At a Paris conference in October 1954, nine Western countries signed agreements on the for-mation of armed forces in the FRG and the FRG's membership in NATO. The Soviet government suggested a conference of European states with the purpose of creating a system of collective security in Europe, but the NATO countries rejected this.

Nevertheless, the conference took place. It was held in Moscow in late 1954 with the participation of delegations from the socialist countries. This conference noted that the Paris agreements had significantly increased the threat of another war. It adopted a declaration which re-emphasized the need for a system of collective security in Europe and called upon all European states to join in considering this question.

This proposal was also rejected by the Western powers. The Paris agreements came into force on May 5, 1955. Upon becoming a NATO member, the FRG, then headed by politicians committed to an openly revanchist policy, joined actively in the arms race. The clouds of war thickened over Europe and there was the direct threat of a military conflict.

In this situation there was a pressing need for the socialist countries to organize cooperation in such a way as to ensure collective action against any aggressor. Representatives of these countries met in Warsaw. Invitations were sent to Western powers to attend the conference, but these were rejected. The Treaty of Friendship, Cooperation and Mutual Assistance, known as the Warsaw Pact, was signed on May 14, 1955, six years after the formation of NATO.

To Communists, the struggle for peace is not in itself a class question. Almost all classes and social strata, including some sections of the monopoly capitalist bourgeoisie, have a vital interest in preventing war. The struggle for peace is a democratic question because it crosses class boundaries. Only those sections of the imperialist bourgeoisie which reap excessive profits from the war industry, want war.

At the same time, the struggle for peace cannot be separated from the class struggle or from the struggle between the socialist and imperialist world systems. The working class constitutes the largest, most stable, most advanced contingent of the democratic forces. As the main enemy of monopoly capital in the class struggle, the working class is the main force in the struggle against imperialism's drive to increase world tensions and foment military conflicts. The world socialist system constitutes those countries where the working class is in power. Having defeated their own bourgeoisie, the working class of the socialist countries in alliance with other social strata must still struggle against imperialist efforts to undermine the achievements of socialism and to destroy socialism itself. As the first and most powerful socialist country, the Soviet Union plays the decisive role in this regard. Thus the struggle of the socialist countries against imperialism merges with the struggle for peace and against the aggressive policies of world imperialism.

CANADIAN TRIBUNE/PAC/PA-93570

2. Fighting the Sell-Out

The LPP also saw Canadian independence as a crucial aspect of the fight for peace; independence from U.S. foreign policy and from NATO was critical for Canada's progress. The need for Canadian independence was expressed in the new draft program adopted by the February 1952 NC meeting. A new program was long overdue considering the fact that the last one had been adopted in 1943 at the time of the LPP's formation. The world had changed radically since then: fascism had been defeated and socialist revolutions had emerged victorious in a number of countries in Europe and Asia.

The draft program pointed to the fact that the development of Canada's economy was being sabotaged by U.S. monopolies. They controlled much of Canada's natural resources and manufacturing industries, a situation which

Left, Tim Buck. Right, Joe Zuken, Winnipeg school trustee from 1941 to 1961, succeeded Jacob Penner as alderman and has held this office since then.

had a long-term impact on Canadian economic and political independence.

The growth of our industry is systematically and deliberately prevented by the U.S. monopoly control of our resources and their shipment to the U.S. as raw materials to be dumped back as finished goods at higher prices.[10]

Canadian monopolies were an integral and willing accomplice in the betrayal of Canada's independence. It was not surprising that Canada's foreign policy so slavishly echoed the foreign policy of the U.S. State Department. In order to protect Canada's interests and make Canada a force for world peace, it was necessary to end U.S. control over the Canadian economy. In this context the LPP projected the building of an anti-monopoly people's coalition which would represent the genuine interests of the vast majority of the Canadian people. With a united working class at its core, such a people's coalition would encompass farmers, the middle strata, intellectuals and other anti-monopoly sections of the population.

The struggle for national independence and to defeat the U.S. domination of Canada will weaken the power of the monopoly capitalists of Canada. The democratic forces of the people will challenge them for real state power, for control of the government of the country.[11]

The struggle for peace and independence was in short intimately linked to the struggle against monopoly capital, both U.S. and Canadian.

Although a cease-fire was achieved in Korea in the spring of 1953, world tension remained at an extremely high level. U.S. imperialism still threatened to provoke a world war in its drive for world domination. Any breach which could be made in the U.S.-led imperialist front would be a step toward world peace. Under these circumstances, the March 1953 NC plenum adopted the slogan "Put Canada First!" to highlight the party's campaign in the August federal election. Although the slogan had a bourgeois nationalist connotation which could be misused in a chauvinist direction, it was clearly

Paul Robeson (1898-1976) at the International Peace Arch Park.

understood at the time that the slogan was directed at U.S. imperialism.

Canada, as Leslie Morris explained, was in need of a democratic alternative of peace and socialism to the aggressive policies of world imperialism. The party's electoral slogan expressed the objective fact that peace, democracy and economic progress could not be achieved without Canadian independence and the defeat of U.S. and Canadian monopoly capital.[12]

In order to publicize its alternative to the maximum, the LPP put forward a record number of 100 candidates in the federal election. In the best of times, pressure on both the leadership and membership of the party during elections is intense; but running 100 candidates at the height of the cold war taxed the membership to the full. It was a great accomplishment in itself. The LPP was the only party to advance a genuine democratic alternative to the policies of the monopolies.

The LPP mustered 59,622 votes, but no communists were elected. This result compared unfavorably with those of the two previous federal elections.[13] Analyzing the outcome of the 1953 election, Leslie Morris reported to the September 1953 NC plenum that Canadians were "showing unmistakable signs of the effect of 'prosperity' and the cold war" and that this effect was "quite profound."[14] As Tim Buck later explained at the fifth LPP convention in March 1954, the party "was not able to break the barrier of lies and misrepresentation set up by the press and other organs of capitalist propaganda set up to confuse the majority of the electorate."[15] The LPP did not have the resources to counteract this massive barrage of anti-communist propaganda.

Throughout the cold war, the party also lost votes and seats provincially. In 1951, A.A. MacLeod lost his seat in the Ontario provincial election. His colleague, J.B. Salsberg, suffered the same fate in the 1955 provincial election. In the 1958 Manitoba provincial election, W.A. Kardash lost the LPP's last seat in any provincial legislature. Party fortunes in municipal elections plummeted everywhere except in Winnipeg, where losses were less severe. The LPP's electoral decline reflected its waning influence in the mass movements, especially in the trade unions where anti-communist purges were still in progress. A further indication of the party's problems was reflected in the loss of party members and in the falling circulation of the *Canadian Tribune*.[16]

While the LPP did its best to inform the Canadian public of the truth of imperialism's activities around the world, conditions in Canada militated against the party's ability to influence the situation. Anti-Soviet and anti-communist agitation reached unheard-of heights. The political savagery of McCarthyism spilled over into Canada from the United States.

In early 1952, Paul Robeson, world-renowned singer and peace activist was invited by the Canadian Mine-Mill to be a guest at its Vancouver convention. The U.S. State Department, however, refused to allow him to leave the country on penalty of permanent exile. Consequently, Mine-Mill, under the leadership of Harvey Murphy, organized a concert to be held at the International Peace Arch Park near Blaine, Washington. From the U.S. side of the border, Paul Robeson sang to an audience of 40,000 people gathered on the Canadian side of the border. This event was repeated in subsequent years and contributed to the partial lifting of Paul Robeson's travel ban in late 1953 and its complete lifting a few years later.

The Paul Robeson open-air concerts demonstrated that the desire for peace remained strong among Canadians despite the cold war. Nevertheless, the bourgeoisie was able to shift substantial sections of public opinion in its favor. Peace became a dirty word; it was "communistic." For Canadian Communists, the struggle for peace was a very difficult and demanding task. It required great personal strength and a deep understanding of the principles of Marxism-Leninism to withstand monopoly's propaganda of hate against peace and progress.

Despite tremendous pressure, the LPP refused to deviate from its principles with regard to the basic laws of capitalist development in Canada. The LPP program adopted by the 1954 convention reaffirmed that capitalism was doomed by the logic of its own contradictions. Class struggle was still a fact of capitalist life and would ultimately lead to working class power and the establishment of socialism.

The program also paid a great deal of attention to the question of U.S. domination over key sectors of the Canadian economy.

In its drive for world mastery it has selected Canada as its first and richest prize. In fact, U.S. penetration and domination have gone further in our country than in any other.[17]

Canadian monopoly capital was an accomplice in the betrayal of Canada because it was "fearful of the deepening crisis of the world capitalist system" and expected to gain maximum profits by obeying U.S. dictates.[18]

The LPP carried out an intense struggle against the St. Laurent government's betrayal of Canadian interests to U.S. imperialism during this period. Two of the most important struggles revolved around the issues of an all-Canadian pipeline and an all-Canadian St. Lawrence Seaway. Both projects, if developed under Canadian control, would facilitate Canada's economic integration on an east-west basis and therefore boost Canada's economic independence.

For 50 years, United States imperialism had obstructed the construction of the St. Lawrence Seaway because

Top, LPP car cavalcade demanding that the St. Lawrence Seaway be built and controlled by Canada on Canadian territory, 1954. Bottom, Harry Hunter showing the all-Canadian pipeline route proposed by the LPP.

CANADIAN TRIBUNE/PAC/PA-93727

CANADIAN TRIBUNE/PAC/PA-93635

such a shipping route would encroach on the interests of U.S. railway companies. Faced with the fact that Canada needed and intended to go ahead with the Seaway, the U.S. government then demanded participation in a route which would straddle the Canadian-U.S. border between Kingston and Cornwall, Ontario, thus giving the USA a grip on Canada's economic lifeline. The LPP — and public opinion — demanded that the Seaway be built and controlled by Canada on Canadian territory.[19] Despite Canada's interests and the demands of the Canadian public, the St. Laurent government capitulated to the pressure of U.S. imperialism.

A similar betrayal of Canadian interests was threatened when the federal government considered constructing the much-needed gas pipeline from Alberta to Ontario along a route which went south of the border. The LPP demanded that a publicly-owned pipeline be built north of the Great Lakes as the only guarantee of Canadian control over the flow of Canadian gas.[20] Together with the CCF and organized labor throughout northwestern and northern Ontario, the party undertook an energetic campaign which culminated in the summer of 1955. In July of that year, Prime Minister St. Laurent and Trade Minister C.D. Howe were forced to meet a delegation from 46 cities, towns and municipalities of northwestern Ontario. Soon after, the government announced its decision in favor of an all-Canadian route. Mass pressure had proved victorious.

The theme of Canadian independence was further developed in the LPP's submission to the Royal Commission on Canada's Economic Prospects in 1956. The submission outlined the historical background of Canada's dependence on the United States. It gave a detailed exposure of U.S. domination as well as the dangers inherent in the policies of Canadian monopoly capital.[21] Although both the 1954 party program and the submission neglected to mention the existence of contradictions between Canadian and U.S. imperialism, this weakness did not prevent the LPP from proposing positive measures to regain Canadian independence and raise the living standards of Canadian working people in a world at peace. However, the party's warnings and alternative proposals were buried under an avalanche of cold war propaganda.

3. McCarthyism in the Labor Movement

Cold war policies imported from the United States had a harmful effect on the Canadian trade union movement. In manoeuvres that were first directed against Communists, the monopoly bourgeoisie created an atmosphere of intimidation and distrust with the aim of dividing and weakening the entire labor movement.

McCarthyism was in full swing in the USA. In 1949, 11 leaders of the Communist Party of the United States of America, among them Gus Hall and Henry Winston (later to be General Secretary and Chairman respectively), were framed and imprisoned on charges of advocating force and violence.[22] The House Committee on Un-American Activities organized witch-hunts to sup-

The Ontario Joint Council of the Lumber and Sawmill Workers' Union at Port Arthur, March 1947. Front row, left to right: Marc Leclerc (vice-president), Jack Quinn (president) and Bruce Magnuson (secretary-treasurer). Back row, left to right: A.T. Hill, Gunwald Espeland, unidentified, unidentified, John Kipien, Charles McClure, Mike Rejsevich, unidentified and Harry Raketti.

press freedom of thought and expression. In the USA, McCarthyism also set the stage for legislation severely restricting the rights of labor. In 1947, the U.S. Congress adopted the Taft-Hartley Act which, among other things, provided for the abolition of the closed shop, the outlaw of mass picketing and the re-establishment of the use of injunctions in labor disputes. Communism was alleged to be the reason for these measures, but in actual fact, the target was the entire labor movement. The provisions of this Act were so extreme that even the right-wing leaders of the AFL and the CIO unions were obliged to express their unhappiness with the bill. The secretary-treasurer of the International Association of Machinists, for example, demanded the removal of the Act.[23]

There was one important provision of the Taft-Hartley Act with which the right-wing leaders of the Internationals fully agreed and willingly complied — the provision prohibiting Communists from holding union office. Alleging that communism and trade unionism were incompatible, the vast majority of the Internationals incorporated anti-communist clauses in their constitutions which not only barred Communists from holding union office but even excluded them from union membership.

The anti-communist clauses were applied to the Canadian sections of the Internationals as well. The right-wing labor leaders in Canada accepted the Internationals' constitutional amendments because they coincided with their

Homer Stevens, secretary from 1948 to 1970 and president from 1970 to 1977 of the United Fishermen and Allied Workers Union.

campaign to oust the left-led unions. By becoming willing, though in some cases unwilling, accomplices in the imposition of McCarthyist U.S. laws in Canada, social-reformism in effect capitulated to foreign imperialist domination and betrayed the sovereignty and independence of many Canadian unions. As W.Z. Foster observed, the Taft-Hartley Act robbed "the trade unions of their customary independence and freedom of action by subordinating them to control by the capitalist government, as never before in their history."[24] The AFL and the CIO effectively made themselves vehicles of U.S. domination of a major part of the Canadian labor movement.

McCarthyism and the Taft-Hartley Act set the stage for the expulsion of the major left-led unions in the late 1940s. The social-reformist assault on the remaining positions held by Communists in the labor movement continued into the 1950s. The CCL adopted a constitutional amendment at its 1950 convention granting the executive council the explicit right to expel unions which allegedly followed the principles and policies of the Communist Party.[25] Significantly, the so-called independent Canadian trade unions also voted for the constitutional amendment.

In April 1951, the International Fur and Leather Workers' Union, led by LPP member Bob Haddow, was expelled from the TLC after it criticized the TLC for betraying Canadian workers by committing itself to a wage stabilization policy.[26] In May 1951, the U.S. leadership of the United Brotherhood of Carpenters and Joiners obtained an injunction from the Supreme Court of Ontario against the executive of Local 2786 of the affiliated Lumber and Sawmill Workers' Union. The injunction prohibited Bruce Magnuson, Marc Leclerc and others, from running the affairs of the local, thereby effectively removing them from office.[27] Despite the support they enjoyed from the union membership, Bruce Magnuson, Marc Leclerc, Harry Raketti, Mike Rejsevich, Jack Quinn, A.T. Hill, Charles McClure, Harry Timchishin and other leaders of the three locals of the Lumber and Sawmill Workers' Union in northern Ontario were soon expelled from the union by the International's leadership because of their membership in the LPP. In 1953, the TLC suspended the United Fishermen and Allied Workers Union for allegedly aiding and abetting the defiance of the TLC constitution. Within a few hours of the announcement, the gangster-ridden SIU launched an unsuccessful raid on this British Columbia based union. The United Fishermen and Allied Workers Union was expelled from the TLC in the following year.[28]

Unions with Communists in their leadership were constantly harassed by other unions led by right-wing social-reformists. Raids were conducted by the USWA and the IUE on locals of the UE; but they had only limited success, mostly in Quebec where Duplessis decertified all the UE locals. In English-speaking Canada, UE's rivals made very little headway, particularly after the IUE's failure in 1950, to capture control of Local 524 in Peterborough, Ontario, one of the UE's largest locals.

Mine-Mill was also a favorite target of union raiding, usually by the USWA. Several attempts by the USWA were unsuccessful until the fateful 1958 Mine-Mill strike against Inco in Sudbury. The local — the union's largest, with 20,000 members — struck at a time when the company was well prepared and when the union was rather isolated from the mainstream of the labor movement. Rent by internal dissension and lacking sufficient resources, the union suffered a serious defeat. A social-reformist executive was then elected. A year later, this executive collaborated with the USWA in a successful raid on the local. (Sudbury was to live with a legacy of bitterness for many years to come, but at the same time, the workers learned from the experience — lessons they used to defeat Inco in 1979.)

Although forced into relative isolation within the labor movement, the effectiveness of Communist trade unionists was never eliminated. The Communist Party regrouped its forces. The many Communists in the trade union movement continued the battle for unity and class struggle policies, defending the immediate and long-term interests of Canada's working class.

McCarthyism contributed to the further splintering of the Canadian labor movement. Even before the anti-communist purges started in earnest, a wide gulf had existed between the French-speaking Quebec-based Confederation of National Trade Unions (CNTU) and the largely English-speaking TLC and CCL. The expulsion of the left-led unions only complicated matters as it split the union movement along political lines as well. Raids and internecine conflicts were the logical by-products of labor disunity.

The problem of inter-union conflicts was serious enough to compel the TLC and the CCL to reconsider their relationship, particularly in the light of the federal government's intention to use an amended Criminal Code against labor as well as Communists, and the merger of the AFL and the CIO in the United States in late 1955. In 1956, the TLC and the CCL merged, forming the Canadian Labor Congress (CLC). The LPP welcomed the move as an historic step with great potential value and importance for the working class and the Canadian people as a whole. The merger would facilitate the growth and advancement of the labor movement and open up possibilities for greater unity and for organizing the unorganized. But the merger plan had some serious limitations. William Kashtan, the LPP's labor secretary pointed out that:

If it is to accomplish what the workers expect, it should include *all unions and trade union centers; guarantee autonomy to its affiliates, and democracy to the membership.* Above all, it should establish a *Canadian Trade Union Congress free of domination and control from any source.* On this basis and with militant policies to inspire the membership, ... organized work-

ing men and women acting in common in a united house of labor would be a mighty force no government could ignore.[29]

However, the attitude of right-wing trade union leaders, whose policies favored further subordination to U.S. and Canadian capital, prevented the formation of such a union center. Social-reformism bore the main responsibility for the labor movement's disunity and its pro-imperialist class-collaborationist policies. As the 1954 LPP program emphasized:

The obstacle to working class unity is the policy of the right-wing leaders of the CCF and the trade union bureaucracy who support the war program of monopoly capitalism and betrayal of our country.[30]

The right-wing leaders of the CCF and the labor movement made themselves the instruments of imperialism's plans to put the working class under its ideological and political control. David Lewis, for example, made no apology for being in the forefront of the struggle against the Labor-Progressive Party and the left wing in general. His policy was to split the labor movement, bringing it under right-wing social-reformist control. Lewis and other right-wing social-reformists played this role while the bourgeoisie laid its plans to limit labor's rights.

History has amply shown that reactionary offensives against the working class are frequently preceded and accompanied by an attack on the democratic rights and political and trade union positions of the Communist Party. Canada's experience has been no different. The groundwork for a new attempt to curtail labor and democratic rights had been laid in the hysteria and anti-communist purges of the late 1940s. The persecution of Fred Rose in 1946 was followed by Duplessis' reimposition of the Padlock Law. Duplessis' immediate aim was to create conditions which would make it impossible for the LPP to function. Under the guise of anti-communism, the Padlock Law was then extended to encompass the suppression of the labor movement as a whole. Meanwhile, Duplessis' efforts were complemented by the activities of a certain Wilfred Lacroix, a Member of Parliament who on three separate occasions in each of the years from 1947 to 1949 introduced a private member's bill aimed at outlawing the LPP. Lacroix's bill met with stiff resistance in the House of Commons, however, because its implications went far beyond the LPP's right to function legally. It threatened the fundamental rights of free speech and assembly. In October 1949, public pressure resulted in the dropping of the bill from serious parliamentary consideration.[31]

In June 1951, Canadians received a rude shock when Parliament rushed through a series of amendments to the Criminal Code which deprived Canadians of many of their most fundamental rights. One amendment made criticism of the government's foreign policy *punishable by death,* whether or not a war had been declared. Another made criticism of the RCMP punishable by

five years in prison. A third defined sabotage in a way which could easily be interpreted to include strikes. "Sabotage" was punishable by 10 years imprisonment.[32] The changes in the Criminal Code had all the earmarks of the McCarthyist Taft-Hartley Act of the United States.

The anti-democratic nature of this legislation soon generated a tremendous groundswell of public outrage. The opposition to the amendments to the Criminal Code included the leaders of the CCF and the trade unions. So strong was the opposition that the federal government was compelled to promise a complete revision of the bill. The League for Democratic Rights was established in late 1951 in response to this struggle for the preservation of existing democratic rights. Replacing the defunct National Council of Democratic Rights, its main task was to mobilize and unite all those organizations and individuals who stood for the protection and extension of democratic rights.

The St. Laurent government introduced its "revised" Criminal Code to the Senate in the spring of 1952. Bill H-8 merely refined those amendments adopted the year before without changing their repressive and anti-democratic essence. Moreover, new sections were added which eroded yet other rights. One proposed section would have effectively banned strikes and picketing. Despite wide protests, the Senate, an unelected body of representatives of monopoly capital appointed by the federal government, passed the legislation.[33] But before the bill could become law, it had to be sanctioned by the House of Commons, an elected body much more sensitive to public opinion. The labor and democratic movements thus had the opportunity to pressure the government into abandoning the bill. This was exactly what happened. As Tim Buck observed in his speech to the 1954 LPP convention, the government's withdrawal of Bill H-8 arose out of its fear of the active opposition of the Canadian people.[34] It was an important victory for labor and democrats.

By this time, opposition to the Padlock Law had deepened considerably. The campaign against the repressive legislation accelerated until finally in 1957, the Supreme Court of Canada ruled that the Padlock Law was ultra vires. Yet another victory in the fight for democratic and labor rights was won.

The LPP always emphasized the close link which exists between the fight for democratic rights and the struggle for peace and Canadian independence. The 1949 convention of the party warned that the erosion of democratic rights under the banner of anti-communism and anti-Sovietism was intended to justify both the imperialist drive toward war and U.S. domination over Canada.[35] This theme remained central to the activities of the Canadian Communists throughout the 1950s and after. Monopoly is fundamentally opposed to genuine democracy which it regards as an obstacle to the implementation of its reactionary policies. Consequently, the struggle for democracy is an integral part of the anti-monopoly struggle. The 1954 program of the LPP therefore called for reversing the erosion of the supremacy of the elected Parliament, for a Bill of Rights and for a democratic constitution.[36]

The struggles for peace, democracy and Canadian independence merged with and were aspects of the anti-monopoly struggle for the everyday needs of the great majority of Canadians. What Canada required was a "democratic national front" which would unite the working class, farmers and other patriotic and democratic forces. The working class would be at the heart of this democratic front, but it would not be able to fulfil this function unless the prevailing state of disunity in the working class movement was overcome. What prevented the formation of such a front was the right-wing policies of the CCF and trade union leadership. Their class-collaboration blocked the achievement of the unity needed to advance the interests of the working class.

The cold war caused a great deal of difficulty for the party, but it was during this period that the connection between the fight for peace and for Canadian independence was clearly articulated and put into action. Usually alone, often jeered at, it was the Communists who demonstration after demonstration tramped the picket lines against U.S. imperialism, against NATO and unfurled the banner reading "Keep Canada Independent!"

1. "Unite for Peace and Canadian Independence!" in *National Affairs Monthly*, Vol. 7, No. 12, December 1950, pp. 6 and 8-9.

2. Committee for a Democratic Far Eastern Policy, *Facts on the Korean Situation* (Toronto, 1950), p. 5.

3. "Unite for Peace and Canadian Independence!", p. 13.
4. *Canadian Independence and People's Democracy* (Toronto, 1952), p. 10.
5. *Canadian Tribune,* July 13, 1946.
6. "A New Stage in the Fight against War" in *National Affairs Monthly,* Vol. 7, No. 7, July 1950, p. 7.
7. B. Mickleburgh, "More Self-Criticism of Our Peace Petition Work!" in *National Affairs Monthly,* Vol. 8, No. 2, February 1951, p. 32.
8. L.T. Morris, "Organize the Will for Peace" in *National Affairs Monthly,* Vol. 8, No. 3, March 1951, pp. 6-7.
9. *Canadian Independence and People's Democracy,* p. 10.
10. Ibid., pp. 5-6.
11. Ibid., pp. 15-16.
12. L.T. Morris, "Put Canada First" in *National Affairs Monthly,* Vol. 10, No. 5, May 1953, pp. 18-19.
13. M.C. Urquhart and K.A.H. Buckley, *Historical Statistics of Canada* (Toronto, 1965), pp. 616-617.
14. L.T. Morris, "Our Federal Election Campaign: a Great Beginning" in *National Affairs Monthly,* Vol. 10, No. 11, November 1953, pp. 7-8.
15. T. Buck, *Put Canada First!* (Toronto, 1954), p. 5.
16. S.B. Ryerson, "In the Fight for Canada — Build the Party — NFLY — Press!" in *National Affairs Monthly,* Vol. 11, No. 6, May-June 1954, pp. 49-50.
17. *Canadian Independence and a People's Parliament* (Toronto, 1954), p. 4.
18. Ibid., p. 5.
19. *Canadian Tribune,* May 17, 1954.
20. Ibid., June 28, 1954.
21. T. Buck, *Canada's Future* (Toronto, 1956), in passim.
22. *Canadian Tribune,* October 17, 1949.
23. *Machinists Monthly Journal,* March 1954, p. 70.
24. W.Z. Foster, *History of the Communist Party of the United States* (New York, 1952), p. 488.
25. I.M. Abella, *Nationalism, Communism, and Canadian Labour* (Toronto, 1973), p. 161.
26. Ibid., p. 162.
27. A.V. Cooper et al, to H. Timchishin et al, 1951, Archives CPC.
28. G. North, revised and edited by H. Griffin, *A Ripple, a Wave* (Vancouver, 1974), pp. 34-35.
29. W. Kashtan, *Unity! Will Organized Labor's Dream Come True?* (Toronto, 1955), p. 9.
30. *Canadian Independence and a People's Parliament,* p. 16.
31. *Canadian Tribune,* February 14, March 7 and October 31, 1949.
32. League for Democratic Rights, *Your Rights and Freedom: IN DANGER* (Toronto, 1952), pp. 4-7.
33. League for Democratic Rights, *It's a Crime!* (Toronto, 1953), p. 2.
34. Buck, *Put Canada First!* pp. 31-32.
35. T. Buck, "A Canadian People's National Policy" in *National Affairs Monthly,* Vol. 6, No. 2, March 1949, p. 57.
36. *Canadian Independence and a People's Parliament,* pp. 12-13.

10. Leninism versus Revisionism

From 1956 to the end of the decade was a most difficult period for Canadian Communists. Bourgeois ideology, which strives constantly to undermine the influence of the Communist Party in the working class movement, strives just as constantly to persuade the party itself to make concessions, to "revise" Marxism-Leninism. In 1956, imperialism seized upon the so-called Stalin revelations and the attempted counter-revolution in Hungary as an opportunity to be fully exploited in a massive ideological offensive. This was a period of intense ideological crisis inside the LPP. Essentially, the party was engaged in a struggle between Leninism and revisionism.

1. The Gathering Storm

The degree to which bourgeois ideology is able to infect the Communist Party depends on the objective and subjective conditions of a particular time. Economic, political as well as ideological factors can and do influence the ideological development and steadfastness of the Communist Party.

In the mid-1950s, the myth of permanent capitalist prosperity provided the breeding ground for crude myths about communism and the Soviet Union. Some party members succumbed to this ideological pressure. It was in this cold war climate that the CPSU held its 20th congress in February 1956. As with previous congresses of the CPSU, the monopoly mass media showed little interest in its proceedings and results. Most of the congress sessions were public, the exception was the day devoted to the election of the Central Committee. As it was and is the custom of Communist Parties to close such sessions to the public and even to fraternal delegates, this evoked no particular interest in the media. Imperialism's open interest in the 20th congress was not expressed until *after* it had ended.

In his speech to the closed session of the congress, Nikita S. Khrushchev included an assessment of the accomplishments and mistakes of J.V. Stalin, leader of the Soviet party and state from 1923 until his death in 1953. A lead article in the March 28 edition of the CPSU newspaper, *Pravda,* summarized these points of Khrushchev's speech. On the one hand, Stalin had violated Leninist principles of party leadership. The cult of the individual had led to administration by injunction, to the disregard of initiatives from below and to cover-ups of shortcomings and mistakes. It had harmed the country's cultural life and the party's ideological work. On the other hand, Stalin had made substantial contributions to the development of his country, his party and the world communist movement. Under Stalin's leadership, the CPSU achieved remarkable progress in the industrialization of the country, in the collectivization of agriculture as well as in other areas. These victories were gained in conditions of capitalist encirclement and an irreconcilable ideological struggle within the party against various anti-Leninist trends. These difficult conditions provided the background for Stalin's rise in the party and for the attribution of the achievements of socialism to his personality. The cult of the individual, however, could not detract from the fundamental strength of socialism in the USSR.[1]

In Canada, the significance of this observation and the fact that genuine democracy is part of and essential to socialism was lost in the torrent of anti-Soviet propaganda that followed the so-called Stalin revelations. While ignoring the Soviet Union's positive achievements in the construction of a socialist society and its unequivocal stance in favor of world peace, nuclear disarmament and peaceful coexistence, imperialism manipulated the Stalin revelations in such a way as to cast doubt on the character of the USSR and on the validity of socialism. The monopoly media deliberately gave the revelations a distorted and one-sided interpretation to prove long-standing bourgeois allegations that by its very nature communism systematically trampled the basic rights of the people underfoot. The ultimate aim of this propaganda was to undermine faith in and support for socialism, the Soviet Union, and by extension, the LPP.

In the context of the intensification of the imperialist ideological offensive against the USSR, the revelations shocked the LPP and the entire world communist movement. Initially, the LPP took a position which accorded with the Soviet view. In the March 19 edition of the *Canadian Tribune,* the first issue to deal with the question of the cult of the individual, Leslie Morris wrote an article outlining the historical significance of the 20th congress. The article treated the congress' criticisms of the cult as a correction of a serious error arising in the course of socialist construction in the conditions of a hostile imperialist world. The main feature of the congress was that it took place at a time when socialism had become a world system of states and colonialism's end was in sight. The following week, the *Canadian Tribune* drew attention to imperialism's stepped-up campaign against the Soviet Union and in an editorial agreed with Leslie Morris' estimation of the 20th congress.[2]

Some Communists were able to place the violations of socialist democracy in their historical context and maintained their confidence in the ability of the socialist system to make the necessary corrections. Articles and reports by Tim Buck, Leslie Morris, Norman Freed and others reflected this point of view. The May 1956 NC plenum adopted a resolution to this effect.

Others, who had idolized Stalin, at first refused to believe that he had committed the crimes attributed to him. They were unhappy with the May plenum's frank admission that "we accepted and promoted the cult of the individual. ..."[3] Some of these people would later leave the party in disillusionment.

A third group consisted of those who advanced revisionist positions. Their criticism of the cult of the individual was a cover for anti-Sovietism and the signal for moving against the party line. Their viewpoint surfaced during the May NC plenum, but as they were in a minority, their view did not generally prevail. However, they did achieve two notable victories. A paragraph was included in the resolution which implied that isolated cases of anti-Semitism under Stalin's rule were actually part of an official campaign of discrimination against Jews. This set the stage for the revisionists' second success

Left, Norman Freed (1906-1977), Toronto alderman from 1944 to 1950. Right, Bruce Magnuson.

— the restoration of J.B. Salsberg to his former position on the National Executive Committee (NEC) from which he had been removed in 1953 for his Zionist sympathies.[4]

Given the general line adopted by the May plenum, one might have expected the party leadership to carry out its decisions. But this was not to be the case. While the revisionists were in a minority in the NC, they enjoyed a majority in the NEC. The NEC and the *Canadian Tribune*, under its direction, defied the spirit of the NC's resolution. Their main aim was to divert the LPP in a right-opportunist direction.

2. The Ideological Crisis Breaks

On June 4, 1956, a doctored version of Khrushchev's speech to the 20th CPSU congress on the Stalin personality cult was released, significantly, by the U.S. State Department. It was published on the following day in a number of monopoly bourgeois newspapers including the *New York Times* and the *Montreal Star*.

The U.S. State Department, it will be recalled, was the chief architect of imperialism's cold war policies, of the campaign of lies, slanders and distortions against the Soviet Union. In view of this record, it was indeed remarkable that the majority of the NEC decided to republish the State Department version of Khrushchev's speech, unquestioned, in the *Canadian Tribune* two weeks later. In fact, 9 whole pages of the 16-page June 18 issue were devoted to it "as a service to the *Tribune's* readers" even though it was readily available from the bourgeois press. The *Canadian Tribune* did devote a nominal half-page editorial in support of the CPSU, but it was written in rather ambiguous terms and did nothing to diminish the feeling among many party members that the NEC was making a qualitative change in its attitude toward the CPSU.

These suspicions were aroused even

more the following week, when an editorial in the *Canadian Tribune* attacked the CPSU for failing to make Khrushchev's speech available to the public. Another on the same page criticized the CPSU for failing to mention Stalin's alleged systematic discrimination against Jews.[5] Meanwhile, the NEC's Leninist minority was given little opportunity in the party newspaper to defend the May plenum's resolution which *all* NEC members were obliged by party rules and discipline to uphold.

On June 26, the revisionist NEC majority issued a statement which went even further. It regarded Soviet explanations of the violations of socialist democracy by Stalin as inadequate and unsatisfactory. Ignoring the fact that the CPSU had given a thorough historical analysis of the cult of the individual in March, the NEC statement falsely accused the CPSU of not giving a Marxist explanation of the Stalin phenomenon.[6] The NEC's accusation tended to coincide with imperialism's current anti-Soviet propaganda line and thus objectively served to undermine faith in and support for the basic soundness of socialism in the Soviet Union as well as to undercut the LPP's internationalist policies.

The rightward shift in the policies of the party leadership met with stiff resistance from the minority in the NEC and from many party members. Thus during the summer of 1956, NEC statements were vague, in order to paper over the fact that the NEC was deeply divided. An NEC statement released on August 1, for example, greeted the June 30 statement of the CPSU as "a Marxist analysis of the objective and subjective factors which made it possible for the Leninist standards of party democracy and collective leadership to be undermined and the cult of the individual around Stalin to arise and assume monstrous proportions." On the other hand, the statement expressed the continuing doubts of the NEC majority when it called on the CPSU to "press further and deeper its Marxist-Leninist study of all questions involved in reassessing the last period and eliminating the consequences of the cult of the individual."[7]

Toward the end of August, the NEC announced the highly unusual step of convening an extraordinary session of the NC in order to discuss the party's growing disunity. An even more unusual step was taken when the NEC opened up pre-convention discussion not just prior to the convention but also prior to the NC plenum. The format of *National Affairs Monthly* was changed from a theoretical journal to a tabloid-size discussion bulletin.

The debate on the cult of the individual took place in the pre-convention discussion. The Quebec LPP provincial committee, for example, expressed the opinion that the NEC's statement of August 1 did not go far enough in its criticisms of the CPSU.[8] This was an openly anti-Soviet position which formed the pretext and justification for an attack on the LPP's Leninist line.

The executive committee of the Quebec party organization had revived a 1947 inner-party controversy about the national question in Canada. At that time, three leading members of the Quebec LPP, Henri Gagnon, Emery Samuel and Evariste Dubé, had been ex-

Left, Harry Hunter (1903-1969). Right, George Harris (1910-1978).

pelled for factionalism. In 1956, an LPP commission was established to re-examine the 1947 events. The LPP was motivated by the desire to restore party unity in Quebec. In the meantime, Gagnon, Samuel and Dubé were reinstated as party members. The Quebec provincial executive used the 1947 events as evidence that Stalin's violation of party democracy had a Canadian counterpart. It supported the three's reinstatement in order to legitimize its new-found "insight" into the 1947 events and its opposition to the party's Leninist policies.

In August, Gui Caron testified to the party's commission investigating the 1947 events that he was "deeply upset" by the Stalin revelations because he did not believe that such things were possible in a socialist society. He rejected explanations that Stalin's crimes could be attributed to the cult of the individual or even to the situation created by imperialist efforts to undermine socialism. Caron went on to say that the Stalin cult arose out of mistaken ideas concerning the understanding and application of

democratic centralism. He re-evaluated his own positions and the decisions of the party surrounding the 1947 inner-party conflict, he claimed, because the LPP was "itself based on democratic centralism."[9] Starting with an anti-Soviet premise, Caron passed over to a denial of the validity of democratic centralism.

In this context, the commission investigating the 1947 events concluded that the 1947 split was caused by "the incorrect practice of leading committees in the party of solving ideological differences by the employment of administrative measures."[10] This conclusion passed over the ideological roots of the 1947 inner-party crisis in Quebec and thus played into the hands of the revisionists. It reflected the fact that the commission itself was subject to the ideological and political confusion to which it drew attention.

Rather than promote party unity, the commission's conclusion actually aggravated disunity. The LPP's Quebec

Ross Russell, veteran of the Mackenzie-Papineau Battalion.

executive decided that the time was ripe for a full-scale assault on the program and organizational principles of the LPP. On October 15, Caron and five other executive members of the Quebec LPP suddenly and simultaneously resigned from their posts and from the party. The reasons for their defection were revealed in Caron's letter to the NC a few days later. That letter exposed his deep-seated anti-Sovietism and his profound opposition to the principles of Marxism-Leninism. In it, Caron expressed the desire to dissociate himself from the Soviet Union by resigning from the LPP because it "has come to represent the Soviet Union in the eyes of the Canadian people." He then called for "a decisive break with the ideological subservience to the CPSU which had characterized our party."[11] He demanded the renunciation of the concept of the dictatorship of the proletariat as foreign and undemocratic, and the transformation of the LPP into what amounted to an educational association similar to Browder's Communist Political Association.

Caron's mistaken ideas of socialist and party democracy and the role of a Marxist party were not unique. The LPP in English-speaking Canada, particularly in Ontario, had its share of party members who wanted to "revise" the program and organizational principles of the party.

Norman Penner, for one, felt that the party was to blame for the failure to establish close relations with the CCF. Ignoring the right-wing course of the CCF leadership and its role in purging Communists from the labor movement, Penner thought that the LPP would benefit by encouraging labor's move in the direction of official support for the CCF because "the CCF is winning increasing support in the new Canadian Labor Congress and will probably become its political arm." He argued that "the problem facing us now is not competition with the CCF, but cooperation to advance labor's political role in the nation."[12] Based on the illusion that the right-wing CCF leadership would defend the class interests of the workers, Penner's thesis amounted to a call for the liquidation of the independent revolutionary role of the LPP in favor of the CCF leadership's class collaborationism. Penner called for making the party "more democratic" in order to overcome alleged negative influences of the cult of the individual in the LPP. Mixing up the specific conditions which gave rise to Stalin's violations of socialist and party democracy with Leninist principles of democratic centralism, he proposed a number of reforms such as referendums on all important questions and the conducting of so-called "open debates" which, if implemented, would have purged the centralism out of democratic centralism, deprived the party leadership of the very function of leadership and reduced the LPP to a debating society.

Such social-reformist views were expressed by others as well. Robert Laxer, for example, while claiming adherence to Marxism-Leninism, called for "a systematic cleaning out of the Augean stables of wrong concepts that have been woven (by the Stalin cult) around correct Marxist doctrine. . . ." He wanted to remove from the concept of the dictatorship of the proletariat "those unique and destructive elements which are historically associated with the Soviet experience."[13] In his opinion, this meant that the LPP should pursue only the parliamentary path to socialism. In the process of "mass experience and learning through the democratic parliamentary struggle, through the struggle of the unions and the people's organizations," the working class "gradually comes to the head of the nation." He asserted that the LPP was "leftist" in its approach to the significance of the reforms proposed by the CCF. It was wrong, he claimed, "to fail to see that the qualitative change to socialism will be the result of quantitative changes. . . ."[14] His theory was reminiscent of the gradualist theories advanced by Karl Kautsky and other right-opportunists decades earlier.

The views expressed by Caron, Penner, Laxer, Salsberg and others were representative of a whole gamut of revisionist ideas plaguing the party. Perhaps the best known of the revisionists, however, was Stewart Smith, the former Toronto Controller and leader of the Ontario LPP. It will be recalled that 16 years earlier, he had advocated turning Canada's participation in the war against Nazi Germany into a civil war in Canada. From ultra-leftism, Smith now found himself in the camp of extreme right-opportunism. Quite typically, the revisionists used Stalin's violations of socialist and party democracy as the pretext for attacking proletarian internationalism and the role of the LPP as the revolutionary party of the Canadian working class.

The ideological crisis in the party as a whole, but particularly in Quebec, was accompanied by the sharpening of ideological differences within the NEC. Discord existed on a number of key questions but found its clearest expression in differing attitudes toward the cult of the individual. In early October, a delegation consisting of Tim Buck, Leslie Morris, William Kardash and J.B. Salsberg went to the Soviet Union for talks with the CPSU on Stalin's personality cult and other questions of mutual interest. They were joined by William Kashtan who was already in Moscow. On their return, they delivered a report to the NEC which provoked several days of exceptionally sharp debate. Finally, on October 12, the NEC unanimously adopted a statement which was noncommittal in both tone and content.[15] Unanimity in this case did not imply unity. It only temporarily hid serious differences.

Two days later, the NEC sent Tim

Left, Nelson Clarke, provincial leader in Saskatchewan from 1945 to 1957. Right, Ben Swankey, LPP provincial leader in Alberta from 1945 to 1956.

ARCHIVES CPC/PAC

ARCHIVES CPC/PAC/PA-125084

Buck, J.B. Salsberg and later Harry Binder, a former Quebec party leader, to Montreal to resolve the crisis. But to no avail. The effort was doomed from the start because neither the six former Quebec provincial executive members nor the revisionist majority on the NEC were genuinely interested in achieving a solution. The NEC declined to go beyond the expression of regret at the actions taken by the six. In fact, it actually agreed with some of their criticisms.[16] As the LPP lacked solid ideological leadership in its Quebec organization, the six resignations precipitated defections from the party membership as well.

Following the resignation of the six Quebec leaders, the crisis within the NEC became so acute that the revisionist majority adopted resolutions submitting the resignation of the NEC effective as of the forthcoming NC plenum, and calling for Tim Buck's resignation as General Secretary. The latter resolution was rescinded just before the plenum

began.[17] As far as the revisionists were concerned, the moment had arrived to launch a major offensive against the party line. Their actions created an atmosphere of confusion, deep distrust and acrimony in which the NC meeting had to take place. They resulted in two of the longest NC meetings in the party's history.

3. Two Plenums — 20 Days

Testifying to the depth of the ideological crisis in the LPP, two plenums lasting a total of 20 days took place within the space of eight weeks. This period marked the most critical phase for the party since the ideological crisis of 1929. The LPP's leadership was paralyzed. The membership was confused and uncertain.

Under normal conditions, party conventions and CC plenums hear a report or political resolution from the party's executive committee, usually delivered by the General Secretary. However, the

13-day plenum which began on October 28 heard no such formal report or political resolution because of the acute differences within the NEC. Instead, Tim Buck delivered a self-critical contribution expressing his personal opinions on the inner-party situation. His address drew attention to the fact that the crisis in the party was fundamentally a crisis of ideas. Influential circles of workers, including party members, were suffering a crisis of confidence in the Soviet Union and in the ideology of Marxism-Leninism.

Any weakening of confidence in Marxism-Leninism is a challenge to our party. As Lenin pointed out, there are only two ideologies in the civilized world, bourgeois ideology and Marxist ideology. There is no third ideology. The battle for men's minds is above all a battle of each communist party to convince its members, supporters, and all those workers who want a new life and a new world, that Marxism provides the key to its future. [18]

Before elaborating on this, his main theme, Tim Buck made an extensive self-critical appraisal of his own role as party leader and a critical examination of the NEC. He admitted that he had "allowed a cult of the individual to develop around myself" and that it was now necessary for the plenum to re-examine the concept, method and practice of leadership.[19] These statements were made while under severe pressure from the revisionists who wanted him removed from his post. He was their special target because of his life-long record as a staunch defender of Marxism-Leninism and proletarian internationalism.

Tim Buck's analysis of the events leading up to the open ideological split in the party showed that there were irreconcilable differences within the NEC on the reports of the October delegation to the USSR and on the evaluation of the party meeting in Montreal where the opposing views of Tim Buck and J.B. Salsberg had been aired.[20] Salsberg's report to the Montreal meeting had given the opportunist elements there the occasion to openly express their disillusionment with the USSR and their doubts about the validity of Marxism-Leninism. In particular, the concept of the dictatorship of the proletariat had come under attack and the party had been accused of not being Canadian.

These events, Tim Buck argued in his address, revealed that there was a widespread tendency to revisionism and liquidationism in the party. He then unequivocally defended the concept of the dictatorship of the proletariat as an essential principle of the revolutionary working class party, although the wording of the principle could vary. Working class power is a prerequisite for the overthrow of the capitalist system, the abolition of the exploitation of man by man and the construction of a socialist society.

He also criticized those NEC members who declared that the LPP was not in competition with the CCF. Competition exists between the two parties because the CCF is not a Marxist party fighting for genuine socialism. To deny this is revisionism.[21] Tim Buck's personal report thus drew the battle lines on these and other basic issues at the very beginning of the NC plenum.

Following Tim Buck's speech, each member of the NEC was given the opportunity to outline his or her position. NC members then defined their attitude in terms of the speeches made by Tim Buck and the other NEC members. It was agreed that during the first session of the plenum there would be no time limit to the discussion. That, too, was a highly unusual step, but it did give the party the chance to debate all the questions thoroughly.[22]

Just as the debate began in earnest, international developments intervened, once more making an impact on the LPP. The first was the Suez crisis. Britain, France and Israel launched an invasion of Egypt to seize the Suez Canal. On the evening of October 30, the plenum sent a telegram to the then Minister of External Affairs, L.B. Pearson, endorsing the Canadian government's appeal to Britain and France calling for the withdrawal of their armed forces from Egypt. Several days later, however, the St. Laurent government decided to abstain from a United Nations vote calling for a cease-fire and the withdrawal of foreign troops from Egyptian territory. In response, the NC meeting sent telegrams of protest to both St. Laurent and Pearson.[23]

The second major event which deeply affected the LPP, was the attempted counter-revolutionary coup in Hungary. It occurred almost simultaneously with the Suez crisis and required Soviet military assistance to frustrate it. Imperialist propaganda cleverly manipulated the Hungarian events in such a way as to give the false impression that the Hungarian people as a whole, rather than reactionary and even fascistic anti-socialist elements, were rebelling against an allegedly unpopular "totalitarian" regime. The preceding 10 years of cold war had paved the way for such propaganda. Coming so soon after the Stalin revelations, even some members of the LPP viewed the troubles in Hungary as confirmation that "Stalinism" had not died with Stalin. For these members, Hungary was either the final blow to their faltering faith in the Soviet Union and socialism, or the long-awaited pretext for quitting the party which they had come to regard as an embarrassment in a society enjoying seemingly endless prosperity. So divisive was the issue that the NC decided not to take a position on the events in Hungary. Instead, the matter was referred to the incoming NEC.[24]

For 13 days, intense and often rancorous debate raged in the NC meeting. Deep splits over a large number of questions were revealed. Opposing views were expressed regarding interpretations of proletarian internationalism, whether the Marxist party was indispensable to the achievement of socialism, the validity of democratic centralism, the policy of the USSR toward Soviet Jews, the dictatorship of the proletariat and Tim Buck's leadership.[25] At one point in the proceedings, criticisms of Tim Buck were so severe that he offered not to stand for the NEC. On the urging of some NEC members, he withdrew this proposal.[26]

The NC plenum appeared to be not only deeply divided but also evenly divided, a situation which was complicated by the high abstention vote on a number of motions. Until the evening of the very last day, November 9, it was almost impossible to discern which side would prevail. In its final session, the NC voted on a motion by Nigel Morgan to, in effect, withdraw criticisms of the

Left to right: Gregory Okulevich (1907-1974), for many years a leader of the Federation of Russian Canadians and editor of the Russian-language newspaper Vestnik; Stanley Dobrowolsky; and Peter Prokop (1903-1981), for many years a leader of the Association of United Ukrainian Canadians.

CPSU made to that party in a cable a month earlier. An amendment by Stewart Smith was defeated by a vote of 18 to 12, while Nigel Morgan's original motion passed by 18 to 11 with 1 abstention. It was clearly a decisive victory for the Leninists and thus augured well for the election to the NEC, in which the Leninists did indeed obtain a majority.

In the election to the 13-member NEC, MacLeod and Salsberg were tied for the last two places with Dave Kashtan. Refusing to consent to a tie-breaking vote, MacLeod and Salsberg withdrew their nominations. Under the circumstances, Dave Kashtan chose not to stand. Unhappy with the fact that the Leninists had obtained a majority on the NEC, Harry Binder and Norman Penner withdrew from the NEC to which they had just been elected. The NC thereupon decided that the NEC would consist of nine members.[27]

The new NEC then proceeded to formulate a draft political resolution for the December NC plenum. The draft resolution drew attention to the fact that international reaction had seized upon the Stalin revelations "to divert attention from the historic contributions of the congress on the possibility of avoiding war and overcoming the split in the working class movement."[28] The crisis in the LPP had arisen out of its inability to come to grips with the changing situation in the country which was advantageous to the monopoly bourgeoisie. There existed a sectarian and dogmatic tendency which displayed reluctance to employ a creative Marxist-Leninist ap-

Left, Joe Wallace (1890-1975), Communist poet. Right, Margaret Fairley (1885-1968), editor of the progressive Canadian literary magazine New Frontiers.

ARCHIVES CPC/PAC

proach to the new tasks facing the party. On the other hand, a more dangerous right-opportunist tendency had surfaced which, in the name of independence from the CPSU, in essence abandoned Marxism-Leninism. It reflected a surrender to pressures of anti-communism and anti-Sovietism.

Not surprisingly, the revisionists were unhappy with the draft resolution's characterization of their ideological positions. Norman Penner, for one, proposed an amendment replacing the first section of the resolution so as to reverse its meaning and content. Criticizing the mistakes of previous party leaders for mechanically applying the experiences of the CPSU to the Canadian situation, he advocated an "independent," that is, a revisionist "Canadian" path to socialism. He then repeated his previously stated ideas on the CCF, the LPP's relation to it and his interpretation of the united front. Significantly, the December plenum rejected Penner's amendment by a vote of 21 to 7.[29]

Toward the end of the seven-day marathon meeting, Salsberg, Binder and Stewart Smith submitted a letter objecting to the decision to withdraw the former NEC's criticisms of the CPSU and demanding the formulation of a "Canadian" path to socialism. In their opinion, such a path could not be discussed "without feeling free to dissociate ourselves from the incorrect relationship between socialism and democracy during the past 30 years in the USSR."[30] In other words, like Penner, they wanted to repudiate the Soviet Union and, by extension, existing socialism and its great achievements, in favor of what they called "democratic socialism." The conclusion of their letter was entirely correct in declaring that there were two opposing lines in the party. They characterized these lines as "old dogmatic thinking" based on the "policies of the Stalin period," on the one side, and "creative Marxism-Leninism," on the other. The two opposing lines were actually Marxism-Leninism and revisionism. These three were later to abandon even the pretense of believing in Marxism.

The struggle between the two opposing lines continued vigorously in the period up to and including the LPP convention of April 1957. However, in a very real sense, this stage of the struggle was anti-climactic since the outcome had already been indicated by the November and December NC plenums. Indeed, the new NEC felt strong and confident enough to issue a statement on January 21 on the events in Hungary which noted that "the legitimate and fully justifiable movements of the Hungarian people ... for the correction of sore grievances were seized upon by internal and external reactionary and fascist elements to stage a counter-revolution aimed at destroying the Hungarian socialist state."[31] It rejected the imperialist lie that the USSR had unilaterally intervened and pointed out that the Hungarian government had requested Soviet military aid under the terms of the Warsaw Pact to suppress the fascist-inspired attempted coup. With this statement, the LPP placed itself solidly on the side of world socialism and proletarian internationalism and against imperialism and revisionism.

In the months immediately preceding the sixth LPP convention, contributions to the pre-convention discussion in *National Affairs Monthly* indicated that the sentiments of the party membership were definitely swinging in favor of maintaining the party's Leninist ideological and political line. Any revisionist hope that lost ground could be regained at the convention was dashed. One of the convention's first tasks was to elect a convention committee of 11 members. Being able to choose from 19 names, the delegates handed the revisionists a stern defeat. Charles T. Sims, Norman Penner, Stewart Smith and Henri Gagnon were all substantially short of election. In the afternoon session, the same fate befell the latter three when they stood for the policy committee. With five to be elected and eight standing, the evening session rejected Salsberg's bid for election to the resolutions committee. The revisionists received little consolation when Norman Penner barely achieved election to the program committee.[32] These committee elections set the tone for the entire convention.

Of even more importance were the votes on the draft policy resolution and the party declaration. An amendment to the draft resolution proposed by Sims was overwhelmingly defeated. Penner's amendment suffered a similar fate with only 15 voting in favor and 1 abstention. Finally, in a recorded vote on the draft policy resolution as a whole, 122 delegates voted in favor and 20 against.

In another recorded vote, this time by a margin of 121 to 9 with 14 abstentions, the convention adopted a "Declaration of the Party."[33] This Declaration reaffirmed that the LPP was "that part of the labor movement of Canada which accepts the science of Marxism-Leninism as the guide to the winning of socialism in Canada...."[34] It rejected proposals advanced by some to dissolve or restrict the role of the LPP; a Communist Party is essential if the ideas of Marxism-Leninism are to be fused with the struggles of the working people against monopoly capitalism. An attempt to replace the Declaration with a substitute statement supported by the Quebec provincial executive was easily voted down.[35] There could be no doubt that the Leninists enjoyed the support of the great majority of the party membership as expressed at the convention and that support for the revisionists was shrinking.

The elections to the new NC merely formalized the outcome of the previous votes. Eighty-six delegates were nominated to fill 51 positions. Sims, Gagnon, Salsberg and Smith were all denied re-election. In fact, the latter two had the dubious distinction of obtaining the lowest votes.[36] The revisionists were reduced to a tiny minority on the incoming NC.

The new NC met in the two days immediately following the convention. The first item on the agenda was the election of an 11-member NEC. Tim Buck was re-elected General Secretary. Leslie Morris replaced John Stewart, who declined nomination, as editor of the *Canadian Tribune*. William Kashtan was assigned the additional task of organizational secretary. John Weir was assigned the task of coordinating work in the national groups field. Other full-time posts were held in temporary abeyance until the newly-elected members of the NEC living in western Canada (Alfred Dewhurst, Sam J. Walsh and Nelson Clarke) could move to Toronto.[37]

Consolidation of the party was essential to further advance. The party's internal crisis had had several negative consequences. Some party members, disillusioned by international and domestic events, left or were leaving the

ARCHIVES CPC/PAC/PA-124364

party. Most of the revisionist leaders resigned from the party after their defeat at the convention. Problems persisted in the LPP's Quebec organization. The public work of the party suffered badly. The circulation of the *Canadian Tribune* was dropping sharply, forcing it to reduce the number of pages from 12 to 8.

The NC plenum in late summer 1957, prepared to take measures to improve the situation. Absolute priority was given to the *Canadian Tribune*.[38] A special resolution underscored the fact that "in this period we must lay stress on the role of the *Tribune* in recouping our losses and solidifying our base."[39] The struggle for the newspaper's circulation and efforts to improve its content were regarded as inseparable aspects of the fight to save the *Canadian Tribune* itself. *National Affairs Monthly* ceased publication with its June 1957 issue and did not appear again until January 1958, as *Marxist Review*.[40]

The plenum also paid particular attention to the improvement of its relations with the CPSU. Warmly congratulating the CPSU on the occasion of the 40th anniversary of the Great October Socialist Revolution, the NC noted that the power and achievements of socialism were exerting a great deal of influence on the peoples of the imperialist and colonial countries and were contributing to the deepening general crisis of capitalism. Its resolution emphasized the fact that the USSR was in the vanguard of the struggle for peaceful coexistence, a policy which coincided not only with the vital interests of the USSR and the international working class movement but also, given the very real danger of nuclear war, with the most fundamental interest of all mankind — life itself. The Soviet Union's considerable achievements as well as its fearless exposure of mistakes and shortcomings, arose out of its adherence to the principles of Marx-

ism-Leninism. These principles are valid internationally, but at the same time, they must be applied creatively in the specific conditions of each country.[41]

In Tim Buck's report to the plenum, much emphasis was placed on the need to strengthen the party's ideological work. It led to a special resolution being submitted by the NEC to the February 1958 NC meeting.

The party must strengthen its understanding of Marxism-Leninism — the universal principles of scientific socialism and the creative application of these principles to conditions prevailing in Canada. This is one of the main lessons of the recent party crisis.[42]

The defeat of the revisionists had been achieved by the party's firm adherence to the basic principles of scientific socialism. It was with a heightened awareness of the dangers of any deviation from these principles that the LPP began the slow and difficult task of rebuilding in the conditions of the cold war.

---

1. *Canadian Tribune*, April 9, 1956.
2. Ibid., March 26, 1956.
3. Ibid., May 28, 1956.
4. *Decisions of the Meeting of the National Committee May 17-21, 1956*. Archives CPC, p. 6.
5. *Canadian Tribune*, June 25, 1956.
6. Ibid., July 2, 1956.
7. Ibid., August 6, 1956.
8. "Resolution of the Quebec LPP Committee" in *National Affairs Monthly*, Vol. 13, No. 7, September 1956, p. 2.
9. *Contribution du camarade Gui Caron devant la Commission d'enquête sur les événements de 1947*, August 7, 1956.
10. *Majority Report on 1947*, 1956, Archives CPC.
11. *Canadian Tribune*, October 29, 1956.
12. N. Penner, "Correct Policy Starts with Real Life, the Experience, Opinions of People" in *National Affairs Monthly*, Vol. 13, No. 8, October 1956, p. 2.
13. R. Laxer, "New Conceptions for a New Period — a Fresh Approach to Canadian Democracy" in *National Affairs Monthly*, Vol. 13, No. 8, October 1956, p. 10.
14. Ibid., p. 18.
15. *Canadian Tribune*, October 22, 1956.
16. Ibid., October 29, 1956.
17. "Meeting of the National Committee, Labor-Progressive Party" in *National Af-*

fairs Monthly, Vol. 13, No. 9, November 1956, p. 1.

18. *Speech by Tim Buck to the National Committee Meeting: October 1956,* Archives CPC, p. 2.

19. Ibid., p. 3.

20. Ibid., p. 11.

21. Ibid., pp. 14-16.

22. "Meeting of the National Committee, Labor-Progressive Party," p. 1.

23. *Summary of Proceedings, National Committee Meeting October 28-November 9, 1956,* Archives CPC, pp. 3 and 5; T. Buck, B. Magnuson and W. Ross, telegram to L.B. Pearson, October 31, 1956, Archives CPC; T. Buck, B. Magnuson and W. Ross, telegram to Louis St. Laurent, November 2, 1956, Archives CPC; and T. Buck, B. Magnuson and W. Ross, telegram to L.B. Pearson, November 2, 1956, Archives CPC.

24. *Summary of Proceedings,* p. 15.

25. "Meeting of the National Committee, Labor-Progressive Party," p. 15.

26. *Summary of Proceedings,* p. 8.

27. Ibid., pp. 13-15; and "Meeting of the National Committee, Labor-Progressive Party," p. 2.

28. "Draft Policy Resolution" in *National Affairs Monthly,* Vol. 14, No. 1, January 1957, p. 1.

29. "Comrade Norman Penner's Amendment" in *National Affairs Monthly,* Vol. 14, No. 1, January 1957, p. 9.

30. "Letter of Comrades J.B. Salsberg, Harry Binder and Stewart Smith" in *National Affairs Monthly,* Vol. 14, No. 1, January 1957, p. 8.

31. "Statement on the Events in Hungary" in *National Affairs Monthly,* Vol. 14, No. 2, February 1957, p. 2.

32. *Summary of Proceedings, 6th National Convention, Labor-Progressive Party,* April 19-22, 1957, Archives CPC, pp. 1-6.

33. "Summary of Proceedings, Sixth National Convention of the Labor-Progressive Party" in *National Affairs Monthly,* Vol. 14, No. 6, June 1957, p. 7.

34. "Declaration of the Party" in *National Affairs Monthly,* Vol. 14, No. 6, June 1957, p. 1.

35. Quebec LPP Executive Committee, *On the Crisis in the Party,* March 14, 1957, Archives CPC; and "Summary of Proceedings of Sixth Convention," p. 7.

36. *Summary of Proceedings, 6th Convention,* pp. 15-17; and the *Canadian Tribune,* May 6, 1957.

37. *Minutes of the National Committee,* April 23-24, 1957, Archives CPC; and the *Canadian Tribune,* May 6, 1957.

38. *Resolution on LPP Policy and the Work of the Party,* NC Plenum, August 31-September 2, 1957, Archives CPC; and also "Resolutions of the National LPP Committee" in *Marxist Review,* Vol. 15, No. 7, October-November 1957, p. 22.

39. *Resolution on the Canadian Tribune,* NC plenum, August 31-September 2, 1957, Archives CPC; and also "Resolutions of the National LPP Committee," p. 26.

40. In 1961, *Marxist Review* ended publication and was replaced in the new year by *The Marxist Quarterly.* The latter was replaced in its turn by *Horizons* in 1966. As *The Marxist Quarterly* was intended "to stimulate Canadian study and research in the light of the world-outlook and method of Marx and Lenin: in economics and political science, inquiries into social conditions, culture, history, natural science, philosophy," (No. 1, Spring, 1962, p. 2), it was necessary to publish a special journal for party documents. In 1964, *Viewpoint* began the first of three years "as an information and discussion bulletin for Communist Party members" (Vol. 1, No. 1, April 1964, p. 1).

41. "Resolutions of the National LPP Committee," pp. 23-24.

42. *Resolution on Ideological Work,* NC plenum, February 15-16, 1958, Archives CPC; and also "Resolution of the National Committee, LPP" in *Marxist Review,* Vol. 16, No. 160, April-May 1958, p. 30.

11. A Period of Transition

The difficult task of overcoming the effects of the 1956 ideological crisis in the party was complicated by developments internationally. The cold war continued, providing the necessary atmosphere for U.S. brinkmanship which threatened to plunge the world into war. But neither the isolation engendered by the cold war, nor the weakened state of the party, prevented Canadian Communists from addressing themselves to the tasks brought about by international and domestic events. Due to the tense international situation, much time and energy was devoted to the struggle for world peace. The dramatic changes unfolding in the world, underscored the need for greater unity and cooperation between Communist Parties.

1. The Diefenbaker Years

Following the party's 1957 convention, the new NEC was faced with the immediate task of participating in the federal election in June. Given the grave crisis through which the party had just gone, the LPP was able to muster only 10 candidates. In this election, widespread dissatisfaction with the St. Laurent government led to the formation of a minority Tory government under John G. Diefenbaker, the first Tory Prime Minister since "Iron Heel" Bennett.

The LPP did not envisage any real change in the new government's policies as compared with the Liberals because the Conservative Party was, as always, dominated by reactionaries. As Tim Buck observed in his report to the NC meeting that September, there were signs of an approaching crisis of production in Canada. Given the fact that the Tories were in a minority position, concessions beneficial to working people could be extracted provided there was a great deal of popular pressure, especially from the organized labor movement, farmers and the CCF group in the House of Commons. But as monopoly could not tolerate such a situation, a new federal election could be expected within the year.[1] That forecast proved correct. A new election was called. Demagogically blaming the previous Liberal government for monopoly capitalism's economic ills, the Tories succeeded in obtaining the largest parliamentary majority in Canadian history in March 1958.

The Diefenbaker era was a period of economic recession. While production slumped and unemployment rose, the Tories took measures to force the working class to shoulder the main burden of the recession. The 1959 Communist Party convention observed that the "main direction of government policy has been to reinforce monopoly's stranglehold over the economy and assure it maximum profits at the expense of the welfare of the people."[2]

Canadian experience thus illustrated the tendency of monopoly to rely more heavily on the state for economic and political support. In the context of the deepening crisis of capitalism, the growth of the world socialist system and the national liberation movement narrowed the scope of imperialism's international activities. The concentration and centralization of capital continued its vigorous progress leading to the intensification of the internal contradictions of capitalism. The monopolies were unable or unwilling to invest in certain industries which required huge amounts of capital with relatively little guarantee of high profits. The state was therefore needed in order to bail out the monopolies and had to expand its ownership of certain sections of the economy.

The LPP's seventh convention in October 1959, took these new features of monopoly capitalism into account in the adoption of the new party program. This convention also featured the decision to change the party's name back to the Communist Party of Canada. The 1959 convention was accordingly renumbered, becoming the 16th convention.[3] Monopoly capital, the new program stated, subordinates the state apparatus more and more directly to its interests and control. It merges with the state and uses it to extend still further monopoly capitalist control over the country's economic life.

> This is state-monopoly capitalism. It leads to further deepening of the contradictions between the interests of the overwhelming majority of the people and those of a handful of immensely wealthy finance capitalists.[4]

Although state involvement in the capitalist economy helped to postpone crises, it could not overcome the objective laws and contradictions of capitalist development. On the contrary, in the long run, the merger of the monopolies with the state deepened capitalism's contradictions and created new ones.

As the 1959 convention noted, the monopoly policies of inflation, price-fixing and increased resistance to workers' wage demands were supported by government policies to hold the line on wages and curb trade union rights. Several provincial governments, for ex-

ample, planned to amend their labor legislation with the aim of limiting the right to strike. Monopoly's attack on the economic interests of the workers was therefore accompanied by an increasingly dangerous tendency to open reaction.

Labor would find no ally in Ottawa in defending their rights from provincial attacks. In spite of Diefenbaker's demagogic propaganda, his proposed Canadian Bill of Rights, passed in 1960, excluded the right of association, to bargain collectively and to strike from its provisions.[5] A simple act of Parliament without constitutional authority, the Bill of Rights did not affect matters within provincial jurisdiction.

Although it was the main victim, the

Left, William A. Tuomi, Alberta provincial leader of the Communist Party since 1957. Right, Mary Kardash, Winnipeg school trustee in 1961-62, 1966-69, and again elected at the end of the 1970s.

working class was not alone in suffering the consequences of the policies of state-monopoly capitalism. Militarization of the economy in favor of the big monopolies, higher monopoly profits through exorbitant prices to consumers, price-fixing and heavier taxation affected the material conditions of all the non-monopoly sections of the population.

The process of the extension of monopoly control over all sectors of the economy was also apparent in agriculture. Monopoly, with the help of the state, pursued a policy of either forcing the family farmer off the land to make way for larger, more mechanized farms, or, if he was kept on the land, virtually making him a hired hand of the monopolies who would control his funds, sources of farm supplies, his production and sales.

In short, state-monopoly capitalism was redistributing the country's wealth in favor of the monopolies. Monopoly therefore stood in opposition to the vast majority of the population and, by extending its sphere of exploitation, contributed to the growth of the objective basis of the anti-monopoly alliance. An anti-monopoly people's movement for policies in the interests of the working people and against U.S.-Canadian monopoly plans was the necessary alternative.[6]

The struggle for working class and people's unity was central to the program of the Communist Party.

It is the way in which the party serves the best interests of the working class; strengthening its ability to defend its immediate interests and steadily building the unity and political understanding which will enable the working class to curb and defeat monopoly capital. The fight to develop the united front of the working class and democratic forces is the overriding task confronting the party today.[7]

Throughout the 1950s, the LPP advocated the formation of a federated labor-farmer party as the organizational form for achieving such unity. The LPP believed that the objective conditions existed for including the labor movement, farmers' organizations, cooperatives, the CCF and the LPP in such a party. It would not have a socialist platform but rather a platform of immediate social reform. Through mass struggle around these reforms, the working class and its democratic allies would gain confidence, strength and experience. In such a process, they would realize the need to struggle for socialism.[8]

The LPP's campaign in favor of the formation of a federated labor-farmer party appeared to receive a boost at the 1958 CLC convention in Winnipeg. A resolution on political action was adopted calling on organized labor to take the initiative in bringing together all democratic forces into a broad people's movement open to all parties and individuals who accepted its program. The right-wing leadership of the CLC and the CCF, however, gave the resolution a narrow interpretation. They wanted to restrict labor political action to support for the CCF.[9]

Nevertheless, they were stimulated to move toward the formation of a new party because of pressure from the CLC and CCF rank and file to set up a political body capable of counteracting the anti-labor policies of the Tories. The right-wing leadership believed that a new party which combined the forces of the CLC and the CCF would strengthen their influence in the working class.

Although excluded from the process of founding a new labor-based party, the Communist Party continued its campaign around the theme of a federated party of the working people which would fight the monopolies. In the par-

ty's estimation, the CLC's and CCF's plans offered the two organizations a chance to break with the past. As a concrete contribution to this process, the party offered to support the new party in the next federal election in all except a few constituencies where the party was traditionally strong.[10]

The party's 17th convention welcomed the formation of the New Democratic Party (NDP) in 1961 "as a major development in the struggle to break the political domination of the parties of monopoly capital" and as "an expression of the historic need of the Canadian people for an independent mass political instrument to advance their interests."[11] But the NDP's full potential could only be realized if genuine working class policies were fought for. It could not be realized under the leadership of the dominant right wing, whose class-collaborationist policies curbed the struggles of the workers.*

Right-wing social-reformism's refusal to pursue policies leading to working class unity was further illustrated by the attitude and activities of the right-wing leadership of the labor movement. The

---

* The 17th convention also saw changes in the party leadership. At the September 1961 NC plenum, Tim Buck, then 71, had announced his intention to step down at the next convention with the recommendation that Leslie Morris be his successor as General Secretary. Leslie Morris, who had played a very prominent role in the Communist Party since the 1920s, had previously been editor of the *Canadian Tribune*, a long-time member of the party leadership and the main author of the party program. The 17th convention elected an NC of 51 members which duly elected Leslie Morris as General Secretary and Tim Buck as chairman.

formation of the CLC initially lessened internecine union competition, but in the early 1960s, raiding once again became part of the policy of a number of unions. Some CLC unions attacked not only unions outside the CLC such as the UE, Mine-Mill and the CNTU, but also their fellow affiliates inside the CLC. Some, such as the Teamsters and the Operating Engineers, were so brazen that the CLC was forced to expel them. Using jurisdictional differences in the labor movement as justification, raiding was often instigated by the head offices of the U.S.-based Internationals. This phenomenon was ultimately inspired by the cold war policies and divisive activities of the employers and the U.S. and Canadian governments.

In the Communist Party's opinion, the expulsion of the delinquent unions did not really solve the problem. What was needed was a full-scale CLC educational campaign directed toward restoring and strengthening the concept of working class and trade union unity. The CLC constitution, the party argued, ought to be amended to allow all unions without exception to join the CLC. Immediate negotiations ought to be opened with the CNTU to unite the two Quebec labor bodies (the CNTU and the QFL) with full respect for the autonomy of the CNTU in such a confederation. Unions ought to work together with the aim of creating favorable conditions for eventual mergers or federations in each industry. Only then could the labor movement end raiding, stop its general retreat, and create the conditions for great advances.[12]

The times demanded progress in the struggles of the working class. The 17th convention of the party characterized this particular period in Canada's history as a time when Canada was undergoing a crisis of national policy which permeated not only the economy but all aspects of Canadian life, a crisis aggravated by U.S. domination over Canada's economic, political, military and cultural life.[13]

Communists had been among the first Canadians to warn of the dangers of increasing U.S. domination. In this period, the party's fight to stop the sell-out of Canada's resources could be seen in its energetic campaign around the Columbia River treaty. The Columbia River was one of the largest untapped hyrdo-electric sources in the Americas at that time. The availability of cheap, abundant energy was a decisive consideration in locating new industry. Throughout the 1950s, the party had fought for the use of the Columbia River in the development of an east-west power grid as the basis for large-scale industrialization. Simultaneously, the party fought against plans to export the Columbia's power to feed U.S. industry.

In 1952, British Columbia Premier W.A.C. Bennett had tried to turn over the Columbia to the U.S. Kaiser Company for one million dollars. The Communist Party immediately took up the campaign to save the Columbia for Canada. From the time that the Vancouver *Daily Province* "blazoned Premier Bennett's charge that 'Only the Communists Oppose Columbia Plan' in an eight-column banner across its front page, popular opposition to the massive giveaway rose and broadened significantly."[14] Nine years later, plans for the sell-out climaxed in the Columbia

The car cavalcade protesting the Columbia River treaty reaches the banks of the Columbia River.

River treaty. Signed by the Diefenbaker and U.S. governments in January 1961, the treaty symbolized the policy of continentalism, of integration with the United States at the expense of Canadian industrial development.

What's happening goes far beyond the Columbia River. The future of Canada itself is on the scales. Shall we grow industrially or become a mere supplier of raw materials and resources to be processed into goods by the U.S. while our living standards decline? This is the choice facing all Canadians today.[15]

From the signing of the treaty to its final passage in Parliament in 1964, the Communist Party conducted a country-wide campaign against its ratification and for the alternative McNaughton plan designed to develop the Columbia River for Canada. Through pamphlets, leaflets, the party's press and a dramatic 1,000-mile car cavalcade through the B.C. interior to the Columbia River itself, Communists advanced a program for Canada's industrial expansion and exposed U.S. economic domination.

Consistent with its sell-out of the economy to U.S. imperialism, the Diefenbaker government subordinated Canada's interests to U.S. foreign policy objectives. Even before they had won their overwhelming majority in Parliament, the Tories finalized agreements with the United States, prepared by their Liberal predecessors, for the creation of the North American Air Defense Command (NORAD). The agreement provided for the integration of the Royal Canadian Air Force into a continental air defense system. Under direct U.S. command, NORAD controlled the aircraft warning system of both countries and would be responsible for the deployment of nuclear missiles.

Canadian Communists realized that NORAD, like NATO, undermined rather than enhanced Canada's "national security" and independence because it made Canada a staging ground for U.S. imperialism's aggressive anti-Soviet plans. By putting Canada at the disposal of the Pentagon, the Diefenbaker government was turning Canada into a likely battleground in the event of nuclear war between the USSR and the USA. Hence the demand of the party's 16th convention for Canada's withdrawal from both NATO and NORAD.

The 16th convention placed a great deal of emphasis on the problem of achieving world peace and how Canada could make a positive contribution to it. The delegates adopted a political resolution calling for decisive action to compel imperialist governments to accept peaceful coexistence and stop the fomentation of war. The convention gave its fullest support to the efforts of the Soviet Union to bring about general and complete disarmament and an end to tests of nuclear bombs. Canada, the political resolution explained, could help strengthen world peace by pursuing an independent foreign policy (an idea first formulated in this way in the 1954 LPP program) including a ban on the construction of missile launching sites on Canadian soil, a vast reduction in military expenditures and the transfer of these funds to peaceful development. An independent Canadian foreign policy would make it possible for Canada to advance the cause of world peace while making substantial progress toward the achievement of genuine Canadian in-

dependence. These concepts and policies were incorporated in the new party program adopted by the convention and have been consistently upheld, with minor amendments, ever since.[16]

A particular focus of the fight for peace was the nuclear missiles the U.S. planned to place in Canada within the NORAD framework. In 1959 and 1960, the Communist Party organized very successful demonstrations and car cavalcades against the Bomarc missile sites at North Bay, Ontario and Macassa, Quebec. By the beginning of the 1960s, the campaign for a nuclear-free Canada had spread far beyond the ranks of the Communist Party. By October 1961, the Canadian government had received 10,000 letters opposing nuclear weapons for Canada. A petition on the same question, initiated by the Canadian Committee for Control of Radiation Hazards, had received the support of over 142,000 signers.[17]

Against this background of growing public pressure, NORAD and the question of nuclear missiles also became a source of conflict between the ruling classes of Canada and the United States. The Canadian government had planned, as early as 1951, to build its own made-in-Canada jet fighter, the Avro Arrow. However, the U.S. administration strenuously objected and brought heavy pressure to bear on the Diefenbaker government to cancel the Avro Arrow in favor of the U.S.-built Bomarc nuclear missile. While the USA finally forced the cancellation of the Avro Arrow in 1959, this was not achieved without antagonizing sections of the Canadian monopoly bourgeoisie, including a number of cabinet ministers. They were

Demonstration against nuclear weapons at the missile base in Comox, B.C. Nigel Morgan, B.C. provincial leader of the party, is on the right.

unhappy with the fact that a burgeoning Canadian industry was sacrificed to U.S. interests, an industry which would have reaped considerable profits from the NORAD alliance. While the Tory government agreed to install Bomarc missiles on Canadian soil, it refused to allow them to be equipped with nuclear warheads. Resentful of U.S. imperialism's arrogant encroachment on the sovereign rights of the Canadian government over its own territory, the "nationalistic" cabinet ministers threatened to split the government if it capitulated entirely to U.S. imperialism's demands. As the Bomarc missiles could carry only nuclear warheads, the government's decision made the Bomarc missile program functionally useless, a decision that infuriated Washington.

U.S. pressure caused the emergence and aggravation of contradictions between sections of the Canadian bourgeoisie, notably between "national" bourgeois interests which found expression in Diefenbaker and his group in the Conservative Party, and the Liberal Party's strategy of fitting Canadian bourgeois interests into U.S. demands. Once raised publicly between the capitalist parties and their leaders after U.S. government publicity, the nuclear arms dispute could no longer be confined to the backrooms of the Liberal and Conservative Parties.[18] A vote was forced in Parliament, resulting in the defeat of Diefenbaker's position. A general election was called.

The April 1963 federal election was largely fought on the issue of nuclear missiles for Canada and Canadian-U.S. relations. It was marked by direct U.S. interference in Canadian internal affairs in support of the Liberals. The Communist Party conducted a vigorous campaign showing that both world peace and Canadian independence were threatened. L.B. Pearson the spokesman for nuclear arms, won the election but was denied the majority so frantically sought by the pro-U.S. circles of the Canadian ruling class. Although the majority of voters cast their ballots for candidates opposed to nuclear arms, the new Liberal government kept its promise to U.S. imperialism. Nuclear warheads arrived in Canada in early 1964.

The contradictions within the Canadian monopoly bourgeoisie revealed in the election, reflected in part contradictions between Canadian and U.S. imperialism. They arose not from any challenge to basic capitalist objectives but rather from opposing methods of how to best protect Canadian capitalist interests in the conditions of the cold war and the growing isolation of U.S. imperialism.

The fact that the administration of President John F. Kennedy did not hide its glee when Diefenbaker was defeated, was not due solely to the nuclear arms issue. Relations between the two governments had soured over a number of questions. Despite U.S. pressure, the Diefenbaker government had refused to join the Organization of American States, an instrument of U.S. domination of the economies and politics of Latin America. Added to this, the Diefenbaker government had maintained diplomatic and trade relations with socialist Cuba in defiance of the U.S. demand for a total boycott. The U.S. had also attempted to prevent delivery of Canadian wheat to China.

The Communist Party opposed any kind of encroachment on Canada's sovereignty and independence and linked the struggle for peace and independence to the struggle against U.S. and Canadian monopoly capital. However, prior to this period, the party had tended to underestimate the existence of contradictions between Canadian and U.S. imperialism. Relations between these two imperialist countries were in fact both collaborative and competitive. As the collaborative side of this contradiction was overwhelmingly dominant in the late 1940s and throughout the 1950s, it was not so easy to discern that a shift to the competitive side was occurring.

The policy resolution of the 17th convention determined that the main enemy of the Canadian people was the U.S.-Canadian monopoly class which ruled Canada in the interests of U.S. imperialism. Thus the main thrust of the Canadian people's struggle was against U.S. domination and for Canadian independence. This struggle was termed "the Canadian expression of, and contribution to, the world-wide anti-imperialist struggle for national independence, peace and democracy."[19] Correction of this one-sided characterization was made at the 18th convention in 1964. As Leslie Morris pointed out in his keynote address:

Canadian monopoly capitalism cannot be considered to be only a junior partner of U.S. monopoly capitalism, not only intertwined with U.S. monopoly, not just an appendage of U.S. capitalism, but possesses its own special class interests (as seen in the trade with the socialist countries), its own ambitions (as seen in its growing conflict over the inequality of trade between the U.S. and Canada) and its own independent policies.[20]

2. New Stage in the World Communist Movement

The fact that opposition to U.S. imperialism's manoeuvres was developing even within the ranks of the bourgeoisie was indicative of the significant changes which had occurred in the post-war period. Following World War II, imperialism, dominated by the USA, appeared in many ways to have consolidated its positions. The economic and military might of U.S. imperialism led it to strive for world hegemony. Imperialist ideology gained considerable ground among large sections of working people in the capitalist countries and even in some Communist Parties. This situation underscored the urgency of greater unity and cooperation among Communist Parties.

In the immediate post-war period, the world communist movement set up an informal structure for the exchange of views and information in the form of the Communist Information Bureau or Cominform (the Comintern had been dissolved in 1943). Yet this was not enough. In the summer of 1957, the LPP's NC plenum expressed the opinion that ties could best be improved by the continued exchange of official party delegations in order to discuss matters of mutual interest, by the publication of materials carried in the fraternal press and by the foundation of an international communist journal.[21]

The celebration of the 40th anniversary of the Russian Revolution brought the leaders of the international communist movement to the Soviet capital. The occasion was used to hold two important multilateral conferences: the first, consisting of representatives of 12 of the 13 socialist countries (the exception was Yugoslavia); and the second, composed of representatives of 64 Communist and Workers' Parties from all parts of the world.

The continuing cold war could not mask the great advances made by socialism. World events were no longer determined primarily by the contradictions between imperialist states, but by the competition between the two world systems, socialism and capitalism. The growing economic strength and political influence of socialism, the upsurge of the national liberation movement and the growth of the labor movement in the capitalist countries were features of the new period. The times were further characterized by the widening front of opposition to war, by the crisis of the colonial system and by the marked relative decline of imperialist power.

The first conference adopted a declaration incorporating the analysis of these new features of the world situation, which was summarized in the statement that "the main content of our epoch is the transition from capitalism to socialism. ... In our epoch, world development is determined by the course and results of the competition between the diametrically opposed social systems."[22] On the basis of this characterization, the declaration deepened the analysis of the new possibilities in the world previously examined by the 20th congress of the CPSU. The 12 parties upheld the thesis that more favorable conditions for the victory of socialism created by the decisive shift in the international balance of forces, resulted in the possibility —

Tom McEwen, A.A. MacLeod and Leslie Morris arrive in Peking to attend the eighth congress of the Communist Party of China in September 1956.

given certain conditions — that the working class might achieve state power in some countries without civil war. The declaration also highlighted the new proposition that war was no longer inevitable, that concerted action of the forces opposed to war could prevent such a calamity. The conference declared that the Leninist principle of peaceful coexistence of the two social systems was the sound basis of the foreign policy of the socialist countries.

The second conference concentrated mainly on the question of world peace, the unity and solidarity of the socialist countries and the world communist movement. The 64 parties present adopted the *Manifesto on Peace*. Declar-

ing that world war was not inevitable, the manifesto appealed for joint action of all people of good will, irrespective of their political and religious convictions, to support the program for peace and peaceful coexistence and actively struggle for the prevention of war.

The February 1958 NC plenum welcomed the positions taken by the LPP delegates at the conference and expressed its full agreement with both the declaration and the manifesto.[23] The new theses advanced at the two conferences were subsequently embodied in the party program adopted by the 16th convention.

The conference of the 64 Communist and Workers' Parties also reached a con-

Leslie Morris speaking to the eighth congress of the Popular Socialist Party of Cuba in August 1960.

sensus on the need to found an international communist journal as a permanent means of exchanging the views and experiences of the fraternal parties. In March 1958, 12 parties including the LPP, met in Prague, Czechoslovakia, to establish *World Marxist Review (Problems of Peace and Socialism)* which began publication in September under the joint editorship of the participating parties. The journal provided a forum for the analysis of new problems and further elaboration of Marxist-Leninist theory.

In confirmation of the conclusions drawn at the 1957 conferences, the face of the world continued to change rapidly in the late 1950s and early 1960s. Despite imperialist efforts to turn back the clock of history, the economic and military might of the world socialist system headed by the Soviet Union continued to grow. This was reflected, for example, in the victory of the revolutionary forces in Cuba under the leadership of Fidel Castro in January 1959. On U.S. imperialism's doorstep, Cuba became the first country in the western hemisphere to take the road of socialism.

Change was also expressed in the achievement of political independence by a large number of colonial territories, especially in Africa. Some of these former colonies took the non-capitalist path of development despite fierce resistance from the imperialist powers.

Yet other developments threatened peace and social advance. The congress of the Romanian Workers' Party in Bucharest in July 1960, utilized by the delegations of the parties from the socialist countries "to exchange opin-ions on pressing questions of the current international situation and the conclusions that stem therefrom," took place in a disturbing context.[24] Tension had increased in the world due to an accelerated arms race, the capture of a U.S. reconnaissance plane over Soviet air space, the U.S. boycott of revolutionary Cuba, the French imperialist war of aggression in Algeria, and preparations for military intervention in the newly independent Belgian Congo (now Zaire) where, half a year later, the Congolese progressive forces were crushed, Patrice Lumumba murdered and a pro-Western dictator was installed. The Bucharest communiqué, which received the unqualified support of the LPP's NC, reiterated the socialist countries' adherence to the principles outlined in the declaration and the manifesto of 1957.[25]

A conference of all Communist and Workers' Parties was also needed, to generalize the experiences of the fraternal parties and characterize the present historical stage of the world revolutionary process. In November 1960, the most representative gathering of Communists to that time, took place in Moscow to discuss the world situation. The unity of views reached in the 1957 conference was maintained. The 81 fraternal parties present, unanimously adopted a statement which drew the conclusion that "a new stage has begun in the development of the general crisis of capitalism."[26] This crisis was entering its third stage and was characterized by the fact that the world socialist system and all anti-imperialist forces were determining the main content, trend and features of historical development. The balance of world forces was shifting in favor of world socialism, the international working class movement and the national liberation movement. While socialism was scoring major economic, social and scientific successes, the world capitalist system was displaying signs of growing economic instability. Under the impact of the national liberation movement, the collapse of the colonial system was imminent.

On the question of world peace, the most burning problem facing the world, the meeting noted that, although imperialism, especially U.S. imperialism, had lost none of its aggressiveness, world war could be prevented by the joint efforts of all countries and forces opposed to war.

The NC plenum of the Communist Party of Canada in February 1961, wholeheartedly approved its delegation's contribution to the conference and with equal enthusiasm endorsed the conference statement and its Appeal to the Peoples of the World for peace and disarmament.[27]

The Communist Party of Canada took unequivocal positions on the international issues of the day. One hotbed of world tension was the divided city of Berlin. For U.S. imperialism and German revanchism, West Berlin was the staging point for keeping the so-called "problem of Germany" alive. They retained ambitions of reuniting Germany on the basis of its pre-war frontiers, that is, to seize, however possible, the entire GDR and large areas of Poland for the re-establishment of a greater, armed imperialist Germany. This amounted to rejection of the results of the Second World War which had led to the restoration of certain lands to Poland and the foundation of a socialist state on German soil.

The Soviet Union had repeatedly made constructive proposals to solve the German problem. These included recognition of two German states with differing social systems, the establishment of a nuclear-free demilitarized zone in central Europe and the normalization of the situation in occupied West Berlin. However, in the summer of 1961, the United States and other NATO powers chose to step up their subversive activities against the GDR by resorting to economic sabotage, thereby compelling the GDR to close its borders with West Berlin. Frustrated that their plans had been thwarted, the NATO powers made preparations for military action against

Communists demonstrate on Parliament Hill against imperialist provocation over West Berlin and for disarmament, October 1961.

the GDR. Tension escalated. World War III loomed on the horizon. When the USSR made clear its determination to help the GDR preserve its sovereignty and territorial integrity, the NATO powers were forced to back down. Praising the USSR and GDR for successfully upholding the cause of world peace, the September 1961 NC plenum called for taking up the struggle to prevent war over Berlin and win general and complete disarmament.[28]

Another potential source for a world conflagration was the U.S. attitude toward revolutionary Cuba. Soon after the revolution, Cuba began to take a democratic and anti-imperialist course. This development greatly angered U.S. imperialism which for so long had dominated the island.

The 16th party convention expressed its solidarity with the Cuban revolution and called for the mobilization of wide support for the demand that the USA desist from its threatened intervention in Cuba's internal affairs. When the USA imposed its economic blockade on Cuba in the summer of 1960, the Communist Party demanded that Canada ship Canadian oil to Cuba as "an act of practical solidarity with the Cuban people."[29]

In April 1961, repeated U.S. threats of intervention in Cuba became a reality. Supported by the CIA, Cuban counter-revolutionary forces landed at the Bay of Pigs. They were quickly defeated by the people and armed forces of Cuba. The NEC of the Communist Party of Canada added its voice to those around the world who condemned the U.S. adventure.[30]

Cuba, with the fraternal aid of the Soviet Union and the other socialist countries, continued to forge ahead. The U.S.-inspired economic boycott could not prevent Cuba's progress. Determined to defeat the Cuban revolution, the U.S. administration attempted to impose a military blockade of the island in October 1962. The U.S. navy was ordered to sink the ships of any country that disobeyed U.S. orders. Given the

Toronto YCL members protest at the U.S. consulate against interference in Laos, 1961.

lifeline provided by the goods and materials brought by Soviet ships, the U.S. action amounted to an act of war. However, due to the initiative of the Soviet government, nuclear war was averted. It was the USA which backed down. Kennedy was compelled to make an agreement with the USSR in which it pledged not to invade Cuba and to end its military blockade in exchange for the removal of Soviet missiles which had been installed to help Cuba defend itself.

The Cuban crisis brought the differences which the Maoist leadership of the Communist Party of China had with the world communist movement into the open. The Maoists were highly criti-

cal of the result because, in their view, the USSR should have pursued a policy of no compromise with U.S. imperialism. Given the very tense atmosphere of the confrontation between the USA and the USSR, to follow the Maoist line would have led to nuclear war. The PRC's leadership characterized all those who sought peace through negotiations as "modern revisionists." In its letter to the membership dated September 17, 1962, the NEC of the Communist Party of Canada pointed out that the Cuban crisis was resolved through a compromise which avoided nuclear war while compelling U.S. imperialism to promise not to intervene militarily against socialist Cuba. Compromise and flexibility in tactics in no way led to compromise in principles, in this case the preservation of socialism in Cuba which U.S. imperialism had sought so actively to destroy.

The Maoist attitude toward the Cuban crisis reflected the emergence of a dangerous trend. The victory of the Chinese revolution in 1949 had been a great event in the development of the world revolutionary process — the most populous country in the world had gone over to socialism. Throughout the 1950s, the LPP had shown great respect and admiration for the Communist Party and people of China. The LPP was at the forefront in the demand for recognition of the PRC by the Canadian government, but that would not come until 1970. By the beginning of the 1960s, however, Maoist policies were clearly at variance with those of the world communist movement.

3. Maoism — Its Break with Socialism

Even though the statement of the 1960 conference of Communist and Workers' Parties was unanimously adopted, discussions during the conference revealed the existence of a "leftist" and nationalist deviation. At that meeting, the Albanian Party of Labor bitterly attacked the line of the 20th congress of the CPSU and the propositions of the 1957 declaration.[31] Despite Soviet assurances to the contrary, the Albanian party was convinced that the CPSU intended to achieve a rapprochement with the League of Yugoslav Communists at Albania's expense. In 1961, Albania broke party relations with members of the international communist movement and state relations with the socialist countries, with the notable exception of China.

The Communist Party of China joined the Albanian party in the attack on the CPSU and the general line of the communist movement. According to the 1960 statement, the supreme task of the Communist and Workers' Parties was the struggle for peace and peaceful coexistence, the struggle to avert nuclear war. Contrary to this view, the Communist Party of China under the leadership of Mao Zedong claimed that as imperialism had not changed its bestial nature and as the "east wind now prevails against the west wind," peaceful coexistence would amount to accomodation with imperialism and the renunciation of the class struggle. In its view, the dangers and consequences of nuclear war were exaggerated. Given this incorrect estimation of the situation in the world, Mao and the leadership of the Communist Party of China drew a whole series of tactical conclusions such as the primacy of the national liberation movement in the world revolutionary process and the tendency to dismiss the working class in imperialist countries. The majority at the conference rejected these unscientific and dangerous opinions.[32]

The Communist Party of Canada added its voice to those who opposed the Maoist theses on the world situation. In his report to the 17th convention, Tim Buck denied that peaceful coexistence meant the renunciation or the relaxation of the class struggle. Quite to the contrary, peaceful coexistence could not eliminate the class struggle, which arises out of the operation of the objec-

Leslie Morris and William Kashtan visit the Dr. Norman Bethune Peace Hospital between sessions of their talks with representatives of the Communist Party of China.

ARCHIVES CPC/PAC

tive internal laws of capitalist development. Placing the struggle for peace and peaceful coexistence as the crucial task of the international communist movement does not in any way imply minimizing the struggle for socialism. Peaceful coexistence actually facilitates the struggle for socialism.[33]

The differences which the Maoist leadership of the Communist Party of China had with the general line of the world communist movement sharpened during 1961 and 1962 until, finally, in late 1962, they broke out into the open over the Cuban crisis and China's border war with India. While most Communist Parties agreed with the PRC that some revision of the border between China and India might be warranted, to go to war was no way of settling the problem. A peaceful negotiated settlement would have been more consistent with the interests of world peace.

Warning that a split in the international communist movement would be disastrous for working people and for the cause of peace, the NEC of the Communist Party of Canada, in its September 1962 letter, called on the Communist Party of China to re-establish its unity with the world communist movement. Such unity "would accelerate the victory of peace and the establishment of the conditions of peaceful coexistence."[34] Instead, the Maoists stepped up their attacks on the CPSU and the world communist movement. Objectively, the Maoist Chinese leadership was aligning itself with the most reactionary cold war elements in the USA and NATO who opposed peaceful coexistence and wanted to keep the world on the brink of nuclear war.

Despite its differences with the Communist Party of China, the Communist Party of Canada actively sought to heal the growing split within the international communist movement. At the February 1963 NC plenum, a resolution was adopted calling for the cessation of public polemics among the fraternal parties and the convening of a conference of parties of socialist countries followed by a world conference of Communist and Workers' Parties.[35]

In the meantime, the NEC arranged to have bilateral talks with both the Soviet and Chinese parties. In April 1963, a delegation consisting of Leslie Morris and William Kashtan set out for Peking by way of Moscow. In Moscow, the two Canadian Communist leaders held some preliminary discussions with the representatives of the Central Committee of the CPSU. The Soviets expressed full agreement with the objectives of the Canadian delegation. In Peking, the two Canadians met with four members of the Central Committee of the Communist Party of China, including its General Secretary Deng Xiaoping.[36]

Much of the discussion between the two sides in the first two sessions revolved around the place of Yugoslavia in the world communist movement. The League of Yugoslav Communists had broken party relations with the CPSU in 1948 and as recently as the 1960 conference had been accused of revisionism and betrayal of Marxism-Leninism.[37] The Chinese CC representatives interpreted the conference statement to mean that there would be no relations with Yugoslavia. To improve relations with Yugoslavia would amount to nestling up with revisionism. The Canadian Communists argued that the statement did not negate the fact that socialist gains had been won in Yugoslavia, nor

did it preclude efforts to bring Yugoslavia closer to the world socialist system. In terms of the ownership of the means of production, the two Canadians noted, Yugoslavia was still a socialist country, a characterization with which the Maoists had strongly disagreed from as far back as the 1960 conference.

The Chinese party representatives also vigorously objected to the characterization of the Albanian Party of Labor as dogmatic and nationalistic. They implied that the CPSU's attitude toward the Albanian and Yugoslav parties was indicative of alleged revisionist tendencies of the CPSU and that these tendencies existed in other fraternal parties as well. But, as William Kashtan reported to the NC on his return, it was the Communist Party of China that was actually moving away from the 1960 statement while striving to take over the leadership of the communist movement.[38]

The discussion in the next session dealt with a whole series of questions of vital concern to the world revolutionary forces. The Chinese representatives denied that a socialist revolution could be achieved by any other means than armed struggle. The Canadian CC representatives noted that while a socialist revolution may result in armed struggle because of the violent activities of the deposed ruling class, it would be wrong to deny or exclude the possibility of a relatively peaceful transition to socialism. In fact, in some countries, a relatively peaceful transition to socialism was a real possibility. Such was the case in Canada, given its specific historical conditions.

The Maoists further argued that the

main contradiction in the world was between imperialism and the so-called third world. This position placed the question of the struggle for world peace on a secondary level. As well, it completely ignored the role in the world revolutionary process of the socialist countries and of the working class movement in the advanced capitalist countries.[39]

It was becoming increasingly obvious that the line of the Maoist-led Chinese party was at variance with the strategy and tactics of the great majority of the fraternal parties. On their way back from Peking, Leslie Morris and William Kashtan informed the leadership of the CPSU of the character and results of their talks with the representatives of the CC of the Communist Party of China. While it was encouraging that the Chinese party appeared to be willing to hold talks with the CPSU, the fact remained that very wide differences continued to exist.

With respect to these differences, the NC of the Communist Party of Canada, in a statement adopted by its May 1963 plenum, declared that the positions of the CPSU were consistent with the 1957 declaration, the 1960 statement and the principles of Marxism-Leninism. It was also clear that the Communist Party of China stood in opposition to the general line of the international communist movement.[40]

The talks between the Soviet and Chinese parties confirmed the "leftist" course of the Maoist leadership. The Maoists were not at all interested in genuinely resolving their differences with the CPSU. They had decided to embark on the road of nationalism, expansionism, adventurism and the splitting of the world revolutionary forces. The Maoists worked hard in their drive to achieve hegemony over the Communist and Workers' Parties of other countries. In some cases such as Albania and Indonesia, they succeeded and in other cases they provoked damaging splits.

With regard to the Communist Party of Canada, the Maoist Chinese leadership failed to achieve either aim, although Maoism did influence some individuals in the party. As in other countries where they were unable to effect a split, the Chinese Maoists sponsored the formation of ultra-left violence-prone splinter groupings based on petty-bourgeois fringe elements mainly in the universities. In China, Maoist policies brought great harm to the construction of socialism and led the PRC closer and closer to the imperialist camp in international affairs, thus undermining possibilities of ensuring peace in the world.

Despite this dangerous development, encouraging steps toward world peace were made.

So close did the world approach the brink of nuclear annihilation during the Cuban crisis that even the USA was forced to see the disastrous consequences of its policy of direct military confrontation with the USSR. U.S. imperialism realized that its own survival was also at stake. On August 5, 1963, the Soviet Union, the United States and Great Britain signed a nuclear test ban treaty prohibiting all but underground nuclear tests.[41] It was a major victory for world peace and the first concrete step toward détente and a thaw in the cold war. This was not to say that imperialism abandoned either its goals or its aggressiveness. Far from it. In the months that followed, U.S. imperialism actually stepped up its efforts to roll back the tide of history.

1. "Meeting of the National Committee, Labor-Progressive Party" in *National Affairs Monthly*, Vol. 13, No. 9, November 1956, p. 15.
2. *Summary of proceedings, National Committee Meeting October 28-November 9, 1956*, Archives CPC, p. 8.
3. "Resolutions" of the 16th convention in *Marxist Review*, Vol. 18, No. 170, December 1959, pp. 31-32.
4. *The Road to Socialism in Canada* (Toronto, 1960), p. 6.
5. "The Struggle for Total Disarmament, Peace and Independence" in *Marxist Review*, Vol. 18, No. 170, December 1959, p. 22.
6. *Documents of the 17th National Convention, January 19-21, 1962* (Toronto, 1962), p. 18.
7. "The Struggle for Total Disarmament, Peace and Independence," p. 23.
8. L.T. Morris, *Labor-Farmer Political Action* (Toronto, 1959), p. 8.
9. "The Struggle for Total Disarmament, Peace and Independence," p. 23.
10. L.T. Morris, *Communists and the New Party* (Toronto, 1961), pp. 5 and 21.
11. *17th Convention*, p. 19.
12. W. Kashtan, *Stop Union Raiding* (Toronto, 1962), pp. 27-28.
13. *17th Convention*, p. 17.
14. *Canadian Tribune*, July 20, 1964.
15. B. Magnuson, *Save Millions of Jobs: Stop the U.S. Power Grab* (Toronto, 1963), p. 4.
16. "The Struggle for Total Disarmament, Peace and Independence," pp. 16-17; and *Road to Socialism* (1960), pp. 14-15.
17. *Canadian Tribune*, October 16, 1961.
18. L.T. Morris, *Look on Canada, Now* (Toronto, 1970), pp. 175-176.
19. *17th Convention*, p. 15.
20. L.T. Morris, *Challenge of the '60s* (Toronto, 1964), p. 10.
21. "Resolutions of the National LPP Committee" in *Marxist Review*, Vol. 15, No. 7, October-November 1957, p. 29.
22. "The 12-Party Declaration" in *Marxist Review*, Vol. 17, No. 174, July-August 1960, p. 62.
23. *Canadian Tribune*, December 9, 1957; and "Resolutions of the National Committee, LPP" in *Marxist Review*, Vol. 16, No. 160, April-May 1958, pp. 32-33.
24. *Canadian Tribune*, July 11, 1960.
25. "Communist Party National Committee Meeting, October 1960" in *Marxist Review*, Vol. 17, No. 176, November-December 1960, p. 30.
26. *Statement of the Meeting of 81 Communist and Workers' Parties* (Toronto, 1960), p. 6.
27. "Communist Party Policy" in *Marxist Review*, Vol. 18, No. 178, March-April 1961, pp. 12-13.
28. *Unite to Prevent War over Berlin*, National Committee plenum of September 8-10, 1961, Archives CPC.
29. *Canadian Tribune*, July 11, 1960.
30. Ibid., April 24, 1961.
31. Ibid., January 21, 1963.
32. Ibid., December 24, 1962.
33. *17th Convention*, p. 8.
34. *Canadian Tribune*, December 24, 1962.
35. *Resolution Adopted by the National Committee Meeting*, February 16-17, 1963, Archives CPC.
36. W. Kashtan, *Report of Delegation to the Communist Party of China and to the Communist Party of the Soviet Union*, May 1963, Archives CPC, pp. 2-3.
37. *Statement of the 81 Communist Parties*, p. 29.
38. Kashtan, *Report of Delegation*, pp. 9-13.
39. Ibid., pp. 16-20.
40. *Statement on the Situation in the World Communist Movement*, May 1963, Archives CPC.
41. *Canadian Tribune*, August 12, 1963.

12. The Challenge of the Sixties

In April 1961, Soviet cosmonaut Yuri Gagarin became the first person to travel in space. The USSR thus became the first country to develop a technology capable of breaking through man's earth-bound limitations. In many ways, Gagarin's flight symbolized new triumphs of socialism.

As man entered the space age, the world was examined with a new perspective. Technological progress made the Earth seem smaller as it brought events thousands of miles distant to Canada's television screens. International developments were increasingly felt directly, immediately. Many did not like what they saw — poverty, exploitation and war. The U.S. civil rights movement, the somewhat romantic but nevertheless powerful response to the Cuban revolution and the growing anger at the U.S. role in Vietnam combined to produce an unprecedented radicalization throughout North America, particularly among the youth. The mid to late 1960s was a period of the growing questioning of capitalism and its values, increasing opposition to the status quo, and search for change. Communists, after the relatively solitary demonstrations of the cold war years, were now in the midst of an extraordinary upsurge of protest against U.S. imperialism.

1. From Selma to Saigon

The inhumane brutality of U.S. policies provoked indignation among Canadians and people throughout the world. People were outraged by the racism which was running rampant in the United States, particularly in the South.

A wave of sit-ins in the USA greeted the beginning of the 1960s and was directed toward breaking segregationist laws and practices. Solidarity actions in Canada with the U.S. civil rights movement attracted thousands of supporters. By the mid-1960s, Canadians had participated in sit-ins, marches, fund-raising concerts, and picket-lines in support of the struggles of Black Americans for their human and democratic rights.

While the U.S. government resisted democratic changes in its own country, it attacked democratic and liberation movements in other countries. In the spring of 1964, U.S. imperialism, with the complicity of Canadian monopoly capital, engineered a fascist coup in Brazil. The U.S. government backed Turkish and British intrigues in Cyprus, a country which had great strategic value for imperialism as a springboard of subversion in the Middle East. In 1965, the United States invaded the Dominican Republic on the grounds that the new, democratically-elected government of Juan Bosch, a social-democrat, was "communist dominated." In Indonesia, the U.S. administration of President L.B. Johnson gave its support to the bloody military coup which carried out reprisals against the progressive forces, slaughtering 500,000 Indonesian patriots. In Europe, U.S. imperialism encouraged West German militarism. In 1967, the CIA and the Pentagon backed a fascist coup in Greece. Throughout the 1960s (and for that matter the 1970s), the USA gave covert and sometimes open assistance to the white supremacists of Rhodesia (now independent Zimbabwe) and the apartheid regime of South Africa.

Demonstration in support of civil rights in the United States, Montreal, March 1965.

In Canada, the Communist Party and other democratic organizations kept up a consistent barrage of protest against U.S. imperialist actions around the world. The monopoly bourgeois media greeted each new act of aggression with propaganda justifying "the defense of freedom." The *Canadian Tribune* took on the enormous task of exposing this propaganda.

The most critical center of world tension was in Vietnam, where U.S. imperialist policy sharpened the danger of a world war. The defeat of French imperialism in 1954 by the Vietnamese liberation forces had struck a major blow against world imperialism. It not only consolidated the triumph of the socialist revolution in the northern half of the country but also demonstrated that the peoples of the oppressed countries could, with the active assistance of the world socialist system headed by the Soviet Union, achieve their political and economic independence even in the face of direct imperialist military intervention. Along with the Cuban revolution of 1959, Vietnam's victory over France was strong evidence that a significant shift was taking place in the balance of world forces in favor of the revolutionary process.

The desire to "contain communist expansionism" and secure the rich re-

Demonstrators in Vancouver protesting the U.S. invasion of the Dominican Republic in May 1965.

sources of Indochina induced U.S. imperialism to fill the political and military vacuum left by France's departure from Southeast Asia. U.S. imperialism wanted to prevent the liberation of Vietnam from spreading to the southern half of the country and thus took the fateful decision to prop up the faltering Saigon regime. Economic and military aid extended to the Saigon regime throughout the last half of the 1950s was complemented by direct U.S. military involvement. The number of U.S. military "advisers" rose from about 2,000 in December 1961, to over 15,000 by the end of 1963.

By 1964, the National Liberation Front of Vietnam had made so much progress that the USA decided to substantially increase its military commitment in the south. In March of that year, the Johnson administration hinted that it might escalate the war by bombing Hanoi and invading northern Vietnam. The *Canadian Tribune* warned that such actions would result in the involvement of the USSR and China in the conflict and would greatly increase the danger of a nuclear war.[1]

In August, the Pentagon's threats became a reality when it staged the Gulf of Tonkin incident. Inventing a North Vietnamese attack on U.S. naval forces off the coast of northern Vietnam, the USA "retaliated" by attacking North Vietnamese ships and ports

The Communist Party of Canada warned of the dangers of escalating the conflict and demanded the withdrawal of U.S. military forces from Vietnam.

April 1965 demonstration in Ottawa against the U.S. bombing of North Vietnam.

Those forces then numbered 25,000.[2]

Initially in Canada, there was considerable confusion about what was actually happening in Vietnam and who the real aggressor was. The Communist Party was the only political party which understood the truth and significance of U.S. involvement in Vietnam. In a wire to Prime Minister L.B. Pearson, William Kashtan, who had been elected General Secretary at the NC's January 1965 plenum,* accused the United States of committing a flagrant act of calculated aggression against North Vietnam. He called on the Canadian government, which as usual had been echoing U.S. policies, to demand the reconvening of the Geneva conference (which had ended French colonialism in Southeast Asia) in order to indict U.S. aggression and arrive at a settlement in the interests of the peoples of Southeast Asia and world peace. As he pointed out, there was a real danger of the war spreading throughout Southeast Asia and developing into a world war.[3]

Canadian Communists willingly assumed the enormous task of bringing the truth about the conflict in Vietnam to the working class movement and democratic forces. At first, the party's support for the struggles of the Vietnamese people was met with derision and hostility. In attempting to expose the real role of U.S. imperialism in Vietnam, Communists were frequently subjected to verbal and sometimes physical abuse. But as the war dragged on and as the barbarism of the U.S. military became

---

*Leslie Morris had died in office in 1964.

Tim Buck meets Ho Chi Minh in Hanoi, December 1965.

known in the USA and throughout the world, Canadians gradually became conscious of the fact that the USA and not North Vietnam was the aggressor.

Realizing that U.S. public opinion strongly favored peace and opposed the escalation of U.S. military involvement in Vietnam, Johnson deliberately gave the impression during the presidential election campaign of November 1964 that he would hold the line on U.S. military commitments abroad. He thus obtained the largest majority in U.S. history, defeating war hawk Barry Goldwater, an advocate of the use of the nuclear bomb in Vietnam. It was, as a statement of the Communist Party of Canada observed, a mandate for Johnson to move toward nuclear disarmament and the withdrawal of U.S. armed forces from Vietnam.[4]

In February 1965, however, the Johnson administration began full-scale military actions against both North and South Vietnam. North Vietnam was subjected to saturation bombing while hundreds of thousands of U.S. troops were sent to South Vietnam to fight the National Liberation Front forces. U.S. imperialism conducted a massive propaganda campaign throughout the world to give the impression that Vietnam, the victim, was the aggressor.

The U.S. government received the tacit support of the Maoist Chinese leadership.[5] There could be no doubt that U.S. imperialism took advantage of Maoism's split with the world communist movement to carry out its policy of armed aggression in the belief that it could do so with impunity.[6] The policy resolution adopted by the 19th convention of the Communist Party of Canada accused the Maoist Chinese leaders of encouraging U.S. imperialism and of obstructing the cause of world peace.

Divisions in the world communist movement and among socialist states have facilitated U.S. imperialism's aggressive drive. It is unity of action which can defeat it. It is all the more serious that unity of action has been rejected thereby weakening the common front against imperialism. We condemn such a policy which plays into the hands of imperialism.[7]

The party reiterated this position in three subsequent CC plenums and in the 20th convention in April 1969.[8]

In April 1965, the first NC meeting to take place after the bombing of North Vietnam called on the Pearson government to "speak now for an end to U.S. intervention in the internal affairs of Vietnam, for an end to air strikes, for the withdrawal of U.S. troops, for the strict adherence to the Geneva agreement, and for the right of the Vietnamese people to decide their own destiny."[9] In a letter to the Vietnam Workers' Party, the NC pledged "all its efforts toward the building of a powerful movement of the Canadian people against U.S. aggression, and for the right of the Vietnamese people to settle their own affairs."[10]

U.S. imperialism had miscalculated badly. The Vietnamese people would not be beaten. U.S. public opinion understood more and more that their country had been dragged into an unjust bloody war against a small country striving for national unity and social liberation. An outraged world voiced its condemnation of U.S. bombings and atrocities. Demonstrations in every major city of Canada became massive expressions of anger. Not since then has the city of Toronto, for example, closed down Yonge Street, its main street, to accommodate the thousands who marched. Teach-ins, sit-ins, sing-ins, pickets and demonstrations brought thousands of Canadians into the streets.

The anti-war sentiment of most Canadians developed in sharp contrast to the Pearson government's refusal to dissociate itself from the USA. The Communist Party fought to put Canada on the side of world peace and peaceful coexistence. The Pearson government, however, still placed its support behind the United States. Using its position as a member of the International Control Commission, Canada ran interference for U.S. aggression in Vietnam. Canadian complicity in the war extended to the supply of war materials to the USA, including a "defense" production sharing agreement between the two countries.

The Communist Party's 19th convention called on the Canadian government to contribute to world peace rather than to U.S. imperialist aims. It sharply condemned U.S. imperialism for its role in bringing about a serious deterioration of the international situation and for taking the path of open war and intervention against peoples striving for independence and social change. Vietnam was the focus of this struggle.

The struggle to end the war in Vietnam and force U.S. withdrawal on the basis of the 1954 Geneva Agreements is the most urgent task confronting all progressive mankind. It must be at the center of attention and work of our party and of all progressive forces in this country.[11]

Canada's complicity with U.S. aggression in Vietnam could only make it more dependent on the USA and threatened to further undermine Canada's economic and political independence. The working class and democratic forces had to struggle for an independent and democratic foreign policy as part of the struggle to curb Canadian and U.S. monopoly domination over Canada.[12]

As Canadians became more aware of the true character of U.S. military involvement in Vietnam and Canada's complicity in it, opposition to the "dirty war" grew. By early 1967, it was becoming clear that the majority of Canadians wanted to see an end to the war.

The united struggle of the Vietnamese people and the widespread and growing opposition to U.S. aggression throughout the world promised the possibility of its defeat. Vietnam had the unconditional support of the Soviet Union and other socialist countries. While providing Vietnam with huge amounts of mili-

Demonstration in Toronto, May 1966, against Canada's complicity in U.S. imperialism's war against Vietnam.

tary and other material aid, the socialist world pursued a persistent struggle for world peace and disarmament. As well, many developing countries and some imperialist countries, most notably France, refused to back U.S. policies in Vietnam. The USA therefore found itself increasingly isolated in the world, a situation which compelled it to refrain from widening the conflict into a world war. However, U.S. imperialist intrigues against world peace and the national liberation movement continued, and extended to the Middle East as well.

Ever since the Suez crisis, the United States had consistently increased its support for the reactionary Zionist government of Israel. U.S. imperialism regarded Israel as a bulwark against the rising tide of the national liberation movement in the Arab world, a movement which threatened to undermine U.S. control of this strategic region and deprive it of the area's rich oil resources. Israel's Zionist ruling circles willingly accepted U.S. economic and military aid because it facilitated Zionism's own ambitions to create a Greater Israel at the expense of its Arab neighbors. This was what motivated Israel when, from 1948, it forcibly expelled the Palestinian Arab people from their lands and from Israel without compensation or regard for their human and democratic rights. And this was what motivated Israel when in 1967, it launched the six-day war against Syria, Jordan and Egypt, seizing substantial portions of their territories.

The September 1967 meeting of the CC of the Communist Party of Canada, in unison with the vast majority of the progressive forces around the world, condemned Israeli aggression as a threat to world peace. The CC endorsed United Nations Resolution 242 which called on Israel to withdraw from all occupied Arab territories, for the recognition of the rights of the Palestinians and for the recognition of the right of Israel to exist within secure borders.[13]

Meanwhile, the war in Vietnam kept grinding on. After three years of heavy bombing of North Vietnamese ports and cities, the Pentagon found itself no closer to the victory it had so confidently expected. In February 1968, the Tet offensive led by the National Liberation Front testified to the determination of the people of Vietnam to win their country's freedom and independence. Opposition to the war assumed massive proportions throughout the world. In the United States, the anti-war movement had become a powerful force capable of organizing demonstrations of hundreds of thousands of people. The Vietnam war had become so unpopular that Johnson was forced to suspend the bombing of North Vietnam, agree to begin negotiations with the liberation forces and decline to seek re-election as

President. On his promise to end the war in six months, Richard M. Nixon was elected U.S. President in November 1968.

2. In Defense of Communist Principles

The depth and breadth of the anti-war movement was all the more significant given the intense ideological campaigns conducted by imperialism against socialism. Imperialism worked particularly hard to produce splits in the world communist movement. In this, it had an objective ally in Maoism. The leadership of the Communist Party of China was diverging further and further from the principles of Marxism-Leninism and proletarian internationalism. In 1964, the 18th convention of the Communist Party of Canada noted that what had begun as ideological differences was being transformed into organized attempts to split the international communist movement and place it under Maoist hegemony.[14]

Imperialism continued to exert direct ideological pressure on the working class and communist movement throughout the 1960s. Its aim was to maintain its ideological control over the working class and to isolate the Communist Party. Wherever possible, it also encouraged the resurgence of the kind of right-opportunism which had afflicted the party in the mid-1950s. The ideological thrust was to convince workers that capitalism was a system capable of meeting their demands and that reforms alone were sufficient to resolve difficulties which might arise in the course of the economy's development.

Political and economic conditions in Canada in the 1960s militated against the party's efforts to re-emerge fully on Canada's political scene. Though thousands of Canadians were in political motion, and though party members worked in and with many groups and organizations, anti-Sovietism and anti-communism were effective barriers between the party and the new generation of activists. The extensive audience of the mass media was denied to Communists, which blacked out publicity of their activities, positions, history of struggle and even their very existence.

The cold war had exacted its toll on the party. The party was not growing; press and literature sales remained at a low level; the membership's average age was in the fifties, all indicative of the fact that the cold war had cost the party an entire generation. Working people did not believe that serious crisis was possible nor did they see socialism as an immediate or necessary prospect. The atmosphere of anti-communism encouraged the development of a certain degree of sectarianism in the party, of self-imposed isolation which served as a way of avoiding a public fight for the program and policies of the party in the mass movements. In his report to the 19th convention, William Kashtan called on the delegates to "re-establish confidence in our party, in the truth of our policies and the science of Marxism-Leninism upon which it is based."[15]

Canadian Communists were under heavy ideological pressure to capitulate to the difficulties confronting them in their political activities. The decision to disband the YCL in 1964 arose out of its apparent inability to make appreciable headway among young people. While it was true that the main cause of the YCL's and party's problems stemmed from cold war conditions, a part of the responsibility also lay with the NEC and NC. The January 1965 NC plenum criticized the NEC and itself for being indecisive and slow in discussing and working out a policy for youth. But given that the YCL was defunct, the plenum decided to establish a National Youth Commission to take on work in this field. It also agreed to begin the publication of a youth magazine entitled Scan.[16] In time, however, despite vigorous opposition by some members of the Commission and of the Editorial Board, these two bodies became not so much organizers of youth as centers of opposition to the party.

Retreats due to political difficulties were also expressed in the ideological sphere. Monopoly made every effort to weaken the Communist Party's influence in the ethnic communities and direct them toward narrow bourgeois nationalism. After World War II, Canada was made a haven for all kinds of reactionary and anti-socialist elements. The government opened Canada's doors to right-wing Ukrainians including those who, in the name of Ukrainian nationalism, had collaborated with the Nazis. (Despite indisputable evidence of their war crimes and the demands of the Soviet government for their extradition, the Canadian government to this day continues to shelter pro-Nazi war criminals from justice.[17]) The self-styled "nationalists" and "freedom fighters" received the considerable material assistance of the government and the bourgeois mass media to spread their slanderous charges of Soviet oppression — the alleged Russification of the Ukraine. They of course downplayed or tried to conceal their connections with the most reactionary circles of world imperialism.

In the conditions of the cold war, the Ukrainian right-wing nationalists succeeded in making some impact on the community and thereby pressured Ukrainian Canadian Communists to make some concessions to bourgeois nationalism. The problem was serious enough to warrant attention at the April 1965 NC plenum and again at the 1966 convention.[18] Those who were succumbing to nationalist influence had become convinced that there was national oppression in the Ukraine. So in early 1967, the party asked the CPSU for the opportunity to see conditions in the Soviet Ukraine first hand. The CPSU granted this request and in the spring a delegation of six headed by Tim Buck embarked on a 22-day tour of the Ukraine.

Reporting back to the CC in September, the delegation concluded that "the Ukrainian nation has, after centuries of oppression, finally achieved a viable and flourishing culture."[19] A grave weakness in the Kiev report, however, was that despite its positive conclusions, it tended to dwell on negative phenomena, on past and present mistakes and shortcomings. The report consequently tended to give a distorted picture of life in the Soviet Ukraine. A great deal of publicity was given to the report by the capitalist media, but in a one-sided, anti-Soviet way. It caused a great deal of harm to the party.

The Kiev report and the disbanding of the YCL were symptomatic of a tendency to falter or yield on questions of principle in the face of enormous difficulties. The deterioration of the party's ideological vigilance became evident in 1968, at the time of the Czechoslovakian events.

The history of imperialism is littered with mass exploitation, subversion, war and the cruelest barbarities including genocide. Never a year passes without imperialism committing new crimes as it seeks to maintain its domination over the peoples of the world, or, in other instances, to regain lost ground. From the very first day of the triumph of the socialist revolution in Russia in 1917, world imperialism has done everything it could to undermine, and if possible, destroy socialism. In short, its aim is to reverse the objective course of world development at the expense of peace and the welfare of millions of people. Imperialism's reactionary and dangerous policies lead, in their extreme form, to military intervention. Indeed, U.S. aggression against Vietnam was in its fourth year when the crisis in Czechoslovakia broke out in 1968.

Just as imperialism had no scruples about waging a genocidal war against the people of Vietnam, so too it had no compunction in using other, non-military means to subvert socialism wherever it existed. Czechoslovakia was a case in point. In the course of its socialist development, mistakes were made which were beginning to undermine the prestige of the Communist Party of Czechoslovakia among the people and which enabled a revisionist trend to seize important positions in the party and state apparatus. Taking advantage of these internal problems, imperialism which at that moment was slaughtering hundreds of thousands of Vietnamese men, women and children, conducted a massive propaganda campaign against Czechoslovakia, urging it to adopt "socialism with a human face" and "market socialism." As the struggle between the revisionists and Leninists intensified within the Communist Party of Czechoslovakia, counter-revolutionary groups in the USA and the FRG were proceeding with their plans to subvert that country's socialist system. Utilizing both revisionism and these counter-revolutionary groups, imperialism hoped to restore capitalism in Czechoslovakia and to bring it back into the imperialist camp.

Over the years, the ideological vigilance of the Communist Party of Canada with respect to anti-Sovietism and anti-communism had been weakened. Some party members were confused as to the class nature of the events taking place in Czechoslovakia. They tended to regard democracy as an abstract concept. They failed to see that the exercise of democracy is conditioned by existing class relations, including the need to defend working class power and socialism. In April 1968, the CC even adopted a resolution warmly greeting the revisionist changes in Czechoslovakia which, it said, "are not confined to the correction of past errors and distortions but represent a new departure with the aim of realizing in life the widest and deepest democracy."[20] The resolution expressed elements of both confusion and opportunism. It failed to make a distinction between changes of a genuinely democratic and socialist character and those which were geared to compromise the continued existence of socialism.

By August of 1968, the danger of capitalist restoration in Czechoslovakia had become very real, consequently the Leninist section of the leadership of the Communist Party of Czechoslovakia called on the Warsaw Pact to forestall an imminent imperialist takeover of the country. Fulfilling their internationalist commitments, Warsaw Pact countries successfully helped defend socialist Czechoslovakia.

The Czechoslovakian events brought developing ideological differences within the CEC to a head and thereby revealed the existence of opportunist tendencies among some members of the party leadership. Some CEC members such as John Boyd, former editor of the *Canadian Tribune* and at the time of the Czechoslovakian events, the party's representative on the editorial board of *World Marxist Review;* Stanley B. Ryerson, editor of *Horizons* and its predecessor *The Marxist Quarterly* and the CEC member responsible for ideological and educational work; and Rae Murphy, the first editor of *Scan* and, in 1968 editor of the *Canadian Tribune,* supported a position condemning the Soviet Union and the Warsaw Pact for their entry into Czechoslovakia. This was the position they fought for in the CEC meeting of August 22-23.

This CEC meeting took place at a time when several key members were away either on vacation or on assignment. Such was the situation for Alfred Dewhurst and Norman Freed. As a result, the opportunists constituted a majority. Nevertheless, their position met with stiff resistance from other CEC members. A "compromise" resolution was then formulated expressing the opinion that the CEC was "deeply disturbed" by the situation which "five parties of the Warsaw Pact judged to constitute a threat of counter-revolution and to necessitate military intervention. . . ." Although the statement observed that the entry of the Warsaw Pact troops into Czechoslovakia "was undertaken at the request of the majority of the presidium of the Communist Party of Czechoslovakia," the statement then went on to say that "both this judgment and declaration were at variance with the estimation and declaration of leading bodies in Czechoslovakia."[21] Bruce Magnuson, Harry Hunter and Jeannette Walsh asked to be recorded as opposing this latter phrase. William Kashtan asked to be recorded as opposing the entire statement, because it "changed the essence of the paragraph." He explained that:

> Imperialism understands quite well that what is involved is a struggle between socialism and capitalism. The change in the paragraph objectively gives grist to the mill of imperialism.[22]

On the question of the Czechoslovakian events, the majority of the party membership and the lower party bodies proved to be in advance of that particular CEC meeting in grasping the fact that socialism itself was at stake. On August 25, the British Columbia Provincial Executive adopted a resolution accepting what it referred to as an "interim" statement of the CEC "pending a fuller and more decisive statement from the forthcoming Central Committee meeting."[23] The September 16 meeting of the Communist Party of Quebec was much less delicate. It urged the CC to adopt a declaration "which will have as its point of departure the expression of our solidarity with the military action of August 20-21, 1968 of the five governments of the Warsaw Pact in order to defend socialism from internal and external attack. . . ." A meeting of the party's Winnipeg membership on September 19 passed a resolution expressing its disagreement with the August 22 CEC statement because it "failed to characterize the central issue in these events to be the defense of socialism against the threat of counter-revolution."[24] The Toronto party membership curtly referred the statement back to the CEC "for strengthening."

The October CC plenum proceeded to correct the ambiguities of the CEC's original statement. It adopted a resolution which "rejected those aspects of the Central Executive statement of August 22nd which gave expression to the false position that the entry of the Warsaw Pact troops into Czechoslovakia was not in the interests of socialism."[25] The resolution noted that the CEC statement did not reflect the real situation in Czechoslovakia where the political power of the working class and the leading role of the party was threatened by counter-revolution. Some CC members strongly opposed this resolution, claiming that the Warsaw Pact's action was a mistake. The CC rejected the opportunists' arguments and unequivocally placed itself on record in defense of socialism's right to protect itself, by whatever means necessary, from internal and external enemies. Shortly after the April 1969 convention, Murphy was replaced by W.C. Beeching as editor of the *Canadian Tribune*. At the end of

1969, *Horizons* was replaced by *Communist Viewpoint* under the editorship of Norman Freed. Boyd, Murphy and other supporters of the anti-Soviet line on Czechoslovakia subsequently quit the party. Later, Ryerson quit the party as well.

The struggle against retreats to right-opportunist positions, especially around the events in Czechoslovakia, coincided and merged with a left-sectarian opposition based in the Vancouver City Committee led by Charles Caron. In October 1967, for example, the Vancouver City Committee issued a leaflet to the peace movement that "as a Marxist party we extend our struggle against war, such as in Vietnam, to the struggle against the capitalist system which is the source of war."[26] It was such a serious departure from the party's policies that it evoked immediate and sharp criticisms from both the British Columbia Provincial Executive and the CEC. The CEC objected to the fact that the line expressed by the leaflet contradicted the party's estimation that "at this stage the main blow should be directed against monopoly and not against capitalism in general."[27] By obliterating the difference between the anti-monopoly and the anti-capitalist stages of the struggle, the leaflet in effect overestimated the level of the struggle in Canada, a position which led to the denial of the need to form the united front. As well, in the framework of the Canadian peace movement's struggle against U.S. imperialist aggression in Vietnam and Canada's complicity in it, to overestimate the political consciousness of the peace movement would mean the isolation of the party from the mainstream of the struggle for peace and could do great harm to the newly developing peace movement. Both the British Columbia Provincial Committee and the CC passed motions in support of the CEC. The Vancouver City Committee agreed to review its positions and for the moment the crisis seemed to have passed.[28]

It soon became obvious that, rather than seek reconciliation with the provincial and central leadership, the Vancouver City Committee, particularly in the person of Charles Caron, chose to continue its left-sectarian opposition to the party line. It conducted an especially fierce campaign against the British Columbia Provincial Committee which was accused of reporting distortions and innuendo to the CEC concerning the City Committee's role in the federal election, of "bureaucratic centralism" and of being bent on removing all opposition to itself.

In actual fact, it was Caron and his sympathizers who consistently violated the principles of democratic centralism. Although a member of the Provincial Committee, he refused to carry out its decisions and used the City Committee as a vehicle for organizing opposition to the party and its program. When the Czechoslovakian events revealed the existence of a deep split in the CEC, the left-sectarians on the City Committee forged an alliance with the right-opportunists of the CEC against the central and provincial leadership of the party. The City Committee's invitation to Rae Murphy to speak on Czechoslovakia, made over the heads of the higher party bodies, clearly demonstrated their conscious and deliberate anti-party factionalism.[29]

The differences between the City Committee, and the Provincial Committee led by Nigel Morgan, were irreconcilable. The party had no choice but to convene a special convention of the British Columbia wing of the party. Realizing that they had no hope of winning a majority in a convention whose delegates were elected by the British Columbia party membership, Caron and his followers staged a show for the monopoly mass media by publicly bolting the party as a group the day before the opening session of the convention. To justify themselves, they issued a statement characterizing the party's wholehearted support for the Warsaw Pact's military assistance to Czechoslovakia as "in fact a denial of not only the sovereignty of that people but also the denial of Canadian self-determination as well."[30] Their nationalistic, anti-Soviet and anti-communist declarations thus revealed that the "left" had found common ground with the right. The special provincial convention formally and unanimously expelled Caron and three others from the party. In Toronto, Charles Boylan, a CC member and the third editor of Scan, was also expelled for his involvement in this anti-party factionalism. The January 1969 CC meeting unanimously endorsed both Nigel Morgan's report and the expulsions.[31]

The 20th convention in April 1969, reaffirmed the principled unity of the party and began the correction of mistakes made in previous years. The convention declared its intention to re-establish the YCL. The October 1969 CC plenum retracted the Kiev report and expressly rejected the false suggestion that the CPSU had deviated from a Leninist position on the national question.[32]

Having overcome "left" and right-opportunism, the Communist Party was able to devote special attention to strengthening its political and ideological unity — the necessary basis for fully understanding and correctly responding to the new conditions and new ideological problems emerging in the 1960s.

Arising out of the groundswell of popular anti-war protest which the Communist Party had helped to stimulate, a movement came into being which questioned the social and political status quo. This movement, called the New Left, was a petty-bourgeois political movement which originated in the USA and spilled over into Canada. It was based among young intellectuals and university students. While anti-capitalist, the New Left was eclectic in philosophy, containing elements of Marxism, Maoism, anarchism and idealism. It was also strongly anti-Leninist, anti-communist and anti-Soviet. Opposed to the bourgeois parties and the reformist NDP, the New Left was largely influenced by the erroneous anti-Leninist ideas of Herbert Marcuse. Marcuse claimed that the working class had become "bourgeoisified," that it had lost its ability to be the vanguard of social revolution. He argued that the progressive intelligentsia was the only social force capable of taking up the struggle for revolutionary change. This characteristic caused Communists to tend toward a sectarian approach to the New Left with the result that the party did not adequately estimate the New Left's positive aspects in furthering the fight for peace and social change. Though it was given to anarchy in organization and was isolated from the working class movement, the New Left did made a substantial and positive contribution to the struggle to end the war in Vietnam. By the early 1970s, however, the New Left was clearly on the decline, a victim of its own ideological and organizational fractiousness.

3. Revival of the Mass Movements

Influenced by the rapid expansion of the anti-war movement and its questioning of imperialist policy, Canadians of all walks of life began to examine their own conditions and take action accordingly. Students were marching to abolish tuition fees and for the democratization of the universities. Concern was growing at the fact that Canadian culture was being strangled by U.S. control. Thousands of farmers in Ontario and Quebec, often in tractor parades, pressed for government action to protect their living standards. An upsurge in strike activity in 1964 continued throughout the decade. Trade unionists fought against injunctions and strikebreaking. Canada was in motion.

The scientific and technological revolution was bringing about significant change in Canadian industry. For example, in 1957 there were no computers installed in Canada, but by 1960, there were 89 and by mid-1964, almost 700. The revolution in science and technology raised new challenges in the lives of Canadian workers, to society as a whole. Through the process of automation, machines replaced workers, causing unemployment. Entire skills and occupations were threatened with elimination while new though fewer, highly technical jobs came into being. Communists supported union struggles to protect workers' job security and demanded that workers be guaranteed a voice in production and in the introduction of new technology.

The new technology had a far-reaching impact on the composition of the work force. While the number of industrial workers remained relatively static, there was a rapid increase in the number of office, professional and technical workers. Governments sponsored a tremendous expansion of post-secondary education to service industry's demand for trained workers. Although the labor force was growing, the trade union movement was not keeping pace with it. Communists stressed the urgency of initiating a new campaign to organize the unorganized, particularly the growing numbers of non-industrial workers.

Advances in technology stimulated the trend to merger among unions, typified in the public sector. Following the merger of the National Union of Public Employees and the National Union of Public Service Employees into the Canadian Union of Public Employees (CUPE), destined to become the biggest union in Canada, an immense upsurge took place among public service employees at all levels. Collective bargaining with the right to strike for public service employees was won in 1967.

Communists played a significant role in the struggle for these advances.

The Communist Party responded to the immediate economic effects of automation with an action program to protect jobs and living standards. Simultaneously, the party conducted an in-depth discussion of the profound social implications of the unprecedented advance in technology. The party's general approach had been formulated in its 1959 program.

> Only socialism can successfully meet the challenge of such new productive powers as automation, electronics and nuclear energy, and use them for the well-being of all Canadians.
>
> In this era of atomic energy and space travel, and inspired by the achievements in the socialist countries, Canadians are determined that the new achievements of science, industry and technique shall lead to a better life for all instead of being used for war and the enrichment of a few.[33]

The party began detailed study of the theoretical and practical implications of automation in 1961. Party study and activity on the question was a highlight of the party's work in 1964. The 18th convention in April of that year devoted considerable attention to economic policy and social change in "the electronic age." Pointing out that "the extent to which the people as a whole secure the benefits from this great revolutionary change will depend entirely upon who controls its introduction, and to what extent society as a whole assumes responsibility for its consequences," the convention outlined the necessity of the working class waging a political struggle against monopoly control of the new technology.[34]

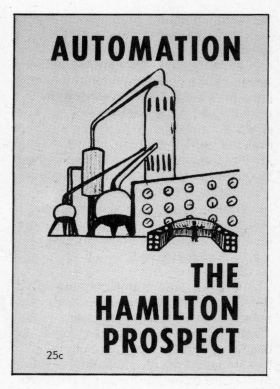

AUTOMATION

THE HAMILTON PROSPECT

25c

The measures that must be fought for now to protect even the most elementary interests of the workers affected by automation and the communities in which they live, go beyond purely economic demands such as shorter hours, higher wages and such, vital as these demands are. Indispensable, in addition to these defensive measures, is the demand for democratic public control of the introduction of automation and its effects. *This must be won.*[35]

To publicize its positions, the Communist Party held a series of public forums on "Automation and its Implications," and featured the question in its publications.[36]

Canada was experiencing a turbulent period in its history, and no less so in Quebec where the Quiet Revolution brought about profound political changes and stimulated a new phase in the development of the national movement.*

The upsurge of the national movement in Quebec paralleled the growth of national awareness in English Canada. Preparations for the celebration of Canada's centennial in 1967, including the adoption of a new flag in 1964, promoted a re-examination of Canada's heritage, its past, present and future. The widespread anti-imperialist sentiment engendered by the Vietnam war and the campaigns of Communists and others against U.S. domination, led many Canadians to criticize Canada's relationship with the United States. This process was further stimulated by the continuing government policy of subordinating Canada to U.S. interests.

Following on the heels of the Columbia River Treaty of 1964, came a new threat to the independent development of the Canadian economy: the 1965 Canada-U.S. Auto Pact, negotiated by the Pearson government to overcome a balance of payments deficit with the USA in auto transactions.

The Communist Party opposed the pact from its inception, arguing that Canada's sovereignty and independence were involved "inasmuch as the application of this agreement and decisions concerning capital investments, production, marketing and employment will rest mainly in the hands of U.S. companies and their Canadian subsidiaries. . . ." The alternative, Communists suggested, was "to regain control of our industries for

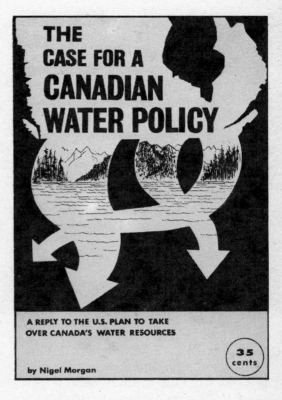

THE CASE FOR A CANADIAN WATER POLICY

A REPLY TO THE U.S. PLAN TO TAKE OVER CANADA'S WATER RESOURCES

35 cents

by Nigel Morgan

independent Canadian development, to seek other markets in newly independent and developing countries and the socialist world, and to refuse to put our trade into a single basket." The party called for "the nationalization of the automobile industry in Canada together with the design and production of a 100 per cent Canadian car."[37]

The Auto Pact reflected the continentalist policies of the Liberals who were reviving proposals for free trade between Canada and the United States. U.S. monopoly was also eager to accelerate the integration of the economies of the two countries. From south of the border came calls for a "continental" approach to water management.

---

*See Chapter 13.

Termed the North American Water and Power Alliance, the plan prepared by the U.S. Ralph M. Parsons Company would divert Canadian rivers to supply U.S. water requirements. Campaigning against the plan, the Communist Party outlined proposals for a National Water Policy, to develop Canada's water resources "for economic expansion and the advancement of Canadian industry, agriculture and the welfare of the Canadian people."[38]

The plan was never implemented. Conditions in the mid-1960s were markedly different from those in 1947 when the Communist Party stood alone in opposition to the economic integration and U.S. domination formulated in the Abbott Plan. Even within the capitalist class, there were rumblings of discontent reminiscent of the furor over the Avro Arrow. Although these rumblings were growing louder, continentalism reigned supreme in the Liberal government. When in 1963, Finance Minster Walter Gordon proposed some limited provisions restricting U.S. takeovers, the government bowed to monopoly protest and withdrew his budget. In 1966, Gordon published a book entitled *A Choice for Canada: Independence or Colonial Status* in which he expressed his nationalistic views. Despite its political limitations, the book contributed to growing public concern over U.S. domination of the economy, a concern which finally forced the government to at least appear to take action. In 1967, Gordon was re-admitted to the Liberal cabinet. A Task Force was assigned to examine "Foreign Ownership and the Structure of Canadian Industry." Headed by Mel Watkins, the Task Force's report, delivered in 1968, confirmed what Communists had long maintained, namely the extensive and harmful character of foreign ownership. Although effectively shelved by the Liberal government, the Watkins Report helped to heighten public awareness of the need for Canadian independence from U.S. economic domination.

This Task Force was not the only body to submit a report in 1968. Pressure across the country for government action on women's issues had led to the appointment of the Royal Commission on the Status of Women in Canada. The number of responses at the Commission's hearings had been one of the largest ever received by a Royal Commission. Delegation after delegation representing women's groups, community organizations, trade unions, political parties, farm organizations and others had appeared to testify to the continuing and growing inequality of women.

The Communist Party's submission pointed out that although women had made some important gains, social and economic inequalities persisted. Women still faced job discrimination and served as a source of cheap labor, and therefore of bigger profits, for the employers. Public opinion had forced provincial governments to enact equal pay legislation, but loopholes were left so that any significant step toward pay equality could be frustrated. The submission recommended the adoption of enforceable equal pay legislation based on a common minimum level of pay for all establishments and rates set on job content only.[39]

The submission also exposed other

forms of discrimination faced by women. The party demanded, among other measures, maternity leave with pay established in law, nurseries and day care centers financed by the federal and provincial governments and an educational Bill of Rights to eliminate discrimination against women in the educational system and the professions.

While the Task Force and Royal Commission dealt with important issues in their reports, equally important issues were being raised by the struggles of Canadian working people. The fight against the war in Vietnam continued to intensify. The Hemispheric Conference to End the Vietnam War brought 1,800 delegates and observers from Canada, the United States, Latin America and the Caribbean to Montreal in November 1968. The following April, 10,000 Torontonians marched through the streets, in one of the largest Vietnam demonstrations to take place in Canada.

Workers were also on the move to advance labor's rights. In Quebec, 20,000 teachers demonstrated at the National Assembly in May 1969 to further their contract demands. The same month, 15,000 Ontario trade unionists brought their demands to end injunctions to the Ontario Legislative Assembly in a demonstration characterized by militancy, unity and membership initiative.

The roots of the Ontario demonstration could be traced to the 1966 campaign against injunctions launched by the CLC and the provincial labor federa-

ARCHIVES CPC/PAC/PA-125056

tions. That year had witnessed particularly bitter struggles in which employers used the courts to slap injunctions in the face of striking workers. In British Columbia, the International Longshoremen's and Warehousemen's Union successfully defied a far-reaching injunction which ordered the union to prevent its members from taking a statutory holiday. In Peterborough, 26 people were imprisoned for peacefully picketing in contravention of an injunction. To take the heat off the injunction battle, the Ontario government appointed a Royal Commission Inquiry into Labor Disputes (the Rand Commission).

By the end of 1968, the Rand Report was completed. Branding the report's recommendations as "a formula for employer dictatorship," the Communist Party immediately began mobilizing opposition. Communists argued that the alternative to the unacceptable and dangerous path prescribed by Rand in labor-management relations was to bring democracy to the workplace, forcing governments to adopt and enforce laws that would restrict corporate management and give labor a greater voice and power in industry. The party outlined this alternative in its Labor Bill of Rights adopted by the 20th convention in April 1969.

Effective resistance to the anti-labor policies of monopoly calls for coordinated and united action by the whole trade union movement, ... which seeks the broadest support to block the

ARCHIVES CPC/PAC

attempts of governments to impose anti-strike and compulsory arbitration laws on the labor movement such as those incorporated in the Rand Report. . . . Above all, anti-labor legislation should be met with a united labor demand for legislation which upholds the rights of labor. . . . United labor action for A Bill of Labor Rights, enshrined in the laws of the land, is inseparably tied to the battle for wages, hours and conditions.[40]

The Communist campaign helped spark a trade union struggle against the Rand Report and for a Labor Bill of Rights. While the right-wing trade union leadership resisted mass action, many local leaders, Communists among them, took the initiative. The 5,000-strong anti-Rand demonstration on March 29, 1969 in Hamilton served

notice on all labor politicians and union leaders as well as the Ontario Tory government that the trade union membership had the will to struggle to victory. Top union officials could not afford to stay away from this struggle and lent official support to the May 31 demonstration of 15,000 workers in Toronto.

The mass demonstrations and trade union deputations forced the NDP legislative caucus to retreat from its initial support of the majority of the Rand recommendations, and won major and fundamental changes to the report from the Conservative government.

The campaign against the Rand Report, like so many of the struggles waged in the 1960s, showed clearly that the new decade approaching held the promise of stormy battles ahead. These actions also showed that the party, having from the beginning played a key role in the organization of many of these campaigns, whether peace marches, labor demonstrations or on women's rights, was once more becoming an effective force in the mass movement.

A highpoint of the last year of the decade for Communists in Canada and throughout the world was the June 1969 Conference of Communist and Workers' Parties. Attended by 75 parties, the international meeting had a dual task: to draw political conclusions from past events and outline a clear perspective for the period ahead, and on that basis strengthen the unity of the world communist movement.

The conference recognized that imperialism would continue to use all means possible to halt and reverse the revolutionary process. It resorts to war

The conference of Communist and Workers' Parties which took place in Moscow, June 1969.

ARCHIVES CPC/PAC

as in Vietnam, and to political and ideological subversion as in Czechoslovakia. Thus imperialism is a dangerous enemy to the forces of peace and progress. In view of imperialism's efforts to split the communist movement, the meeting drew the conclusion that to mount an effective offensive against imperialism, *"cohesion of Communist and Workers' Parties is the most important factor in rallying together all the anti-imperialist forces."*[41] Also, *"the main link of united action of the anti-imperialist forces remains the struggle for world peace. . . ."*[42]

The main document concluded:

Tense class battles lie ahead and they cannot be avoided. Let us step up the offensive against imperialism and internal reaction. The revolutionary and progressive forces are certain to triumph.[43]

In analyzing the perspective for the period ahead, the conference's main document stressed that "imperialism can neither regain its lost historical initiative nor reverse world development."[44]

This high note of optimism was to take the Communist Party of Canada into the 1970s.

1. *Canadian Tribune*, March 9, 1964.
2. Ibid., August 10, 1964.
3. *Pacific Tribune*, February 12, 1965.
4. *Canadian Tribune*, November 16, 1964.
5. Ministry of Foreign Affairs, Socialist Republic of Vietnam, *The Truth about Vietnam-China Relations over the Last Thirty Years* (1979), p. 32.
6. "For Unity of the World Communist Movement" in *Viewpoint*, Vol. 2, No. 1, January 1965, p. 37; and W. Kashtan, "The International Crisis" in *Viewpoint*, Vol. 2, No. 2, May 1965, p. 7.
7. "The 19th Convention, Communist Party of Canada, May 21-24, 1966" in *Viewpoint*, Vol. 3, No. 5, June 1966, p. 5.
8. *On the Unity of the World Communist Movement*, CC resolution, January 14-16, 1967, Archives CPC; *On Consultative Meeting*, CC resolution, January 19-21, 1968, Archives CPC; *Resolution on the Convening of an International Conference of Communist and Workers' Parties*, CC resolution, April 19-21, 1968, Archives CPC; and *The 20th Convention, Communist Party of Canada, April 4-6, 1969: Resolutions, Reports, Policy Resolutions* (Toronto, 1969), p. 61.
9. CPC press release, April 25, 1965, Archives CPC.
10. Untitled resolution of the NC plenum of April 23-25, 1965, Archives CPC.
11. "The 19th Convention," p. 4.
12. Ibid., p. 6.
13. *Canadian Tribune*, September 25, 1967.
14. "For the Unity of the International Communist Movement" in *Viewpoint*, Vol. 1, No. 1, April 1964, pp. 36-37.
15. W. Kashtan, *A New Course for Canada* (Toronto, 1966), p. 25; and also W. Kashtan, *Toward Socialism* (Toronto, 1976), p. 28.
16. "Motions on Youth Work" in *Viewpoint*, Vol. 2, No. 1, January 1965, pp. 33-35.
17. M. Hanusiak, *Lest We Forget* (Toronto, 1976), in passim.
18. "Memorandum on Work in National Group Communities" in *Viewpoint*, Vol. 2, No. 2, May 1965, pp. 36-39; and "Resolution on Work in National Group Communities" in *Viewpoint*, Vol. 3, No. 5, June 1966, p. 72.

19. "Report of Delegation to Ukraine" in *Viewpoint*, Vol. 5, No. 1, January 1968, p. 13.
20. Untitled CC resolution, April 19-21, 1968, Archives CPC.
21. *Canadian Tribune*, September 11, 1968.
22. *CEC Minutes: Situation in Czechoslovakia*, Archives CPC.
23. British Columbia Provincial Executive, *Resolution re Czechoslovakian Situation*, August 26, 1968, copy distributed to the CC plenum of October 4-7, 1968, Archives CPC.
24. Copies of resolutions sent to the CEC and distributed by the CEC to the CC plenum of October 4-7, 1968, Archives CPC.
25. "Resolution on Czechoslovakia" in *Viewpoint*, Vol 5, No. 4, November 1968, p. 12; and also *Canadian Tribune*, October 9, 1968.
26. Vancouver City Committee, *Peace*, October 1967, Archives CPC.
27. N. Clarke, letter to the British Columbia Provincial Committee, October 27, 1967, Archives CPC.
28. British Columbia Provincial Committee, *Resolution*, November 12, 1967, Archives CPC; *B.C. Provincial Committee Resolution on the Internal Situation*, January 13, 1968, Archives CPC; untitled CC resolution, January 19-21, 1968, Archives CPC; *Vancouver City Committee Statement*, January 4, 1968, Archives CPC.
29. *Motion & Letter of the City Committee on the Federal Elections*, August 19, 1968, Archives CPC, p. 1; *To the Central Committee, Communist Party of Canada — The City Committee's View of the Inner Party Struggle*, no date, Archives CPC, p. 6; and N. Morgan, letter to the CEC, September 29, 1968, Archives CPC.
30. *This Is a Statement of Members of the Communist Party of Canada Including Members of the Central Committee, Central Youth Committee, B.C. Provincial Committee, B.C. Youth Commission and the Majority of the Vancouver City Committee*, December 13, 1968, Archives CPC.
31. N. Morgan, *Resolution*, December 15, 1968, Archives CPC; and "Resolutions & Decisions" in *Convention 69*, No. 1, January 20, 1969, p. 15.

32. *Defeat the Government's Austerity Program* (1969), pp. 10, 19 and 22; and *Draft Statement on the Report of the Party Delegation to the Soviet Ukraine, for CC meeting,* October 4-6, 1969, Archives CPC.
33. *The Road to Socialism in Canada* (Toronto, 1960), p. 3.
34. "A new economic policy for Canada" in *Viewpoint,* Vol. 1, No. 1, April 1964, p. 15.
35. Ibid., p. 17.
36. See for example: W. Kashtan, *Automation and Labor* (Toronto, 1964); and *The Marxist Quarterly,* No. 11, Autumn 1964, which is devoted to "Automation: prospect and policy."
37. *Canadian Tribune,* February 1, 1965.
38. N. Morgan, *The Case for a Canadian Water Policy* (Toronto, 1966), p. 26.
39. A Dewhurst, *Submission to the Royal Commission on the Status of Women from the Central Executive Committee of the Communist Party of Canada,* March 14, 1968, p. 20.
40. *20th Convention,* p. 67.
41. "Tasks at the present stage of the struggle against imperialism and united action of the Communist and Workers' Parties and all anti-imperialist forces" in *World Marxist Review,* Vol. 12, No. 7, July 1969, p. 23.
42. Ibid., p. 19.
43. Ibid., p. 25.
44. Ibid., p. 7.

13. The National Question in Canada

Canadian history has witnessed the development of two nations — French Canadian and English-speaking — reflecting the fact that before Confederation in 1867, Canada was at different times under French and British colonial domination. Canada's colonization by these two European powers was done at the expense of the Native peoples. In a number of cases, there was physical genocide of whole tribes.

The French Canadian nation is largely descended from French immigrants who came to Canada in the 17th and 18th centuries when most of eastern Canada was under the rule of feudal France. In 1759-60, New France (as Quebec and Ontario together were then called) was conquered by Great Britain. In 1763, France ceded almost all its territories in the northern part of North America to Britain under the terms of the Treaty of Paris which ended the Seven Years War. Thus began the oppression of the French Canadian people — at first by the British colonialists who unsuccessfully attempted to assimilate them forcibly into British culture and colonial society, and then by the Canadian English-speaking capitalists. The British North America Act refused to recognize French Canada as a distinct nation and enshrined its inequality in Confederation.

The English-speaking nation was initially descended from British and Irish immigrants who came to Canada in the 18th and 19th centuries either directly from Britain or indirectly through the United States. In fact, after the American Revolution of 1776, thousands of pro-British Americans flooded into what is now southern Ontario and parts of modern Quebec to avoid persecution from the new republican government in the former British colonies to the south.

From the second half of the 19th century to the present time, hundreds of thousands of immigrants from around the world, but mostly from Europe, have immigrated to Canada. These immigrants, whose mother tongue was neither English nor French, have tended to assimilate with Canada's two founding peoples, particularly English Canada.

1. The Communist Party's Initial Approach

Confederation formalized French Canada's inequality. Despite Canada's development as an advanced industrialized capitalist country since then, the national question has not been solved and consequently continues to play a central role in Canadian political life. It has become a highly complex and acute problem.

In working out a program of struggle against national oppression in an advanced capitalist country, a Communist Party has three points of reference: (1) unity of the working class regardless of national origin against the main enemy, the monopolies and imperialism; (2) social, economic, cultural and language equality; and (3) the right to self-determination up to and including the right to secession.

From its beginnings, the Communist Party of Canada adopted the principle of working class unity regardless of national origin, in the fight against the capitalist class.

But the national question in general and its particular expression in Canada was not fully understood by the party in its early years. Although Lenin had written classics on the national question and the right of nations to self-determination as early as 1913 and 1914, they were not easily available in Canada until the late 1920s and early 1930s. By that time, the struggle to defend the economic and political interests of the working class against the reactionary capitalist offensive had assumed paramount importance for Canadian Communists. Although the national question was first raised at the Communist Party's sixth convention in 1929, it was not given extensive examination because of the convention's preoccupation with a difficult and bitter struggle against North American exceptionalism. The defeat of the right-opportunist MacDonald faction was, moreover, soon followed by the controversy around the definition of Canada's status in the world imperialist system. As the right to national self-determination was not demanded as such in French Canada, the national question as it applied to Canada was given little attention.

It was the ECCI that raised this question in its letter of fraternal greetings to the 1929 convention of the Communist Party of Canada. The letter made a passing reference to the fact that "the guarantees for complete self-determination (French Canada) can only be achieved through revolutionary action."[1] In its conclusion, it called for "active recruiting and the establishment of Communist influence among French Canadian workers" and also "a systematic drive amongst French Canadians by special language papers and literature. ..."[2] Neither the ECCI letter nor the party convention delved into the theoretical aspect of the national question; the convention concluded that what the party needed was to "establish party organization among French Canadian workers."[3] Despite the limitations of this position, it was an important step forward for the Communist Party on the road to a fuller understanding of the national question in Canada. This was made clear in the convention's political theses in which it was declared that "particular attention must be given to work among the French Canadian masses, work that has been almost wholly neglected by the party."[4] And it was in the course of this work that the party began to grapple with the national question.

The national question as an active issue under discussion by the Communist Party, lay dormant during most of the first half of the 1930s. It was a time when the party was deeply concerned with the struggle against Section 98 under which the party was banned and eight of its leaders imprisoned, and with the organization of the unorganized into the militant industrial unions of the

WUL. Then, in the spring of 1934, a contributor to the party's underground theoretical journal, the *Review,* pointed out that French Canadians formed a nation and therefore had the right to self-determination up to separation.[5] Officially, however, the party maintained its previous position. The seventh party convention in July 1934, for example, called for unity of the Canadian working class against the bourgeoisie and declared its support for the demands of the French Canadian masses against the English-speaking and French Canadian bourgeoisie.[6]

That the above-mentioned contributor to the *Review* could come to this conclusion was made possible by the growing availability of Lenin's and Stalin's contributions on the national question. The Leninist definition of a nation is as follows:

A nation is a historically constituted, stable community of people, formed on the basis of a common language, territory, economic life, and psychological make-up manifested in a common culture.[7]

In an article published in *The Worker,* Fred Rose attempted to apply this definition to French Canada and came to the conclusion that French Canada fulfilled all of the conditions but one. He denied that there was such a thing as a French Canadian economy; there was only a Canadian economy.[8] And since according to the Leninist definition of what constitutes a nation "it is sufficient for a single one of these characteristics to be lacking and the nation ceases to be a nation," French Canada could not be considered a nation.[9] Fred Rose was mistaken, for if he had more carefully studied what was meant by a common

economy in this context, he would have realized that it *did not signify a separate economic life from other nationalities.*[10] A common economy is one which is *no longer separated into feudal principalities* (or *seigneuries* as it was termed in New France under the *ancien régime*). It comes about as a consequence of the rise of capitalism which, in the course of its development, integrates these small isolated feudal economies into a larger, territorially-defined capitalist economy. In its early phase of development, the common capitalist economy stimulated the formation of nations and nation-states.

The contributions made by the *Review* writer and by Fred Rose signified the fact that the party was coming to grips seriously with the national question. They signified the Communist Party's recognition of the fact that French Canada constituted a distinct entity.

During this period, Fred Rose was given the specific task of building the party among French Canadian workers. His unwavering defense of the French Canadian people's struggle against economic, political, social, cultural and language discrimination won a place for him in the hearts of many French Canadians, particularly in the Montreal working class district of Cartier.

The defense of the French Canadian people's struggle against discrimination and for equality was an important aspect of the Communist Party's brief to the Rowell-Sirois Commission on federal-provincial relations in 1938. As the party pointed out in its brief, Confederation maintained French Canada in a degraded position in relation to English-speaking Canada and deprived French

ARCHIVES CPC/PAC/PA-125152

Canadians of their political, social, economic and cultural rights. The party charged that the Duplessis government was no defender of French Canadian rights either, because it carried out measures that prevented the French Canadians from enjoying genuine equal rights. Under these circumstances, the party believed that the federal government had to play a much larger role in guaranteeing and ensuring equal rights for the French Canadian people.[11]

Aiming to overcome both the effects of the Great Depression and national antagonisms in Canada, the party's brief had three unique and outstanding features: (1) it represented the accumulation of 17 years of struggle by the party for a program of immediate demands for workers and farmers; (2) it outlined a comprehensive program to overcome the effects of the economic crisis in a way beneficial to working people; and (3) it responded to the question of constitutional reform and indirectly, the national question. The party proposed, among many other measures, that the federal government assume complete responsibility for unemployment insurance, social welfare, health and crop insurance, family allowances, old age pensions and the establishment of minimum educational standards for all of Canada.[12] In addition to helping the Canadian working people as a whole, these measures would help French Canadians overcome "their discriminatory exclusion from the economic, social and cultural rights of the Canadian people."[13]

With respect to constitutional change, the Communist Party's brief demanded the amendment of the BNA Act to permit "the establishment of equality of the rights of the French Canadian people, without which there can be no economic progress and social security for the Canadian people as a whole."[14]

The brief urged the adoption of a Canadian Bill of Rights which would "guarantee the economic, social and cultural rights of the French Canadian people."[15] Clearly, the Communist Party's contribution to the Rowell-Sirois Commission marked an important step in the development of the party's program for the equality of the French Canadian nation in a united Canada.

The party had taken up the struggle for equality, but the particular circumstances of the period in Quebec militated against a more detailed examination of the question of the right to self-determination. The monopoly-controlled Hepburn government in Ontario and the reactionary, nationalist and even pro-fascist Duplessis government in Quebec formed an axis to combat all social reform behind the slogan of provincial rights. Duplessis cleverly played on French Canada's national aspirations to come to power in 1936. He used reactionary bourgeois nationalism to justify the repression of the working class movement and opposition to social welfare schemes sponsored by the federal government, thus perpetuating French Canada's inferior living standards and working conditions. All this was done, not to protect the French Canadian nation, but to ensure that the monopolies, which were overwhelmingly owned and controlled by English-speaking capitalists, would have a continuous source of cheap, unorganized labor. Duplessis' nationalism was therefore fundamentally opposed to the real interests and aspirations of the French Canadian nation.

Although some party members, including some leaders, called for the recognition of the right to national self-determination, the Communist Party as such had not yet officially come to the theoretical conclusion that this was a valid demand. The third element, self-determination, became a focus of discussion in the party throughout the 1940s.

2. The Nation and the Right to Self-Determination

The key to the recognition of the right to national self-determination was recognition of the fact that French Canadians constituted a nation. Reflecting the growing theoretical maturity of the party, this idea was more or less grasped by the end of the 1930s.[16] This conclusion was not reached without, at times, sharp controversy.[17] Nevertheless, recognition of French Canada as a nation was formalized, at the February 1942 party conference in Montreal. That con-

ference declared that "the Communist Party stands for the fullest satisfaction of the *national* [author's emphasis] aspirations of the French Canadians."[18]

The constituent convention of the LPP in August 1943 further developed the party's position on the national question in Canada.

The Labor-Progressive Party stands unreservedly for the establishment of full national equality for the French Canadians. The party presses the government, provincial and federal, to take immediate measures to redress the burning grievances of the French Canadian people. It fights for the establishment of explicit constitutional guarantees of the cherished language rights of the French Canadians. It works to win the support of English Canada for the achievement of full national equality for the French Canadian people. This is a common responsibility of all Canadians and the key to real and enduring national unity.[19]

Another indication of the party's growing theoretical maturity on the national question was reflected in the publication of Stanley B. Ryerson's book, *French Canada,* in September 1943. In it, Ryerson pointed out that "it is important to understand the fact that the democratic struggle of the French Canadian people during the whole of the preceding period had been *a struggle for the right of national self-determination,* for their right as a nation to choose their own form of state."[20]

At the May 1947 NC plenum, the LPP formally recognized French Canada's right to national self-determination. To achieve Canadian unity and national equality for French Canada, it was necessary to abolish the economic and social inequalities existing between Canada's two nations. The NC concluded that genuine national self-

In April 1965, Quebec Communists demonstrate in Montreal against the massive U.S. bombing of North Vietnam.

determination could be achieved through united action of all democratic forces in the struggle against the monopolies and reaction. This was the way for French Canada to win more advanced social services, social security and higher education standards. Winning these reforms would eventually lead to the realization of the need for "democratic modernization" of the constitution.[21]

Although the right to national self-determination was recognized, the LPP's main emphasis was unquestionably on the abolition of the economic and social inequalities existing between English and French Canada. "Democrat-ic modernization" *without weakening* constitutional guarantees for French Canada became an important part of the party's program. However, there was nothing as yet about the necessity of struggling for a new constitution for Canada with an emphasis on the right to national self-determination. This continued emphasis on equality of Canada's two nations was politically sound because, in the post-war period, Duplessis continued to wage total war against social reforms on the all-Canada basis proposed by the King government. The latter was under heavy pressure from the working class and democratic forces to implement social reforms. Once again,

Duplessis posed as a champion of French Canadian nationalism fighting for Quebec's provincial rights against the centralism of the federal government. As there was as yet no national democratic mass movement that saw through the hypocrisy of Duplessis' reactionary nationalism, it was thus hardly the time for the LPP to stress the right to national self-determination.

In the Quebec party organization, some French Canadian members had a different, essentially nationalist point of view. A nationalist deviation was first manifested in 1945 when Emery Samuel declared that "it was impossible to have a single Leninist strategy for two nations. ..." Claiming that the political strategy for English Canada was the affair of English-speaking Canadians, Samuel wanted only to discuss "the political strategy of my country, French Canada."[22] Henri Gagnon's nationalist tendencies were not so easily discernible. During the Quebec LPP convention of 1947, Gagnon and his group hid their nationalist inclinations behind an acrimonious debate in which they fought for the exclusive right of the French Canadian delegates to name the French Canadian half of the incoming provincial committee. Resorting to open factionalism, they pursued a line which in essence tended to separate the party membership along national lines. When the majority of the 1947 convention voted to abolish national distinctions in the election of the provincial executive, Gagnon and his supporters walked out. Gagnon then took his differences with the party to the bourgeois press. A few weeks later, he was expelled for organizing an anti-party grouping within the

ARCHIVES CPC/PAC/PA-124363

party with a nationalist orientation.[23] In confirmation of both his factionalism and his nationalism, Gagnon proceeded to form the Communist Party of French Canada, an organization which did not survive for long.

Within a year, Gagnon revealed the real source of his differences with the LPP on the national question (which he had up to then denied). Not only did he oppose the party's primary emphasis on equality rather than national self-determination, but he was opposed to the transfer of Quebec taxation points to the federal government to enable it to enact the proposed social legislation. This definitely put him in the Duplessis camp on the issue. These events were to resurface in the inner-party conflict of 1956, when they were used as a cover for attacking the general Marxist-Leninist line of the party.

It was not until the Asbestos strike of 1949 that significant sections of democratic and Catholic opinion began to break with Duplessis and inject a democratic content into Quebec's national movement. Only then did the movement for national self-determination take on a certain mass character. This played a significant role in the inclusion of the following formulation in the draft program adopted by the NC in 1951:

Such a union of both Canadian nations can be achieved and preserved only if it is voluntary and based on the free choice of the people of each of the two nations. That is why the recognition of the existence of the French Canadian nation by the English-speaking Canadians, of its full rights and sovereignty, including the right of secession, is the path along which the friendship and close union of the two peoples can become firm and lasting. There must be no imposition upon French Canada of any institution, social changes or policies against the will of the Quebec people. The future of French Canada will be decided by the French Canadian people themselves.[24]

The third point of reference, self-determination, was thus solidly entrenched. What remained was the further application of the Leninist approach to the national question in the specific, complex conditions of Canada.

A major step forward in the detailed development of the LPP's policy on the national question was the new program's proposals for a democratic constitution. In the course of preparing its lengthy submission to the Royal Commission on Constitutional Problems, the LPP had come to the conclusion that French Canada's struggle for national equality was an important component of the democratic struggle of the Canadian

working people as a whole. Confederation had failed to meet the demand of the French Canadian nation for full national equality. Just as Canadian monopoly and U.S. imperialism sought to undermine the democratic rights of the Canadian people as a whole, so it also denied the democratic and national rights of the French Canadian nation. In contrast, the LPP demanded the right to national self-determination for French Canada up to and including the right of secession.

Victory for this democratic principle will open the way for the free and voluntary association of French Canada with English-speaking Canada in a federal state based upon the complete national equality of both peoples.[25]

Although not demanding a new, made-in-Canada constitution, the party believed that very substantial changes were required in order to secure genuine democracy for both nations. The LPP had the distinction of being the only political party in Canada to suggest a democratic solution to the national question.

At the 16th convention of the Communist Party of Canada in October 1959, the party made important amendments to its program with regard to the national question. The program, in addition to expressing support for French Canada's right to self-determination up to and including the right to secession, now demanded the replacement of the BNA Act with a made-in-Canada constitution buttressed by a Canadian Bill of Rights. A new Canadian constitution would guarantee the inviolability of the rights of the Canadian people.[26] However, the program did not sufficiently spell out the need for unity of the working class and democratic forces of both nations in the struggle against the common enemy, monopoly and U.S. domination. Accordingly, an amendment was adopted in the 1962 program which observed that only in this way could an equitable basis be created for a lasting voluntary union within one bi-national state.[27]

The Communist Party's demand for a new made-in-Canada constitution was further developed in its submission to the Royal Commission on Bilingualism and Biculturalism. This Commission was appointed by the Pearson government in response to the rapid growth of Quebec nationalism. The party's submission criticized the federal government for reducing the problem of relations between Canada's two nations to questions of language and culture and for ignoring the fact that French Canada was oppressed *as a nation*.[28] Standing for the unity of the working class and people of French and English Canada, the submission demanded the unfettered right of both nations to self-determination and the replacement of French Canada's unequal status by national equality.[29] To achieve unity in a bi-national Canada, it proposed the convocation of a Constituent Assembly elected on the basis of equal representation from French and English Canada.

In such an assembly, the representatives of the two nations would negotiate a new constitution *on a completely equal footing*, with the principles of unanimity prevailing as between the delegations from French and English Canada.[30]

A referendum would then be held and the proposed constitution would require the endorsement of a majority in each of the two nations before being adopted.

The Communist Party's submission to the Royal Commission also outlined the features that this new constitution would have to include, in order to be acceptable to both nations. One of its features would be to spell out clearly and unambiguously, the voluntary character of the union between French and English Canada. The new constitution would have to contain explicit guarantees of the right of each nation to self-determination. The new Bill of Rights would outlaw all forms of discrimination on the basis of national or ethnic origin.[31] In its proposals for a new confederal pact, the party's submission called for an end to the situation in which a parliamentary majority based on the English-speaking majority of Canada's population could impose its opinion on the French Canadian minority.

We see as the most satisfactory solution to this problem, the establishment of a *bi-cameral* confederal parliament, one house based upon representation by population as is the present House of Commons, the other house, also elective (unlike the present Senate), but composed of an *equal number* of representatives from each of the two nations. Each house should have equal authority, and all legislation would require the endorsement of both.[32]

Such a structure would protect the equality of rights of both nations and the democratic principle of majority rule. (This proposal was subsequently incorporated into the party program adopted in 1971.)

The Communist Party's submission to the Royal Commission on Bilingualism and Biculturalism was a substantial con-

The Communist Party of Canada and the Communist Party of Quebec lobby for the creation of one million jobs, November 1970.

tribution to the full development of the position of the party on the national question. It showed that Communists were able to apply Marxist-Leninist theory on the national question to the conditions prevailing in Canada and in such a way as to serve the interests of Canada's working people and promote Canada's unity. The party brought forward concrete proposals for the democratic solution of the crisis of Confederation at a time when the national movement in Quebec was on the ascent.

3. The Crisis of Confederation

After Duplessis' death in 1959 and the victory of the Liberal Party under the leadership of Jean Lesage in 1960, Quebec underwent profound changes.

The Lesage government proceeded to secularize and modernize Quebec's state structure, its functions and institutions. This included revamping the educational system and nationalizing a multitude of hydro-electric companies, amalgamating them into the newly-formed Hydro-Quebec. The vigor of these reforms was facilitated by the fact that all the preconditions for the full-scale development of monopoly capitalism had been ripe for some time. In fact, under Duplessis, a contradiction had arisen between the objective needs of monopoly capital, particularly with respect to the interventionist function of the state in Quebec's economic and social life, and Duplessis' stubborn resistance to any meaningful change.

The Lesage government made a con-

Communist Party of Quebec candidate Claude Demers speaking to a voter in the provincial riding of St. Jérôme, 1972.

scious effort to use the Quebec state apparatus as a lever "to increase the role of French Canadian capital in the monopolies already existing and in rapid process of formation but by no means to the exclusion of U.S., Anglo-Canadian or European capital."[33] A special NEC report to the April 1965 NC plenum, delivered by Sam J. Walsh (who had been a Toronto school trustee in 1949 and 1950 and had become the new leader of the party's Quebec wing) stated:

In order to develop Quebec on the basis of modern state-monopoly capitalism, many stifling institutions inherited from the patronage-ridden, stagnant regime of the Union Nationale had to be renovated or replaced. In some cases this renovation, which Premier Lesage likes to call the quiet revolution, brought about reforms which were beneficial to the masses of the people. And these were welcomed, indeed they had been fought for. But the primary objectives of the government were clearing the way for the full-scale development of state-monopoly capitalism in Quebec.[34]

Popular pressure and support for continued reforms were part of a revival of Quebec nationalism. For many years, French Canadians had protested their national oppression. The unequal status of the French Canadian nation was at the root of the crisis of Confederation and of the unresolved national question in Canada.[35] The resurgence of nationalism in this period contained a new quality. Under Duplessis, national consciousness had been channelled into reactionary, bourgeois nationalism. A land-owning class (including the Catholic Church) whose material basis had long since been undermined by the development of monopoly capitalism, was its historical source. In the 1960s, the situation was quite different. The working class was becoming more aware of its specific class interests. However, because the working class was still in the process of organizing itself, it was not yet able to distinguish its class and national interests from those of the French Canadian bourgeoisie. In contrast, the French Canadian bourgeoisie, particularly its more radical petty-bourgeois section, was keenly aware of its class interests. Allied with the middle strata in the Quebec state apparatus, bourgeois and petty-bourgeois nationalists assumed the leadership of the struggle of the French Canadian nation against national oppression.

The bourgeois and petty-bourgeois nationalists aspired to join the world of monopoly capital but were confronted by the fact of U.S. and Anglo-Canadian monopoly domination. They therefore relied on the Quebec state apparatus to provide the wherewithal to achieve their class aims. The contradiction between the nationalist section of the French Canadian bourgeoisie and the U.S. and Anglo-Canadian monopolies led to the exacerbation of the contradiction between the two nations, and consequently to the formation of separatist groups which regarded secession as the only solution to the fulfillment of their class ambitions.

While supporting the French Canadian nation's right to self-determination up to and including the right to separate from Canada, the party conducted a vigorous campaign against separatism.

It challenged separatist notions that Quebec was a colony of English-speaking Canada. The April 1965 CC plenum rejected this concept on the grounds that Quebec did not have the essential features of a colony. While it was true that only a small percentage of French Canadian capitalists participated in the effective control of big industrial and financial monopolies, it was equally true that a section of the French Canadian bourgeoisie was showing unmistakable signs of developing into an imperialist bourgeoisie. To say that Quebec was a colony was to characterize French Canada's struggle as a national liberation struggle, a theory which in practice served as a cover for the French Canadian bourgeoisie's drive to gain economic and political advantages at the expense of both the Canadian working people and the Anglo-Canadian monopolies. Separation was actually an extreme form of the policy of the Lesage government and reflected the existence of differences within the rising French Canadian bourgeoisie as to how to strengthen their specific class interests. The Communist Party opposed separatism because it would divide and weaken the working class of both nations and prejudice their interests in the common struggle against monopoly domination and U.S. imperialism.[36]

The Communist Party's stance in favor of the right to national self-determination, of genuine equality between the two nations of Canada and of unity between the two nations on an equal, voluntary and negotiated basis stood in sharp contrast to the NDP's refusal to even acknowledge the existence of two nations in Canada. In 1964, the

Three of the leaders of the Communist Party of Quebec. From left to right: Claire DaSylva, Jeannette Walsh and Claude Demers.

NDP suffered the consequences of its short-sighted policy when the majority of its French Canadian members split from the party to form the separatist-oriented Parti socialiste du Québec.[37]

Given the rising national consciousness of the French Canadian people, it was more important than ever for the Communist Party to bring its organizational structure into harmony with Canada's bi-national character. The party constitution, it was pointed out, did not reflect this fact of Canadian history and political life.[38] The NC therefore adopted a resolution expressing its agreement with the proposal that "the party in Quebec be established as a distinct entity and be called the Parti communiste du Québec."[39] Furthermore, the NC instructed the NEC to establish a Quebec Solidarity Fund which would give the Communist Party of Quebec the means to strengthen its work in French Canada. It also instructed the NEC to draft amendments to the party constitution for submission to the next party convention. The 19th convention in 1966 agreed to the relevant amendments. The amended constitution declared the Communist Party of Quebec to be a distinct entity within the Communist Party of Canada, having "complete control over its policies and structure within Quebec as decided by the National Convention and the National Committee of the Communist Party of Quebec."[40] The constitution further stated that as members of the Communist Party of Canada, the members of the Communist Party of Quebec "participate fully, on the basis of equality, in its life and activities, in its Conventions, Central Committee and leadership, take

part in the collective formulation of policy and share in the common responsibility for action in the interests of the working class of Canada."[41] In order to make the nomenclature of the leading party committees correspond with Canada's bi-national character, the National Committee and the National Executive Committee were renamed the Central Committee and the Central Executive Committee respectively. With these changes, the Communist Party was in a better position to rebuild its strength and influence among French Canadians.

The 1960s saw an upsurge of activity in the Quebec working class movement. Strikes and rallies, marked by increasing militancy, became regular features of the Quebec labor scene. However, the labor movement in Quebec had some serious weaknesses, the most damaging being its lack of unity. The Quebec Federation of Labor (QFL) and the CNTU raided each other constantly. The QFL supported the NDP federally but was unable to decide whether to support the NDP provincially or work toward the formation of a mass party of labor, to include left organizations, as decided by its 1967 convention. This situation was complicated by the fact that many of the old-time leaders, especially of the craft unions, still had political ties with the Union Nationale. The CNTU for its part was dominated by people like Jean Marchand, its president, who argued that the formation of a workers' party could not be morally justified.[42] Significantly, he became a cabinet minister in Pierre E. Trudeau's Liberal government a few years later.

Neither the Liberal Party, nor the Union Nationale which came to power in the 1966 provincial election were able to satisfy the demands of the working class or of the nationalist petty-bourgeoisie. Both parties alienated the working class because of their anti-labor, pro-monopoly bias. Both alienated the nationalist petty-bourgeoisie and middle strata. Reflecting the interests of the monopolies, the two parties, particularly the Liberals, moved to cleanse their ranks of petty-bourgeois nationalist spokesmen. This action was designed to avoid coming to grips with the national question; instead, the idea of increasing the rights and powers of *all* the provinces at the expense of the federal government was supported. As the January 1968 CC meeting pointed out, the shifting of social and economic responsibilities to all the provinces in the name of provincial rights could "only assist monopoly capital in its obstruction of such measures as medicare and leads in the direction of the balkanization of English Canada."[43]

A just and democratic solution to the crisis of Confederation, the party added, required full and unconditional recognition of the right of the French Canadian nation to decide for itself the course of its national development. At the same time, it was necessary to ensure the centralization of education and social welfare schemes for English-speaking Canada while not infringing on Quebec's legitimate demand to handle its own affairs. Also, unity on an equal and voluntary basis was necessary for the common struggle against U.S. imperialist domination which threatened the vital interests of both nations.[44] The struggle for the right to self-determination was therefore an aspect of the struggle for an independent united Canada and also for a democratic anti-monopoly coalition. The Communist Party of Canada and the Communist Party of Quebec (founded on November 26-27, 1965) were to play a substantial role in fighting for this policy in the working class movement.

The Communist Party took into account the prevailing political situation in Quebec in determining its tactical approach. The political ferment of the Quiet Revolution had spawned not only new forms of Quebec nationalism but

The 1975 May Day parade organized by Quebec's three trade union centers.

also a myriad of left-wing, socialist groups and journals, most of which believed that socialism could not be achieved without independence. At first, Communists thought that possibilities existed for a rapprochement with these groups. It was instrumental, with the leadership of the Parti socialiste du Québec, in setting up the Comité de coordination de mouvements de gauche. Its aim was to unite the efforts of the left to influence the trade union centers and other mass popular organizations to join in the formation of a mass federated party of the working people around a common program of immediate demands in defense of the interests and national rights of Quebec's working people.[45] The Comité de coordination de mouvements de gauche succeeded in organizing Canada's first post-war mass May Day meeting in Montreal in 1966, with speakers from the QFL, the CNTU, the Communist Party, the Parti socialiste du Québec and several of their affiliated groups.

When the 1967 convention of the QFL decided to call a conference of progressive groups in order to reach agreement on a political program for a mass party of labor, the doors were opened for the possible formation of a party with direct support from at least one section of the labor movement. Such support would have helped to give the federated party the distinct working-class character it needed. The Communist Party of Quebec warned, however, that pseudo-leftists could effectively sabotage the formation of such a party.[46]

The clearing of petty-bourgeois nationalists from the ranks of the Liberal Party and the Union Nationale led to the formation of the separatist Mouvement Souveraineté-Association headed by the purged Liberal cabinet minister, René

The Communist contingent in the 1976 May Day parade in Montreal.

Lévesque. This movement's aim was to unite all the "respectable" separatist groups around its nationalist program. But from the beginning, it was able to attract a significant section of the trade union leadership who saw the new group as a way to advance labor's aims in opposition to the Liberals. This development, together with the divisive activities of the pseudo-left, did result in the QFL convention resolution remaining a dead letter — much to the relief of the reformists and nationalists in the QFL who were also opposed to a mass federated party of labor.

The Communist Party of Quebec realized that the formation of a mass federated party of labor uniting the labor unions and Quebec's progressive and socialist groups was still on the agenda, even though it had moved farther down in the order of business. As for the left-wing groups, many of them eventually folded. But the party retained the idea of a mass federated party of the working people through which the Quebec working class could express its independent class and political interests.[47] This proposition was elaborated and developed in subsequent pamphlets and books.

In the meantime, monopoly capital and its representatives in federal and provincial governments persisted in ignoring the national question. Although it provided ample evidence to support contentions that French Canada's status in Confederation was inferior to that of English Canada, the Royal Commission on Bilingualism and Biculturalism avoided the conclusion that French Canadians collectively constituted a nation whose homeland was Quebec

and who therefore had the right to national self-determination and equality with English Canada.

It became increasingly clear that relations between Canada's two nations were deteriorating rapidly. By installing a French Canadian as Prime Minister, namely Trudeau, monopoly hoped somehow to assuage French Canada's belief that Confederation served as a vehicle for the oppression of the French Canadian nation. The Liberal strategy was to avoid dealing with the main issue of *national* oppression by reducing it to its manifestations such as language and cultural discrimination, differences between Quebec and the federal government over taxation powers, and so on.

Although some piecemeal reforms were made to promote what is called

"Quebec needs jobs, not the army" — Communists protest the War Measures Act on Parliament Hill.

bilingualism and biculturalism, the Trudeau government's policies failed to stem the growth of Quebec's national consciousness or the sharpening of relations between the two nations.[48] This became more obvious when the Parti Québécois (PQ) made a very significant breakthrough in the Quebec election of April 1970. Seven Péquistes were elected; the party as a whole garnered 23 per cent of the total vote. However, the Liberals under Robert Bourassa, were returned to power.

Rather than deal with Canada's national antagonisms in a democratic and rational way, the Trudeau government opted for a policy of confrontation and repression. In October 1970, the terrorist Front de Libération du Québec kidnapped James Cross, a British trade commissioner in Montreal, and Pierre Laporte, Quebec's Minister of Labor who was subsequently killed. Condemning the kidnappings and other acts of terror as "not the forms of struggle that the working class and the Communist Party adopt in striving for social change," the CEC warned that such acts would "merely give reaction a pretext to perpetuate its anti-people and anti-national policy."[49]

Within days of the kidnappings, the federal government invoked the War Measures Act, brought Quebec under military occupation and suspended the human and democratic rights of *all* Canadians. The government justified these actions on the grounds of an alleged threat of an "apprehended insurrection" even though it was clear that no such "apprehended insurrection" existed.[50] In actual fact, the intent was to frustrate the working class and national

ARCHIVES CPC/PAC

movements in Quebec and to intimidate the working class and democratic forces in both French and English Canada. The anti-working class and anti-French Canadian essence of the War Measures Act was demonstrated by the fact that of the more than 450 people who were detained without charge, only two were known to have been members of the Front de Libération du Québec; the majority of those arrested were trade unionists, civic activists, Québécois personalities and cultural figures, Communists and other left-wingers.

The reaction of the Quebec working class in the months that followed was unprecedented in the history of French Canada. Quebec's three trade union centers, the QFL, the CNTU and the Centrale de l'Enseignement du Québec (CEQ — the Quebec teachers' union) organized the Common Front whose aims were to defend democracy and the French Canadian nation. Initially, a large part of the leadership and membership of the three union centers did not support the Common Front. They had fallen prey to the massive propaganda campaign which equated the Common Front's aims with support for terrorism. Nevertheless, the working class briefly came forward as an independent political force and a leader of the national and democratic struggle.[51] The second stage of the Common Front came in October 1971 as a result of the unity achieved around support for the striking workers of the Montreal bourgeois paper, *La Presse*. This stage was characterized by a strong anti-capitalist sentiment. The third stage of the Common Front opened with the one-day general strike of 210,000 public and parapublic employees on March 28, 1972, followed by an 11-day strike by the same workers in April. The latter strike was broken by Bill 19, a heavy-handed back-to-work order of the Quebec government which threatened crushing fines and up to a year in prison. These two strikes were characterized by a high level of unity.

Although the unity and militancy of the Quebec labor movement was growing, forces were at work to split the Common Front and divert it from its course of independent labor political action. Right-wing elements wanted to bring the labor movement back to a

class-collaborationist course. The CNTU suffered a split of right-wing elements who formed the Centrale des Syndicats Démocratiques. The right-wing leaders of the QFL building trades carried out raiding against the CNTU building trades provoking a split between the CNTU and the QFL.

Nationalists in all three union centers worked hard to bring the labor movement under the influence of the petty-bourgeois PQ. The petty-bourgeois nationalists opposed the formation of a mass federated party of the working people because it would place the working class in the position of leading the national and democratic movements.[52]

The efforts of the nationalist and right-wing elements to divide the Quebec labor movement did meet with some success. The Common Front was weakened; cooperation declined. The

QFL decided to give conditional support to the PQ rather than to the formation of a political party expressing the independent interests of the workers. This conjuncture of events made it possible for the PQ to pose as the defender of the French Canadian nation. The result was that in the October 1973 Quebec election, the PQ won six seats and 31 per cent of the vote, and thus became the Official Opposition. The Liberals won 102 of the 110 seats in a demagogic, anti-labor campaign.

The re-election of the Bourassa government did nothing to solve Quebec's many problems. The province continued to suffer from unemployment, inflation, slow growth and government corruption. The Bourassa government continued its anti-labor policies. In fact, the government's aggressiveness toward the trade unions obliged the latter to intensify its struggles, which had ebbed somewhat in 1973. The most significant action of this period was the UAW strike against United Aircraft in Longueuil which began in January 1974. The company refused to bargain with the workers in good faith, a stance which was facilitated by the support given to the company by the Trudeau and Bourassa governments. The strike reached its peak in May 1975, when 34 workers peacefully occupied one of the plant's shops. The police charged in, savagely beat the workers and arrested them. A week later, 100,000 members of the QFL held a "study session" in support of the striking UAW workers. After 20 months, the strike was settled leaving the union weakened; but this and other struggles by Quebec's working people left the Bourassa government with a severely tarnished image.

As the Quebec labor movement still lacked a mass party of its own and as disillusionment with the Liberals and the remnants of the Union Nationale and Créditistes was extremely high, the electoral conditions were created for the stunning upset victory of the PQ in the Quebec election of November 15, 1976.

The February 1977 CC plenum pointed out that the PQ's victory created a new situation in Quebec and Canada. French Canadians had prevented the election of a party directly tied to monopoly and had instead voted for a petty-bourgeois nationalist party whose basic goal was Quebec's separation from Canada. The vote reflected a turn away from right-wing policies and in this sense the PQ's victory represented a certain advance for the progressive forces in Quebec.[53]

The CC resolution warned the Quebec working class not to rely on the PQ and criticized those, such as the NDP, who characterized the PQ as a social-democratic party.

The Parti Québécois is not a social-democratic party with a nationalist flavor based on the working class and trade union movement. It is a party representing the interests of the petty-bourgeoisie, the professional middle class, particularly those in the state sector. This stratum of Quebec society is the source of the nationalism through which the petty-bourgeoisie advances its class interests. This results in the Parti Québécois' rejection of the class struggle even though in its program there are elements of social reform which are progressive and which merit support.[54]

It was still necessary for the Quebec working class to establish its own mass party which would advance its independent interests against both monopoly capital and the petty-bourgeoisie.

The CC resolution criticized the monopoly bourgeois parties and the right-wing social-reformists for failing to come to grips with the fact that Canada was a bi-national country. The PQ victory demonstrated that Trudeau's policy of substituting recognition of Canada's bi-national character with bilingualism and regional development was completely bankrupt. Yet the Trudeau government made clear its intention of pursuing such policies. The Tory approach was to dilute the question by calling for the decentralization of federal powers to all the provinces. Their evasion of the basic root of the crisis of Confederation was designed to strengthen the provinces so that U.S. monopolies and multinationals could strengthen their grip on the Canadian economy. It was a policy of dividing Canada and making it easier prey for U.S. imperialism. As for the NDP, it was at this moment veering toward the idea of "special status" for Quebec, a concept which ignored the existence of the French Canadian nation and justified its opportunist flirtation with the PQ. Subsequently, the NDP veered back to its old policy of tailing the Liberal Party on the national question.

All of these approaches, and variations of them, had one common characteristic: they refused to recognize Canada as a bi-national state and consequently the right to national self-determination was ignored. These policies amounted to the perpetuation of the status quo, in other words, to the perpetuation of national antagonisms in Canada and to the exacerbation of the crisis of Confederation.

Only a comprehensive all-sided program, a new economic and social policy geared to full employment and to constitutional reform, based on a democratic restructuring of the constitution, can create conditions for real Canadian unity and thereby cope with the crisis.

The firm foundation for a united Canada lies through recognition of the French Canadian nation and its right to self-determination up to and including the right to secession. It lies in establishing a bi-national state based on an equal, voluntary partnership of the two nations — English and French Canada — and the adoption of a made-in-Canada constitution with guarantees of the language and culture of the two peoples.[55]

The CC resolution pointed out that a firm foundation for a united Canada would require unity of the working class of both nations around economic and social policies aimed at improving the conditions of the working people and overcoming national inequality.

4. The Native Peoples

The Communist Party has an outstanding record in the fight for the rights of the French Canadian nation. So, too, Communists have paid — and still pay — special attention to the oppression of the Native peoples, Indian, Inuit and Métis.

When the European capitalist exploiters and settlers came to Canada, they found a sparsely-populated country that was already occupied by distinct peoples who spoke many different languages and stood at varying levels of economic and social development. For some of these peoples, agriculture formed the basis of tribal life, but for most, subsistence was sustained through hunting and fishing. This situation enabled the Europeans to conquer the new world with relative ease and caused the wholesale displacement of the original inhabitants from the choicest land. The coming of the Europeans interrupted the independent historical development of the Native peoples. Capitalist Europe's conquest of the new world began an era of savage racial oppression of the indigenous peoples. In some cases, the drive for capitalist profit led to wholesale genocide. The Beothuks of Newfoundland, for example, were exterminated to the last individual. In most cases, the indigenous peoples were forcibly deprived of their lands and rights and were driven into reservations where the bourgeoisie systematically deprived them of their language, culture and few remaining rights. Capitalism's policy was the cultural, if not physical, genocide of the Native peoples. As Tim Buck observed at his trial in 1931, the bourgeois state was created in Canada "first to enforce the robbers' will on the suppressed Indians, and later on the working class."[56]

The eighth convention of the Communist Party in October 1937 drew attention to the oppression of the Native peoples in a special resolution. This resolution noted that extreme poverty and disease were rampant on the reserves, that there was little provision for adequate cultural, educational and vocational training, that there were repeated infringements of treaties entered into with the Native peoples and that they were disenfranchised in the country of which they were the original citizens. The resolution therefore demanded that the government take measures to reverse this situation and pledged the party's support toward this end.[57]

Just as Communists fought for the equality of nations, so also they fought for the equality of peoples and an end to all forms of racial, ethnic and national discrimination. In 1943, the constituent convention of the LPP adopted a resolution "fully supporting the Métis and Indian people in their struggle for full equality with other citizens of Canada, and records its sympathy for the program of democratic reforms as put before the authorities by the organizations of the Métis and Indian peoples of Canada."[58]

The party's position on the rights of the Native peoples matured as the years went by. One of the LPP's demands in the 1953 federal election was "full democratic rights for North American Indians and Canadian Arctic peoples, including equal rights and facilities for education and employment."[59]

The 1954 party program demanded full equality for Native peoples, including the possession of tribal lands and hunting and fishing rights, material aid for the growth of their economic life and culture and the abolition of all forms of discrimination.[60]

In the spring of 1959, the NEC issued a statement which, in protesting certain racist actions by the RCMP against the Six Nations Iroquois Confederacy, demanded "recognition by statute of the identity of the Indians as a people, with the full right of self-government on their lands, including control of property and civil rights, finances, welfare services,

Communists protest the federal government's Green Paper on immigration policy.

education and cultural development; in short, of their fundamental right to determine their own way of life, including their association as Indians."[61] This principle was incorporated in the amended program adopted by the 16th convention of the Communist Party. As a distinct people, the Native peoples had the right to self-government and to their languages and culture.[62]

The Communist Party made a particularly in-depth study of the conditions of the Native peoples in its submission to the Joint Committee of the Senate and the House of Commons which was examining the Indian Act in 1961. The party's submission characterized the Act as the legal expression of "the system of oppression and racist discrimination to which the Indian people are subjected."[63] Discrimination against the

Native peoples was a special form of oppression within the framework of monopoly capitalist relations whose basis was the exploitation of man by man. Outlining the historical roots of the oppression of Canada's indigenous peoples, the submission pointed out that the appalling living conditions and state of health and education, rampant racial discrimination, the suppression of the linguistic and cultural heritage of the indigenous peoples which includes forcible assimilation into white society, were all aspects of the government's policy. Demanding the abrogation of the Indian Act, the party also demanded the outlawing of all forms of discrimination and a constitutional amendment that would "accord explicit recognition of the identity of the Indian people, reaffirm their rights as embodied in the Treaties and proclaim their right to self-government in all areas where they comprise a majority of the local population."[64]

The party's submission also examined the place of the indigenous peoples in terms of the national question. The party concluded that the Native peoples constitute a people and as such have certain rights, rights which the Indian Act continuously sought to undermine in the interests of monopoly capital.[65] This principle was reaffirmed by the 18th convention in May 1964, which observed that "at the heart of the struggle for equal rights is the insistence on equality without loss of identity as a people."[66]

In April 1969, the Communist Party's 20th convention called for the adoption of a Native Bill of Rights which would codify in Canada's laws the full and equal rights of the Native peoples, equality in opportunity, full recognition and protection of all historic and treaty rights, self-government and full freedom to move off the reserves without loss of treaty rights. Demanding the just settlement of land claims and adequate financial and other government assistance to the Native peoples, the convention pledged its complete support for the struggles of the indigenous peoples.[67]

The convention's policy statement came at an opportune time, for, a few months later the federal government announced a new policy with respect to the Indian Act, whose aim was to break up the bands, force the Indian people off the reserves, allow the big corporations and land speculators to take over reserve lands and compel the Native peoples to migrate to the slums of city and town where they would be assimilated into the country's poor population as a whole. As former Alberta provincial leader of the Communist Party, Ben Swankey, pointed out, "the Indian people justifiably characterized this policy as genocide."[68] The government's proposals provoked an upsurge of unity and militancy in the Native people's long fight for survival. At the heart of this fight for survival was the demand for self-government and control over their own lands, lands which the monopolies coveted for their resources and speculative value. Pointing to the ambivalence of the NDP, Ben Swankey noted in his pioneering pamphlet on the conditions and struggles of the Native peoples, that the Communist Party "more than any other political party, has consistently played an active public part in supporting full equality for the Native peoples of Canada."[69]

The validity of Ben Swankey's remarks was confirmed not only by the party's past positions but also later ones. In its submission to the Mackenzie Valley Pipeline Inquiry, for example, the party demanded that the pipeline not be built unless the justness of the land claims of the Native peoples of the Northwest Territories was recognized. It was incumbent on the federal government, which had complete control over the Yukon and the Northwest Territories, to come to a principled agreement with the Native peoples with respect to their rights and land claims. Such an agreement would have to include preferential treatment for Native peoples in jobs, training programs, housing, education and medical services as the guarantee of their equal treatment in practice.[70]

The Communist Party's principled defense of the national rights of French Canada, and the democratic rights of the Native peoples was consistent with the reputation the party had earned in defense of immigrants. The Communist Party is the defender of the individual and collective rights of all peoples no matter what their national, racial or ethnic origin. And this fact makes the Communist Party of Canada a steadfast fighter for the democratic and human rights of the Canadian working class and people as a whole.

Throughout its history, the Communist Party of Canada has maintained the supremacy of the class and social question over the national question, without prejudice to a democratic solution to the national question. The national question is subordinate to the class question because the attainment of working class power and the construction of socialism are the only guarantees for permanently overcoming antagonisms between nations. The Leninist position makes it possible for the Communist Party to be a consistent fighter for the interests of the entire Canadian working class while upholding the special democratic interests of Canada's two nations.

1. *Report of the Sixth Convention of the Communist Party of Canada*, May 31-June 7, 1929, Archives CPC, p. 9.
2. Ibid., p. 13.
3. Ibid., p. 16.
4. Ibid., p. 25.
5. "Canadian Communists and the French Canadian Nation" in *The Marxist Quarterly*, No. 15, Autumn 1965, p. 27.
6. *The Way to Socialism* (Montreal, 1934), pp. 49-50.
7. J.V. Stalin, *Works* (Moscow, 1953), Vol. 2, p. 307.
8. *The Worker*, January 19, 1935.
9. Stalin, p. 307.
10. Ibid., p. 306.
11. *Toward a Democratic Canada* (Toronto, 1938), p. 12.
12. Ibid., p. 41.
13. Ibid., p. 11.
14. Ibid., p. 101.
15. Ibid., p. 110.
16. S.B. Ryerson, "French Canada: Thorn in the Side of Imperialism" in *Monthly Review*, March 1940, p. 27.
17. T. Buck, *Thirty Years* (Toronto, 1952), pp. 182-183.
18. *Resolution of the National Party Conference* (1942), p. 15.
19. *Program of the Labor-Progressive Party* (Toronto, 1943), pp. 9-10.
20. S.B. Ryerson, *French Canada* (Toronto, 1943), p. 63.
21. T. Buck, "French Canada versus Duplessis" in *National Affairs Monthly*, Vol. 4, No. 7, August 1947, p. 206.
22. *Submission of Harry Binder to the Commission on the Events of 1947*, August 20, 1956, Archives CPC, p. 2.
23. *Canadian Tribune*, January 10, 1948.
24. *Canadian Independence and People's Democracy* (Toronto, 1952), p. 12.
25. *Canadian Independence and a People's Parliament* (Toronto, 1954), p. 13.
26. *The Road to Socialism in Canada* (Toronto, 1960), pp. 12-13.
27. *The Road to Socialism in Canada* (Toronto, 1962), p. 12.
28. *Submission to the Royal Commission on Bilingualism and Biculturalism by the Communist Party of Canada* (Toronto, 1964), pp. 3-5.
29. Ibid., pp. 17 and 20.
30. Ibid., p. 21.

31. Ibid., p. 22.
32. Ibid., p. 24.
33. S.J. Walsh, "French Canada" in *Viewpoint*, Vol. 2, No. 2, May 1965, p. 19.
34. Ibid.
35. Ibid., p. 16.
36. Ibid., pp. 15-17.
37. S.J. Walsh, "New Socialist Left in Quebec" in *Viewpoint*, Vol. 2, No. 1, January 1965, p. 47.
38. Walsh, "French Canada," pp. 29-31.
39. "Motion on French Canada" in *Viewpoint*, Vol. 2, No. 2, May 1965, p. 33.
40. *Constitution of the Communist Party of Canada* (Toronto, 1966), p. 20.
41. Ibid., pp. 3-4.
42. Walsh, "French Canada," p. 23.
43. *The Crisis of Confederation*, CC statement, January 19-21, 1968, Archives CPC, p. 1.
44. Ibid., p. 4.
45. Walsh, "New Socialist Left in Quebec," p. 59.
46. Communist Party of Quebec, *The Working People of Quebec Need Their Own Political Party* (Montreal, 1968).
47. Communist Party of Quebec, *Les Prochains pas* (Montreal, 1968), p. 14.
48. *The 20th Convention, Communist Party of Canada, November 27-29, 1971* (Toronto, 1971), p. 32.
49. *Canadian Tribune*, October 14, 1970.
50. W. Kashtan, *The Fight for Democracy and Social Advance* (Toronto, 1970), pp. 4-6.
51. S.J. Walsh, "Quebec working class reaches new dimensions" in *Communist Viewpoint*, Vol. 4, No. 4, July-August 1972, p. 21.
52. S.J. Walsh, *For a Mass Federated Party of the Working People* (Montreal, 1973), p. 10.
53. "For a Democratic Solution to the Crisis of Confederation" in *Communist Viewpoint*, Vol. 9, No. 1, January-February 1977, p. 58.
54. Ibid., p. 59.
55. Ibid., pp. 61-62.
56. T. Buck, *An Indictment of Capitalism* (Toronto, 1932), p. 13.
57. *We Propose . . .*, resolutions of the eighth convention of the CPC, October 8-12, 1937, p. 67.
58. *Resolutions of the Labor-Progressive Party* (Toronto, 1943), p. 40.
59. "Federal Election Platform of the Labor-Progressive Party" in *National Affairs Monthly*, Vol. 10, No. 6, June 1953, p. 12.
60. *Canadian Independence and a People's Parliament*, p. 14.
61. *Canadian Tribune*, April 27, 1959.
62. *Road to Socialism in Canada* (1960), p. 26.
63. "Canada's Oppressed People" in *Marxist Review*, Vol. 18, No. 179, May-June 1961, p. 3.
64. Ibid., pp. 13-14.
65. Ibid., pp. 12-13.
66. "Other Resolutions" in *Viewpoint*, Vol. 1, No. 1, April 1964, p. 44.
67. "Native Peoples' Bill of Rights" in *Convention 69* (Toronto, 1969), p. 91.
68. B. Swankey, *National Identity or Cultural Genocide?* (Toronto, 1969), p. 5.
69. Ibid., p. 35.
70. *Mackenzie Pipeline: Development or Sellout?* (1975).

14. Unity in Action

In the 1970s the people of Vietnam won a long and hard-earned victory over U.S. imperialism. Progressive people around the world greeted this victory with deeply-felt joy. It was the culmination of years of struggle in support of Vietnam and proved that a mighty imperialist force could be beaten. It strengthened the optimism of a period of resurging people's movements in the capitalist countries, of expanding struggles for national and social emancipation and of the growing strength of the socialist community. Shortly afterward came the signing of the Helsinki Agreement and the world rejoiced at this triumph for peace which opened a new stage of détente.

As the cold war crumbled, the Communist Party of Canada was able to overcome much of the isolation imposed by the capitalist class, emerging as a vital and increasingly influential force in the working class and democratic movements.

It was becoming increasingly difficult for the bourgeoisie to rely on the rhetoric of the cold war — Canada and the capitalist world as a whole was shaken by a deep crisis. There was not an aspect of society immune to the symptoms of a system in decay. For working people the crisis heralded a constant assault on labor's rights, social and working conditions; an assault countered by growing labor militancy.

1. The Road to Socialism

When Pierre Elliott Trudeau became Prime Minister of Canada in 1968, there were clear indications that Canada was about to enter a difficult period in its economic and political life. There was widespread desire among Canadians for change, which monopoly successfully channelled into the election of a majority Liberal government around Trudeau's slogan for a "just society." During this election, Communists warned that "the Canadian people were being offered an illusion of change instead of real change required to solve the deepening problems confronting the country."[1]

An urgent problem facing the country as Trudeau assumed office, was the increasing opposition to national oppression in Quebec. However, the Liberal government had no intention of seeking a democratic solution to the crisis of Confederation; rather, Trudeau moved to curb the rising national movement in Quebec. When in 1970, the terrorist Front de Libération du Québec (FLQ) kidnapped British trade commissioner James Cross and Quebec Minister of Labor Pierre Laporte, the federal government seized the opportunity to invoke the War Measures Act, an Act with an established history as a weapon against democracy and the working class. While its use this time was mainly directed to suppress the struggle for national self-determination in Quebec, the Act was also intended to intimidate the working class and democratic movements throughout Canada.

Before, during, and after the imposition of the Act, the RCMP on their own initiative or under the direction of as yet unnamed powers, perpetrated illegal acts, such as Operation Checkmate. On the grounds of protecting Canada from subversion, democratic organizations such as the Communist Party, trade unions, farm organizations, Native

On the day after the invocation of the War Measures Act, the Communist Party answered the government's intimidation by taking their protest to Parliament Hill.

peoples groups, the Parti Québécois and the NDP were harassed and victimized by RCMP arson, break-ins, wire-tapping, forgeries, letter openings, invasion of privacy. RCMP provocations included the issuing of a false communiqué allegedly drawn up by the FLQ.

In the first few days of the October Crisis the country was confused and fearful due to the hysterical media reports of subversion and the uncertain implications of living under a War Measures Act. But the Communist Party of Canada refused to be intimidated by the government's repressive measures and violations of even the most fundamental of bourgeois-democratic rights. In bold

defiance of the government, the party, led by its General Secretary William Kashtan, demonstrated on Parliament Hill in Ottawa on October 17, the day after the invocation of the War Measures Act. True to the party's long tradition as a consistent fighter for the democratic rights of the Canadian people, the demonstrators demanded the repeal of the notorious War Measures Act and the restoration and extension of democratic rights through a united movement of the trade union, progressive and democratic forces. They placed the blame for the crisis where it belonged — on monopoly and its government for having "completely failed to recognize and act on the root causes of the social, economic and constitutional crisis in our country."[2]

The initial response of the social-reformist leadership of the NDP to the October Crisis ranged from unqualified support for the imposition of the War Measures Act (Edward Schreyer, Premier of Manitoba and later Governor General of Canada) to opposition (Andrew Brewin, the NDP's external affairs critic in the House of Commons). Caught between the government-sponsored English-Canadian jingoism, and concern expressed by the CLC among others that the War Measures Act could be used to empower the government and the police to suppress all dissent, the federal NDP parliamentary caucus at first attempted to steer a middle course and avoid taking a definite position.

In early November, the Trudeau government sought Parliament's approval for its actions. It received the support of the Liberals, Tories and Social Credit Members of Parliament in

Members of the party's Central Executive Committee, 1971. Left to Right: William Stewart, Bruce Magnuson, Alf Dewhurst, Norman Freed, William Kashtan, Jeannette Walsh, Sam Walsh, George Harris, Misha Cohen.

their entirety, as well as four NDP Members of Parliament. The remaining 16 members of the NDP's federal parliamentary caucus voted against the government's measures. The Communist Party welcomed the vote of the majority of the NDP parliamentary caucus as a triumph for the growing mass democratic movement in Canada which opposed the government's repressive measures.

Realizing the significant extent of public opposition to the peace-time use of the War Measures Act, the government attempted to enact the equally anti-democratic Public Order Act. Initially, this move received the support of the NDP and CLC leadership, who claimed that the new act was not as repressive as the War Measures Act. The party condemned the new government move, and criticized those social-reformists who supported it, pointing out that "such wavering, vacillation and

sheer opportunism ... played into the hands of the government."[3]

A Canada-wide effort of democratic forces was needed to accomplish the repeal of the War Measures Act and prevent the enactment of the Public Order Act. Given the federal NDP's rejection of the War Measures Act despite right-wing, chauvinist pressures, the Communist Party drew the conclusion that the conditions existed for persuading the NDP to reverse its tentative support for the Public Order Act. Growing public opposition to the government's bill did in fact lead to its withdrawal.

During the October Crisis, three members of the CEC, led by W.C. Beeching, approached the question of the party's relationship to the NDP in a one-sided, left-sectarian manner. For example, in the October 28, 1970, issue of the *Canadian Tribune*, Beeching wrote an editorial which made the attitude toward communism of federal NDP leader

T.C. Douglas a criterion for unity in the fight against the War Measures Act and its proposed substitute.[4] This meant that, although Douglas opposed the War Measures Act, Communists ought not to work with him, and others like him, because of their anti-communism. As the party leadership and the CC realized, W.C. Beeching's position amounted to a renunciation of work with reformist-minded people on specific issues unless they agreed with the policies of the Communist Party, and to a rejection of the need to fight for the formation of a united front. In practice, it was a formula for the self-inflicted isolation of the Communist Party from the working class and democratic movements which at this stage in Canadian history were still very much under the influence of bourgeois and reformist ideology. W.C. Beeching, Don Currie (the party's central organizer) and Charles McFadden (YCL General Secretary) pursued this left-sectarian opportunist line as a faction. The CEC censured the three and ordered them to dissolve their group. These decisions were upheld by the CC plenum of November 1970.[5] Immediately afterward, the three, in defiance of the CC decision, resigned from their posts and from the CEC.

Although the national question and the 1970 October Crisis were major preoccupations of the Communist Party at the beginning of the 1970s, close atten-

tion was also given to general economic and political developments. Analysis of such developments was necessary to maintain a correct strategy, the party's course toward the socialist transformation of Canada. Indeed, one of the main tasks facing the 21st convention in November 1971, was the amendment of the party program to take into account changes which had taken place since the program had been last amended in 1962.

A rich and extensive pre-convention discussion throughout the party had deepened the Communists' understanding of new features of Canadian capitalism. Within capitalist society, monopoly had come to be the dominant factor in economic and political life, the main enemy of all non-monopoly sections of the population. The new program emphasized that breaking monopoly control was the first stage toward the socialist transformation of Canada.

The ability to forge a democratic anti-monopoly and anti-imperialist coalition and a government based on it, directed to curbing and restricting monopoly, extending democracy and consolidating Canadian independence, creates the best conditions for a relatively peaceful advance to socialism.[6]

The 21st convention elaborated its analysis of the role played by monopoly by adding an entirely new section to the program which stressed that "monopoly capital not only exploits the working

Jim Leech, editor of the Canadian Tribune since 1973.

CANADIAN TRIBUNE

of the state and monopoly into a single mechanism. The new 1971 program deepened the analysis of this phenomenon and gave it a more central place in the document as a whole.

The government has virtually become the political instrument of the small group of top monopolies to control the rest of society. Monopoly uses the state to provide orders, capital and subsidies, to secure foreign markets and investments, and to mitigate the consequences of economic crises. The principal aim of modern state-monopoly capitalism is the salvation of the capitalist system, the enrichment of the monopolies, the destruction of the socialist sector of the world, the suppression of the working class movement and the national liberation struggle.[9]

The program examined the increasingly reactionary nature of the state-monopoly capitalist system.

State-monopoly capitalism deepens the crisis of capitalist politics and ideology, generates political reaction, and seeks to strengthen all the reactionary features of capitalist society. State-monopoly capitalism means a shrinking of democratic forms of control, with parliament increasingly by-passed.[10]

The events of October 1970 provided glaring proof of the fragility of even bourgeois-democratic rights in modern capitalist society. It was perfectly accurate for the program to add that "state-monopoly capitalism undermines democracy."[11]

class, but through its dominant position in the economy and financial system and merger with the state, it rigs prices and taxes, manipulates credit, and extracts huge profits from the vast majority of Canadians."[7] It endangers the future of the young generation, denies equal rights and opportunities to women and brings about the ruination of the small farmers and small and medium businessmen. At the heart of the monopoly capitalist system is of course the exploitation of the working class which is "the source of all material wealth and cultural values."[8]

Monopoly capital uses its power to increasingly subordinate the state machinery to its aims, thus extending monopoly control over all sectors of economic life and aggravating the contradictions between monopoly and the overwhelming majority of the people. The 1962 program had devoted only one paragraph to the emergence of state-monopoly capitalism, the merger

In strengthening and deepening the main theses of the program, the convention also made a significant correction to one thesis. The 1962 program had stated that monopoly capital in Canada had fused with the U.S. monopolies with the result that Canada was a U.S. satellite, a dependent of U.S. imperialism. Canada's monopoly élite was linked to the U.S. monopolies as junior partners.[12]

William Kashtan speaking to a rally on Parliament Hill organized by the Communist Party to protest President Nixon's policies in Vietnam and toward Canada.

ARCHIVES CPC/PAC/PA-12437B

The main enemy was therefore "the U.S.-Canadian monopolist oligarchy, in which U.S. capital is dominant."[13] In effect, the 1962 party program underestimated the fact that Canada was and is an imperialist country in its own right.

The 1971 convention recognized that this formulation did not accurately correspond to the economic and political reality in Canada. While still stressing the continuing domination of U.S. imperialism over the Canadian economy, the convention decided to eliminate the implication that Canadian monopoly capitalism had no imperialist interests of its own. Canada's political life proved that Canadian monopoly "is

more than a junior partner to U.S. imperialism."[14] It was certainly true that U.S. monopolies controlled key sectors of the Canadian economy, particularly natural resources, energy and manufacturing industries. But Canadian monopolies advanced their own specific interests in their determination to maintain control over banking, transportation, communications and other vital industries.

The growing strength of Canadian finance capital increased interimperialist competition between the two countries. In his report to the 1971 convention, William Kashtan observed that the special relationship between the USA and Canada had been rudely shattered by the Nixon administration's unilateral demands for further revaluation of the Canadian dollar, for adjustments in trade policy, especially the auto pact and armaments production, and for a continental energy policy. All these measures were intended to strengthen U.S. imperialism at the expense of the Canadian economy.[15] In 1971, the U.S. government established the Domestic International Sales Corporation. It provided tax concessions to companies which could demonstrate that such concessions would increase exports of their products. As the Communist Party noted, this program encouraged U.S.-owned companies to move their operations from Canada to the USA with a resultant loss in jobs for Canadians.[16] In 1973, a proposal was made to the U.S. Senate to end the duty-free status of goods partially manufactured in the USA and then sent to Canada for finishing. Known as the Burke-Hartke bill, this proposal threatened thousands of Canadian jobs.[17]

The Trudeau government sought to counter U.S. demands for closer economic integration by making some timid steps toward a more independent foreign, trade and investment policy. The creation of the Foreign Investment Review Agency in late 1973, was designed to screen foreign takeovers of enterprises in Canada. However, in practice FIRA neither reversed nor halted increasing foreign penetration of the economy. Another step was the agreement between Canada and the USSR to strengthen their relations in various fields.[18] Canada's decision to reduce its troop commitment to NATO coupled with recognition of the People's Republic of China met criticisms from the U.S. government.

Clearly, Canadian imperialism's relationship with U.S. imperialism "is an antagonistic partnership, that of simultaneously collaborators and competitors." Furthermore, the amended program warned, Canadian imperialism's struggle with U.S. imperialism "is directed to achieve maximum profits for Canadian monopoly, not to establish genuine Canadian independence. It reflects the growing rivalry over who will get the bigger share of the profits through the intensified exploitation of the Canadian working class."[19] The main enemy of the Canadian people is therefore monopoly capitalism, both U.S. and Canadian.[20]

Canada's contradictory status as an imperialist country dominated by another imperialist country was reflected in its political life as well. Monopoly in Canada was divided into two main opposing sections which expressed themselves in both the main political parties of monopoly. One section favored closer integration with the United States and opposed any steps to curb U.S. takeovers in Canada. Its policies tended to veer to the right in both domestic and foreign policies. The other section, while not opposed to a certain degree of integration with the U.S. economy, favored greater industrialization of Canada, a lessening to some degree of U.S. domination and the strengthening of Canada's competitive position in the world imperialist economy. Its policies contained an element of bourgeois nationalism leaning toward a more independent economic and foreign policy. These policies, however,

Alf Dewhurst mans the Communist Party's information table at the annual Labor Festival.

would not guarantee genuine Canadian independence or higher living standards for working people.

The differences between the two main sections of the monopoly bourgeoisie were important to the struggles of Canadian working people, "in order to utilize them in the interests of the struggle for genuine Canadian independence, peace, democracy and the well-being of the Canadian people."[21] This did not mean that the working class ought to pursue a policy of trailing behind the bourgeoisie or a section of it. The aim of monopoly capital was still the perpetuation of monopoly capitalism and the maintenance of its system of exploitation. All that Canadian monopoly wanted was a better deal for itself in

relation to U.S. imperialism, a greater opportunity to exploit its own working class and working people. As such, Canadian monopoly was as much an enemy of the vast majority of the Canadian people as the foreign monopolies and transnationals.

The new program thus clearly exposed the forces which stood in the way of progress in Canada, the forces against which the party and working class had to direct their main fire: monopoly capital. On this basis, the party proposed the building of a democratic, anti-monopoly, anti-imperialist coalition led by the working class and its parties, to curb the power of monopoly and achieve genuine Canadian independence. The anti-monopoly struggle is a distinct and related stage in the struggle for socialism.

The immediate aim and program of the anti-monopoly coalition is not socialism. A program to curb monopoly would include: long-term and balanced all-Canadian industrial development based on public ownership under democratic control of the key sectors of the Canadian economy, particularly energy and natural resources; the extension of trade with the socialist and newly liberated countries; an active policy of peaceful coexistence; economic and social policies directed toward achieving full employment, rising living standards, decent health care, housing and education as a right for all Canadians, equal rights for women; and the adoption of a new made-in-Canada constitution based on the equal, voluntary partnership of the French Canadian and English-speaking nations including the right to national self-determination and a Bill of Rights.

To defeat the political domination of monopoly capital requires united action of all those feeling the effects of monopoly rule. The unity of the working class is the indispensable factor making for people's unity against the monopolies. The main policy resolution of the party's 1971 convention paid particular attention to unity of action of the left, unity which would "make it possible to change the present relationship of forces in the labor and democratic movement, defeat right-wing class-collaborationist policies, and take the country on a new course of far-reaching economic and social advance." In this sense, unity of action of the left was "the key link at this stage to bring into being the democratic, anti-monopoly, anti-imperialist alliance."[22] The non-communist left was to be found mainly in the NDP, the trade unions, the farm movement and among youth and women activists who were striving for fundamental solutions to the country's vital problems. The convention discussed the main obstacles to working class and democratic unity, particularly in the trade union movement and the NDP, where anti-communism, anti-Sovietism, and right-wing social-reformism persisted.

In the labor movement, the right wing of some trade unions still pursued the persecution of Communists and even denied their basic democratic rights as at the height of the cold war. The right-wing leadership willingly used the anti-communist clause in the constitutions of the International unions against party members, clauses dictated by U.S. anti-labor laws. The leadership of the AFL-CIO, headed by George Meany and Jay Lovestone, aligned itself unequivocally with the aims and policies of U.S. imperialism. It had brought the cold war into the trade union movement, supported U.S. imperialist aggression in Indochina and U.S. government measures to make the working people pay for the capitalist economic crisis. Thus, the defeat of the anti-communist clause would also be a defeat for the reactionary leadership of the AFL-CIO.

The Communist Party successfully fought for freedom of political belief and against the imposition of U.S. laws in Canada, obtaining wide support from the left and democratic forces of the labor movement. The fight against the anti-communist clause centered on two well-known Communists. In 1969, Jim Bridgewood was denied office in his UAW local although he had been duly elected by his fellow workers. In 1974, John Severinsky was expelled from the USWA because of his membership in the Communist Party. However, a vigorous campaign compelled the leaders of the UAW and the USWA to reinstate the two Communists in their respective unions. In 1970, a court order forced the UAW to reinstate Jim Bridgewood. Preferring to avoid a similar embarrassing court case, particularly in view of the Canadian USWA membership's support for the deletion of the anti-communist clause from the union's constitution, the USWA leadership decided to voluntarily readmit John Severinsky into the union. These were victories for democratic rights in general and for the legality of the Communist Party in the labor movement, although, as William Kashtan noted in his report to the October 1974 CC plenum, anti-communism and anti-Sovietism continued to be used by monopoly to divide the working class and democratic movements and therefore had to be systematically combatted.[23]

The struggle against the U.S.-imposed anti-communist clause emphasized the need to fight for democracy and for membership control of unions in Canada. This need was further underlined by the preparedness of the AFL-CIO leadership to support measures by the U.S. administration which would hurt the Canadian economy and put Canadian members of the AFL-CIO unions out of work. Thus Canadian workers' struggle for control of the Internationals in Canada was an aspect of the struggle against U.S. imperialism and for genuine Canadian independence and was therefore an important facet of development toward an anti-monopoly coalition.

As in the past, Communists played an important role in stimulating the fight for Canadian control of Canadian union affairs. The party campaigned for an independent, sovereign and united Canadian trade union movement as the best protector of the interests of the Canadian working class. At the same time, U.S. and Canadian workers faced a common enemy, the U.S. transnationals. This common struggle required the continuation of strong fraternal ties, but on the basis of genuine equality rather than domination. In this way, the workers of the two countries could coordinate efforts in bargaining and other relations with corporations, for the exchange of ideas and information and for mutual assistance in struggles involving transnationals.[24] An independent, sovereign and united trade union movement is still to be won, although some notable victories were achieved during the 1970s.

In discussing working-class unity and the fight against monopoly, the 1971 convention also examined the role of social-reformism, particularly as expressed in the NDP, a party which represents a substantial political trend within the working-class movement. The party program adopted by the delegates noted that the NDP "fulfills a positive role in challenging the monopoly of the two old-line parties, detaching working people from their influence and furthering the process of independent labor-farmer political action."[25]

William Kashtan, Alf Dewhurst and Sam Walsh having a few words with Leonid Brezhnev at the 24th congress of the CPSU, 1971.

However, right-wing social-reformism as expressed by many leaders of the NDP, pursues class-collaborationist, anti-communist policies which divide the working class and subordinate the workers' class interests to those of finance capital. Further, the NDP is a movement limited to reforms under capitalism. Social-reformism views the state as an institution above classes, as an impartial authority which could be made to work if only "good" people were in power. This attitude disarms working people, preventing the understanding that under capitalism the state is the instrument of the monopoly capitalist class.

Communism is fundamentally opposed to social-reformism — the system of opportunist practices and views incorporating policies of class collaboration between workers and capital-ists. Social-reformism seeks to perpetuate the capitalist system, limit people's movements to narrow parliamentary aims and partial reforms.[26]

Although Communists support reforms, reforms alone will not solve the fundamental problems of the working people. The Communist Party therefore works to persuade the NDP to go beyond these reforms, to adopt anti-monopoly policies.

In these efforts, Communists are very mindful of the fact that the NDP is not homogeneous. This was particularly evident in the early 1970s; a significant section of the NDP membership was moving leftward. The "Waffle," an organized left current within the NDP, reached its height in this period, only to be broken up as an organized force by the NDP's right wing. The administrative defeat of the Waffle within the NDP, did not entail the political defeat of left views within that party critical of right-wing social-reformism. While class-collaborationism has dominated the NDP, the struggle between left and right views continues.

Given the heterogeneous character of the NDP and of the general reformist current in the working class, the Communist Party guards against a one-sided approach. To refuse to have anything to do with the NDP (a left-sectarian approach), would lead to the isolation of the Communist Party from reform-minded workers and, in practice, would abandon these workers to the influence of bourgeois and reformist ideology; it would endanger the ability of the working class to unite in its interests. On the other hand, to sacrifice principles for the sake of unity with those espousing reformist ideology (a right-opportunist approach), would lead to the liquidation of the Communist Party's independent political position. Therefore, Communists carry out a consistent struggle against reformist ideology, while seeking ways and means to work with social-reformists around immediate aims and objectives.

The Convention stressed that to build a united front between revolutionary and reform-minded workers based on the interests of the Canadian working class requires a strong and influential Communist Party.

The more effectively the Communist Party works for the united front and strengthens its independent political activity, propagating its Marxist-Leninist program and policies, the more it will encourage and strengthen the left wing in the New Democratic Party and the struggle for genuine socialist policies.[27]

The decisive task for Communists, and the prerequisite for the formation of the united front against monopoly capital, is to build the Communist Party, the YCL and the communist press. The 50th Anniversary convention of the party noted that the Communist Party plays a distinctive role in the unremitting struggle to integrate Marxism-Leninism into the working class movement, defends and advances the daily needs of the people and in the course of these struggles strives to create the necessary conditions for the development of the revolutionary movement against capitalism and for a socialist Canada.[28]

The convention delegates also discussed the international situation in much detail. By 1971, the trend to peaceful coexistence and international détente had been noticeably strengthened: "New winds are blowing ... more favorable conditions exist for compelling imperialism to retreat ... the imperialist drive to aggression can be curbed providing there is the maximum of unity and coordination of efforts of all the anti-imperialist forces of the world."[29] Despite defeats, U.S. imperialism still wielded considerable strength, and clearly had no intention of withdrawing from Indochina. Vietnam remained at the center of the global struggle against imperialism, particularly U.S. imperialism.

2. The Struggle for Détente

Instead of ending the war as he had promised during the 1968 presidential election campaign, Nixon decided to prolong and even escalate it. While participating in the Paris Peace Talks as a concession to Vietnamese and international pressure, U.S. imperialist policy was based on the so-called Nixon Doctrine. This doctrine assumed the "right" of the USA to use its military might in Indochina so that it could negotiate with the liberation forces "from a position of strength." U.S. imperialist strategy was based on continuing the war through "Vietnamization." In other words, U.S. troops were to be withdrawn from active combat and replaced by South Vietnamese puppet troops with U.S. fire power. This strategy was intended to pacify the growing opposition at home and abroad to U.S. involvement in Vietnam.

The other side of Nixon's strategy was to undertake a rapprochement with Maoist China which had launched a military attack on the Soviet Union in 1969 and was then pressuring North Vietnam to adopt a pro-Maoist line in its foreign policy and domestic affairs. Secretary of State Henry Kissinger's two visits to Peking in 1971 laid the groundwork for President Nixon's visit in February 1972, and for the establishment of what has since developed into political and military collusion between the two countries. U.S. imperialism and the Maoist Chinese leadership were clearly motivated by their common hatred for socialist Vietnam and the Soviet Union, both of which were major obstacles to their expansionist ambitions.

Nixon's strategy also included a reactionary pro-U.S. coup in Kampuchea in the spring of 1970, followed by a massive invasion of Kampuchea and Laos.

At the June 1970 CC meeting, William Kashtan warned that the invasion of Kampuchea and Laos added a dangerous quality to the international situation because, unlike the U.S. puppet regime in South Vietnam, these two countries had never invited U.S. military intervention. The escalation of the war was a desperate measure taken by U.S. imperialism to resolve the crisis of its Indochina policy.

The General Secretary of the Communist Party of Canada condemned the Trudeau government's whitewashing of the U.S. invasion of Kampuchea as a despicable example of servility to the U.S. government. In fact, the Canadian government had shifted from apparent neutrality (with actual complicity) to open support for Nixon's perfidious plans for Southeast Asia. Opposition to U.S. aggression in Indochina grew rapidly in Canada. The task of Canadians opposed to U.S. aggression was "to unite all those forces into a powerful movement centered on the demand for the immediate, unconditional withdrawal of all U.S. troops and their satellites from Indochina and the demand that the Canadian government condemn this aggression and end its complicity by halting the shipment of arms to the USA."[30]

Communists helped initiate and organize a petition campaign demanding an end to the Indochina war and to Canadian complicity. The "Out Now" petition won the support of many peace organizations, trade unions, clerics, women's, youth and student groups. Near the end of the campaign in May 1971, 90,000 Canadians had signed the petition.[31]

Toronto candle-light parade down Yonge Street protesting the Vietnam War, 1971.

Nixon's strategy of escalating the war failed. The combined military forces of the Laotian and Vietnamese liberation movements inflicted serious blows to U.S. plans for Laos' subjugation in 1970 and 1971. In 1972, the liberation forces succeeded in freeing large rural areas of South Vietnam and breaching strong enemy defense lines in several major urban centers. U.S. imperialism suffered extensive military setbacks which severely damaged its international prestige and led to its further isolation in the world community. Mass demonstrations took place constantly in the USA and around the world. Nixon became so frustrated with his inability to achieve a military solution to the war in Indochina that he ordered a renewal of the bombing of North Vietnam and the mining and blockade of its ports lasting from April to December 1972.

At its May 1972 meeting, the CC of the Communist Party of Canada predicted that Nixon's adventuristic policies were doomed to failure. The only way for the USA to get out of its Indochinese impasse was to end its military actions against North Vietnam, return to the negotiating table and get out of Vietnam.[32]

The escalation of the war in Indochina was closely connected to increased racism and repression inside the USA itself. One case which received extensive world attention was the hounding, frame-up and imprisonment of Angela Davis on charges of complicity to murder and kidnapping, charges which could have brought the death penalty. A Black woman and a well-known member of the Communist Party of the United States of America, Angela Davis was victimized for her activity and

Free Angela Davis picketline outside the U.S. consulate, Toronto.

leadership in the Soledad Brothers Defense Committee which defended imprisoned victims of the racist U.S. judicial system. A massive solidarity campaign developed in the USA and around the world. In Canada, as in the USA and elsewhere, Communists played a prominent role in mobilizing public opinion in favor of freedom for Angela Davis. After a world-wide campaign lasting almost two years, she was acquitted of all charges in June 1972.[33] Angela Davis' acquittal was a serious defeat for the repressive Nixon administration. Two years later, the Nixon administration fell victim to its own gross political corruption and its massive systematic violation of the human and democratic rights of the American people.

As the war in Indochina dragged on, the USA found itself more and more isolated in the world. Even some imperialist countries, most notably France, were openly reluctant to support U.S. imperialism's reckless policies. Moreover, some imperialist countries were becoming uneasy about being so closely tied to the U.S. economy which, as a consequence of the war in Indochina and the growing expenditures on armaments, was sinking into a deeper, more acute crisis. They realized that a world at peace in which trade relations with the socialist countries could flourish, would be more beneficial than an unequal relationship with an ailing U.S. economy. In fact, as the main policy resolution of the 21st convention of the Communist Party of Canada in 1971 pointed out, the United States had begun a currency and trade war against its allies in the hope of forcing them to bear the brunt of the U.S. economic recession. In response, the Trudeau government was impelled to take measures to lessen the impact of U.S. domination over Canada.

In May 1971, Trudeau paid an official visit to Moscow. There, an agreement was signed by Prime Minister Trudeau and Premier Alexei Kosygin on cooperation in the industrial application of science and technology, trade, the expansion of ties and exchanges in the fields of the economy, culture and northern development and the maintenance of world peace. At the time, Trudeau stated that the agreement was meant to offset one-sided reliance on the United States.[34] In the wider world context, Trudeau's visit was a significant contribution to the improvement of relations between Canada and the Soviet Union, to a more independent stance on at least some issues on the part of the Canadian government and to the process of détente. In October of the same year, Alexei Kosygin made a return visit to Canada which strengthened agreements and relations between the two countries.

Canadians welcomed both Trudeau's visit to the Soviet Union and Kosygin's visit to Canada. The standing ovation Kosygin received from 17,000 Vancouver hockey fans was one indication of the positive response by the Canadian public.[35] The improvement of Soviet-Canadian relations had a benign effect on the political climate inside Canada, as Canadians became more interested in what the Soviet Union was really like. This development impeded the activity of the most extreme anti-Soviet and anti-communist elements in Canada and had a positive effect on the activity of the progressive forces in Canada, including the Communist Party.

Public concern for peace was heightened in November 1971, by the U.S. nuclear test on Amchitka island, in the northern Pacific Ocean. Canada's west coast was directly endangered by the blast. In October, 15,000 Vancouver high school students protested the planned test. Radio stations sponsored mass protest telegrams, one of which attracted the signatures of 100,000 Torontonians. Demonstrations on the Canada-U.S. border and rallies were held across the country and increasingly the call to "Stop the War" joined the demand to "Stop Amchitka." The trade union movement was a significant participant in the campaign. The 1000 delegates to the annual OFL convention, marched to the U.S. consulate to register their opposition. On the day of the blast, the BCFL called a half-hour protest strike. The campaign to stop Amchitka increased public awareness of the need for peace and disarmament, and contributed to the creation of more favorable conditions for the promotion of détente.

In 1972, détente received a major boost when the FRG ratified important treaties with the Soviet Union, Poland and the GDR recognizing the inviolability of the borders arising out of World War II. Furthermore, the FRG's new *Realpolitik* led to the recognition of the GDR in international law. These were important victories for peaceful coexistence. They signalled West German imperialism's temporary shelving of revanchism, the dangerous policy which strives to re-unite Germany under an imperialist government on the basis of Germany's 1937 boundaries.

The world situation had changed to such an extent that U.S. imperialism was compelled to join the world community in furthering the process of détente. The United States joined the quadripartite agreement on West Berlin (for many years an imperialist springboard for confrontation with the socialist world), which solved the Berlin question on a mutually satisfactory basis. Nixon became the first U.S. president to visit the Soviet Union. These two countries then concluded the first Strategic Arms Limitation Treaty (SALT I), limiting offensive weapons and establishing Soviet-U.S. relations on the principles of peaceful coexistence. They also agreed on the need for economic, scientific and technical cooperation.

These agreements of course did not mean that the USA had changed its aims for world domination. Its commitment to détente was far from certain and arose out of the realities of the international situation. Instead, the Nixon administration changed its methods, temporarily and reluctantly abandoning its attempts to achieve its imperialist aims through cold war and military pressure. The accent was shifted to economic competition with world socialism, a field where the USA also continued to lose ground.

At the beginning of 1973, U.S. imperialism was finally forced to sign a cease-fire agreement with the liberation forces of Vietnam including the withdrawal of its 500,000 troops. It was an agreement which in Canada was hailed by the Communist Party as "a victory for the heroic people of Vietnam in their struggle against imperialist aggression, a victory achieved with the decisive aid of the Soviet Union and other socialist countries, of all progressive and peace-loving forces throughout the world and by the American people."[36] It was proof that even the most powerful imperialist country in the world could not stop the national and social liberation of the peoples or reverse the world's transition from capitalism to socialism. Although the Saigon puppet regime remained in power in the south, the cease-fire agreement marked the removal of the major obstacle to Vietnam's total freedom, the massive United States military presence.

The world was undergoing two simultaneous but contradictory developments — the process of détente and the continuation of international tensions. In 1973, the CIA and U.S. transnationals destabilized the Chilean economy and conducted other acts of subversion against Chile culminating in a bloody fascist military coup which overthrew the democratically-elected Popular Unity government of Salvador Allende. Accusing the U.S. of engineering the coup, the Communist Party of Canada called it a "part of the larger aim of U.S. imperialism to prevent the peoples of Latin America from achieving sovereign control of their lands, their natural resources and their destiny."[37] The party demanded no recognition of the fascist junta. Much to the disgust of many Canadians, the Trudeau government extended recognition to the Chilean fascists in less than a month.

The following year, the fascist junta in Greece, encouraged by NATO and U.S. imperialism, attempted to overthrow the neutral government of Cyprus with the aim of making the island a secure base for NATO activities in the Middle East. The coup failed but it provided the pretext for another NATO ally, Turkey, to invade the country and seize 40 per cent of Cyprus' territory. Also in 1973, Israel, which still enjoyed the massive military and economic support of U.S. imperialism, once again went to war against its Arab neighbors. The Israeli

September 1974 demonstration in Toronto, in solidarity with the Chilean people.

DEFEAT FASCISM!
Solidarity with Chilean people!
YOUNG COMMUNIST LEAGUE

...IDARI...
WITH THE
PEOPLE
OF CHILE!

ASYLUM
FOR
REFUGEES
FROM CHILE

YOUNG WORKER

Zionists held fast to their reactionary dream of creating a Greater Israel. Their ambitions inevitably brought them into conflict with the Arab peoples, especially the Palestinian Arab people, who demanded the recognition of their right to self-determination and the restoration of the occupied territories to the countries from which they had been seized during the 1967 war. These developments were setbacks for détente. They confirmed the observation of the main policy resolution of the 22nd convention of the Communist Party of Canada in 1974 that the process of détente was not an automatic one, that it was being interrupted by new outbreaks of war and tension.[38]

Another source of international tension was the policies of the Maoist leadership of the PRC. China established trade and political relations with the fascist junta in Chile and the racist apartheid regime in South Africa. It joined the United States and South Africa in giving military aid to reactionary pro-imperialist forces in Angola in 1975, with the aim of setting up a pro-Western regime in that country. It openly supported the presence of the U.S. military in Europe and Asia and called for the strengthening of NATO. It sought to establish cordial relations with ultra-right elements in other countries, for example, with the West German revanchists. This scurrilous record demonstrated Maoism's break with Marxism-Leninism, and confronted many people who had been influenced by Maoism with the necessity of rethinking their position. The main policy resolution of the 23rd convention of the Communist Party of Canada in October 1976 concluded that Maoism was hostile to the world revolutionary process.

The Maoists joined the cold warriors in the reckless drive to torpedo détente. In word and deed they became allies of reaction in striving to undermine détente, prevent disarmament in their unprincipled anti-Soviet campaign. By their disgraceful support of the military junta in Chile, and of the imperialist powers and South African racism in Angola, the Maoists further discredited themselves. The Maoists abandoned Marxism and Leninism and became an active reserve of imperialism in the struggle against socialism. From being incompatible with Marxism-Leninism, Maoism became hostile to it.[39]

Despite imperialism's stubborn resistance to face up to the new world reality, and the reactionary turn of the PRC's foreign policy, the dominant trend in the world in the 1970s was the development and deepening of détente. The world revolutionary process continued unabated. Contrary to the assertions of the Maoists, détente did not inhibit the revolutionary process but indeed facilitated it. In 1974, the peoples of Greece and Portugal overthrew the repressive fascist regime in their countries. Portugal's colonies, among them Angola and Mozambique, won their independence and embarked on socialist-oriented development. Several other African countries followed their example. In 1974, the people of Ethiopia ended centuries of feudal rule and began the revolutionary transformation of their country. In 1975, Vietnam, Kampuchea and Laos were victorious in their long struggle for freedom from imperialism. Franco's death accelerated the collapse of fascism in Spain. For the first time since the early 1920s, the entire European continent was free of the yoke of fascism.

The process of détente reached its height in the 1970s with the signing of the Helsinki Agreement on August 1, 1975, by 33 European states, the United States and Canada. The key points of the accords were as follows: (1) sovereign equality including respect for rights inherent in sovereignty, (2) renunciation of the use of force or threat of force, (3) the inviolability of frontiers, (4) territorial integrity of states, (5) the peaceful settlement of disputes, (6) non-interference in internal affairs, (7) respect for human rights and basic freedoms, (8) equality and the right of peoples to decide their destiny, (9) cooperation among states and (10) honoring commitments under international law. As the *Canadian Tribune* noted at the time, the Helsinki accords materialized the results of détente, turned it into a formal international agreement involving most socialist and imperialist countries.[40]

Most of the imperialist countries, including Canada, did not make the text of the Final Act of the Helsinki Conference readily available to the public — in sharp contrast to the socialist countries where the text was published in daily newspapers.[41] Thus, the fight for the implementation of the accords began and was taken up by the party as a key task.

3. The Working Class on the Move

In the early 1970s, Canada, like the rest of the capitalist world, entered a period of growing economic and political instability. The crisis of overproduction was aggravated by the outbreak of a monetary crisis and an energy crisis. At the same time, Canada and the world capitalist system experienced a deepening structural crisis reflected in the fact that both inflation and unemployment became chronic and permanent features of state-monopoly capitalism. The conjuncture of these crises throughout the capitalist world was exacerbated in Canada by the country's inordinate dependence on U.S. imperialism. The objective conditions for an intensification of the class struggle were maturing.

Monopoly sought to force the working people to bear the brunt of the capitalist economic crisis. Growing unemployment, spiralling prices, higher taxes on working people, substantial tax concessions to the giant corporations, cutbacks in health care and education and finally the imposition of wage controls in late 1975 were all designed to make working people pay for the consequences of an economic crisis which had been created by the policies of the monopolies and the governments they controlled. At a time when the big corporations were making record profits, the federal and provincial governments were implementing policies designed to accelerate the redistribution of the national income in favor of the monopolies and the transnationals at the expense of Canadian working people.

The working class and democratic forces responded to the urgent necessity of defending their interests. In a march organized by the BCFL at the British Columbia legislature in January 1971, 2,000 people demanded the adoption of job-creating policies. In June, a demonstration of 1,500 took place in Hamilton around the same issue.[42] As the 1971 convention of the Communist Party observed:

The growing monopoly offensive is leading to an upsurge of working class, trade union and democratic unity in action.[43]

The organized labor movement was at the heart of this struggle against monopoly policies. Not only had the strike movement grown among industrial workers, it also encompassed white collar workers, in particular public employees and teachers who in many cases were participating in strike actions for the first time. In 1972, the public and para-public employees of Quebec conducted a historic general strike under the auspices of the Common Front. In the Common Front, Quebec's three trade union centers overcame the differences which had long divided them, and unified their efforts against the common enemy, the Quebec government of Liberal Robert Bourassa.

This trend toward the adoption of more militant policies and greater labor unity was expressed by the CLC's decision to readmit the UE and the United Fishermen and Allied Workers Union in December 1972. The 1974 CLC convention adopted a resolution recognizing the autonomy of the Quebec Federation of Labor on matters affecting the specific needs of Quebec workers. This demonstrated the willingness of the Canadian working class to achieve unity on the basis of equality between the two nations. Last but not least, the CLC and a number of its affiliates eliminated the anti-communist clause from their constitutions, thus repudiating their previous adherence to the more extreme forms of the cold war ideology of state-monopoly capitalism and promoting greater unity of the labor movement irrespective of the political opinions of union members.

Monopoly's response to the growing militancy of the working class and democratic movements was to utilize the state more directly as a tool for the suppression of the mass struggle. In the spring of 1972, Bill 3 was rammed through the British Columbia legislature to crush collective bargaining for teachers. Bill 88, designed to restrict collective bargaining, to provide penalties for refusing to cross picket lines and to undermine union hiring for the entire British Columbia labor movement, was brought before the legislature but then withdrawn in the face of the exceptionally sharp opposition of the BCFL.[44] Analyzing similar plans in other provinces, the *Canadian Tribune* pointed out that what was under concerted attack across the country, was the fundamental democratic right of the labor movement, the right to strike.[45] This became particularly evident in the strike of Local 173 of the United Brewery Workers against Dare Foods in Kitchener, Ontario. The strike began in May 1972 around the demands for a 40-hour work week, more pay and better working conditions. This long strike was marked by the wide use of the police, professional strikebreakers, scabs and court injunctions in support of the company's efforts to smash the union. On the first anniversary of the strike, 6,000 demonstrators marched through Kitchener in solidarity with the strikers. As its contribution to the solidarity march, the Communist Party organized a car cavalcade from Toronto, Hamilton and other Ontario centers with signs on the cars demanding the outlawing of strike-breaking, a demand warmly welcomed by the striking workers.[46]

Despite public indignation, the federal and provincial governments stepped up their efforts to undermine labor's rights. In July 1972, Parliament ordered striking members of the International Longshoremen's Association in Quebec back to work.[47] In September 1973, a similar order was issued against the striking members of the Canadian Brotherhood of Railway, Transport and

General Workers. Shortly afterward, 3,000 railway workers expressed their displeasure at this arbitrary measure by demonstrating in front of the Parliament buildings.[48]

In late 1973, Bill 41 was passed by the Ontario legislature denying hospital workers the right to strike or to bargain on a wide range of issues affecting their lives. In December, 40,000 teachers marched on Queen's Park protesting Bill 274, which denied teachers the right to resign collectively from their jobs (teachers did not have the right to strike at that time) and which substituted compulsory arbitration for free collective bargaining. Although the provincial Tory government was compelled to withdraw Bill 274 immediately after the demonstration, it introduced Bill 275, which in essence was little different from the previous bill.[49] However, in 1975 the Ontario government was compelled to recognize the teachers' right to strike.

The Communist Party paid special attention to this trend of using arbitrary methods to force the workers to accept monopoly and government policies. In the summer of 1972 in a pamphlet written by George Harris, member of the party's CEC and secretary-treasurer of the UE, the party warned of monopoly's campaign to limit and even take away labor's indispensable right to strike.

The main aim of this campaign is to cripple labor's ability to defend and improve its conditions of life. The big business drive for maximum profits requires a shackled, docile labor movement. It masks this selfish, sinister aim by hiding behind the cry of "defending the public interest." Capitalism always parades under false slogans. It always seeks to make it appear as if its greedy profit interests are synonymous with public interest.[50]

The Communist Party's 1974 convention linked this trend with the general tendency of monopoly capitalism to undermine democratic rights.

As state-monopoly capitalism goes into deeper crisis and as resistance to its policies grows, it tends to throw overboard bourgeois democracy and reinforces and extends its established police and security forces which are directed to act against the working class and democratic forces.

The monopoly offensive on living standards is accompanied by growing attacks on democratic rights. This finds its expression in the campaign to restrict trade union rights, undermine collective bargaining and impose compulsory arbitration.[51]

On several occasions, federal and provincial governments broke legal strikes by legislating workers back to work on penalty of heavy fines and imprisonment. On other occasions, these same governments refused to negotiate in good faith with public employees and teachers. As these workers were relatively inexperienced in the class struggle, the bourgeois state thought that it could defeat them and use them as an example for the entire working class movement. In September 1974, the Ontario Tory government ordered the striking members of Toronto Local 113 of the Amalgamated Transit Union to return to work. Parliament followed with back-to-work orders against the west coast grain handlers in October 1974, and against west coast longshoremen, members of the International Longshoremen's and Warehousemen's Union, in March 1975. This was the third time in less than three years that Parliament had legislated the west coast

The Communist Party protests double-digit inflation, Ottawa, June 1973.

ARCHIVES CPC/PAC

longshoremen back to work — Parliament was being used as an instrument of the British Columbia Maritime Employers' Association. As in several other cases, the NDP supported the legislation although claiming "great reluctance." Communists regarded the NDP's endorsement of the legislation as "tantamount to a stab in the back by the only group in Parliament from whom labor had a right to expect a fight on the principal issue of the right to strike."[52] For its part, the Communist Party demanded "a complete reversal of government policy in labor-management relations, making employers respect the fundamental rights of working people to collective bargaining and the right to strike."[53]

The party's campaign in defense of the right to strike complemented its efforts to defend the living standards of Canada's working people. Double-digit inflation was eating away at people's purchasing power. The federal government tried to allay popular anger by establishing a Prices Review Board, which, however, was given no power to roll back unjustified price increases. The party countered the government's lack of effective policy by participating in the Coalition to Roll Back Prices, formed in September 1973. The coalition's petition and other activities won wide support in the labor movement and communities across the country.

Throughout the 1970s, Communist campaigns and programs for improving

ARCHIVES CPC/PAC

the conditions of working people met with an increasingly positive response. The growing militancy of the working class paralleled a turn in the development of the party. As the cold war atmosphere receded, growing numbers of young people joined the ranks of the Communist Party and Young Communist League. A resurgence of the party's electoral activities resulted in some limited successes, particularly at the municipal level. In the Toronto borough of York, Oscar Kogan who had been elected school trustee in 1966, was elected alderman in 1974. Eunice Parker, Dorothy Lynas and Mark Mosher were elected school trustees in the British Columbia cities of Coquitlam, North Vancouver and Port Alberni respectively. Joe Zuken was consistently re-elected in Winnipeg. Notable successes were also achieved in other British Columbia and Ontario centers.

At the federal level, the party set itself the task of running a maximum number of candidates: to make an impact on Canadian politics, stimulate the labor and progressive movement, focus attention on the central issues, advance the party's alternative policies and strengthen the progressive forces in and outside Parliament. Whereas the party had only fielded 14 candidates in the 1968 federal election, 30 Communists contested seats in the 1972 election, and 69 party candidates were fielded in 1974.

With obvious political motivation, governments moved to restrict the participation in elections of parties other than those already represented in legislatures. In 1975, Ontario became the first province to require registration of political parties. The party was forced to secure the signatures of 10,000 eligible voters in order to campaign in its own name in provincial elections. The Communists' successful door-knocking and street campaign brought the party into direct contact with thousands of people and contributed to the breaking down of cold war barriers in the party's work.

The party's electoral campaigns, although as yet unsuccessful in electing Communists at the provincial and federal levels, helped expose monopoly's policies and popularize the anti-monopoly alternative. The prevailing economic and social crisis underlined the importance of such activity. While workers suffered cuts in real wages, corporate profits reached all-time highs. Monopoly concentration and foreign ownership compounded this problem. In its submission to the Royal Commission on Corporate Concentration, the party emphasized the damage done to the Canadian economy by foreign ownership, particularly by the giant transnational corporations.

The multinationals interfere with our national priorities, distort consumption patterns, income distribution, and redistribution of the national income. They have the capability of affecting governmental, monetary, fiscal and trade policies.... The same is true in respect to energy and the resources industry in general.[54]

To correct the distorted structure of Canada's economy, the party proposed that all transnational corporations be nationalized, as the first step toward the nationalization of the banks, trust, insurance companies and credit system, which would secure the necessary capital for the planned, balanced development of the economy under public ownership and control, serving the public interest.

As in all times of economic crisis, monopoly and its political representatives sought to divert public attention from the source of the crisis. Racism was fostered and economic and social problems were attributed to immigrant workers. In 1975, the federal government published its Green Paper on immigration policy, outlining a more restrictive policy. The qualifications for potential immigrants had built-in racist features, designed to limit the number of immigrants from Asia, Africa, the Caribbean and Latin America. The Communist Party condemned the racist character of the proposals and exposed the government's fraud.

The proposal to change immigration policy and restrict entry of immigrants into Canada is based on the false assumption that unemployment is caused by workers, particularly the immigrant workers, whereas in fact it is caused by capitalism. ... Canada does not have an immigration problem; it has an unemployment problem. What is evident is that immigrant workers are being made scapegoats of a crisis they did not create.[55]

Demographic and immigration policy, the party suggested, must be non-discriminatory, take into account the bi-national character of Canada, and be geared to a policy of full employment, independent economic development, industrialization and an expanding home market. There should be guarantees of employment, adequate housing and social services for all; equality of living and working conditions, job opportunities and equal pay.

The economic crisis also inflicted special hardship on women. International Women's Year, 1975, proclaimed by the United Nations under the slogan "Equality, Development and Peace," helped to increase public awareness of the inequities experienced by women. The Communist Party worked hard to focus attention on the fundamental problems facing women. In seminars, leaflets, resolutions and articles, the party highlighted the key issue of equal pay for work of equal value, and related issues of paid maternity leave, universally accessible child care as a right, elimination of sexual discrimination and inequalities in opportunity and employment. Although this was a year in which much attention was devoted to women, Communists realized that the struggle for the rights of women would not end in 1975, particularly as the economic and political crisis continued and sharpened.

The capitalist crisis severely affected the working class as a whole. In late 1974, the Trudeau government introduced so-called voluntary wage and price controls. It soon became obvious to the labor movement that the government was only interested in controlling wages. The labor movement would not accept such unequal anti-labor terms, and refused to submit to voluntary controls. The federal government then *imposed* wage controls, on October 13, 1975. Controls on prices and profits were a sham. As a consequence of wage controls, Canadian working people experienced a reduction in *real* income while the monopolies and transnationals were permitted to achieve record profits. To the working class, this was an intolerable situation. The organized labor movement fought back. The first demonstration against Bill C-73, the wage control bill, took place two weeks later in Toronto, where Prime Minister Trudeau was to speak to businessmen at the Royal York Hotel. There he was awaited by 2,000 workers voicing their anger at his anti-labor policy.[56] It was the opening shot in the struggle against wage controls.

The Communist Party played a significant role in the struggle. The party immediately condemned Bill C-73, blasting the false premise that wage increases caused inflation and exposing the wage restraint program's attack on collective bargaining and living standards. In union locals, shop and convention floors, Communists worked to mobilize widespread opposition to the government's wage control program.

In contrast, the NDP was divided on the question. In fact, the three NDP provincial governments in British Columbia, Saskatchewan and Manitoba had taken an unequivocal position in favor of wage controls, a position which of course put them into direct conflict with the mass of Canadian workers.

Opposition to Bill C-73 developed quickly throughout the country. Provincial labor federations put themselves on record in opposition to wage controls which they regarded as inimical to workers but beneficial to big business. In Quebec, over 40,000 workers demonstrated their protest in November 1975.

The CLC held a special conference on wage controls in early November and came forward with a 10-point program of reforms favoring working people. The 200 delegates, leaders of the CLC and its affiliated unions, supported the plan for a country-wide educational campaign to last until the Quebec City convention of the CLC in May 1976.[57]

Rank and file and extensive union leadership pressure prompted the CLC to step up the fight against wage controls and extend the form of its activities. Pressure from the workers in favor of mass struggle, which Communists helped to generate, overcame the resistance of right-wing social-reformists in the CLC and the NDP who tended to back away from precisely such a struggle. Responding to the call of the CLC, endorsed by the Quebec Common Front, 35,000 trade unionists carried their demands for an end to wage restraint to

Top, in the bitter cold, 35,000 workers demonstrate in Ottawa against wage controls, March 1976. Bottom, the 23rd convention of the Communist Party of Canada, October 9-11, 1976.

CANADIAN TRIBUNE

The Day of Protest, Toronto.

The Communist contingent in the Day of Protest demonstration, Toronto.

Parliament Hill. Held on a bitterly cold day in March 1976, the demonstration proved that given a fighting class policy and militant leadership, the working class is fully capable of united action in defense of its common interests. The Ottawa march was followed by a demonstration of 25,000 Ontario workers in April.[58]

Against this background of increasing labor militancy, the CLC convention took place in May 1976. The convention overwhelmingly endorsed a resolution giving the CLC Executive Council a mandate to organize and conduct a general work stoppage or stoppages if and when necessary.[59] The Communist Party promised its full support to the CLC in its struggle against wage controls and called on all Canadians "to support the demand of organized labor for a new and meaningful role in economic and social policy-making for a curb on monopoly power and the expansion of the scope of collective bargaining in the interest of democracy and its expansion in Canada."[60] In August, Joe Morris, CLC President, announced plans for a "National Day of Protest" for October 14 against the federal government's wage-cutting program.

The 23rd convention of the Communist Party of Canada took place on October 9-11, 1976, just days before the Day of Protest. For weeks Communists had been working persistently to mobilize their fellow workers to participate in the general strike, fulfilling their promise to the CLC to lend full support. The Canadian working class as a whole was on the move; it was militant and prepared to engage the class enemy in battle. The convention thus took place in an atmosphere of exceptional enthusiasm and militancy.

The 23rd convention drew attention to the fact that the Day of Protest would be an historic event for Canada and the working class movement.

A general strike will, by its very nature, be an important political act on the part of the working class. The organization of such a strike, the first of its kind in Canada, will require great effort and united will. Communists in the trade union movement will work side by side with their workmates to help make it an outstanding success. The Communist Party gives unreserved support to this effort of the Canadian Labor Congress. All democratic forces in Canada must support that strike and its democratic aims.[61]

On that day, October 14, 1976, the protests of one million workers reverberated across the country. The general strike of October 14, was an historic event which struck a high note of working class unity, militancy and confidence. This defiant challenge by Canadian workers was part of the process which had been underway throughout the 1970s in Canada and around the world. International victories for progress and in particular the significant steps toward détente and peace, stimulated an upsurge of political activity. As a member of the world communist movement and an integral part of militant working class action at home, the Communist Party of Canada itself reflected this upsurge; growing in numbers and in influence, an optimistic spirit permeated party activity.

1. "Main Policy Resolution" in *The 20th Convention, Communist Party of Canada, April 4-6, 1969* (Toronto, 1969), p. 29.
2. *Canadian Tribune*, October 21, 1970.
3. W. Kashtan, *The Fight for Democracy and Social Advance*, (Toronto, 1970), p. 16.
4. A. Dewhurst, *On Some Questions of Party Policy*, CC plenum of November 14-16, 1970, Archives CPC, p. 4.
5. Ibid., p. 1.
6. *The Road to Socialism in Canada* (Toronto, 1971), p. 52.
7. Ibid., p. 10.
8. Ibid., p. 5.
9. Ibid., p. 7.
10. Ibid.
11. Ibid., p. 8.
12. *The Road to Socialism in Canada* (Toronto, 1962), p. 6.
13. Ibid., pp. 14-15.
14. *Road to Socialism* (1971), p. 9.
15. W. Kashtan, "Keynote Address" in *21st Convention, Communist Party of Canada, November 27-29, 1971* (Toronto, 1971), pp. 14-16; and W. Kashtan, *Toward Socialism* (Toronto, 1976), pp. 181-185.
16. *Canadian Tribune*, May 3, 1972.
17. Ibid., March 7, 1973.
18. Kashtan, "Keynote Address" in *21st Convention*, pp. 14-16; and Kashtan, *Toward Socialism*, pp. 181-185.
19. *Road to Socialism* (1971), p. 9.
20. Ibid., p. 27.
21. Kashtan, "Keynote Address" in *21st Convention*, p. 16; and Kashtan, *Toward Socialism*, p. 185.
22. "Main Policy Resolution" in *21st Convention*, p. 43.
23. W. Kashtan, *Unite in Struggle* (Toronto, 1974), p. 25.

24. *For an Independent, Sovereign and United Trade Union Movement* (Toronto, 1974).
25. *Road to Socialism* (1971), p. 44.
26. Ibid., p. 43.
27. Ibid., p. 45.
28. "Main Policy Resolution" in *21st Convention*, p. 48.
29. Kashtan, "Keynote Address" in *21st Convention*, p. 5; and Kashtan, *Toward Socialism*, p. 170.
30. *Parliament Must Act to Provide One Million Jobs!*, CC plenum of June 6-8, 1970, p. 10.
31. *Canadian Tribune*, May 19, 1971.
32. W. Kashtan, *A New Direction for Canada* (Toronto, 1972), p. 3; and Kashtan, *Toward Socialism*, pp. 193-194.
33. *Canadian Tribune*, June 7, 1972.
34. Ibid., May 26, 1971.
35. Ibid., October 27, 1971.
36. W. Kashtan, *Report to Central Committee, May 12-13, 1973*, Archives CPC, p. 2.
37. *Canadian Tribune*, September 19, 1973.
38. "The Communist Party in the Struggle for Working Class and Democratic Unity" in *22nd Convention Communist Party of Canada, May 18-20, 1974* (Toronto, 1974), p. 5.
39. "The policy of the Communist Party of Canada for a democratic alternative to the crisis policies of monopoly" in *Convention 76: 23rd Convention, Communist Party of Canada, October 9-11, 1976* (Toronto, 1976), p. 32.
40. *Canadian Tribune*, August 6, 1975.
41. W. Kashtan, "For a democratic alternative to the crisis policies of monopoly" in *Convention 76*, p. 19.
42. *Canadian Tribune*, January 27 and June 16, 1971.
43. *22nd Convention*, p. 18.
44. *Canadian Tribune*, April 5, 1972.
45. Ibid., May 3, 1972.
46. Ibid., May 16 and 30, 1973.
47. Ibid., July 12, 1972.
48. Ibid., September 5, 1973.
49. Ibid., January 2 and February 6, 1974.
50. G. Harris. *The Right to Strike and the Public Interest* (Toronto, 1972), p. 7.
51. *22nd Convention*, p. 24.
52. *Canadian Tribune*, April 2, 1975.
53. Ibid.
54. *Put the Multi-nationals Under Democratic Nationalization* (Toronto, 1975), p. 9.
55. "On the Green Paper and Immigration Policy," Submission to the Special Joint Committee on Immigration Policy by the Central Executive Committee, Communist Party of Canada, in *Communist Viewpoint*, July-August 1975, p. 59.
56. *Canadian Tribune*, October 29, 1975.
57. Ibid., November 5, 1975.
58. Ibid., May 17, 1976.
59. Ibid., May 24, 1976.
60. Ibid., June 7, 1976.
61. *23rd Convention*, p. 42.

Conclusion

Readers of *Canada's Party of Socialism* will, of course, come to their own conclusions on the policies, political activities and long-term aims of the Communist Party. Whether such conclusions are favorable or not, will depend in good measure on what place the reader holds in the production process of capitalist society.

For those who are compelled to sell their labor-power to procure the necessities of life, the book we believe, will invoke favorable interest. To the class-conscious worker, whether laboring by hand or brain, the interest could be of a more fundamental character, perhaps an urge to re-read particularly interesting aspects of the party's consistent search for theoretical clarity as a reliable guide to action. Or, the application of scientific socialism to the study of the impact of economic, political and moral aspects of monopoly capitalist exploitation on the lives of the vast majority of Canadians.

For party members, young and old, study of the party's history, its achievements as well as setbacks, will be an affirmation of ideological and political conviction. At the same time, it will be a source of new inspiration, of a deeper understanding of scientific socialism to clearly illuminate the road to the socialist future.

In achieving these objectives, this history will have made an important contribution to the party's historic task of melding the liberating philosophy, the theory and practice of Marxism-Leninism with the everyday struggles of the broad labor movement — struggles that grow in intensity as monopoly savagely intensifies its exploitation of the working people in its inhuman search for maximum profit, wrung out of the labor and living standards of ordinary Canadians. This search serves imperialist greed for super-profits at the expense of other peoples and nations; the sell-out of Canada's energy and resources to U.S. transnationals; preparations for aggressive military action against living socialism and the national liberation movement, instigated by U.S. imperialism.

Canada's real history, as this book illustrates, is a history of class struggle, at the center of which is the struggle to emancipate the working class and all working people from the exploitation of capital. This will remain the central feature of social development in Canada as long as it remains a part of the world capitalist system.

The history of Canada's party of socialism provides irrefutable evidence that to break the hold of monopoly capitalism over Canada and her people, the Canadian working class needs its own party. A party independent of the class of capitalists — a party of socialism. The Communist Party of Canada has proved itself to be such a party.

Firmly based on the revolutionary theory and practice of Marxism-Leninism, working class internationalism and genuine patriotism, the Communist Party of Canada will add many more honorable pages to the history of working class struggle in Canada, the historic goal of which is socialism.

Abbreviations

ACCL	All-Canadian Congress of Labor
AFL	American Federation of Labor
BCFL	British Columbia Federation of Labor
BNA Act	British North America Act
CCASD	Canadian Committee to Aid Spanish Democracy
CCF	Co-operative Commonwealth Federation
CCL	Canadian Congress of Labor
CIO	Committee for Industrial Organization (also Congress of)
CLC	Canadian Labor Congress
CLDL	Canadian Labor Defense League
CLP	Canadian Labor Party
CNTU	Confederation of National Trade Unions
CSU	Canadian Seamen's Union
ECCI	Executive Committee of the Communist International
FRG	Federal Republic of Germany
FUL	Farmers' Unity League
GDR	German Democratic Republic
IUNTW	Industrial Union of Needle Trades Workers
IWA	International Woodworkers of America
IWW	Industrial Workers of the World
LPP	Labor-Progressive Party
LWIUC	Lumber Workers' Industrial Union of Canada
Mine-Mill	International Union of Mine, Mill and Smelter Workers of America
MWUC	Mine Workers' Union of Canada
NORAD	North American Air Defense Command
OBU	One Big Union
OFL	Ontario Federation of Labor
PFEL	Progressive Farmers' Educational League
PQ	Parti Québécois
PRC	People's Republic of China
QFL	Quebec Federation of Labor
RCWU	Relief Camp Workers' Union
RILU	Red International of Labor Unions
SIU	Seafarers' International Union
SWOC	Steelworkers' Organizing Committee
TLC	Trades and Labor Congress
TUEL	Trade Union Educational League
UAW	United Auto Workers of America
UE	United Electrical, Radio and Machine Workers of America
UMWA	United Mine Workers of America
USWA	United Steel Workers of America
WUL	Workers' Unity League
YCL	Young Communist League

In Lieu of a Bibliography

Given the enormous number of books, pamphlets, documents and other material produced by the Communist Party of Canada, it would necessarily take another volume to list them in a proper way. The footnotes following each chapter include the major documents and publications of the party.

The documents of the Communist Party of Canada are deposited in the Public Archives of Canada and will be accessible to the public under the conditions agreed upon by the Public Archives of Canada and the Communist Party of Canada.

Index

Custance, Florence A. 18, 23 n.43, 26-27, 32, 72
Cyprus 229, 293
Czechoslovakia 131, 238-242

Daily Clarion 117, 120
Daladier, Edouard 131
Dalskog, Ernest 162
Danzig 133
Dare Foods strike 297
Davis, Angela 290-291
Davis, Roy 124
Day of Protest 305-306
Defence of Canada Regulations 136-137
DeLeon, Daniel 3
Democratic centralism 20, 24, 28, 30, 42, 50-51, 53, 57-58, 85, 197, 199, 202, 241
Deng Xiaoping 226
Dewhurst, Alfred 206, 239
Dictatorship of the proletariat 15, 183, 198-199, 201-202
Diefenbaker, John G. 209-210, 216-217
Dimitrov, Georgi 110-112
Dion, Gérard 169
Dolgoy, Max 23 n.43
Dominican Republic 229
Dominion Communist-Labor Total War Committee 142-143, 145
Douglas, T.C. 127, 280
Draper, D.C. 72
Dubé, Evariste 196-197
Dufour, Lucien 119
Duplessis, Maurice 116, 118-121, 136, 169-170, 188, 190, 255-259, 261-262

Egypt 202, 236
Engels, Frederick 3, 6-8, 15, 31
England, Roy 167
Estevan miners' strike 68-72, 87
Estonia 10
Ethiopia 110, 122, 295
Evans, Arthur H. 94-95, 97-98
Ewert, Arthur 16

Fairley, Margaret 204
Farby, Joe L. 58
Farmers 8, 12, 17, 24, 29, 40-41, 68, 73, 81, 83, 88-91, 98, 113, 135, 172, 181, 191, 209, 211-212, 243, 246, 281, 285
Farmers' Union of Canada 40
Farmers' Unity League 41, 88-91
Federal elections 8, 68, 98, 139, 148, 181-182, 209, 216, 241, 272, 300

Federated party 42, 115-116, 211-212, 265-267, 269
Federation of Russian Canadians 203
Ferguson, Dewar 164, 166, 168
Finland 10, 134
Finnish Canadians 5, 29, 37-38, 57, 92, 118
Finnish Organization of Canada 59, 137
Finnish Social Democratic Party 5
First International 2
Flin Flon miners' strike 87-88
Ford strike 160
Foreign Enlistment Act 124, 127
Foreign Investment Review Agency 283
Forkin, M. Joe 70, 116
Foster, W.Z. 187
France 27, 122-123, 129, 131, 133-134, 136, 145-146, 153-154, 202, 230-231, 235, 252, 291
Franco, Francisco 123, 295
Free speech fight 72, 92
Freed, Norman 168, 194, 239, 241
French Canada 8, 30, 117-118, 141, 169, 252-260, 262-265, 267-271, 275
Friends of the Mackenzie-Papineau Battalion 126-127, 129
Front de Libération du Québec 268, 277-278
Furrow 90

Gagarin, Yuri 229
Gagnon, Henri 196-197, 205-206, 258
Gauld, Alex 23 n.43
Gauld, Bella Hall 18
Gélinas, Pierre 169
General Steel Wares Workers' Union 102
German Democratic Republic (GDR) 154, 221-222, 292
Germany 10, 12, 27, 46, 110, 121, 127, 129, 131, 133-134, 136, 146, 150, 152-153, 199, 221, 292
Germany, Federal Republic of 154, 179, 229, 239, 292, 295
Goldstick, David 127
Goldwater, Barry 233
Golinsky, Mike 73
Gompers, Samuel 35
Goodwin, Ginger 21
Gordon, Walter 246
Gouin, Paul 118
Gouzenko, Igor 155-156
Great Britain 3, 8, 17, 50-51, 61-62, 76, 123, 129, 131, 133-134, 136-137, 146, 153-154, 157, 202, 227, 252
Greece 152-154, 229, 293, 295
Green Paper on immigration policy 301